Hedge Funds and Managed Futures

Hedge Funds and Managed Futures

A Handbook for Institutional Investors

Edited by
Greg N. Gregoriou and Dieter G. Kaiser

Riskbooks

Published by Risk Books, a Division of Incisive Financial Publishing Ltd

Haymarket House
28–29 Haymarket
London SW1Y 4RX
Tel: +44 (0)20 7484 9700
Fax: +44 (0)20 7484 9800
E-mail: books@incisivemedia.com
Sites: www.riskbooks.com
www.incisivemedia.com

ISBN 1 904339 53 0

British Library Cataloguing in Publication Data
A catalogue record for this book is available from the British Library

Publisher: Laurie Donaldson
Assistant Editor: Steve Fairman
Designer: Rebecca Bramwell

Typeset by Mizpah Publishing Services Private Limited, Chennai, India

Printed and bound in Spain by Espacegrafic, Pamplona, Navarra

Contents

Foreword

As the hedge fund industry has matured and established itself as a mainstream investment class, the importance of institutions in shaping the industry's future has become increasingly evident. Hedge funds have certainly come a long way from the long/short equity beginnings of Alfred Winslow Jones some 60 years ago. They have evolved through the global macro giants of the 1980s to become a viable fourth asset class in which the pursuit of absolute returns and diversification are the key drivers. The phenomenal growth of hedge fund investments into a US$1.3 trillion industry has brought with it many challenges and provoked much debate. The industry continues to thrive despite the obituaries commentators have regularly written for it over the past decade. Central to its evolution and regeneration is innovation. The quest for new alpha sources is the spur for hedge fund managers to explore new markets and strategies in, for example, energy, insurance and health care. As financial markets develop and investment banks introduce new financial products and instruments, hedge funds look for new ways to capitalise on these opportunities. The chief driver of this evolution has been the institutional investor. To be fully effective, today's hedge fund providers need to work in partnership with institutions to deliver appropriate levels of service, transparency and consistent performance across the risk/return spectrum.

This book, *Hedge Funds and Managed Futures – A Handbook for Institutional Investors* is a measure of the growing sophistication and importance of the sector. The depth and range of topics are testament to the maturity and diversity of the industry. The handbook evaluates four key topics from a critical perspective: benchmarking and performance measurement, risk management, portfolio management and asset allocation. The contributors are well known finance academics, industry commentators and practitioners. The independence of their views reflects an intellectual maturity and confidence which is essential in maintaining a healthy industry.

Of particular interest are comments on how the industry responds to investor needs. My experience, initially as a client and then working closely for some years with one of the largest European fund of hedge funds managers, gave me valuable insights into the needs of investors. It brought home to me the importance of working in partnership with clients to develop a wide range of products, giving institutions the scope to tailor their hedge fund investments for their particular needs. My interest was caught, also, by the comments on CTAs. My experience with these systematic trend followers goes back to the 1980s when my initial involvement was as an institutional investor. To many, CTAs are niche players in the hedge fund industry. Their strategy is not easy to get right consistently but the rewards can be exceptional – impressive alpha generation, a very low (or even negative) correlation to stock markets and excellent portfolio diversification possibilities.

Looking to the future for the hedge fund industry we can be very optimistic. The industry will certainly consolidate – the environment has always been Darwinian in nature. Beta *versus* alpha is a constant debate. The ability to generate alpha and structure genuinely innovative products will be paramount in the growth of the industry. So, we can have confidence that new hedge funds and managed futures strategies will continue to develop and attract considerable investment. Given that, there will always be demand for publications such as this that seek to challenge, debate and inform.

John Morrison
Chief Executive, Man Investments, Pfäffikon, Switzerland

About the Editors

Greg N. Gregoriou is associate professor of finance in the School of Business and Economics at State University of New York (Plattsburgh). He is also an associate member of the Centre for Research in E-Finance (CREF) at HEC Montreal and a fellow member of the Research Center for Operations & Productivity Management supported by the School of Management at the University of Science & Technology of China and the Department of Management at Worcester Polytechnic Institute. A native of Montreal, he obtained his PhD in finance from the joint Doctoral Program in Administration that merges the resources of Montreal's major universities (McGill, Concordia and HEC). Greg has had over 50 academic articles published in peer-reviewed journals. He is hedge fund editor and editorial board member for *Derivatives Use, Trading and Regulation*, a UK-based academic journal since 2003 and editorial board member of the *Journal of Wealth Management*, based in New York City. He has also been invited to present his papers at numerous academic conferences in the US, Canada and Asia. He is the co-author of the book *"Evaluating Hedge Fund and CTA Performance"* and has edited 18 books.

Dieter G. Kaiser is responsible for the institutional research at Benchmark Alternative Strategies in Frankfurt, Germany. Dieter started his professional career in the structured products sector at Dresdner Kleinwort Wasserstein in Frankfurt. Afterwards he joined Crédit Agricole Asset Management in Frankfurt where he was responsible for the fund of hedge funds marketing support. Dieter has written several articles on the subject of alternative investments that have been published in professional as well as academic journals. He is the author of the German book *"Hedge Funds – Demystifying an Asset Class – Structures, Opportunities, Risks"* and co-author of *"Alternative Investment Strategies – Insights into the investment* *techniques of hedge fund managers"*. He is also co-editor of *Handbuch Alternative Investments*. Dieter holds a diploma in business administration and a Master of Arts in banking and finance from the HfB – Business School of Finance and Management in Frankfurt, where he has also lectured on hedge funds since 2003.

List of Contributors

Paul U. Ali is an associate professor in the Faculty of Law, the University of Melbourne. Paul was previously a finance lawyer in Sydney and has published several books and journal articles on finance and investment law. Most recently these have included *Opportunities in Credit Derivatives and Synthetic Securitisation* and articles in *Derivatives Use, Trading and Regulation, Journal of Alternative Investments, Journal of Banking Regulation* and *Journal of International Banking Law and Regulation.*

Bernard Bachmann is a member of the risk management team of RMF Investment Management, a fund of hedge funds based in Pfäffikon, Switzerland. He heads the operational risk management team. Prior to joining RMF in 2004, Bernard worked at KPMG for five years as an external auditor responsible for the financial and the Swiss regulatory audit of a major investment bank. He has extensive experience of performing regulatory audits in the areas of collateral management, equity finance, risk management, OTC derivatives and management controls. Previously, he worked as a research assistant for the University of Zurich and taught economics and law at a Swiss high school in Winterthur. Bernard has a masters degree in business administration and economics from the University of Zurich and is a qualified Swiss CPA.

Jean-François Bacmann is a member of the quantitative analysis group of RMF Investment Management, based in Pfäffikon, Switzerland. Within the group he heads the research and implementation of tools team whose key responsibilities are the development of innovative solutions in the context of alternative investments and the implementation of the quantitative in-house software tools. Prior to joining RMF Investment Management in 2002, he spent five years as a research professional in finance at the Entreprise Institute at the University of Neuchâtel, Switzerland. Jean-François received his engineering degree in computer science and applied mathematics from the ENSIMAG, France, a masters degree in finance from the University of Grenoble, France, and a PhD in finance from the University of Neuchâtel. He has published several articles in professional and academic financial journals.

Zsolt Berényi holds an MSc in economics from the University of Economic Sciences in Budapest and a PhD in finance from the University of Munich. His main interest lies in the risk and performance evaluation of alternative investments: hedge funds, CTAs, credit funds. After working at Deutsche Bank, HypoVereinsbank and KPMG at various locations throughout Europe, Zsolt now leads an independent consultancy in Budapest, Hungary.

Ursula Bosshard is a member of the quantitative analysis group of RMF Investment Management, based in Pfäffikon, Switzerland. She is responsible for the maintenance and development of the extensive hedge funds quantitative database, the construction of new portfolios, as well as measuring and rating hedge funds performance. Prior to joining RMF Investment Management in 2001, Ursula spent two years working for UBS AG, New York, focusing on modifying the private banking proprietary Management Information System (MIS) to capture and analyse customer assets, loans and revenue data. From 1997 to 1999 she worked at UBS Warburg as a business analyst. Ursula received her degree as Economist SEBA from the University of Applied Sciences, Zurich, Switzerland. She holds a US stockbroker licence as well as a US investment advisor licence.

Bernhard Brunner completed his studies in business mathematics at the University of Augsburg with a masters degree. In 2004, he received his PhD in finance on market-consistent option pricing from the Economics Department at the University of Augsburg. Bernhard worked for several years as a working student in the risk management department at HypoVereinsbank AG in Munich. From 2000 to 2003 he was scientific assistant at the Economics Department at the University of Augsburg. Apart from his research activities, he was teaching courses on corporate finance, investment and portfolio management. In 2003, he joined risklab germany GmbH in Munich as a financial engineer. He is primarily responsible for hedge fund analysis and the development of investment strategies. Bernhard has published several articles in renowned professional journals. In 2003, he received the Best Paper Award from the Swiss Society for Financial Market Research.

Irina Y. Butina is a Master of Finance student at the University of Freiburg, Germany. She has a BBA degree in information systems with honours from the International University Vienna (Austria) and Kiev (Ukraine), and is a holder of the Deutscher Akademischer Austauschdienst scholarship. She has also successfully completed an internship at Deutsche Bank AG in Frankfurt, Germany. Iryna conducts a statistics tutorial and is writing her masters thesis at the department of Empirical Research and Econometrics, the University of Freiburg. Her research interests include asset pricing, portfolio management, financial markets, and investor behaviour.

Daniel Capocci is fund of funds manager at the KBL Group. Previously he gained experience on the bond fund management desk and on the risk management desk. Daniel has written a book on hedge funds called "Introduction aux Hedge Funds", and has participated in several other books on the subject and co-written numerous publications on hedge funds that have appeared in professional and academic periodicals such as *Echo de la Bourse, Agefi, the Journal of Empirical Finance* and the *European Journal of Finance.* Daniel is currently a PhD candidate in Sciences de Gestion at HEC-Université de Liège and a research associate with the EDHEC Risk and Asset Management Research Centre.

Donald R. Chambers is the director of Curriculum at KalmAI. He has served since 1992 as the Walter E. Hanson/KPMG Professor of Finance at Lafayette College teaching corporate finance, investments and derivatives. Donald previously taught on the faculties of Penn State, the University of North Carolina at Chapel Hill, Rochester Institute of Technology and the University of Baltimore. He received his PhD from the University of North Carolina at Chapel Hill in 1981. Donald is an experienced teacher in executive education programmes including the programme of the University of North Carolina at Chapel Hill. He has published five books, over 30 journal articles, and serves as a consultant to the public and private sectors including The Bank of New York.

Alain Coën is associate professor of finance at the University of Quebec in Montreal (UQAM). He obtained his PhD in finance from the University of Grenoble and holds a Master of Arts in economics with a major in macroeconomics from Laval University. Alain teaches, researches and consults in the areas of asset pricing and portfolio management. His research interests focus on asset pricing, international finance, real business cycle and financial econometrics. He has published in several international journals and has written a book in financial management.

John E. Dunn III is an international institutional investment advisor living and working in Geneva, Switzerland. Having begun his career in the international investment field in the early 1980s, he worked for a variety of banks including Nomura, Citicorp Vickers da Costa, Barclays de Zoete Wedd in Tokyo, Geneva, and New York, before opening the first office of UBS Securities in Switzerland. John has also taught finance at a variety of international graduate business schools, including the Swiss Finance Academy, and Thunderbird, The Garvin School of International Management, and currently is associated with Terrapinn Financial Training, where he conducts executive training programmes in investment management and hedge fund investment. His career interests revolve around hedge fund investment allocation and institutional portfolio management, and as an international asset management consultant he has advised a variety of institutional investors primarily on their alternative asset allocations. John is a frequent speaker at hedge fund and asset management conferences around the world and is an advisory board member to Infiniti Capital.

Roland Füss is lecturer at the department of Empirical Research and Econometrics and assistant professor at the department of Finance and Banking at the University of Freiburg, Germany. He holds an MBA from the University of Applied Science in Lörrach, MEc and PhD degrees in economics from the University of Freiburg. His research interests are in the field of applied econometrics, alternative investments as well as international and real estate finance. Roland has co-authored several articles in finance journals and book chapters. He is a member of the Verein für Socialpolitik and the German Finance Association.

Florian Haberfelner is quantitative analyst at Benchmark Capital Management GmbH in Vienna, Austria. He develops the quantitative tools that complement Benchmark's investment process and is responsible for the macro-based modelling of market risks as the major input for the tactical asset allocation. Florian studied international business administration at the University of Vienna, where he majored in investment analysis and international management. Furthermore, he took an exchange year where he studied at Lund Universitet in Sweden. During his studies he undertook several internships, among others at Finanzierungsgarantiegesellschaft (FGG) and Deutsche Bank. In the course of his master thesis on the topic "Performanceanalyse bei Hedgefonds" Florian worked together with Benchmark and developed a performance attribution tool.

Reinhold Hafner completed his studies in business administration at the University of Augsburg in 1997 with a masters degree. In 2004, he received his PhD in finance on factor-based stochastic implied volatility models from the Economics Department at the University of Augsburg. In 1997 Reinhold joined RiskLab GmbH in Munich as a financial engineer. He has been head of Market Analytics since 2001. In 2003 he joined newly founded risklab germany GmbH as a managing director. Reinhold heads the business areas "Alternatives" and "Investment Strategy". He has written numerous articles for renowned professional journals and regularly lectures at national and international conferences on topical subjects of asset management and financial engineering. Within the framework of his scientific work, Reinhold has received several awards; in 2003, for instance, he received the Best Paper Award from the Swiss Society for Financial Market Research.

Thomas Heidorn has been professor of banking and finance at the HfB – Business School of Finance & Management in Frankfurt since 1991. He studied economics at the University of Hannover and at the University of California Santa Barbara. He received his PhD degree from Christian Albrechts Universität Kiel. From 1988 to 1991 Thomas worked at Dresdner Bank (New Issues and Underwriting). His main academic and teaching activity lies in the field of investment banking, focusing especially on risk management, derivatives, and treasury. He has published numerous books and articles in this area. Thomas also lectures in various training programmes for investment specialists.

Christian Hoppe is divisional partner of finance and controlling at Dresdner Bank in Frankfurt. In 2003, he completed his economics degree at the University of Essen-Duisburg. Whilst writing his master thesis, Christian worked in the Institutional Research Department of Benchmark Alternative Strategies GmbH in Frankfurt. Christian is the author of the German book *"Derivatives based on Alternative Investments – construction and ways of evaluation"* and is the co-author of numerous working papers on the subject of structured products based on hedge funds and the biases in hedge fund indexes.

Lutz Johanning holds the endowed chair of Asset Management at the European Business School (ebs) in Oestrich-Winkel, Germany. His teaching focuses on capital market theory, derivatives, asset management and risk management. Lutz's research interests are in the areas of best execution and market microstructure, empirical capital market research and risk management. As dean of full-time programmes (2004/2005) he was responsible for coordination of the university's study programme and, in particular, the introduction of the Bachelor/Masters study courses. Lutz is the academic director of XTP GmbH for consultation projects for the financial industry.

Karin Kisling is a managing partner of Benchmark Capital Management. Within the group, as the CIO she is responsible for portfolio management and research. From 1987 to 1994 Karin worked at GiroCredit (now Erste Bank) as head of the Fixed Income Department. Thereafter, as Global Treasurer, she was jointly responsible for the turnaround at HTM AG. Between April 1996 and May 1997 Karin was managing director at Vontobel Asset Management, responsible for the development of the Eastern European Asset Management business. In May 1997 she joined Rabobank International in Budapest as general manager, where she was responsible for the bank's activities in Eastern Europe, and afterwards she took over the trading for Global Emerging Markets Fixed Income in local currency in London. Karin studied social and economic sciences at the Vienna University of Economics and Business Administration. She also is a lecturer at the Finance Institute of the Karl Franzens University in Graz.

R. McFall Lamm Jr is chief strategist for Deutsche Bank's Global Investment Management Group in London/New York. His responsibilities include asset allocation, advising clients, and managing portfolios. He has 20 years of experience in market analysis and investment research, and is well known for his expertise in alternative investments where, in the 1990s, he was instrumental in integrating alternative investments with traditional portfolio assets. He was especially recognised for publishing "Why Not 100% Hedge Funds" in advance of the stock market bubble burst in the early 2000s – advice that saved many investors from significant losses. Dr. Lamm is a frequent speaker at conferences and events around the globe. He also writes market commentary that is disseminated worldwide and is often quoted in the news media. In addition, Dr. Lamm is an energetic writer having published numerous book chapters and professional articles in various academic journals.

François-Serge Lhabitant is responsible for the investment research at Kedge Capital. He was previously a member of senior management at Union Bancaire Privée (Geneva), taking charge of quantitative risk management for trading desks, and then managing all quantitative research and institutional portfolio management activities in the area of alternative investments. He was formerly a director at UBS Global Asset Management. On the academic side, François-Serge is a professor of finance at the University of Lausanne and at EDHEC Business School. His specialist skills are in the areas of alternative investment (hedge funds) and emerging markets. He is the author of five books on these two subjects and has published numerous research and scientific popularisation articles. He is a member of the Scientific Council of the Autorité des Marches Financiers, the French regulatory body.

Lionel Martellini is a professor of finance at EDHEC Graduate School of Business and the Scientific Director of EDHEC Risk and Asset Management Research Centre. A former member of the faculty at the Marshall School of Business, University of Southern California, he holds masters degrees in business administration, economics, statistics and mathematics, as well as a PhD in finance from the Haas School of Business, University of California at Berkeley. Lionel is a member of the editorial board of *The Journal of Portfolio Management* and *The Journal of Alternative Investments*. He conducts active research in quantitative asset management and derivatives valuation, which has been published in leading academic and practitioner journals, and has been featured in major European and global dailies such as *The Financial Times* and *The Wall Street Journal*. He has co-authored reference textbooks on topics related to alternative investment strategies and fixed-income securities. Lionel has served as a consultant for various investments banks and asset management firms both in Europe and in the US on questions related to active asset allocation decisions and alternative investment strategies, and is a regular speaker in seminars and conferences on these subjects.

Pierre-Yves Moix is the chief risk officer of RMF Investment Management, based in Pfäffikon, Switzerland. He is a member of the management committee and the investment strategy committee of RMF Investment Management. Prior to joining RMF in 2000 as a quantitative analyst, Pierre-Yves spent four years as a research assistant with the Institute of Operations Research at the University of St Gallen, focusing on quantitative methods for financial risk management. He previously worked from 1994 to 1996 as a derivatives specialist at Credit Suisse and from 1992 to 1994 as a quantitative analyst with UBS. Pierre-Yves received his masters degree and PhD (Dr lic. oec HSG) in economics from the University of St Gallen, Switzerland, as well as a masters degree in statistics from the University of Neuchâtel, Switzerland. He is a CFA charterholder and a Financial Risk Manager (FRM). He has published many articles on finance related topics and is the author of the book *"The Measurement of Market Risk"*.

Peter Oertmann is co-founder and chief executive officer of Vescore, an asset management company based in Switzerland and Germany with a focus on quantitative investment strategies and alternative asset classes. In addition, he is a member of the advisory boards of several financial market research companies. Peter is also lecturer of finance at the University of Basel and the University of St Gall in Switzerland. His research interests include international asset pricing models, tactical asset allocation strategies, style investing, alternative asset classes, and investments in commodity futures. He has published more than 40 articles in these fields, is the author of the book *"Global Risk Premia on International Investments"* and co-author of the book *"Global Asset Allocation"*. He is a member of the editorial board of the journal *"Financial Markets and Portfolio Management"* and is the chairman of the board of the Munich Finance Forum. Peter holds a masters degree in business administration from the University of Bielefeld, Germany, as well as a masters degree in economics from the University of Georgia, US. He received a PhD in finance from the University of St Gall.

Mehmet Orhan is an assistant professor at the Economics Department of Fatih University, Istanbul. At the same time, he is the director of the Social Sciences Institute that is responsible for the coordination of several graduate programmes. He has a PhD from Bilkent University, Ankara, and has graduated from the Industrial Engineering Department of the same university. He had full scholarship until he got his PhD degree. Mehmet's main interest is econometrics, both theoretical and applied. He has published articles in *Economics Letters, International Journal of Business* and *Journal of Economic and Social Research*. His theoretical research interests include HCCME estimation, robust estimation techniques, and Bayesian inference. Mehmet is working on IPO performances in Turkey, tax revenue estimation and international economic cooperations as part of his applied research studies.

Juliane Proelss is a research assistant at the endowed chair of asset management at the European Business School (ebs) in Oestrich-Winkel, Germany. Her research focus lays on risk management and alternative investments. Juliane also works as an academic assistant in the field of executive educational in alternative investments and finance at the ebs Finanzakademie. Prior to this she studied at the Catholic University of Eichstaett-Ingolstadt, where she graduated in 2005 with a diploma in business administration, and at Lincoln University, New Zealand, where she graduated with a postgraduate diploma in commerce. Her major subjects were financial markets and econometrics. During her studies she worked as a student assistant at the chair for statistics and operations research and as a student trainee for FondsConsult and Siemens Management Consulting.

François-Éric Racicot is associate professor of finance at the University of Quebec (Outaouais) and permanent member of LRSP (Laboratory for Research in Statistics and Probability). He holds an MSc in economics with a major in econometrics from the University of Montreal and received his PhD in finance from UQAM. François-Éric was previously professor at Ecole des sciences de la gestion of University of Quebec (Montreal). He is also consultant in financial econometrics for various banks and investment firms. François-Éric's research interests focus on developing econometric methods applied to financial problems, on corporate governance, on financial engineering and on the analysis of financial projects in the perspective of real options. He has also written several books in computational finance and financial econometrics.

Heinz Rehkugler is professor of finance at the University of Freiburg, Germany. He studied business administration at the University of Munich where he completed his masters degree and PhD. He was then co-founder and, from 1975 to 1977, the owner-manager of a consulting company for business information systems. In 1977 he joined the finance faculty at the University of Bremen as professor and in 1988 moved to the University of Bamberg. Since 1994 he has been chair of banking and finance at the University of Freiburg. Heinz has published more than 140 articles in a wide range of topics in finance. His primary research topics are the financial analysis of companies and financial products with quantitative methods, real estate investments, and private financial planning.

Artus Ph. Rosenbusch studied at the Universidad de Salamanca in Spain and at the Technische Universität Darmstadt, where he graduated with a diploma in mathematics. His major subjects were abstract algebra, domain theory, cryptography, data mining and game theory. In game theory he developed an explanation and solution for the ultimatum game paradox. In 2004 Artus worked for the Commerzbank in Frankfurt, where he developed a risk estimate for swaps on bonds at central credit operations. At that time he also started his second undergraduate degree in financial mathematics. Presently Artus works as a graduate assistant for the ebs Finanzakademie.

Denis Schweizer is a PhD student and research assistant at the endowed chair of asset management at the European Business School (ebs) in Oestrich-Winkel, Germany. His research focus lays on asset allocation and pricing of alternative investments. At the same time he works as an academic assistant in the creation of executive educational programmes in alternative investments and finance at the ebs Finanzakademie. Denis also lectures in those programmes. In 2005 he graduated from the Johann-Wolfgang Goethe University in Frankfurt with a diploma in business administration. During his studies Denis worked for the UBS Investment Bank and for the SEB AG as a student trainee.

Oliver A. Schwindler is a doctoral candidate within the Department of Finance at Bamberg University. He is currently working on his dissertation "Value Added of Funds of Hedge Funds Manager". His research comprises the risk and performance evaluation of alternative investments and hedge funds. Oliver received his Dipl.-Kfm. from the University of Regensburg. He is a member of the Hedge Fund Association (HFA) and the International Association of Financial Engineers (IAFE), as well as the founder of HF-Analytics.

Turker Tekten is the chief operating officer at Standard Yatirim Menkul Kiymetler A.S., a subsidiary of Standard Bank Group, located in South Africa. He has graduated from the Industrial Engineering Department of Bilkent University, Ankara. He had full scholarship until he got his BS degree. Turker has been working in the Turkish banking sector since 1992, when he started as an internal auditor at Turkey's Isbank, worked at several positions ranging from audit to finance and ran the structured products desk, before and after the 2001 financial crisis, at JPMorgan Chase Bank Turkey.

Raymond Théoret is professor of finance at the University of Quebec (Montreal). After having obtained his PhD from the University of

Montreal in economics, he was professor at HEC Montreal and senior financial economist in great financial institutions. Raymond published many academic articles and books and made numerous consultations. His research is oriented towards financial engineering, risk management, portfolio analysis and real options.

Georg Wessling is a senior portfolio manager working for Harcourt Investment Consulting AG, a Zurich-based fund of hedge funds manager. There he is responsible for advising and managing customised hedge fund portfolios. Before joining Harcourt, Georg worked for 10 years as an investment consultant. He was involved in asset liability management, manager selection and monitoring, and he was responsible for alternative investments (hedge funds, private equity and real estate). Georg graduated from the University of Berne in 1995 with a degree in economics. In 2003 he received a PhD in finance from the University of Zurich.

Kathryn Wilkens earned her PhD at the University of Massachusetts at Amherst in 1998 and now serves as the Chartered Alternative Investment Analyst Association's Director of Curriculum. Her primary research interest is in the bases of relative performance among alternative investment strategies. Kathryn has published several articles in the *Journal of Alternative Investments, Managerial Finance,* and *Journal of Financial Education,* amongst others. She has co-authored several book chapters, including "CTA Performance Evaluation with Data Envelopment Analysis," "Classifying Hedge Funds Using Data Envelopment Analysis," and "Maximum Drawdown Distributions with Volatility Persistence." Kathryn is an associate director of research at the University of Massachusetts' Center for International Securities and Derivatives Markets (CISDM). She was a 2002–2004 Teaching Technology Fellow at Worcester Polytechnic Institute.

Guy P. Wyser-Pratte is the chief executive officer and portfolio manager of Wyser-Pratte Management Co, Inc in New York. He graduated from the University of Rochester in 1962, and then served in the US Marine Corps from 1962 to 1966, attaining the rank of Captain. He received an MBA from New York University in 1971. In the course of his 38-year career in investment management,

Guy headed the risk arbitrage department at Prudential-Bache Securities, Inc. In 1991, he resurrected the firm that his father founded in Paris in 1929 as a vehicle for pursuing activities in event-driven investing as an independent firm. Guy is currently a member of the board of directors of Ingenico, SA and Prosodie, SA. He is a member of the board of overseers of the International Rescue Committee, a non-governmental international refugee organisation, a member of the Council on Foreign Relations, a trustee of the Congressional Medal of Honor Foundation, and is the president of the US Marine Corps University Foundation.

Volker Ziemann is a research engineer at EDHEC Risk and Asset Management Research Centre and a PhD student in finance at the University of Aix-Marseille in France. Volker focuses on econometrics in general and applications to asset allocation problems in particular. He holds masters degrees in economics from Humboldt University in Berlin and in statistics from ENSAE in Paris.

Part One

Benchmarking and Performance Measurement

1

Construction Methods, Heterogeneity and Information Ratios of Hedge Fund Indices

Thomas Heidorn; Christian Hoppe; Dieter G. Kaiser

HfB – Business School of Finance & Management; Dresdner Bank AG; Benchmark Alternative Strategies GmbH

INTRODUCTION

Parallel to a steadily increasing interest in alternative investments, especially in hedge funds (from the institutional and private investor), the importance of hedge fund indices in the world of international finance is rapidly growing. On one hand hedge fund indices serve as an underlying asset for a number of derivatives, whereas on the other hand there is a growing demand for transparency of prices and representative benchmarks in the area of hedge fund products which is known as being unregulated. Hedge fund indices allow for the comparability within the asset class and at the same time confirm the advantages with respect to traditional forms of investment.

The core of this chapter is comprised of data from hedge fund indices and their heterogeneous characteristics in the period from January 2001–March 2005. Starting from a discussion of basic properties of hedge fund indices, based on statistic references, the scope of the heterogeneity of these indices is investigated. Apart from a mere descriptive analytical goal, with minimum, average and maximum values of the parameters in question the investor is supposed to be given a benchmarking spread. Depending on the investors' preferences this can be helpful in selecting adequate comparison indices to which a pre-selection of potential investments can be achieved. Finally, it is investigated by calculating the information ratio and how benchmarking of traditional stock and fixed income indices is influenced by the choice of the respective hedge fund index family.

PROPERTIES

Institutionalisation of the hedge fund industry

During the course of time, numerous hedge fund indices have appeared and established themselves in the market. This process was accelerated at the beginning of 1994 when many companies began recording data series of individual hedge funds. Since these companies either did not pursue any recordings prior to 1994 or lost their records, most indices lack time series pre-1990. Specialised companies in the hedge fund industry such as Hennessee, Van Hedge, and Hedge Fund Research (HFR) encountered new competitors from well known US financial institutions (eg, Credit Suisse (CS), Dow Jones, Standard & Poor's, Morgan Stanley Capital International (MSCI)) is a sign for continuing the institutionalisation of the hedge fund industry. At the same time the transparency of index construction increased in the hedge fund industry and Table 1 provides a survey of the most significant hedge fund indices. An interesting note is that 87.5% of the index providers calculate a composite index including the considered sub-strategies, but only 50% offer a fund of funds index.

Access to time series of index providers is granted in most cases after registering online free of charge. Some of the established financial information services such as Reuters or Bloomberg also offer hedge fund index time series from different providers. According to Indjic and Heen (2003), **Credit Suisse/Tremont and Hedge Fund Research (HFR) were established as industry standard in the hedge fund industry**.

Uniqueness, investability, measurability and adequacy

The purpose of indices is serving as a benchmark for investors. Bailey *et al* (1990) and Bailey (1992) named uniqueness, investability, measurability and adequacy as main requirements for a benchmark. In particular the point of investability is further intensified by Sharpe (1992) stating that a benchmark is supposed to be a real investment alternative which can be purchased incorporating only negligible fees. Furthermore, a benchmark should be well diversified

Table 1 Survey of hedge fund indices

Index providers (Establishment)	First published	Number of funds in the indices	Number of indices	Composite index	Provisional values	Fund of funds index	Transparent composition	independent committee	actualisation frequency	Balancing
CISDM / MAR (1990)	1990	1,500	19	–	X	X	–	–	monthly	monthly
Credit Suisse/ Tremont LLC (2003)	1994	900	14	X	X	–	X	X	monthly	quarterly
Dow Jones Hedge Fund Indexes, Inc. (2004)	2001	39	6	X	–	–	X	X	daily	quarterly
Edhec Alternative Indices (2004)	1997	n/a	13	–	X	X	X	X	monthly	quarterly
Evaluation Associates Capital Markets (1996)	1996	100	18	X	X	–	–	–	weekly	yearly
Eureka Hedge (2001)	2000	6,585	200	X	–	X	X	–	monthly	continuously
Feri Alternative Assets GmbH (2002)	2002	30	7	X	X	–	–	–	monthly	quarterly
FTSE International Ltd. (2004)	1998	40	12	X	X	–	X	X	weekly	monthly

Table 1 (continued)

Index providers (Establishment)	First published	Number of funds in the indices	Number of indices	Composite index	Provisional values	Fund of funds index	Transparent composition	independent committee	actualisation frequency	Balancing
Hedge Fund Intelligence (1998)	2000	3,378	43	X	X	X	X	X	monthly	yearly
Hedge Fund Research, Inc. (1994)	1990	1600	37	X	X	X	–	–	monthly	monthly
Hedgefund.net/ Tuna Indices (1997)	1976	4,200	38	X	X	X	X	–	daily	continuously
Hennessee Group (1992)	1987	450	23	X	X	–	–	X	monthly	yearly
Investorforce / Altvest (1993)	1993	2,304	14	X	–	X	–	–	daily	monthly
MSCI Hedge Fund Indices (2003)	2002	2,050	190	X	X	–	X	X	monthly	quarterly
Standard & Poor's (2002)	1998	41	13	X	X	–	X	X	daily	yearly
Van Hedge Fund Advisors (1995)	1988	750	14	X	X	X	–	–	monthly	monthly

and well-known before any investment decisions are made. This implies that the relative index matches the specific investment style and focus and the resulting risk characteristics of the fund manager in question. As regards to the efficiency of the benchmark, the goal for it is to incorporate the best investments in its asset class.

The main prerequisite of an index to be used as a benchmark is to be sufficiently transparent in order to make it clear for investors which characteristics are chosen ie, include calculation procedures and administration principles. It is also necessary to mention the independence of the index committee and that its independence must be ensured to prevent and minimise the risk of future conflicts of interest between index providers and investors. In the year 2000 no index provider could meet this demand but Vaissié (2003) concluded that three years later 47.6% of the index providers featured an independent committee. In 2005 more than half of the index providers had an independent committee. Regarding the transparency of the index composition, more providers publish the individual hedge funds comprising the composition of index.

Another deterrent regarding hedge fund indices is the delay with respect to the publication of the final results. There is a tendency that with individual hedge funds there is a delay of between 30 and 60 days before the final values of the index composite are known, which are essential when calculating the index value itself. To further complicate the issue with individual hedge funds, it is customary to calculate an actualised net asset value every month. Regarding the actualisation frequency of hedge fund indices one can observe that 62.5% of the hedge fund indices publish monthly, 25.0% daily and 12.5% weekly actualised index data. CS publishes the actualised month's end values of their index families on the 15th of the month following the respective valuation day. At HFR actualisation is done on the first business day of the month with a delay of two months relative to the valuation day. Indices publishing daily index data are based on managed accounts and imply a delay of one to two days. Managed accounts are accounts opened by index sponsors in order to convince hedge fund managers to implement their strategies not within the existing fund structure but on the account of the index sponsor. Daily actualised hedge fund indices have existed 2002 and have a much shorter time series history than monthly actualised indices. In order to counter the delay problems, 81.25% of the index providers mentioned here not only publishing final values but also provisional values on an irregular basis. According to Vaissié (2003) the percentage in 2003 was only 76.2%.

The hedge fund indices offered in the market do not provide the stability investors' need for rational investment decisions. This is due to the fact that individual hedge funds are excluded from the indices if they cease to report their monthly valuation data to the respective database in time. Adversely new individual hedge funds are added to the indices only at the next index rebalancing date. Table 1 also shows that index rebalancing occurs quarterly with 31.25%, monthly with 31.25%, yearly with 25% and continuously with 12.5% of the providers. Therefore the risk return profile of the indices is changing in the same rhythm as the rebalancing. Additionally, when a new individual hedge fund is included a part of or even the entire time series of the fund is subsequently integrated into the index. This problem which is also called "backfilling" is raised only with the index families of hedgefund.net and MSCI. At the same time only with indices from www. hedgefund.net valuation data from "dead funds" are eliminated from index data subsequently.

Hedge fund indices are calculated mainly in US currency due to the dominant role of the US$ as base currency of hedge funds. Of course there are also country or region specific indices which may have a differing base currency. In order to incorporate accurate benchmarking, the cost of a currency hedge for the investor for a currency different to the base currency must be taken into account. Concerning consistency of valuation data provided by the hedge funds, it is assumed that due to lack of control not all of the funds report the requested net return, but only partly consider management, performance and administration costs.

Minimum requirements

There are enormous differences concerning the specific requirements of database providers for hedge funds to be included in their indices. Therefore, some databases only select those individual funds meeting certain minimum requirements. Table 2 provides a survey of the different selection criteria of index providers. Only

Table 2 Selection criteria of database providers

Index providers	Minimum fund volume (in Mil. US$)	Minimum track Record (in years)	Closed funds	Managed accounts	Strategy classification
CISDM / MAR	–	–	X	–	Manager
CS/Tremont LLC	10	1	X	–	Manager
Dow Jones Hedge Fund Indexes, Inc.	50	2	–	X	Index provider
Edhec Alternative Indices	–	–	–	–	n.a.
Evaluation Associates Capital Markets	20	2	–	–	Index provider
Eurekahedge			X		Index provider
Feri Alternative Assets GmbH	50	1	–	–	Index provider
FTSE International Ltd.	50	2	–	X	Index provider
Hedge Fund Intelligence	–	–	X	–	Manager
Hedge Fund Research, Inc.	–	–	X	–	Manager
Hedgefund.net / Tuna Indices	–	–	X	–	Manager
Hennessee Group	10	1	X	–	Manager
Investorforce / Altvest	–	–	X	–	Manager
MSCI Hedge Fund Indices	15	–	–	–/X	Manager
Standard & Poor's	75	3	–	X	Index provider
Van Hedge Fund Advisors	–	–	X	–	Index provider

Source: Vaissié (2003) and Heidorn *et al* (2006).

50% of hedge fund indices require an average minimum fund volume of US$35 million from individual hedge funds. Those database providers that also request minimum fund volume in 87.5% of the cases have a minimum requirement with respect to the time series history of the individual hedge funds. Of the index providers 43.75% demand a minimum track record of 1.7 years, on average. Interestingly there are only two providers that have minimum requirements concerning the assets under management and track record and also consider closed funds in their index calculation. Altogether, 56.25% of the benchmarks in question consider closed funds in their index calculation. However, the percentage of closed funds in the respective databases is relatively low. In the TASS database for example 9% of the included hedge funds that are active are closed to new investors. According to Garbaravicius and Dierick (2005) the percentage of closed funds at TASS was 19% in 1994.

All hedge fund indices require specific selection criteria. Concerning the integration of individual hedge funds into the respective strategy indices there are also different approaches. With half of the indices it is the individual fund's choice which index it decides to be associated with. With the remaining half, the decision is made by the respective database provider. The representativity of hedge fund indices correlates negatively with the dimension of the selection criteria requested by the databases. Therefore a huge catalogue of selection criteria is counterproductive for the degree of representativity of hedge fund indices.

Representativity

Although a number of fund managers and investors use indices as a comparison quantity, it is not the primary objective of indices to act as benchmark. Indices mainly serve as a representative of its class and the inherent risks of the respective investment universe. In this function they do not represent the optimal market portfolio, but their goal is to process all available data. Hilpold and Kaiser (2005) realise after their investigation of existing hedge fund strategies that representativity is limited by the lack of consensus regarding the definition and classification of hedge fund strategies. The degree of representativity of the considered indices is now put to the test by comparing them with a comparison index. Following Lhabitant

(2004) an equally-weighted comparison index integrating six indices is constructed to judge the representativity. Apart from the existing overlapping issues of the database providers it is assumed that the constructed index of indices represents the respective hedge fund universe relatively well. The correlation between the single indices and the comparison index is calculated in Table 3. The Edhec Index is based on a comparable methodology. For the Edhec index, the principal component analysis (PCA) is used to identify the optimal set of competing indices and focuses on the representativeness, while the minimum variance analysis focuses on the measurement biases. Therefore the monthly returns of the first three years of the competing indices for each strategy are collected and analysed by the PCA. This process is repeated quarterly.

It is noted that the higher the correlation coefficient the higher the respective degree of representativity. Judging from the indices involved, the HFR databases (Composite and Long/Short Equity), VanHedge (Convertible Arbitrage and Multi Strategy) and Altvest (Merger Arbitrage and Market Neutral) are especially representative. Additionally considering the Edhec-Indices-Index, this index features the highest degree of representativity within the sub-indices distressed securities, event driven, emerging markets, fixed income, fund of funds and Global macro. The main differences are found in the sub-index market neutral between the database providers with the following correlation coefficients of HFR (0.424) and Altvest (0.910).

BIASES

Independent from its construction principle, an index must be able to reproduce a development of value realisable by a special strategy hedge fund in order to be purely in the sense of the hedge fund universe to be represented. That is why the respective indices should not be overly distorted due to biases. Since the data from the various database providers differs with respect to quality and composition, the various indices are subject to different sorts of return distortions (Liang 2000).

Survivorship bias

The most common distorting factor is survivorship bias. It happens every time there are only live funds contained in an index or a

Table 3 Representativity of hedge fund indices

Corr (indices index)	InvestHedge	VanHedge	CS	HFR	CISDM	Altvest	Edhec
Composite	0.886	0.958	0.909	0.966	0.854	0.946	
Convertible arbitrage	0.766	0.981	0.945	0.976	0.974		0.979
Distressed securities		0.930	0.902	0.964	0.920	0.967	0.972
Event driven		0.951	0.949	0.985	0.946	0.980	0.995
Emerging markets	0.987	0.975	0.954	0.989	0.978	0.934	0.997
Fixed income	0.805	0.745	0.751	0.666	0.625		0.824
Fund of funds	0.833			0.950	0.906	0.900	0.956
Global macro	0.774	0.824	0.666	0.913	0.873	0.864	0.982
Long short	0.889	0.953	0.899	0.970	0.771	0.940	0.968
Merger arbitrage		0.930	0.910	0.972	0.955	0.977	0.977
Market neutral		0.838	0.448	0.424	0.890	0.910	0.846
Multi strategy	0.790	0.937	0.802				
Short selling		0.973		0.934	0.967	–	0.986

database at the end of an observation period. Funds that cease operation during the period in question are not taken into account in this case. There are several reasons for reporting returns of a hedge fund to be discontinued: the end of fund operation, bankruptcy, liquidation, name change and merger or fund specific decisions. If the documentation of fund returns is stopped solely due to performance based reasons, this is called "termination bias". Termination bias is based on bad performance and not only does it lead to positive distortions of returns but also to a significant negative distortion of the standard deviation. However, it leads to a positively distorted estimation of skew and a negatively distorted kurtosis of the index return compared with the actual fund universe according to Amin and Kat (2002). The underestimation of variance is backed up by the positive correlation between the volatility of a fund and its survivorship which was investigated by Brown *et al* (1995). In order to adjust the index return, the survivorship bias has to considered and deducted.

The scope of survivorship bias within the area of international equity funds has been investigated and documented already in great detail. The approach of determining the distortion effect usually is to deduct the average return of the surviving funds from the entire fund universe in question. This, however, is not an easy task. Unlike in traditional investments a direct calculation of survivorship bias is not possible since the total hedge fund universe has not yet been grasped. One solution for this problem is to do an estimation based on the data provided by renowned hedge fund databases.

Herein lies the key to the significant differences between various empirical studies (see *Table* 4) which calculates an irrelevant 0.16% (Ackermann et al, 1999) up to 4.41% bias per year (Malkiel and Saha 2005) *depending on the choice of database, the time period examined* and biases encountered. Judging the differing results one must consider that for traditional investments that with increasing time period the survivorship bias per year increases from 0.17% for one year, 0.71% for ten years and 1.24% for 34 years (Carhart *et al* 1997).

The arithmetic mean of the distortion is 2.13% per year and this neglects the positive correlation of the approximation of the hedge fund universe with the size of the sample and the length of the sampling period, thus obtaining 2.34%. Dealing with this problem

Table 4 Investigation of survivorship bias

Authors	Database	Number of funds	Time period of reporting	Survivorship Bias (%)
Ackermann *et al* (1999)	MAR/HFR	547	1988–1995	0.16
Amin and Kat (2002)	TASS	1,721	1994–2001	1.89
Anjilvel *et al* (2000)	FRM	1,130	1990–2000	2.20
Baquero *et al* (2004)	TASS	1,797	1994–2000	2.10
Bares *et al* (2002)	FRM	2,308	1996–1999	1.30
Brown *et al* (1999)	Offshore Directory	395	1989–1995	0.75
Capocci *et al* (2004)	MAR	2,796	1994–2002	1.51
Darst (2000)	MAR	2,202	1995–2000	1.15
Das (2003)	ZCM	2,467	1989–2000	2.16
Edwards and Caglayan (2001)	MAR	1,665	1990–1998	1.85
Edwards and Liew (1998)	MAR	1,456	1989–1996	1.91
Fung and Hsieh (1997)	TASS	901	1989–1995	3.42
Fung and Hsieh (2000)	TASS	1,722	1994–1998	3.00
Ibbotson and Chen (2005)	TASS	4,437	1995–2004	2.74
Liang (2000)	TASS	1,627	1994–1998	2.24
Liang (2000)	HFR	1,162	1994–1997	0.60
Liang (2001)	TASS	1,921	1994–1999	2.43
Liang (2001)	TASS	2,016	1990–1999	1.69
Liang (2002) – CTAs	CISDM	1,510	1985–2001	6.22
Liang (2002) – Fund of Funds	CISDM	597	1985–2001	0.70
Liang (2002) – Hedge Funds	CISDM	2,357	1985–2001	1.52
Liang (2003)	ZCM	2,357	1994–2001	2.32
Malkiel and Saha (2004)	TASS	2,700	1996–2003	3.74
Malkiel and Saha (2005)	TASS	2,700	1996–2003	4.41
Schneeweis *et al* (2001)	TASS	1,722	1998–2000	2.17
Schneeweis *et al* (1996)	TASS	56	1988–1991	1.20

in a realistic fashion, Anson (2002) assumes a distortion of between 2% and 3% per year.

TASS and HFR were the first database providers who realised the importance of a survivorship bias. From 1994 onwards they marked discontinued or dead funds and continued to publish them in a separate database called the "graveyard". Apart from the reasons of fund exclusions from current index calculations, an alternative for survivorship bias is to calculate the attrition rate as an indicator for the rate of funds dying within a yearly time frame. It is calculated as the number of discontinued funds within the year divided by the total number of existing funds at the beginning of the year.

Table 5 Investigation of the attrition rate

Authors	Database	Time period of reporting	Attrition rate (%)		
			min	mean	max
Amin and Kat (2002)	TASS	1994–2001	2.2	–	12.3
Baquero *et al* (2002)	TASS	1994–2000	–	8.6	–
Barès *et al* (2001)	FRM	1992–2000	–	5.0	–
Barry (2002)	TASS	1994–2000	8.0	–	10.0
Brown *et al* (1999)	Offshore Directory	1987–1996	–	14.0	–
Brown *et al* (1999)	Offshore Directory	1989–1995	–	20.0	–
Brown *et al* (2001)	TASS	1994–1998	–	15.0	–
Fung and Hsieh (1997)	TASS	1989–1995	–	19.0	–
Getmansky *et al* (2004)	TASS	1993–2004	1.1[a]	8.8	30.7[a]
Hennessee (2005)	Henneessee	1999–2004	3.8	5.0	6.4
Jenkins (2003)	EuroHedge	2001–2002	8.0	9.0	10.0
Liang (1999)	HFR	1993–1997	–	2.2	–
Liang (2000)	TASS	1994–1998	4.7	8.3	13.4
Liang (2000)	HFR	1994–1997	1.4	2.7	6.2
Liang (2001)	TASS	1994–1999	4.1	–	13.0
MSCI (2005)	MSCI	2004	–	8.0	–

Note: [a] Strategy specific extrema

The unfiltered average attrition rate (ALL) sums up to 8.8% for the time period 1994–2002 based on the TASS database (see Table 5). On the other hand the mortality rate (MR) represents the change in the number of living funds over several years, for example if only 15 funds out of an initial 100 in 1989 survived until 1995 the MR in this case is 15%. The exclusive consideration of the attrition or the mortality rate only provides a distorted picture of the health of the hedge fund industry, since it does not differ between the reasons of exclusion from the index.

Self-selection bias

Contrary to the survivorship bias there may be a negative distortion (downward bias) of the return results of hedge fund indices due to the omission of a database or the discontinuation of reporting (self-selection bias). This type of distortion has its roots mainly in the voluntary character of data providing. It is assumed that there is the tendency of unknown and relatively successful hedge funds trying to avoid being listed in a database due to marketing reasons. At the same time, some hedge funds cease operation of their reporting due to sufficient reputation (based on good performance etc) and/or reaching the maximum investment capacity (fund closure) both leading to a decreasing index return. In the literature this is called "self-selection bias" but the description may slightly differ because fund management has a free choice as to which index provider it has gives its data to or if it wants its data to be published at all. Differences appear even within databases and the desired representation of the hedge fund universe is also distorted. Another form of self-selection bias mentioned in the literature is the confidence in the correct declaration of the investment style from hedge fund managers and the danger of distortions due to non-published changes in investment style (style drift). An alternative characterisation of self-selection bias is representation bias. In view of the fact that some hedge funds do not provide data, this part of the hedge fund universe cannot be included in the index generation, therefore the entire market is not completely represented. Asness *et al* (2001) draw a different conclusion when it comes to performance distortion as a result of self-selection bias. Good performing or under-performing hedge funds stay away from the databases due to various reasons as previously mentioned, hence the net effect of self-selection bias is supposed to be minimal, aside from some persistence.

According to Ackermann *et al* (1999) survivorship and self-selection bias net each other out. Comparing the survivorship bias of traditional indices with a distorted return of about 0.5% to 1.4% per year without the possibility of including self-selection bias yields additional pessimistic assumptions for hedge funds (4.4% per year survivorship bias minus 1.4% per year self-selection bias resulting in an upward bias of 3.0%) (Fung and Hsieh, 2000). Taking the distortion of the traditional indices into account, this would present an advantage of 1.6% up to 2.5% per year for hedge fund indices when used for benchmarking purposes against traditional indices. If one believes the statement of Ackermann *et al* the returns of traditional indices vary only by about 0.3% to 1.2% from those of hedge funds, then hedge fund indices survivorship bias and self-selection bias cancel each other out. Survivorship and self-selection may be reasons for differing performance of indices. Hedge fund index providers take into

Table 6 Annualised returns and Sharpe Ratios of individual sub-indexes

	Annualised returns				Sharpe ratio (4%)			
	Min (%)	Max (%)	Diff.	Mean (%)	Min	Max	Diff.	Mean
Composite	5.60	8.16	2.55	7.30	0.59	1.26	0.67	0.81
Convertible arbitrage	5.82	8.23	2.40	7.09	0.76	1.17	0.41	0.98
Distressed securities	13.72	15.86	2.14	15.06	2.05	2.53	0.48	2.41
Event driven	7.78	11.20	3.42	9.67	1.14	1.75	0.61	1.30
Emerging markets	11.86	17.06	5.20	14.43	0.94	1.57	0.63	1.23
Fixed income	4.90	8.74	3.83	7.15	0.28	2.48	2.20	1.53
Fund of funds	5.23	6.54	1.30	5.72	0.32	0.71	0.39	0.50
Global macro	5.11	14.58	9.46	8.19	0.23	3.15	2.92	1.03
Long short	4.07	8.29	4.22	5.88	0.03	0.99	0.96	0.45
Merger arbitrage	3.20	4.68	1.47	3.93	−0.40	0.26	0.66	−0.04
Market neutral	3.78	7.89	4.10	6.65	−0.09	2.35	2.44	1.45
Multi strategy	5.82	8.30	2.47	6.91	0.38	1.76	1.38	0.98
Short selling	−4.81	9.05	13.86	1.11	−0.58	0.89	1.48	−0.05

account the case of reporting individual hedge funds in their databases in different ways. One provider deletes all past data (www.hedgefund.net), others continue to calculate their indices without the hedge funds in question, but include their past data (CS, HFR, VanHedge). Apart from survivorship bias and self-selection bias, other distortions may exist but are not further discussed here.

HETEROGENEITY

In what follows, different reference numbers for the composite and strategy indices of the following providers Altvest, CISDM, Credit Suisse/Tremont, Hedge Fund Research, InvestHedge and VanHedge during the time period from January 2001–March 2005 are calculated and used as criteria to judge the heterogeneity of hedge fund indices. The aggregated results can be found in the following tables. For each reference number the difference – defined as the maximum value minus the minimum value of the index time

Table 7 Differences in correlation of sub-indices with the S&P 500 and among themselves

	Correlations (S&P 500)				Correlations (indices)			
	Mean	Min	Max	Diff.	Mean	Min	Max	Diff.
Composite	0.648	0.450	0.839	0.390	0.816	0.735	0.864	0.129
Convertible arbitrage	0.071	0.039	0.380	0.341	0.863	0.681	0.883	0.202
Distressed securities	0.462	0.430	0.538	0.108	0.849	0.800	0.882	0.082
Event driven	0.651	0.532	0.725	0.194	0.921	0.905	0.936	0.031
Emerging markets	0.676	0.626	0.739	0.112	0.925	0.897	0.949	0.052
Fixed income	0.169	−0.055	0.624	0.678	0.455	0.291	0.577	0.286
Fund of funds	0.620	0.490	0.647	0.156	0.794	0.610	0.833	0.223
Global macro	0.242	−0.237	0.492	0.729	0.618	0.492	0.685	0.192
Long short	0.683	0.403	0.872	0.469	0.789	0.707	0.843	0.136
Merger arbitrage	0.580	0.471	0.607	0.136	0.879	0.811	0.913	0.103
Market neutral	0.098	−0.336	0.576	0.913	0.552	0.311	0.836	0.525
Multi strategy	0.542	0.442	0.879	0.437	0.682	0.566	0.682	0.116
Short selling	−0.676	−0.928	−0.056	0.872	0.754	0.630	0.913	0.283

series investigated – is given, which can be interpreted as the maximum distortion using one hedge fund index family *versus* another.

Return and Sharpe Ratio

To analyse the return development, the annualised rate of return of the indices is taken and compared. Table 6 shows that there are severe differences between individual hedge fund indices. The maximum yearly return difference is especially high in the sub-index short selling. An average annualised rate of return of −4.81% (HFR) and 9.05% (Altvest) leads to a difference of 13.87%. With 9.47%, the difference in returns is equally high within the sub-index Global macro. The highest average yearly rates of return are achieved in the sub-indices distressed (15.06%) and emerging markets (14.43%). The short selling strategy generates the worst annualised rate of return with 1.1%.

In contrast to the one-dimensional absolute and relative monthly returns, two-dimensional reference numbers in performance measurement have the advantage of additionally considering a risk factor. Sharpe's ratio (1966) is the ratio of excess return over the risk taken and can be interpreted as risk premium per unit of total risk. The excess return is calculated as the difference between actual monthly return and benchmark return. This is usually done by using money market interest rates with matching terms.

These hedge fund indices have been reported as being highly volatile since 1990, the year of first recordings. Kaiser and Kisling (2006) however conclude their investigation that differences on composite level between a Sharpe ratio based on the risk-free rate and a fixed percentage turn out to be very small with a maximum of 0.20. Therefore, the following uses a constant risk-free interest rate of 4%: the higher the Sharpe ratio, the higher the reward for the risk taken. The distressed security strategy overall possesses the most attractive risk-adjusted return. The strategies short selling and merger arbitrage offer the worst Sharpe ratios. Within the different strategies there are noticeable differences between individual databases. They are most noticeable in fixed income arbitrage (2.2), Global macro (2.92) and market neutral (2.44).

Correlation

In order to screen the absolute returns – independent from developments in the traditional money and fixed income markets – published by hedge funds the correlation with indices of traditional investment classes is of central concern. The computation of correlations starts in the first month the index values of the strategies in question are published together. The biggest difference in correlation between individual indices and the S&P 500 is seen in market neutral (0.913). The sub-indices fixed income, Global macro and market neutral show positive as well negative correlation with the S&P 500. The non-directional strategies market neutral (0.098) and convertible arbitrage (0.071) present a very low correlation with the S&P 500. Short selling has a negative correlation (−0.676) as expected. The directional strategies emerging markets (0.676), event driven (0.651) and long/short equity (0.683) show the highest correlation with the equity markets.

Skewness and kurtosis

In general it is assumed that hedge fund returns are not normally distributed (Kat, 2003) and therefore investigations regarding the

Table 8 Differences concerning skew and kurtosis of hedge fund strategy indices

	Skew				Kurtosis			
	Min	Max	Diff.	Mean	Min	Max	Diff.	Mean
Composite	−0.39	0.50	0.89	0.02	−3.74	−1.50	2.24	−2.95
Convertible arbitrage	−0.68	0.19	0.87	−0.20	−3.05	−1.85	1.20	−2.64
Distressed securities	−1.58	0.49	2.07	−0.14	−3.53	1.77	5.30	−1.82
Event driven	−1.27	−0.07	1.20	−0.66	−2.23	0.39	2.63	−1.42
Emerging markets	−0.67	−0.14	0.53	−0.48	−3.38	−2.50	0.89	−3.08
Fixed income	−1.50	−0.30	1.21	−0.82	−3.28	3.10	6.38	−0.36
Fund of funds	−0.21	0.38	0.59	−0.01	−3.12	−0.75	2.37	−2.20
Global macro	0.04	0.55	0.51	0.24	−3.29	−1.58	1.72	−2.59
Long short	−0.75	0.07	0.82	−0.24	−3.62	−1.20	2.41	−2.81
Merger arbitrage	−1.23	−0.41	0.82	−0.91	−1.29	−0.29	1.00	−0.79
Market neutral	−0.40	0.94	1.34	0.16	−3.90	−1.74	2.17	−2.50
Multi strategy	−0.32	0.25	0.57	0.00	−3.19	−2.47	0.72	−2.82
Short selling	−0.47	0.24	0.71	0.02	−3.67	−1.94	1.73	−3.14

skew and kurtosis are necessary. In this chapter only the relative skewness parameters are calculated and compared. A result exceeding zero – a distribution with right-skew – implies a higher probability of positive monthly returns compared to the normal distribution. Table 8 shows the differences of the individual strategy indices. Global macro is the only strategy showing a right-skewed return distribution. All the other strategies vary largely in their skewness values. The Distressed strategy shows the largest differences (−1.58 and 0.49). The strategies fixed income arbitrage, fund of funds, long/short equity and merger arbitrage appear to be unfavourable for the risk-averse investor.

The curvature as measure of concentration of a distribution around its mean is also called kurtosis. A value of three for the relative kurtosis or a value of zero for the excess kurtosis defines the existence of normally distributed returns. On the other hand a positive excess kurtosis characterises so-called fat tails (leptokurtosis). This implies that large deviations around the mean of the distribution occur with a higher probability than they would in a

Table 9 Information ratio (comparison index S&P 500)

Strategy	InvestHedge	VanHedge	CS	HFR	CISDM	Altvest	Edhec
Composite	0.457	0.735	0.621	0.731	0.620	0.715	
Convertible arbitrage	0.464	0.584	0.515	0.514	0.536		0.525
Distressed securities		1.157	1.050	1.130	1.017	1.110	1.109
Event driven		0.826	0.860	0.998	0.632	0.724	0.825
Emerging markets	1.412	1.492	1.184	1.616	1.259	0.979	1.379
Fixed income	−0.632	0.633	0.507	0.528	0.443		0.539
Fund of funds	0.555			0.469	0.482	0.480	0.492
Global macro	0.527	0.459	0.918	0.667	0.461	0.541	0.588
Long short	0.370	0.781	0.499	0.615	0.462	0.718	0.548
Merger arbitrage		0.303	0.370	0.328	0.414	0.408	0.356
Market neutral		0.621	0.554	0.305	0.500	0.566	0.460
Multi strategy	0.472	0.776	0.641				
Short selling		0.123		−0.083	0.047	0.597	0.143

Table 10 Information Ratio (Comparison Index: Global Government Bond Index)

Strategy	InvestHedge	VanHedge	CS	HFR	CISDM	Altvest	Edhec
Convertible arbitrage	–0.085	0.244	0.407	0.220	0.212	0.371	0.286
Composite	–0.034	0.497	0.239	0.267	0.344		
Distressed securities		1.517	1.239	1.593	1.398	1.554	1.677
Event driven		0.560	0.890	0.655	0.379	0.472	0.609
Emerging markets	0.712	0.703	0.762	0.952	1.051	0.824	0.972
Fixed income	1.314	0.751	0.295	0.379	–0.179		0.504
Fund of funds	0.099			–0.119	–0.039	–0.121	–0.056
Global macro	0.537	–0.126	2.129	0.656	–0.057	0.069	0.398
Long short	–0.393	0.099	–0.095	–0.051	–0.039	0.367	–0.147
Merger arbitrage		–0.703	–0.372	–0.562	–0.279	–0.305	–0.469
Market neutral		0.437	0.459	–0.569	0.200	0.368	0.030
Multi strategy	–0.029	0.098	0.564				
Short selling		–0.251		–0.669	–0.412	0.495	–0.168

mesokurtic normal distribution. A platykurtic frequency distribution expressed via an excess kurtosis smaller than zero implies a lower volatility and therefore less risk of the investment in question. The sub-indices show different values depending on the database involved. The strategies distressed securities (5.3), event driven

Table 11 Information ratio (comparison index: Edhec-Index)

Strategy	InvestHedge	VanHedge	CS	HFR	CISDM	Altvest
Composite						
Convertible arbitrage	−0.483	1.325	−0.086	−0.177	0.058	
Distressed securities		0.070	−0.384	0.106	−0.899	−0.132
Event driven		−0.061	0.895	0.668	−1.003	−0.991
Emerging markets	−0.313	0.056	−0.819	0.679	−0.153	−0.959
Fixed income	0.486	0.847	−0.228	−0.160	−0.691	
Fund of funds	0.249			−0.654	0.095	−0.232
Global macro	0.105	−0.945	1.866	0.736	−0.981	−0.466
Long short	−0.154	1.103	0.173	0.499	0.196	1.139
Merger arbitrage		−0.425	0.104	−0.627	0.887	1.056
Market neutral		0.843	0.710	−1.202	0.530	0.830
Multi strategy						
Short selling		−0.313		−1.022	−0.931	0.347

Table 12 Comparison of information ratios (comparison index: S&P 500)

Strategy	InvestHedge	VanHedge	CS	HFR	CISDM	Altvest	Edhec
Composite							
Convertible arbitrage	−0.061	0.059	−0.010	−0.011	0.011		0.525
Distressed securities		0.049	−0.059	0.021	−0.092	0.001	1.109
Event driven	−0.825	0.001	0.034	0.172	−0.193	−0.102	0.825
Emerging markets	0.033	0.114	−0.195	0.237	−0.120	−0.400	1.379
Fixed income	−1.171	0.094	−0.033	−0.012	−0.097		0.539
Fund of funds	0.063			−0.023	−0.010	−0.012	0.492
Global macro	−0.060	−0.129	0.331	0.079	−0.126	−0.047	0.588
Long short	−0.178	0.233	−0.049	0.067	−0.086	0.170	0.548
Merger arbitrage		−0.052	0.014	−0.027	0.058	0.052	0.356
Market neutral		0.160	0.094	−0.156	0.039	0.105	0.460
Multi strategy							
Short selling		−0.019		−0.225	−0.096	0.454	0.143

(2.63) and fixed income arbitrage (6.38) present the largest differences. These are being identified as platykurtic as well as leptokurtic distributions depending on the database used. VanHedge (3.10) and InvestHedge (−3.28) show the biggest difference in the fixed income arbitrage strategy. The remaining sub-indices are completely platykurtic and hence tend to possess unfavourable properties.

A mathematical combination of skewness and kurtosis to examine the existence of a normal distribution can be executed with the Jarque–Bera test (JB). The critical variable of the test is chiquadrat distributed and has a value of 5.991 at a confidence level of 95%. Is the actual value higher than this, the null hypothesis – ie, the existence of a normal distribution – has to be denied. The results reflect those of Ranaldo and Favre (2003) and show that following the Jarque–Bera test, none of the strategies are normally distributed.

INFORMATION RATIO

Especially in the field of hedge funds the generation of alpha, the quality of the fund management to be judged is of central concern. There are already a number of reference numbers in use dealing with this issue. One of them is the Information ratio (IR) which remotely belongs to the family of Sharpe ratios. Not only is this number widely accepted among investor, it is also often the performance benchmark to outperform the fund manager. An IR smaller than 0.25, may lead to the dismissal of the fund manager.

The information ratio is the quotient of the annualised excess return of a fund relative to a benchmark and the annualised standard deviation of the excess returns. An information ratio of 0.5 can be interpreted as good while a value of 1.0 or more is the consequence of the outstanding skill of the fund manager. On the other hand a comparison of two funds with negative information ratios is less to be desired.

For the empirical analysis of the six database providers based on the information ratio three comparison indices were chosen as benchmarks: The S&P 500, the Global Government Bond Index and the Edhec index time series. This is intended to meet the high demands concerning the representativity of diverging investor characteristics. The examination of the time period January 2001–March 2005 yields the following results. Compared with the S&P 500 only the short selling strategy of the database provider CS and Fixed Income Arbitrage of InvestHedge have a negative information ratio. All the other strategy indices have a positive information ratio. The highest information ratio is found in the emerging market indices implying existing alpha with HFR taking the top with 1.616. An explanation for the convincing risk-adjusted out-performance of almost all strategy indices compared to the S&P 500 lies in the fact that there was only an annualised return of −1.38% to outperform. This is due to the fact that the considered period involved the 9/11 incident and therefore strongly decreasing markets which could only recover again in 2005. However it is nevertheless remarkable that an asset class is able to generate positive returns or alpha respectively even in times of exogenous shocks.

When we use the Global Government Bond Index the situation is different and there are 24 more strategy indices with negative information ratios. The CS Global macro index attains the highest information ratio (2.129). If the quality of indices is judged by an information ratio of 0.5 and higher, then only the sub-indices, distressed securities and emerging markets accomplish this demand across all databases. The reason for the hedge fund strategies not performing well is due to the high annualised return of the bond index with 5.8% and to its low volatility. Whether it is meaningful to do this comparison, especially when the benchmark is supposed to have a comparable risk-return-profile, is a guideline for possible future research and investigation.

Comparing the strategy indices with the respective hedge fund based benchmark, the Edhec index family composed of data from various established hedge fund databases, there is a mixed picture. Accordingly in the time frame considered there are 15 strategy indices in with an information ratio exceeding 0.5%. The number of strategy indices with a negative information ratio has risen to 28. Calculating the information ratio of the Edhec indices *versus* the S&P 500 shows that all indices have a positive information ratio except four of the sub-indices – merger arbitrage, market neutral, fund of funds and short selling – have an information ratio exceeding 0.5%.

If subsequently these information ratios are compared with those of the six databases (where the criterion for quality is whether a higher or lower information ratio with respect to the Edhec is achieved) the result is that only the strategy indices of VanHedge and Altvest show a better information ratio than Edhec in 50% or more of the cases. The majority of sub-indices from InvestHedge, CS, HFR and CISDM on the other hand have a lower

Figure 1 Rolling information ratios of the composite indices compared to the performance of the S&P 500 (comparison index: S&P 500)

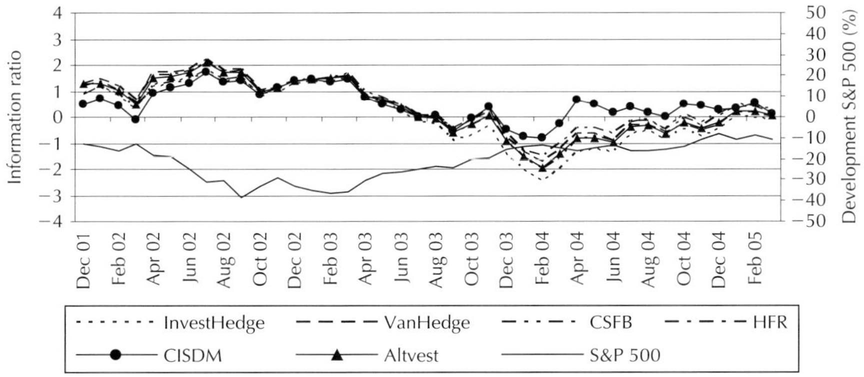

information ratio than that of Edhec. This implies that the six database providers are not competitive with respect to the Edhec indices when the chosen benchmark is the S&P 500.

Especially the positive information ratios in the case of an equity benchmark like the S&P 500 confirms the advantages of hedge fund strategy indices in bearish times. To answer the questions of implicit alphas via information ratio in times of rising stock prices and the expressiveness of the information ratio in general the focus is on rolling information ratios with a time frame of 12 months in the investigation. Confronting the development of rolling information ratios of the composite sub-indices of the six database providers with that of the S&P 500 it is seen that all information ratios show a negative correlation with the S&P 500. The decline of the stock index chosen here is accompanied by information ratios rising asymptotically identical. These tendencies as seen in Figure 1 changed their signal type around March 2003 when the S&P 500 begins to rise steadily. The decline of the information ratios reached their maximum level in February 2004 then they approach zero where they remain thereafter. When examining the information ratios of the index providers it is obvious that their respective development since mid-2003 is different and therefore certain heterogeneity exists and the observations hold for all sub-indices in a similar way. According to the rolling information ratios of the

Table 13 Deviation of the total information ratio *versus* the rolling information ratios (comparison index: S&P 500)

Strategy	InvestHedge	VanHedge	CS	HFR	CISDM	Altvest	Edhec
Composite	0.400	0.332	0.295	0.283	0.117	0.381	
Convertible arbitrage	0.392	0.421	0.403	0.417			0.422
Distressed securities		0.187	0.229	0.083	0.141	0.183	0.139
Event driven		0.213	0.242	0.200	0.321	0.289	0.267
Emerging markets	0.015	0.025	0.072	0.021	0.124	0.282	0.092
Fixed income		0.368	0.359	0.348	0.285		0.367
Fund of funds	0.169			0.370	0.377	0.380	0.365
Global macro	0.518	0.315	0.329	0.287	0.400	0.331	0.333
Long short	0.416	0.303	0.182	0.271	0.422	0.326	0.271
Merger arbitrage		0.473	0.446	0.454	0.427	0.420	0.429
Market neutral		0.357	0.409	0.459	0.389	0.404	0.432
Multi strategy	0.402	0.288	0.331				
Short selling		0.478		0.468	0.370	0.343	0.428

composite indices it is concluded that hedge funds generate alpha and perform better in bearish times than in bullish times with no noticeable alpha.

The results obtained clarify that when judging a fund or a fund manager not only the choice of the comparison index but also the observation period is crucial. Table 13 confronts the deviations of the information ratios over the entire period of time (January 2001–March 2005) with the mean value of the rolling 12-month-information ratios. Numbers above zero can be interpreted as positive distortions of total information ratios *versus* the average rolling information ratios. Hence, the information ratios of all sub-indices of all databases are positively distorted. The most insignificant distortions are observed for the emerging market indices of InvestHedge, VanHedge, CS and HFR as well as for the distressed securities index from HFR. Most considerable is the degree of distortion with 0.518 for the macro index of InvestHedge. Furthermore, all information ratios of the Edhec index family are positively distorted.

CONCLUSION

The fact that an ideal index composition correlates significantly with its respective form of use shows that there is no universal index approach and that homogeneous hedge fund indices remain fiction. The consideration of the hedge fund strategy indices published by six database providers shows that independent from the reference number used for decision; there are distinct differences between the indices with respect to their magnitude. It is astonishing that the statements based on the reference numbers used not only vary significantly in their intensity, but may also lead to contrarian results and hence contradictory investment decisions. Information ratios used as quality criterion to judge a fund manager's skill to generate alpha create largely varying investment signals depending on the chosen comparison index and varying time horizons. This has been shown by comparing the information ratios calculated over the entire time horizon with their rolling counterparts. The existence of a "dynamic" heterogeneity further shows that pure consideration and optimisation based on a single strategy index is not very informative and therefore not advisable as investment decision assistance. Alternatively, interested investors may categorise a strategy index to be judged in the hedge fund universe according to the arithmetic mean, minimum and maximum values discussed in this chapter. The results achieved can be interpreted as a sort of guideline for the assessment of hedge fund strategy indices.

REFERENCES

Ackermann, C., R. McEnally, and D. Ravenscraft, 1999, "The Performance of Hedge Funds: Risk, Return, and Incentives", *Journal of Finance,* **54(3)**, pp 833–74.

Anjilvel, S. I., B. E. Boudreau, M. W. Perkins, and M. S. Urias, 2000, "Why Hedge Funds Make Sense," (New York: Working Paper, Morgan Stanley Quantitative Strategies).

Amin, G. S., and H. M. Kat, 2002, "Portfolios of Hedge Funds", (London: Working Paper, Alternative Investment Research Centre).

Anson, M., 2002, *Handbook of Alternative Assets* (New York: John Wiley & Sons Ltd).

Asness, C., R. Krail, and J. Liew, 2001, "Do Hedge Funds Hedge? Be Cautious in Analyzing Monthly Returns", *Journal of Portfolio Management,* **28(1)**, pp 6–19.

Bailey, J. V., 1992, "Are Manager Universes Acceptable Performance Benchmarks?", *Journal of Portfolio Management,* **18(3)**, pp 9–13.

Bailey, J. V., T. M. Richards, and D. E. Tierney, 1990, "Benchmarks, Portfolios and the Manager/Plan Sponsor Relationship", in: Frank J. Fabozzi, and T. Dessa Fabozzi (eds), *Current Topics in Investment Management,* (New York: Ballinger Pub Co), pp 349–63.

Baquero, G., J. T. Horst, and M. Verbeek, 2004, "Survival, Look-ahead Bias, and the Persistence in Hedge Fund Performance", *Journal of Financial and Quantitative Analysis*, **40(3),** pp 493–517.

Barès, P.-A., R. Gibson, and S. Gyger, 2002, "Hedge Fund Allocation with Survival Uncertainty and Investment Constraints," (Lausanne: Working Paper, Swiss Federal Institute of Technology EPEL).

Barry, R., 2002, "Hedge Funds: a Walk through the Graveyard," (Sydney: Working Paper, Macquarie University).

Brown, S. J., W. N. Goetzmann, and R. G. Ibbotson, 1999, "Offshore Hedge Funds: Survival and Performance 1989–1995", *Journal of Business*, **72(1)**, pp 91–117.

Brown, S. J., W. N. Goetzmann, and J. Park, 2001, "Careers and Survival: Competition and Risk in the Hedge Fund and CTA Industry", *Journal of Finance*, **56(5)**, pp 1869–86.

Brown, S. J., W. N. Goetzmann, and S. A. Ross, 1995, "Survival", *Journal of Finance*, **50(3)**, pp 853–73.

Busack, M. and D. G. Kaiser, 2006, *Handbuch Alternative Investments*, Band 1, (Wiesbaden: Gabler Verlag).

Capocci, D., A. Corhay, and G. Hübner, 2004, 'Hedge Fund Performance and Persistence in Bull and Bear Markets,' (Liege: Working Paper, University of Liege).

Carhart, M. M., J. N. Carpenter, A. W. Lynch, and D. K. Musto, 1997, "Mutual Fund Survivorship", *Review of Financial Studies*, **15**, pp 1439–63.

Darst, E. M., 2000, "Performance Evaluation for Alternative Investments: The Effects of Firm Characteristics and Fund Style on the Performance of Hedge Funds," (Cambridge/Boston: Master Thesis, Harvard University).

Das, N., 2003, "Development of an Analytical Framework for Hedge Fund Investment", (Bloomsburg: Working Paper, Bloomsburg University).

Edwards, F. R., and M. O. Caglayan, 2001, "Hedge Fund Performance and Manager Skill", (New York City: Working Paper, Columbia University).

Edwards, F. R., and J. Liew, 1998, "Hedge Funds and Managed Futures As Asset Classes", (New York City: Working Paper, Columbia University).

Fung, W., and D. A. Hsieh, 1997, "The Information Content of Performance Track Records: Investment style and survivorship bias in the historical returns of commodity trading advisors", *Journal of Portfolio Management*; **24(1)**, pp 30–41.

Fung, W. and D. A. Hsieh, 2000, "Performance Characteristics of Hedge Funds and Commodity Funds: Natural vs. Spurious Biases", *Journal of Financial and Quantitative Analysis*, **35(3)**, pp 291–308.

Garbaravicius, T., and F. Dierick, 2005, "Hedge Funds and their Implications for Financial Stability," (Frankfurt a.M.: European Central Bank, Occasional Paper Series, No. 34).

Getmansky, M., A. W. Lo, and S. X. Mei, 2004, "Sifting Through the Wreckage: Lessons from recent Hedge Funds Liquidations", *Journal of Investment Management*, **2(4)**, pp 6–38.

Heidorn, T., C. Hoppe, and D. G. Kaiser, 2006, "Validität des Benchmarking von traditionellen Marktindizes mit Hedgefondsindizes", forthcoming in *Bank Archiv*.

Hennessee (2005): www.hennesseegroup.com.

Hilpold, C. and D. G. Kaiser, 2005, *Alternative Investment-Strategien – Einblick in die Anlagetechniken der Hedgefonds-Manager*, (Weinheim: John Wiley & Sons Ltd).

Ibbotson, R. G. and P. Chen, 2005, "Sources of Hedge Fund Returns: Alphas, Betas, and Costs," (New Haven: Working Paper No. 05–17, Yale ICF).

Indjic, D. and A. Heen, 2003, "AIMA Survey on Hedge Fund Classification Practise", *AIMA Journal*, **58(September)**, pp 1–6.

Jenkins, I., 2003, "State of the Hedge Fund Industry", *AIMA Journal*, February.

Kaiser, D. G., 2004, *Hedgefonds – Entmystifizierung einer Anlageklasse – Strukturen – Chancen – Risiken*, (Wiesbaden: Gabler Verlag).

Kaiser, D. G. and K. Kisling, 2006, "Einflussfaktoren der risikoadjustierten Wertentwicklung von Hedgefonds", in M. Busack, and D. G. Kaiser, (eds), *Handbuch Alternative Investments Band 1*, (Wiesbaden: Gabler Verlag).

Kat, H. M., 2003, "Hedge Funds vs. Common Sense – An illustration of the Danger of Mechanical Investment Decision Making", (London: Working Paper, City University of London).

Lhabitant, F.-S., 2004, "Testing the Representativity of Pure Style Indices", (Lille: Working Paper, EDHEC Graduate School of Business, Risk and Asset Management Research Centre).

Liang, B., 1999, "Hedge Funds: The Living and the Dead," (Cleveland: Working Paper, Case Western Reserve University).

Liang, B., 2000, "Hedge Funds: The Living and the Dead", *Journal of Financial and Quantitative Analysis*, **35(3)**, pp 309–26.

Liang, B., 2001, "Hedge Fund Performance: 1990–1999", *Financial Analyst Journal*, **57(1)**, pp 11–18.

Liang, B., 2002, "Hedge Funds, Fund of Funds, and Commodity Trading Advisors," (Cleveland: Working Paper Sep. 2002, Case Western Reserve University).

Liang, B., 2003, "On the Performance of Alternative Investments: CTAs Hedge Funds and Funds of Funds," (Amherst: Working Paper, Isenberg School of Management, University Massachusetts).

Malkiel, B. G. and A. Saha, 2004, "Hedge Funds: Risk and Return," (Princeton: Working Paper, Princeton University).

Malkiel, B. G. and A. Saha, 2005, "Hedge Funds: Risk and Return," (Princeton: Reviewed Working Paper).

MSCI, 2005: www.msci.com

Ranaldo, A., and L. Favre, 2003, "How to Price Hedge Funds: From Two to Four Moment CAPM," (Lille: Working Paper, EDHEC Graduate School of Business, Risk and Asset Management Research Centre).

Schneeweis, T., H. Kazemi, and G. Martin, 2001, "Understanding Hedge Fund Performance: Research Results and Results of Thumb for the Institutional Investor," (Amherst: Working Paper, Center for International Securities and Derivatives Markets, University Massachusetts).

Schneeweis, T., R. Spurgin, and D. McCarthy, 1996, "Survivor Bias in Commodity Trading Advisors Performance", *Journal of Future Markets*, **16(7)**, pp 757–72.

Sharpe, W. F., 1966, "Mutual Fund Performance", *Journal of Business*, **39(1)**, pp 119–38.

Sharpe, W. F., 1992, "Asset Allocation: Management Style and Performance Measurement", *Journal of Portfolio Management*, **18(2)**, pp 7–19.

Vaissié, M., 2003, "Detailed Analysis of Construction Methods and Management Principles of Hedge Fund Indices – Are all hedge fund indices created equal?," (Lille: Working Paper, EDHEC Graduate School of Business, Risk and Asset Management Research Centre).

2

Hedge Fund Indices and Passive Alpha: A Buy-Side Perspective

François-Serge Lhabitant

Kedge Capital, HEC Lausanne and EDHEC

INTRODUCTION

Hedge funds have enjoyed extraordinary growth in the past decade, with assets under management increasing from approximately US$25 billion in 1990 to more than a trillion today. The number of hedge funds (now estimated at more than 8,000) exceeds the number of securities traded on the New York Stock Exchange, a phenomenon already experienced by mutual funds in the early 1990s. Several factors have contributed to this tremendous success. Let us mention three years of dismal equity market performance, depressed cash and bond yields, high profile defaults and accounting scandals, but also the investors' quest for new sources of diversification as well as the increased attraction of absolute returns, ie returns that are positive and independent from market conditions.

Traditionally, hedge fund investors have had just two means of investing in hedge funds: "do-it-yourself" manager selection, or investing via a fund of hedge funds. Unfortunately, "do-it-yourself" manager selection is not as simple as investing in a portfolio of traditional securities. First, the lack of transparency in the alternative investments marketplace renders individual hedge fund selection and monitoring a challenge. Note that this is not new – hedge fund managers have always been secretive, and obtaining performance or strategy information often requires patience and perseverance. Second, the absence or quasi-absence of regulation imposes the conduct of a thorough initial due diligence process on each selected hedge fund. This due diligence process is costly, difficult, resource-intensive and time consuming, but it should be a pre-requisite to any investment. Third, selecting individual hedge funds is only the first part of the process. Much attention should be devoted to the portfolio construction process in order to ensure sufficient diversification, reasonable liquidity and an adequate risk/return profile. The best ingredients do not turn into the best dish without a chef's intervention, and the same goes for hedge funds. Finally, hedge funds are actively managed, which means that investors need to monitor them on a continuous basis to assess whether they fulfil their mandate and justify their fees. In particular, investors have to remember that beta is for free, and that hedge funds should primarily focus on alpha generation rather than on free-riding betas. All these features and requirements often represent a significant barrier to direct hedge fund investment, as most investors lack the time, resources and/or expertise required to sift out the charlatans from the honest and the skilful from the lucky.

The second alternative, fund of hedge funds, has therefore naturally emerged as the solution to externalise the burden of hedge fund due diligence and portfolio construction. Against an additional layer of fees, fund of hedge funds offer easy access to a diversified portfolio of hedge funds, most of the time with better liquidity terms and lower minimum investment requirements. For most investors, they represent the only possible way to invest in hedge funds while fulfilling their role as fiduciaries and keeping staffing levels reasonably low. As a result, in a few years, the number of fund of hedge funds has grown exponentially. According to Hedge Fund Research, there are now more than 2,000 funds of hedge funds worldwide and they control more than a third of the assets deployed in the hedge fund industry. If this trend continues at the same pace, it is likely that investors will soon find the process of picking fund of hedge funds as challenging as the process of selecting individual hedge funds. Of course, at that point, fund of fund of hedge funds might help, but again at the expense of an additional layer of fees.

When facing these never ending increasing frictional costs of hedge fund investing, buy-side investors should recall Warren Buffet's 2005 newsletter, and particularly his comments on the proliferation and rising greed of types whom he calls "Helpers" and

"Hyper-Helpers". Buffet saved his greatest sarcasm for "the recent pandemic of profit arrangements, under which helpers receive large portions of the winnings when they are smart or lucky, and leave [investors] with all the losses – and large fixed fees to boot – when the helpers are dumb or unlucky (or occasionally crooked)". In a few years' time, these words of wisdom will be likely to strike a particular resonance in investors' minds, when the Super-Hyper-Helpers will step in.

In the meantime, a third method of delivery for hedge fund returns has become available: hedge fund indexing. Rather than handpicking hedge fund managers, this latest evolutionary step in hedge fund investing uses the hedge fund market – or one of its representations – as the basis for manager selection and portfolio construction. The goal is no longer to allocate to the best hedge fund managers, but rather to get a low-cost efficient exposure to hedge funds in aggregate. At first glance, the debate seems familiar – we already had it for several years in traditional asset classes. Those who believe they can select a better than average fund of funds manager will take the active route. Those who lack the necessary degree of self confidence will opt for an index fund. However, hedge fund indexing is fundamentally different from equity or bond indexing. In fact, our opinion is that it is a rather flawed concept, both for practical and theoretical reasons, because:

(a) creating a good hedge fund index is nowhere near as easy as it is in equity land; and
(b) investors should not be willing to pay active fees to obtain *below* average performance. This chapter will justify our views and explain why we believe that from the buy-side point of view, investing in an index of hedge funds seems like the ultimate oxymoron.

The chapter is structured as follows. The next section describes the essential characteristics of the existing hedge fund indices and in particular, their construction methods and key management principles. The third section discusses the biases that affect these indices, and their impact from an investor's perspective. The final section concludes and opens the door to further research.

HEDGE FUND INDICES

While traditional equity indices date back to the 19th century, hedge fund indices are a relatively recent innovation. Indeed, the first indices grew out of hedge fund advisory firms such as the Hennessee Group (Hennessee), Hedge Fund Research (HFR) or Managed Accounts Reports (MAR) in the early 1990s. They were initially developed as in-house basic averages designed to occasionally gauge the hedge fund industry's general direction. But rapidly, the growing interest in benchmarking hedge fund returns convinced their creators to publish them regularly and on a wider basis. Since then, a growing number of firms have been involved in the creation and publication of hedge fund indices. These firms now include small boutiques specialising in hedge funds, hedge fund data providers, publishers, but also leading traditional index providers and companies with hedge fund products to sell.

Today, the initial lack-of-index issue that once deterred many institutions from embracing hedge funds is now slowly being swept away. In fact, the proliferation of new hedge fund indices has even resulted in a new difficulty for investors: that of choosing an appropriate one. At the time of writing, there were 24 hedge fund index providers, several composite indices and hundreds of single-strategy indices – see Table 1.

Interestingly, none of these hedge fund indices has really managed to become accepted as the industry's standard for measuring performance. This is not really surprising, given the disparity of their track records. As an illustration, Amenc and Martellini (2002) found that differences in monthly returns between hedge fund indices from different providers supposedly representing the same strategy were sometimes greater than 20%. For instance, Zurich reported a 20.48% return for the long/short equity strategy in February 2000, while EACM reported a −1.56% return in the same month for the same strategy. Discrepancies of a similar magnitude are also observed in dedicated short, emerging markets and global macro-strategies. Last, but not least, some competing indices on the same strategy were negatively correlated to each other, which seriously question their ability to represent a common behaviour. Hedge fund indices were definitely not all created equal.

Needless to say, such disparities have provided a somewhat confusing picture of the hedge fund investment universe, and one may

Table 1 Major hedge fund index providers

Index provider	Index launch date	Start of historical data	Web site
Altvest	2000	1993	www.investorforce.com
Barclays	2003	1997	www.barclaygrp.com/indices/ghs
Bernheim	1995	1999	www.hedgefundnews.com
Blue X	2002	2002	
CISDM/MAR	1994	1990	www.cisdm.org
CS/Tremont	1999	1994	www.hedgeindex.com
Dow Jones	2003	2002	www.djindexes.com
EACM	1996	1996	www.eacmalternative.com
Edhec	2003	1997	www.edhec-risk.com
Eurekahedge	2002	2000	www.eurekahedge.com
Feri	2002	2002	www.feri-alta.de
FTSE	2004	1998	www.ftse.com
Hennessee	1987	1987	www.hennesseegroup.com
HF Intelligence	2001 to 2003	1998	www.hedgefundintelligence.com
HF Net (Tuna)	1998	1976–95	www.hedgefund.net
HFR	1994	1990	www.hedgefundresearch.com
LJH	1992	1989	www.ljh.com
MondoHedge	2003	2002	www.mondohedgeindex.com
MSCI	2002	2002	www.msci.com
S&P	2002	1998	www.spglobal.com
RBC	2005	2005	www.rbchedge250.com
TalentHedge	2003	2003	www.talenthedge.com
Van Hedge	1994	1988	www.vanhedge.com
Zurich	2001	1998	Discontinued

wonder how such differences are possible. The answer is twofold. First, as will be seen, hedge fund indices are usually calculated from different samples and databases, which do not necessarily overlap. As an illustration, if one considers four of the largest hedge fund databases (Hedge Fund Research, TASS, CISDM and MSCI), only 3% of the funds report to all four databases, and only 10% report to three databases – see Figure 2. Second, due to the important theoretical and practical barriers to implementing a hedge fund index, index providers often had to take subjective decisions, and these resulted in strong heterogeneity in the construction approaches used to calculate these indices – see for instance Heidorn *et al* (this volume).

At this stage, readers may simply ask which hedge fund index they should use. But there is no universal answer, because the

Figure 1 Maximum monthly performance spread between competing hedge fund indices on the same strategy

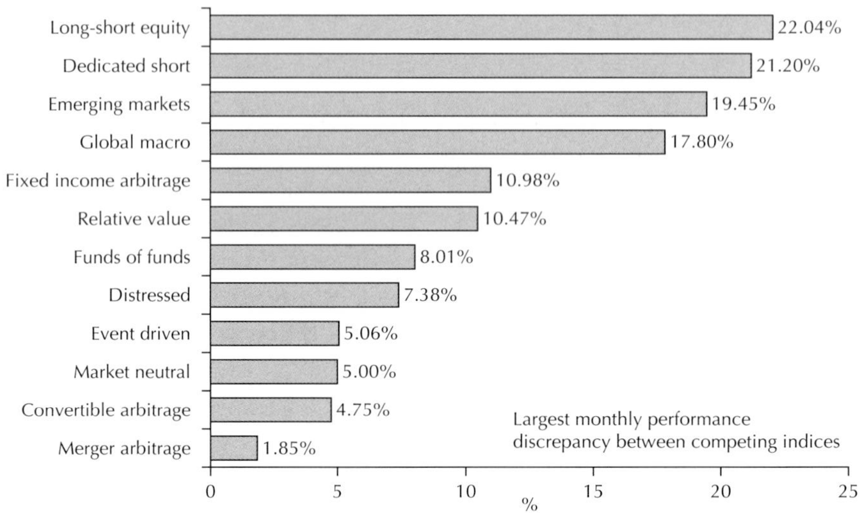

Figure 2 The overlap in terms of hedge funds between four of the largest commercial hedge fund databases is small, which means that hedge fund indices will often diverge in terms of components

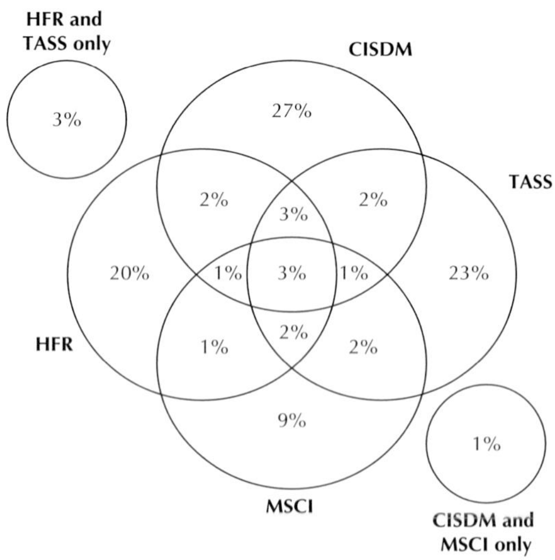

quality of an index should imperatively be evaluated in the light of the use that will be made of it. The following section will therefore focus on *one* particular use of hedge fund indices, namely, indexing.

WHY HEDGE FUND INDEXING IS NOT A GOOD IDEA

Many investors and consultants consider indexing as the best and least costly solution to implement an asset allocation. While we generally agree with them when dealing with traditional asset classes, our opinion is that indexing in the world of hedge funds is a minefield for the unwary. The reason is that the majority of hedge fund indices suffer from serious biases, both conceptually and in their implementation, so that tracking a given hedge fund index is often sub-optimal and does not correspond to the initial intentions of investors. Let us now explain why.

Lack of representativity

Successful indexing pre-supposes that one has identified an index which is representative of an investment universe. In traditional asset classes, this is usually not a concern, because the investment universe is well-defined and the underlying securities are exhaustively identified. In hedge funds, however, the situation is different. Hedge funds have no obligation to report their performance or even their existence beyond the circle of their investors. They can operate in complete secrecy, whatever their size. Consequently, the hedge fund universe is not observable, and index providers need to work with small samples of hedge funds rather than with the entire universe. At best, their indices will therefore be representative of the sample they originated from. But few investors ask the right question – how representative are these samples used?

If one wants to get a passive exposure to an asset class using an index, the question of the index coverage becomes essential. Ideally, a hedge fund index should cover the entire universe of hedge funds, or at least a large majority of its assets. Unfortunately, no hedge fund index yet fulfils that criterion. In fact, all existing indices are subject to at least three sampling biases:

(1) The *voluntary reporting bias*: the hedge fund managers that report their performance to a commercial database do it only on

a voluntary basis and primarily for marketing purposes – this constitutes the easiest way for them to appear on the radar screen of consultants. This creates a significant self-selection bias, ie the most successful hedge funds will typically not be included in databases because they do not actively seek new capital, and they will therefore not be included in indices.

(2) The *database selection bias*: most database providers have defined specific criteria to accept hedge funds in their universe. These criteria may include a minimum asset size, a minimum track record, a minimum liquidity, the appurtenance to specific strategies, etc. They create another bias because some hedge funds will systematically be excluded from the database and therefore from the resulting indices.

(3) The *index selection bias*: most index providers have also defined their own set of criteria to include hedge funds in their indices. In some cases, this selection will even be delegated to a third party service provider, eg Lyxor in the case of the MSCI investable indices or PlusFunds for S&P's hedge fund indices. This results in another sampling bias, which is similar to the database selection bias but applies at the index level. It is often more difficult to quantify, because several index providers do not explicitly disclose the rules they use when they build or rebalance their index.

The importance of these three sampling biases varies from one index to another, but it is relatively easy to observe that the coverage ratio of most indices is remarkably low. Indeed, if one admits that the hedge fund universe counts approximately 8,000 *active* managers and more than US$1 trillion of assets, it should be obvious that a sample of 40 or even 100 hedge funds will have a hard time representing the universe, whatever the index construction approach – see Table 1 (Heidorn *et al*, this volume).

But the disparity between indices is even more visible when one considers their individual components. Competing hedge fund indices, which are extracted from small samples of their respective databases, have very few hedge funds in common. As an illustration, Lhabitant (2006) compared the hedge funds used in the six so-called "investable indices", and observed that the large majority of them (246 funds) were only found in one index, 32 funds were members of two indices, nine funds were in three indices, and 10 funds were in four indices. And no fund was found in more than four indices. On average, only 7.8% of the funds covered by two investable indices were common to both of them. It is therefore not surprising if the performance of various hedge fund indices diverge: not only their construction methodologies differ, but in addition they are not based on the same investment universe.

Survivorship bias

The majority of hedge fund indices are affected by survivorship bias. That is, when an index is created, its pro-forma historical track record is usually backtracked from its component funds' track records. The problem is that these component funds are actually survivors. Defunct funds which typically stopped reporting due to bankruptcy, liquidation or poor performance are ignored. Once the index is launched, survivorship bias is no longer a concern for the future track record, but most investors will base their investment decisions based on the *historical* track record, which is biased.

How important is this bias? The academic literature has investigated and documented survivorship bias already in great details, and the answer varies from 0.16% to 6.67% pa depending on the observation period, the database or even the definition used to calculate the survivorship bias – some researchers analyse the return of dead funds versus surviving funds, while others compare all funds (dead and alive) to surviving funds – see Table 4 (Heidorn *et al*, this volume). The magnitude of survivorship bias varies also greatly across strategies. According to Malkiel and Saha (2005), survivorship bias is as high as 15.24% per annum for emerging market funds and 14.97% per annum for global macro-funds, but as low as 2.55% per annum for funds of hedge funds.

Although these numbers are calculated at a database level and not at a hedge fund index level, it is obvious that indices will inherit some of the survivorship bias from the database on which they are built. Investors are therefore likely to select indexing because of its superior historical performance over an actively managed fund of hedge funds, while most of its dominance was actually generated by survivorship bias.

LACK OF ALPHA, ON AVERAGE

Having a truly representative hedge fund index is highly desirable, if only for benchmarking purposes. But assuming that such an index existed, would gaining exposure to that index be a recommended strategy? In our opinion, the answer is again negative. The reason is that allocating to hedge funds using a representative hedge fund index approach implies gaining exposure to a large and potentially growing pool of unskilled managers. This leads to what we call the *representativity conundrum*: the more representative an index is, the more attractive it is for benchmarking purposes, but the less attractive it becomes as an investment. Although hedge funds are one of the few areas in asset management where all managers claim to belong to the first quartile, reality is that a representative hedge fund index *has no particular reason to exhibit any alpha*. In fact, we believe that there are several reasons to exhibit a negative alpha. Let us explain why.

First, we believe that contrary to the situation that prevailed in the early days of hedge funds, the average hedge fund manager today has no proven skills. The higher level of fees charged by hedge funds combined with the absence of barriers to entry and the relative opaqueness of the hedge fund industry have attracted a large number of new players who have opened their own hedge fund. It is hard to believe that so many talents were hidden for so long and suddenly found their way. Reality is more that with a few exceptions, these new managers still have to demonstrate their ability to generate alpha and control risk. Of course, several of them had a successful career in asset management (long only funds) or in investment banking (traders), but there is no guarantee that they will be able to replicate this in the hedge fund space. And many have no particular experience of shorting securities, or even failed miserably to generate alpha in the long-only industry.

Second, being called a hedge fund does not guarantee a positive alpha, at least from the investor's perspective. In fact, if one assumes that alpha is a zero sum game at the industry level, then uninformed investments in hedge fund managers should have a zero expected excess return before fees, with half of the funds outperforming the market and the other half underperforming. Needless to say, this zero-sum game becomes extremely unattractive for the

Figure 3 The decline of the average hedge fund alpha over time. Alpha is defined as the intercept of a regression of the HFR Global hedge Fund Index returns on the S&P 500 returns over a 36-month rolling window

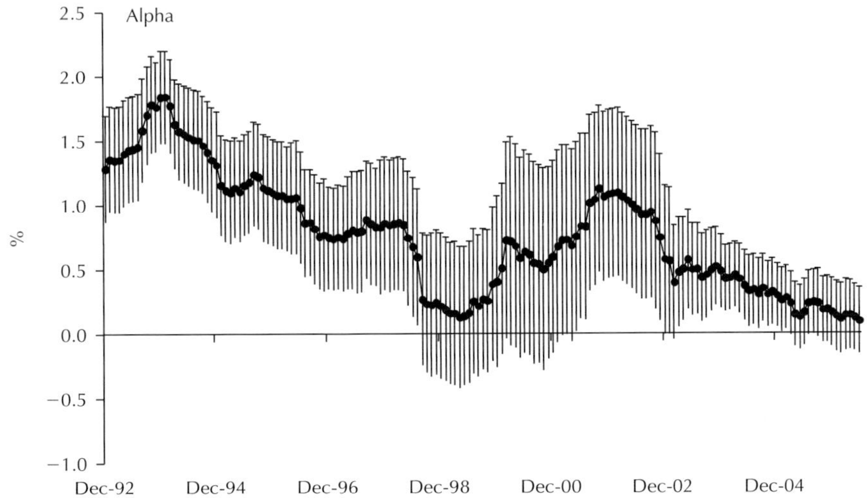

investor if each player charges a 2% management fee and a 20% performance fee.

Third, even if we accept that a small portion of hedge fund managers are actually skilled, their ability to extract profits due to market inefficiencies is becoming increasingly challenged. The massive inflows of capital are chasing the same opportunities, so that the initial pie needs to be split into more slices. The best hedge funds are facing capacity constraints, and have closed their doors to new investors – they do not want to accept additional capital if the marginal profit is lower. Needless to say, these highly successful hedge funds are usually not found in indices.

As an illustration of this declining performance effect, let us consider the following experiment. A simple regression of the HFR Global Hedge Fund Index is run against the S&P 500 index from January 1990 to June 2006, using a rolling 36-month window. The resulting alpha from this regression is displayed in Figure 3, as well as its 95% confidence interval. It is clear that hedge funds have experienced *on average* a significant decline of their alpha over time. The R^2 of the regression, by contrast, seems to be slightly increasing over time – see Figure 4.

Figure 4 The explanatory power (R^2) of the rolling regression used in Figure 3

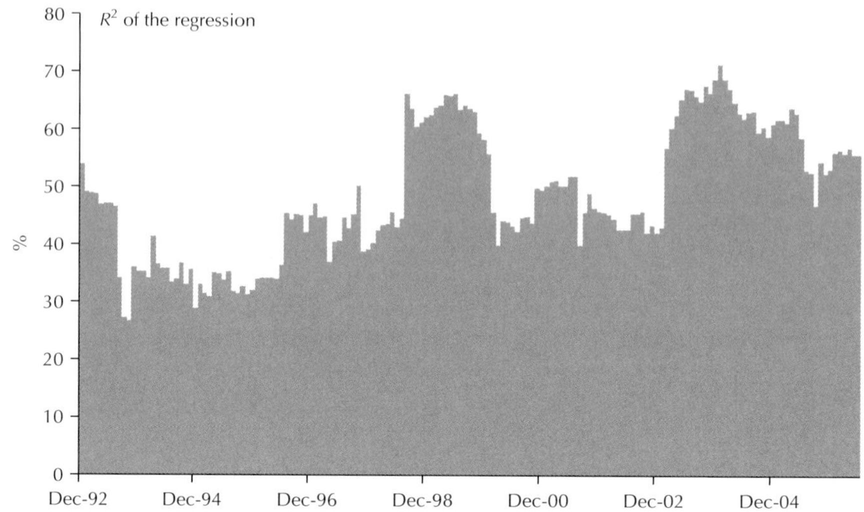

Figure 5 Impact of the number of components in a fund of hedge funds portfolio on its correlation with the S&P 500

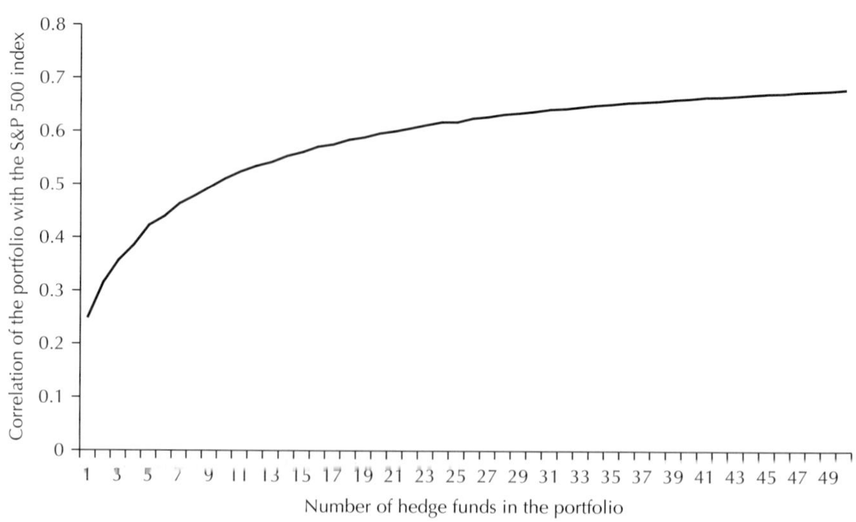

Figure 6 The correlation between the HFR Fund Weighted Composite Index and the S&P 500, based on different samples of months over the January 1990 to May 2006 period

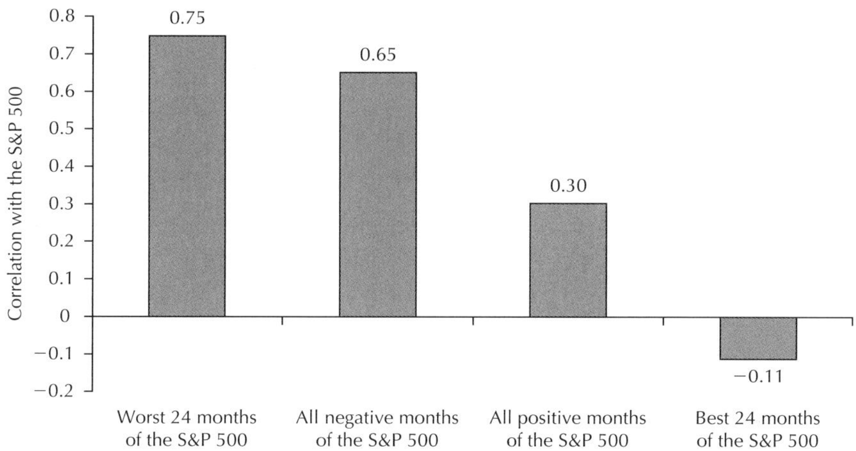

Now, these results do not imply that *all* hedge funds have lost their golden touch and no longer generate alpha. It means that alpha has declined *on average* at the industry level. Whether this lower level of alpha generation will stabilise, continue to decline, or increase is difficult to say definitively. But in the meantime, this is precisely what the problem of hedge fund indexing is: it provides an exposure to the average of the industry, not the best alpha providers. Is this really what investors like when they consider hedge funds? We have strong doubts about it.

OVER-DIVERSIFICATION EFFECTS

Most investors are drawn to hedge funds because they offer a unique combination of attributes, and in particular a low correlation to traditional asset classes. However, when pooling several hedge funds in an index, these attributes may not survive. The over-diversification that prevails in most hedge fund indices often makes the result look poor, although the original components were individually attractive.

As an illustration, consider Figure 4, which shows the link that exists between the number of hedge fund managers in a portfolio and its correlation with the S&P 500. The hedge fund managers are randomly selected in the Altvest database and receive an initial equal dollar allocation, and the process is repeated 5,000 times to calculate the average correlation for each portfolio size. Clearly the correlation with the S&P 500 increases as the number of funds increases. In a sense, this should be expected, since the specific risk of each hedge fund is diversified away while the systematic risk remains in the portfolio. The more hedge funds are in the portfolio, the higher the diversification impact … and the higher the correlation with the S&P 500.

This increase of correlation is also observable as the single strategy level. For instance, Lhabitant and Learned (2002) documented that market neutral hedge funds had on average a low correlation to the S&P 500, while a portfolio of market neutral hedge funds was usually highly correlated. This phenomenon was also confirmed over different time periods, which simply shows that the diversification of specific risk is obviously time-resistant. Of course, this correlation behaviour arises as soon as there is more than one fund in a portfolio. Consequently, it also affects actively managed funds of hedge funds. But it the impact is likely to be more important in hedge fund indices because of their larger number of managers and their absence of portfolio construction. In a sense, by including more hedge funds in a hedge fund index to make it more representative, index providers are actually losing the initial desirable property offered by their *individual* components.

Note that this also explains why so many studies found that investing in hedge fund indices actually provided so few benefits from a risk management perspective – see for instance Liew (2003) and Lhabitant (2004). In particular, in bearish environments, the aggregate market exposure of hedge fund indices tends to increase rapidly and even dominates the skill component. As an illustration, the correlation of the HFR Fund Weighted Composite Index has been calculated with the S&P 500 over different samples of month. The result clearly shows that correlation with traditional equities increases when diversification benefits are most needed.

Consequently, when there are periods of severe market dislocation, hedge fund indices fail to provide adequate protection. Most investors are aware of vanishing diversification benefits in these circumstances and attempt to create portfolios that reduce downside risk under extreme market conditions. But this is not what index providers are doing, as their construction approaches, rather they aim at diversifying the specific bets taken by hedge fund managers and retaining their systematic risk. Investors should therefore be cautious before extending any conclusion from a study based purely on indices to individual managers, as from a risk perspective, a basket of hedge funds does not necessarily behave as the average of its components.

Inefficient fee structure

Finally, there is one crucial difference between the indexation of hedge funds and the indexation of traditional asset classes. In the latter case, indexation is free or available at a *very low* cost. Indexers are trying to free ride on an asset class's features, and it is hard to justify paying any fee for that. By contrast, hedge fund indexing – ie free-riding on the selection abilities of active managers – is *extremely* expensive. First, the underlying hedge fund managers will charge their usual 2% management fee and 20% performance fee. Second, the hedge fund indexers will charge practically the same as actively managed fund of hedge funds – see Table 2. Third, investors should be cautious with hidden costs such as subscription and redemption fees, index calculation fees, administration fees, and bid-ask spreads. At the end of the day, an indexed hedge fund portfolio is sometimes more costly than an actively managed portfolio, and this without offering the same services, eg asset allocation, access to high quality closed funds, extensive due diligence, etc. Of course, fees are a result of supply and demand, and time will tell if investors are willing to pay active fees for getting an average performance.

CONCLUSIONS

The aim of the chapter was to explain why we believe that hedge fund indices should not be considered as attractive investment opportunities from a buy-side perspective. In our opinion, the verdict is clear: (a) most hedge fund indices do not currently represent adequately the alternative investment universe; (b) representative hedge fund indices, if they exist one day, will increasingly be exposed to mediocre and unskilled managers; and (c) trackers on hedge fund indices are as expensive as actively managed portfolio of hedge funds without offering the same services and advantages.

3

History Bias Factor: A Definition

Daniel Capocci

HEC, University of Liège

INTRODUCTION

Hedge funds have been studied since the late 1990s. Fung and Hsieh (1997) are the pioneers. Today, the literature on the subject is rich and more and more aspects of the subject are studied. Hedge funds databases have some specific biases. The two most recognised are the *survivorship bias* and the *instant return history bias* (also called the *backfill bias*). The survivorship bias is measured by the performance difference between living and all funds in a database (as defined by Brown *et al*, 2001). The same definition applies to mutual funds databases. The second bias, specific to the hedge fund world is called the *instant return history bias*. It exists because hedge funds are not allowed to advertise. Because of this managers consider inclusion in a database primarily as a marketing tool. This creates a positive *instant history bias* or *backfilled bias* (Fung and Hsieh, 2000) that occurs because a fund's performance history is backfilled after inclusion. The upward bias results from the fact that funds with a poor track record are less likely to apply for inclusion than funds with good performance history.

The presence of this bias can be estimated using a two-step methodology (defined by Park, 1995; Brown, Goetzmann and Ibbotson, 1997; Fung and Hsieh, 2000). On the one hand, the average monthly return of the "observable portfolio" which invests in all funds from the database each month has to be estimated. On the other hand, the average monthly return of the "adjusted observable portfolio" obtained from investing in all these funds after deleting the first 12, 24 and, if possible, 36, 48 and 60 months of returns should be calculated. Then, the difference in performance between the observable portfolio and the adjusted observable portfolio is estimated.

The measure of the instant history bias has three main problems. The first is that the performance of the funds at the start of their existence and global performances are not compared over the same time frame. In order to estimate the bias, the first months of existence of each fund are removed and then, the figures are aggregated to compare the performance of the global database with the funds without the first months of existence. Market conditions can be fundamentally different (1999 and early 2000 compared with 2001 and 2002). If, over a specified period many more funds are created and the global performance of these new funds is significantly better or worse than other funds (because a new strategy that is developing rapidly – with a growing number of funds – works particularly well or because on previous performance one does not work any more – see eg, convertible arbitrage in 2004 and early 2005), the results obtained can be biased by the time period analysed. Second, since in the estimation we have to remove funds with less than 12, 24, 36, 48 or 60 months of existence, survivorship bias can also intervene in the estimation since badly performing funds dissolved after 12, 24, 36, 48 and 60 months will not be included in the estimation and the survivorship bias of these funds will clearly intervene in the estimation. It is not easy to determine which of the two biases contribute most to the instant return bias estimation. Finally, and maybe less importantly, estimation of the bias needs a lot of calculation and manipulation. In the estimation process a portion of the monthly return for each fund should be removed first. Then, performance should be aggregated. Finally, the figures should be compared. Moreover, the figures are not easy to compare because various percentages are obtained (when removing 12, 24, 36, 48 and 60). The new measure proposed in this chapter will address these issues.

This chapter is organised as follows. The next section presents the data used. The third section introduces the definition of the instant history factor. The fourth section reports the estimation of this factor before explaining how this factor corrects the problems of the classical instant return history bias estimation in the penultimate section. The final section concludes the chapter.

DATABASE

Four main hedge fund databases are available for empirical studies, the Managed Account Reports, Inc/Center for International Securities Derivatives Markets, Hedge Fund Research, Inc, Tass Management and the Barclays database. The same dataset is used as Capocci (2005) combining MAR/CISDM data with Barclays hedge fund data. There is a total of 3,060 individual funds and 903 funds of funds. This is one of the greatest databases ever used in hedge funds performance studies. These funds include 1,873 (61.15%) survived individual funds, 1,190 (38.85%) dissolved individual funds, 653 (72%) surviving funds of hedge funds and 254 (28%) dissolved funds of funds.[1]

HISTORY BIAS FACTOR DEFINITION

Ratios and factors have been used for a long time in the financial world. Their first use has always been to compare portfolio managers' performance and/or risk. The best-publicised is the Sharpe ratio (see Sharpe, 1994). This ratio is defined as the ratio of excess return (over the risk-free rate) over the risk of the portfolio analysed (measured by the standard deviation) as defined by Sharpe (1994). This ratio has been widely used in hedge fund academic studies (see eg, Ackermann *et al*, 1999; Liang, 1999; Amin and Kat, 2003). Other well-known factors are the Jensen alpha (1968), the Treynor ratio (1965), which have been defined to compare specific aspects of the data analysed. The death ratio for example defined as the ratio of death funds over all the funds in the database over a specified period has been widely used in hedge fund studies (see eg, Liang, 2003).

The *history bias factor* aims at determining if new funds tend to outperform existing ones. Stated differently, it aims at determining if funds tend to outperform over their first months of existence. This factor is defined as follows:

> The *history bias factor* is the ratio of the yearly performance of the funds over the period considered divided by the net number of new funds over the period studied.

The *history bias factor* has the following formula:

$$HBF = {R_{HF_t}}/{NF_t} \tag{1}$$

where HBF = *history bias* factor, R_{HF} = performance of the funds in the database over the period t (1 year), NF = net number of funds in the database at period t (number of new funds less number of dissolved funds).

This factor is higher when:

- ❑ the absolute performance of the funds in the database over the period is higher; or
- ❑ when the net number of funds in the database over the period decreases.

The factor is lower when:

- ❑ the absolute performance of the funds in the database over the period is lower;
- ❑ when the net number of funds in the database over the period increases.

This factor is a good approximation of the presence of backfill bias because it links the two ingredients intervening in this estimation: the returns of the funds and the number of funds in the database. On the one hand, when there are a lot of new funds, if the performance of these funds is no better than the one of existing funds, the ratio will decrease. On the other hand, when new funds have a better performance, the ratio will increase (because the returns increase more rapidly than the number of funds) and this will prove that there is a difference between existing and new funds.

INSTANT RETURN HISTORY BIAS ESTIMATION

Before reporting the estimation of the *history bias factor*, we estimate the instant return history bias using the classical methodology. Then, we quantify the drawback of this current methodology in the second part of this section.

Estimation

Instant return bias can be estimated using the two-step methodology as defined by Park (1995), Brown *et al* (1997) and Fung and Hsieh (2000). On the one hand, the average monthly return of the "observable portfolio" is estimated which invests in all the funds of the database each month. On the other hand, the average monthly return of the "adjusted observable portfolio" obtained is estimated

Table 1 Instant return history bias

	Mean monthly return (%)	Monthly difference (%)	Annual difference (%)	No of obs. per year
All	1.02	NA	NA	21,723
Without 12 M	1.00	0.01	0.17	17,639
Without 24 M	0.90	0.12	1.43	14,972
Without 36 M	0.77	0.24	2.91	12,638
Without 48 M	0.64	0.38	4.53	10,547
Without 60 M	0.69	0.33	3.91	8,696

from investing in all these funds after deleting the first 12, 24 and, if possible, 36, 48 and 60 months of returns. The bias is estimated for the whole period and for the bullish and bearish sub-periods in order to compare the results with those obtained by Fung and Hsieh (2000). Results are reported in Table 1.

Table 1 indicates that the mean monthly return of the funds tend to decrease when the first years of returns of the fund are removed. These results are in line with the one obtained in previous studies. Interestingly, this mean monthly return is marginally higher when we remove 60 months of data compared with 48 months. This result is due to the lower number of data available when 60 months of data are removed. Only 34% of the funds in the database have more than 60 months of data. Moreover, a further analysis indicates that only 25% of the dissolved funds existed for more than 60 months confirming that survivorship bias could also impact this result. At the global level, the backfill bias obtained range from 0.17% when 12 months of data are removed to 4.53% when four years of data are removed.

Instant return history bias drawbacks

As stressed in the introduction of the chapter, the backfill bias estimation has two main drawbacks. The first regards the comparability of returns used with and without the first months of existence of the funds. The second regards the presence of survivorship bias that also intervene in the quantification of the instant return history bias, since the first months of performance of each are removed and bad performing funds dissolved early because of their bad performance will also be removed from the database.

Bias 1: Comparability

First, the estimation can be biased because performances with and without the first months of existence are not compared over the same time frame. Three methods are used to check this point. First, we report the yearly number and percentage of new funds, dissolved funds in Panel A of Table 2 to determine if more funds have been created or dissolved over some years. Since the instant return history bias estimation is based on funds and not percentage we focus attention on the new and dissolved columns. The new column indicates that many funds have been created between 1997 and 2001. In aggregate, 60% of the funds of the database have been created in or after 1997. These funds will intervene in the estimation of the bias and will bias it. Panel B reports the reason why. With the current methodology of estimating the instant return history bias, the first months of existence of each fund are removed. Funds created over the last five years of data consequently will have been removed and will not or only partially be considered in the estimation. When more data are removed, the effect is even more important.

Second, we report the average return of the two categories used in the estimation (with and without the first months of existence) in Panel A and B of Table 3. Panel A indicates that as data are removed from the estimation, the performance decreases as expected. Panel B clearly indicates that the difference in performance is mainly due to the bullish years. The difference in performance is much higher when the net performance of the industry is high than when it is relatively low. 1999 is the best example with a difference in performance that can reach 6.6% when 5 years of data are removed. This result indicates that the current way of measuring the bias can be biased.

Finally, we estimate the correlation between the number of funds and the monthly performance, then we perform the same calculation using a 3-year rolling period. This analysis is interesting, helping us to prove that it is important to compare the returns over the same period because as more and more new funds report to the database, the global performance of the industry is impacted. Results are reported in Table 4 and Figure 1.

Table 5 is interesting because it indicates that at a global level the number of funds is negatively correlated to the performance of these funds, indicating that the global performance of the industry

Table 2 Comparability of the instant return bias estimation – birth and death rate

	Year start	New	Birth rate (%)	Dissolved	Attrition rate (%)	Year end	Hedge funds performance(%)
Panel A: Birth and attrition rate							
1994	728	237	32.55	24	3.30	941	2.1
1995	941	277	29.44	91	9.67	1127	19.6
1996	1127	359	31.85	66	5.86	1420	21.4
1997	1420	414	29.15	104	7.32	1730	20.0
1998	1730	387	22.37	163	9.42	1954	5.1
1999	1954	411	21.03	163	8.34	2202	34.6
2000	2202	424	19.26	225	10.22	2401	9.1
2001	2401	448	18.66	245	10.20	2604	5.3
2002	2604	282	10.83	360	13.82	2526	0.5
	Total	3239	23.91	1441	8.68	1878	13.10

	Period covered	New	Proportion of all the new funds (%)
Panel B: Percentage of new funds at the end of the period analysed			
12 months	2002	282	9
24 months	2001–2002	730	23
36 months	2000–2002	1154	36
48 months	1999–2002	1565	48
60 months	1998–2002	1952	60

1996) it was significantly positive. Then it decreased rapidly after the start of the Asian crisis in the second half of 1997 before returning to positive values during the technology bubble in 1999. The value of the factor turns back to negative when the bear market started before being negative in 2001. Its value then remained very low. The figures reporting the same results while removing 12, 24, 36 or 48 months of data indicate the same patterns.[2]

Bias 2: Presence of survivorship bias

Second, survivorship bias can also intervene in the estimation since badly performing funds dissolved after 12, 24, 36, 48 and 60 months will not be included in the estimation and the survivorship bias of these funds will clearly be included in the estimation.

The survivorship bias has been estimated in the database (calculated as the performance difference between living and all funds, see Fung and Hsieh, 2000). The value obtained is 1.1% annually. This means that funds that exist over the whole period studied offer 1.1% performance more than the global database. To check for the presence of survivorship bias in the estimation of the instant return history bias the backfill bias analysis is performed with dissolved funds, without dissolved funds and for dissolved funds only. Results are reported in Table 5.

There are two very important points. First, Panel C clearly indicates that dissolved funds have a much higher instant return history bias and that the current methodology used to estimate it does not take this aspect into account. The backfill bias of dissolved funds is much higher than that of funds that exist over the global period. Second, the difference in performance between living funds and the global database is very low, confirming that most dissolved funds are not included in the estimation of the instant return history bias and that these funds contribute to the estimated instant return bias. The bulk of the difference in the performance of funds, when their first months of existence can be explained by the presence of survivorship bias in the data, also contributes to the estimation of the instant return history bias.

THE HISTORY BIAS FACTOR ESTIMATION

The *history bias factors* are reported in Table 6. The table indicates that 1994 and 2002 have the lowest values and that 1999 and 1995

Table 6 History bias factor estimation

	1994	**1995**	**1996**	**1997**	**1998**	**1999**	**2000**	**2001**	**2002**
Performance (a)	2.14	19.62	21.42	20.04	5.07	34.57	9.15	5.34	0.52
Nb funds at year-end (1)	*941*	*1127*	*1420*	*1730*	*1954*	*2202*	*2401*	*2600*	*2526*
Nb funds at start (2)	*724*	*1013*	*1201*	*1519*	*1794*	*2007*	*2271*	*2432*	*2656*
Nb of new funds (1)−(2)=(b)	217	114	219	211	160	195	130	168	−130
History Bias Factor (a)/(b)*1000	**9.8**	**172.1**	**97.8**	**95.0**	**31.7**	**177.3**	**70.4**	**31.8**	**−4.0**

the highest. In 2004, there were a very high number of new funds and their performance has been relatively low. This result indicates that new funds have not created significant value over this year. The history bias factor is relatively low (around 10). In 2002, there was a net decrease in the number of funds (few new funds) and the performance of the funds in the database was relatively low (close to 0). As a consequence the instant history bias estimated is very low.

In 1995 and 1999, the net number of new funds were relatively high (particularly compared with the global number of funds in the database at this time) and the performance was high (close to 20% for 1995 and higher for 1999). These results lead to a particularly high history bias factor that comes from the fact that over this year of creation of many new funds, performance was strong. New funds help to create good returns.

This history bias factor is of interest because every year with a good performance and a lot of new funds (1995–1997, and 1999), the factor reported is high. This proves that new funds help to create absolute returns. On the other hand, when performance is more difficult (1994) or when few funds have been created (2002), the factor has a low absolute value. Finally, when performance is disappointing and many new funds have been created (1998 and 2001), the value of the factor is relatively low. The year 2000 is a special case because absolute performance (around 9%) was correct but lower than over the best years of the period. Relatively few new funds were created indicating that the effect is mitigated of which few funds have added marginally to the performance.

It is interesting to note that the figures reported are not only due to the performance of the funds in the database. The *history bias factor* and the performance evolve the same way despite the fact that the number of funds and their performance evolve over time.[3] The table indicates that the performance of the funds or the number of funds created has been negative in 1994 and 2002 and that they have been both positive or negative (in our case both positive) over the other period covered and that the creation of new funds does clearly not lead to worse performance for hedge funds considered as a whole but that other factors should intervene.

CONCLUSION

Biases are of particular concern in analysing quantitative data. Instant history bias is an important issue in hedge fund studies. This chapter aims at defining a factor that helps estimating this bias. We first present the main drawbacks of the current estimation methodology. The first is the fact that performance is compared independently of the period analysed. We illustrated the estimation problem in three ways. The second issue with the current way of estimating the backfill bias is linked to the fact that the survivorship bias also intervenes in the estimation and that this bias can also induce a bias in the results obtained. The results indicate that dissolved funds tend to be removed when the instant return history bias is estimated and that the estimation of the backfill bias obtained in the past has been impacted by the presence of survivorship bias.

We present an alternative to the current way of estimating the backfill bias and the *history bias factor* is defined as the ratio of the yearly performance of the funds over the period considered divided by the net number of new funds over the period studied. This ratio addresses the drawbacks of the current methodology because it estimated the bias over a same time frame without aggregating the non-comparable analysis period. Second, dissolved funds are not removed from the analysis. There is no combination of the backfill and the survivorship bias.

This study opens the door to a new way of determining the presence of the backfill bias in hedge funds studies. The next step will be to test this ratio further using other databases and other analysis periods and to compare the results obtained.

1 See Capocci (2005) for a complete discussion of the database and its construction.

2 They are not reported for the sake of brevity but can be obtained directly to the author.

3 Please note that the total number of funds evolve monastically but that the net number of new funds range from 219 new funds in 1996 (the maximum) and 130 funds less in 2002.

REFERENCES

Ackermann, C., R. McEnally, and D., Ravenscraft, 1999, "The Performance of Hedge Funds: Risk, Return, and Incentives", *Journal of Finance*, **54(3)**, pp 833–74.

Amin, G.S. and H. M. Kat, 2003, "Hedge Fund Performance 1990–2000: Do the 'money machines' really add value?", *Journal of Financial and Quantitative Analysis*, **38(2)**, pp 251–74.

Brown S. J., W. N. Goetzmann, and R. G. Ibbotson, 1999, "Offshore Hedge Funds: Survival and Performance 1989–1995", *Journal of Business*, **72(1)**, pp 91–118.

Capocci, D., 2005, "The Sustainability in Hedge Fund Performance: New Insights", Working Paper, Université de Liège, www.ssrn.com

Fung, W. and D. A. Hsieh, 1997, "Empirical Characteristics of Dynamic Trading Strategies: The Case of Hedge Funds", *Review of Financial Studies*, **10(2)**, pp 275–302.

Fung, W. and D. A. Hsieh, 2000, "Performance Characteristics of Hedge Funds and Commodity Funds: Natural vs. Spurious Biases", *Journal of Quantitative and Financial Analysis*, **35(3)**, pp 291–307.

Jensen, M., 1968, "The Performance of Mutual Funds in the Period 1945–1964", *Journal of Finance*, **23(2)**, pp 389–416.

Liang, B., 1999, "On the Performance of Hedge Funds", *Financial Analysts Journal*, **55**, pp 72–85.

Park, J., 1995, "Managed Futures as an Investment Set", Ph.D. Dissertation, Columbia University.

Sharpe, W., 1994, "The Sharpe Ratio", *Journal of Portfolio Management*, **21(1)**, pp 49–58.

Treynor, J., 1965, "How to Rate Management of Investments Funds", *Harvard Business Review*, **43**, pp 63–75.

There may be many causes to specification errors. According to Spencer and Berk (1981), these errors may originate from numerous phenomena: omission of relevant explanatory variables, errors in variables, inappropriate aggregation over time, simultaneity and incorrect functional form. Numerous studies have tried to modify the Fama and French model for eventual specification errors without really identifying these errors or creating tests for them, however, this chapter will try to fill this gap.

In the econometric literature, specification errors give way to an absence of orthogonality between the explanatory variables of a model and its innovation. This problem may be identified by a Hausman test and can be corrected by the use of appropriate instruments. As mentioned by Watson (2003), this approach is quite rare in finance. There exists some chapters on the estimation of financial models using the generalised method of moments (GMM) however numerous authors are not very concerned by the choice of appropriate instruments[2]. However, this choice is fundamental to obtain good performance of an estimation process. Watson (2003) suggests using the Chen–Roll–Ross (1986) factors as instruments to remove specification errors.

In this chapter, we pursue the studies on specification errors in the Fama and French model, using the GMM method to correct for these errors. The originality of our exercise lay in the choice of new instruments based on the recent risk literature, which deals with higher moments and co-moments of returns and even higher cumulants and co-cumulants. We relate this financial literature to the econometric works of Dagenais and Dagenais (1997) which were later generalised to financial applications by Racicot (2003)[3]. We propose the higher moments as instruments for running our GMM estimations. We then compare the results to those ones of ordinary least squares and of GMM involving classical instruments, eg, predetermined variables of the model and the Chen–Roll–Ross (1986) factors which are usually used to discard specification errors in the Fama and French model.

The literature about specification errors proposes that a way to correct them is to make the alphas and the betas of the CAPM, or the augmented Fama and French model conditional. We will complete our study by showing that the procedure may improve the results already obtained by using our instruments.

Our chapter is organised as follows. In the second section, we justify our choice of instrumental variables to purge the Fama and French model from its specification errors. In the third section, we study the specification errors in the augmented Fama and French model by comparing the indexes of two databases of hedge funds: Hedge Fund Research Inc. (HFR) and Van-Greenwich. Comparing both databases allows us to rank the strategies of the hedge funds not yet attempted in the hedge fund literature. We do so by running two-stage least squares (TSLS) and generalised method of moments (GMM) estimations using as instruments the higher moments of the explanatory variables. The analysis of the contribution of conditional alphas and betas to the reduction of specification errors in our samples completes our study.

THE CHOICE OF INSTRUMENTAL VARIABLES TO ESTIMATE THE AUGMENTED FAMA AND FRENCH (F&F) MODEL[4]

The augmented F&F (1992, 1993 and 1997) model is a purely empirical model which may be written as:

$$R_{pt} - R_{ft} = \alpha + \beta_1(R_{mt} - R_{ft}) + \beta_2 SMB_t + \beta_3 HML_t + \beta_4 UMD_t + \varepsilon_t \quad (1)$$

with $R_{pt} - R_{ft}$ the excess return of a portfolio, R_{ft} being the risk-free return; $R_{mt} - R_{ft}$ the market risk premium; *SMB* a portfolio which mimics the "small firm anomaly", which is long in the returns of selected small firms and short in the returns of selected big firms; *HML* a portfolio which mimics the "income stock anomaly", which is long in returns of stocks of selected firms having a high (book value/market value) ratio (income stocks) and short in selected stocks having a low (book value/market value) ratio (growth stocks); *UMD* a portfolio which mimics the "momentum anomaly", which is long in returns of selected stocks having a persistent upper trend and short in stocks having a persistent downwards trend.

To explain the return of a stock or of a portfolio of stocks, the F&F model adds to the unique factor retained by the CAPM, the market risk premium, three other factors which are assumed to represent market anomalies: the small firm anomaly, the book value to market value anomaly and the momentum anomaly[5].

We postulate that equation (1) contains specification errors, which may be due to many causes but the main plausible reasons could be the omission of relevant variables, the aggregation level of the data or simply an incorrect functional form. Following these errors, the risk factors become endogenous and the condition of orthogonality between these factors of risk and the innovation term in equation (1) is violated: the estimators of these coefficients of equation are no longer unbiased and consistent. To eliminate these coefficients from these biases, we must regress in a first attempt the independent variables on instrumental variables, whereby the problem remains in the selection of these instruments.

It is difficult to find valuable instruments for the excess returns of the mimicking portfolios. Being long in some stocks and short in others, renders their cash flows similar to those of hedge funds. Higher moments of returns, like asymmetry and kurtosis, might have a great influence on these returns suggesting the use of higher moments of the variables on the RHS of equation (1) as instrumental variables. An econometric theory is indeed in construction on this subject. Following Durbin (1954) and Pal (1980), Dagenais and Dagenais (1997) showed that higher moments[6] of independent variables of a regression might be valid instruments to remove errors-in-variables. However instead of defining higher moments as in the above chapters, we adopt a method more akin to asset pricing theory which defines higher moments of returns by the power of these returns.

The method of asset pricing based on higher moments is not new. Rubinstein (1973) and Kraus and Litzenberger (1976) put the foundations of the three-moment and four-moment CAPM. The three-moment CAPM integrates asymmetry of returns in the analysis while the four-moment CAPM adds kurtosis.

Some authors, like Kraus and Litzenberger (1976), use a general utility function to derive the moment-CAPM. Others use a Taylor expansion of the utility function which, following Samuelson (1970) and Rubinstein (1973), allows expressing utility in terms of the higher moments of returns.

Let us assume that the expected utility of wealth, $E[U(W)]$, is function of the n first moments of the distribution of wealth:

$$E[U(W)] = \varphi[\bar{W}, \sigma_W, skew_W, kur_W, \ldots, sm_{nW}] \quad \textbf{(2)}$$

with $\bar{W}$ the expected value of wealth; σ_w, the volatility of wealth; $skew_W$, its skewness; kur_W, its kurtosis and sm_{nW}, the nth moment of the distribution of wealth. We incorporate moments of order 5 and greater because we know that they may be important to explain the returns of long-short portfolios similar to mimicking portfolios which are the foundation of the F&F model. The returns of these portfolios depend on the tails of their distribution which are described by the entire set of higher moments.

The expected utility of end-of-period wealth is maximised over the one period horizon subject to the constraint of initial wealth, which is:

$$a_0 + \sum_{i=1}^{n} a_i = w_0 \tag{3}$$

According to equation (3), the initial wealth w_0 is allocated between the risk-free asset a_0 and n other risky assets designated by a_i. To maximise the utility of end-of-period wealth subject to (3), we form the usual Lagrangian:

$$L = E[U(W)] - \phi\left(a_0 - \sum_{i=1}^{n} a_i - w_0 \right) \tag{4}$$

Taking the first-order conditions for a maximum, we have:

$$\frac{\partial L}{\partial a_0} = \varphi_{\bar{W}} \times \frac{\partial \bar{W}}{\partial a_0} - \phi = 0 \tag{5}$$

$$\frac{\partial L}{\partial a_{i,i\neq 0}} = \varphi_{\bar{W}} \times \frac{\partial E(w)}{\partial a_i} + \varphi_{\sigma_W} \times \frac{\partial \sigma_W}{\partial a_i} + \varphi_{skew_W} \times \frac{\partial skew_W}{\partial a_i} + \varphi_{kur_W} \times \frac{\partial kur_W}{\partial a_i} + \cdots + \varphi_{sm_{nW}} \frac{\partial sm_{nW}}{\partial a_n} - \phi = 0 \tag{6}$$

with $\varphi_x = (\partial E[U(X)] / \partial x)$.

End-of-period expected wealth is equal to:

$$\bar{W} = (1 + R_0)a_0 + \sum_{i=1}^{n} [(1 + E(R_i))a_i] \tag{7}$$

We thus have:

$$\frac{\partial \bar{W}}{\partial a_0} = 1 + R_0 \quad \textbf{(8)}$$

$$\frac{\partial \bar{W}}{\partial a_i} = 1 + E(R_i) \quad \textbf{(9)}$$

We can therefore express the moments of wealth in terms of the moments of returns of the portfolio as:

$$\sigma_W = \sum_i a_i \beta_{ip} \sigma_p \quad \textbf{(10)}$$

$$skew_W = \sum_i a_i \gamma_{ip} skew_p \quad \textbf{(11)}$$

$$kur_W = \sum_i a_i \theta_{ip} kur_p \quad \textbf{(12)}$$

$$sm_{nW} = \sum_i a_i \omega_{ip} sm_{np} \quad \textbf{(13)}$$

with $\sigma_p = \sqrt{E(R_p - \bar{R}_p)^2}$, the volatility of the return of the risk assets; $\beta_{ip} = (E[(R_i - \bar{R}_i)(R_p - \bar{R}_p)] / \sigma_p^2)$, the beta of risk asset i with the investor's portfolio of risk assets; $skew_p = \sqrt[3]{E[(R_p - \bar{R}_p)^3]}$, the asymmetry of the return of the portfolio and $\gamma_{ip} = (E[(R_i - \bar{R}_i)(R_p - \bar{R}_p)^2] / sk_p^3)$, the gamma of risk asset i with the investor's portfolio of risk assets . It is easy to generate all the other variables by following this pattern.

Equating equations (5) and (6) to delete ϕ and taking into account equations (10) to (13), we arrive at an expression for E(R_i) in terms of the moments of the distribution of the return of an investor's portfolio:

$$E(R_i) - R_0 = -\left(\frac{\varphi_{\sigma_W}}{\varphi_{\bar{W}}}\right)\beta_{ip}\sigma_p - \left(\frac{\varphi_{skew_W}}{\varphi_{\bar{W}}}\right)\gamma_{ip} skew_p - \left(\frac{\varphi_{kur_W}}{\varphi_{\bar{W}}}\right)\theta_{ip} kur_p - \cdots - \left(\frac{\varphi_{sm_{nW}}}{\varphi_{\bar{W}}}\right)\omega_{ip} sm_{np} \quad \textbf{(14)}$$

with $(\varphi_{moment}/\varphi_{\bar{W}})$ being an investor's marginal rate of substitution between expected wealth and a specific moment. According to Scott and Hovarth (1980), these marginal rates of substitution are positive for odd moments, like mean and positive asymmetry, and negative for even moments, like variance and kurtosis. From equation (14), odd moments have, ceteris paribus, a negative impact on expected return from the point of view of investors. Even moments have a positive impact because they represent risk.

Moving from equation (14) to the condition of market equilibrium for $E(R_i)$ requires making, according to Kraus and Litzenberger (1976), the strong assumption of homogeneous expectations for investors. Following this assumption, equation (14) becomes, assuming that p is the market portfolio:

$$E(R_i) - R_0 = \left[\frac{d\bar{W}}{d\sigma_W}\right]\sigma_m\beta_{im} + \left[\frac{d\bar{W}}{dskew_W}\right]skew_m\gamma_{im} + \left[\frac{d\bar{W}}{dkur_w}\right]kur_m\theta_{im} + \cdots + \left[\frac{d\bar{W}}{dsm_{nW}}\right]sm_{nm}\omega_{in} \quad \textbf{(15)}$$

The terms in brackets in expression (15) are the slopes of the efficient frontiers whose arguments are expected wealth and the respective moment. We obtain finally the n-moment CAPM:

$$E(R_i) - R_f = \psi_1\beta_{im} + \psi_2\gamma_{im} + \psi_3\theta_{im} + \cdots + \psi_n sm_{nm} \quad \textbf{(16)}$$

We may directly use expression (16) to define our instruments for removing specification errors by the methods of higher moments in the F&F model. Assume we want to correct the mimicking portfolio *SMB* for specification errors. In the first pass of our regressions, we regress this variable on the co-moments of the lagged excess return of the market portfolio. The variable *SMB* corrected for specification errors would be:

$$S\hat{M}B_t = \kappa_0 + \kappa_1\beta_{im,t-1} + \kappa_2\gamma_{im,t-1} + \kappa_3\theta_{im,t-1} + \cdots + \kappa_n sm_{nm,t-1} \quad \textbf{(17)}$$

We must also introduce the co-moments of the mimicking portfolios, however, this approach would be laborious and would require computing rolling windows of co-moments, but there is a procedure for simplifying equation (17). Kraus and Lintzenberger (1976)[7] have shown that a three-moment CAPM is consistent with the following quadratic form:

$$R_i - R_0 = \alpha_0 + \alpha_1(R_m - R_0) + \alpha_2(R_m - R_0)^2 \quad \textbf{(18)}$$

and consequently a n-moment CAPM can be written as:

$$R_i - R_0 = \alpha_0 + \alpha_1(R_m - R_0) + \alpha_2(R_m - R_0)^2 + \alpha_3(R_m - R_0)^3 + \cdots + \alpha_{n-1}(R_m - R_0)^{n-1} \quad \textbf{(19)}$$

A test on α_2 is a test on skewness preferences in asset pricing and a test on α_3, a test on kurtosis preferences, and so on. The higher moments are consequently powers of returns in this approach. We therefore use a financial theory, the n-moment CAPM, to give an object to the method of Dagenais and Dagenais (1997) for correcting errors-in-variables and more generally specification errors. Let us return to the variable *SMB*, which we want to correct for the problem of specification errors. In the first pass of the regression, this variable will be regressed on:

$$\hat{SMB}_t = f(F_{it-1}, F_{it-1}^2, F_{it-1}^3, \ldots, F_{it-1}^5, \ldots) \quad \textbf{(20)}$$

where F_i are the variables in the RHS of the equation of Fama and French (equation 1) including *SMB*. They stand for the higher moments of these variables and F_{it-1}^2 represents the skewness of factor F_i; F_{it-1}^3, for its kurtosis and so on. The variables appearing on the RHS of equation (20) will serve as instrumental variables.

EMPIRICAL RESULTS

Description of the samples

Our sample of hedge funds comprises the monthly returns of 11 Hedge Fund Research, Inc. (HFR) indexes and 11 Van-Greenwich (VG) indexes representing various strategies. The starting date of the sample was conditioned by the beginning date of the Van-Greenwich (VG) indexes, January 1995. The observation period thus runs from January 1995 to December 2005, for a total of 132 observations. The sample includes also a composite index of VG and HFR hedge funds. The risk factors which appear in the F&F

equation – that is the market risk premium and the three mimicking portfolios: SMB, HML and UMD – are for their part drawn from the French's website[8]. We use as instruments, the Chen–Roll–Ross (1986) factors: the industrial production and the consumer price index expressed in monthly and annual growth rates; the spread between long and short term bonds; the spread between BBB and AAA corporate bonds and the dividend yield of the S&P 500. These factors are drawn from the database of the Federal Reserve Bulletin and the Federal Reserve Bank of St-Louis.

A first glance at the strategies analysed

In table 1, we classify hedge funds strategies in two groups: directional and non-directional strategies. Directional strategies aim to benefit from large movements of the market. The beta of these funds is quite high but usually below 1, because hedge funds, according to their vocation, hedge a part of their market positions. Following Table 1, this category gathers together the following strategies: aggressive, emerging markets, long-short, macro, market timing and short-selling. The long-short group was placed in the directional strategies because its beta is quite high. The non-directional strategies are generally neutral with regard to the market. The beta of the hedge funds following these strategies is low and they maintain a minimal position relative to the market and try to exploit market inefficiencies. The non-directional strategies include: convertible arbitrage, distressed securities, event driven, equity market neutral and fixed income. In Table 1, we find the symbols retained in this study for the various strategies.

Table 2 reports the descriptive statistics of the chosen strategies for both databases that is VG and HFR. We note that the statistics of the strategies are quite comparable from one database to the next. In both databases, the directional strategies identified in Table 1 have a standard deviation exceeding 2% and, as we will see in the next section, they also have a higher beta than the non-directional strategies, thereby conforming to finance theory. There is also a positive but weak relation between the mean return and the standard deviation of the strategies, and there is no relation between the mean return and the kurtosis of the strategies.

The mean return of the composite index of VG group is quite high at 12.8% over the period 1995–2005, which is quite comparable to

Table 1 Hedge funds strategies analysed

Directional strategies		Non-directional strategies	
Group	**Description**	**Group**	**Description**
Aggressive (AG)	Investments in companies experiencing strong growth in earnings per share	**Convertible arbitrage (CONV)**	Purchase of a portfolio of convertible securities, generally convertible bonds and hedging a portion of the equity risk by selling short the underlying common stock
Emerging Markets (EM)	Investments in securities of companies or the sovereign debt of developing or "emerging" countries	**Distressed Securities (DIS)**	Investments in companies which experiment financial or operational difficulties
Long-Short (LS)	Strategy that characterised hedge funds at their beginnings. Long positions in some securities and short positions in others. Other name of this strategy: equity hedge	**Event Driven (ED)**	Investments in opportunities created by significant transactional events such as spin-offs, mergers and acquisitions, bankruptcy reorganisations, recapitalisations and share buybacks

Macro (MACRO)	Funds which have a particular interest for macroeconomic variables. They take positions according to their forecasts of macro. variables: exchange rates, inflation…	**Equity Market Neutral (EQMN)**	They exploit pricing inefficiencies between related equity securities and neutralise market exposure by combining long and short positions
Market timing (MT)	They switch into investments that begin an uptrend and switch out of investments that start a downtrend	**Fixed Income (FINC)**	Investments in a variety of fixed income strategies like exploiting relative mispricing between related sets of fixed income securities
Short selling (SHORT)	They take advantage of declining stocks		

Table 2 Descriptive statistics of VG and HFR indexes, monthly, 1995–2005*

	AG	CI	CONV	DIS	ED	EM	EQMN	FINC	LS	MACRO	MT	SHORT	Average	Market	CI
VG															
Mean	1.31	1.07	0.96	1.09	1.09	0.88	0.99	0.68	1.24	0.65	0.98	−0.12	0.90	1.02	1.07
Median	1.00	1.10	1.10	1.20	1.20	1.40	0.90	0.80	1.60	0.60	0.60	−0.40	0.93	1.62	1.10
Maximum	18.40	9.00	3.80	5.70	7.90	20.00	5.10	3.30	11.80	10.50	11.70	24.90	24.90	8.47	9.00
Minimum	−12.20	−7.90	−3.40	−4.70	−7.20	−19.90	−3.70	−7.20	−7.90	−9.60	−6.00	−24.30	−24.30	−15.56	−7.90
Std. Dev.	4.54	2.17	1.08	1.40	1.73	5.03	1.13	1.17	2.72	2.79	2.61	6.43	2.73	4.51	2.17
Skewness	0.59	0.19	−0.83	−0.10	−0.42	−0.23	0.11	−2.28	0.38	0.36	0.99	0.13	−0.09	−0.75	0.19
Kurtosis	5.09	6.05	4.68	5.70	7.51	5.93	5.82	17.17	5.33	5.57	5.76	5.45	6.67	3.65	6.05
Jarque-Bera	31.5	51.4	30.7	39.9	115.0	48.0	43.6	1210.6	32.8	38.7	62.9	33.1	144.9	14.7	51.4
Probability	0.00	0.00	0.00	0.00	0.00	0.00	0.00	0.00	0.00	0.00	0.00	0.00	0.00	0.00	0.00
HFR															
Mean	1.37	1.12	0.82	1.07	1.16	1.28	0.77	0.49	1.29	0.88	1.04	0.10	0.95	1.02	1.12
Median	1.84	1.31	0.94	1.11	1.29	1.76	0.69	0.57	1.57	0.81	0.93	−0.35	1.04	1.62	1.31
Maximum	12.50	7.62	3.65	5.34	5.93	15.75	3.88	7.46	11.54	6.24	6.91	26.43	26.43	8.47	7.62
Minimum	−15.52	−8.31	−4.29	−8.88	−9.81	−22.07	−3.90	−9.14	−7.42	−5.10	−3.20	−21.00	−22.07	−15.56	−8.31
Std. Dev.	4.51	2.22	1.06	1.70	2.07	4.54	1.11	1.64	2.95	2.18	2.23	6.98	2.77	4.51	2.22
Skewness	−0.40	−0.43	−1.18	−1.54	−1.28	−0.98	−0.12	−1.03	0.19	0.07	0.17	0.42	−0.51	−0.75	−0.43
Kurtosis	3.91	4.90	6.92	11.08	8.19	7.77	5.10	13.11	4.03	3.04	2.36	5.32	6.31	3.65	4.90
Jarque-Bera	8.1	23.6	114.2	407.6	182.8	145.4	24.5	581.7	6.5	0.1	2.9	33.3	127.6	14.7	23.6
Probability	0.02	0.00	0.00	0.00	0.00	0.00	0.00	0.00	0.04	0.94	0.24	0.00	0.10	0.00	0.00

* The symbols used in this table are defined in table 1. CI: hedge funds composite index for the VG and HFR groups; Market: market index (S&P 500).

the 13.4% observed for the mean return of the composite index of the HFR group over the same period. Among the strategies, only the short-sellers display a very low performance for both groups over the period reported. The standard deviation of the returns of the composite indexes of the VG and HFR groups, is about 2.2% for both, which is half the standard deviation of the S&P 500 index. Therefore, as we will see in the following section, the beta of the composite index of each database will be sensibly below one. The lower standard deviation may be explained by the hedging activities of the funds. Moreover, the composite index of each group of hedge funds has greater kurtosis than the market; a characteristic shared by almost every strategy. The Jarque–Bera test of normality also indicates that returns are not normal for the majority of the indexes appearing in Table 2 implying that rare or extreme events are more frequent than in a normal distribution and that nonlinearities of payoffs are present.

The choice of instruments

As mentioned previously, the choice of instruments is fundamental for the estimation of the IV methods. We will examine the performance of the two groups (classical instruments and higher moment instruments) of instrumental variables of our sample during the 1995–2005 period.

The classical instruments are the Chen–Roll–Ross (1986) factors mentioned earlier and the explanatory variables of the model of F&F model lagged one period. The regression of the endogenous variables of the model on these instruments appears at Table 3. The R^2 of these regressions do not exceed 0.10: these instruments are obviously quite poor.

Table 3 R^2 and adjusted R^2 of the regressions of the endogenous variables of the Fama and French model on the instrumental variables constituted by classical instruments

	R^2	R^2 adj.
$R_m - R_f$	0.09	0.01
SMB	0.08	0.00
HML	0.10	0.02
UMD	0.06	0.00

Table 4 R^2 and adjusted R^2 of the regressions of the endogenous variables of the Fama and French model on the instrumental variables constituted by classical instruments and higher moments

	R^2	R^2 adj.
$R_m - R_f$	0.36	0.13
SMB	0.35	0.11
HML	0.49	0.31
UMD	0.41	0.20

Table 4 adds to classical instruments the higher moments of the explanatory variables up to the fifth power and we note that the R^2 of these regressions improve considerably. What must be explained are the returns of the market portfolio and that of the mimicking portfolios, nevertheless it tends to be rather tedious to explain the returns of a model which are stochastic by nature. With R^2 between 0.35 and 0.49, we may consider that higher moments of the factors of risk are quite good instruments over our sample.

The composite index of each group of hedge funds and the average strategy

For the following evaluation of specification errors, the OLS method will serve as benchmark to estimate equation (1). Three classical IV (instrumental variables) methods using as instruments predetermined variables of the model and the Chen–Roll–Ross factors are used: the two-stage least squares (TSLS), the non-iterated GMM (GMM clas. nit) and the iterated GMM (GMM clas. it.). For the GMM, we use the Newey-West matrix as weighting matrix. Besides these estimations, we run the higher moment versions of each of these GMM. The latter GMM uses as higher moments the one-lagged explanatory variables of the model up to the fifth power and the same Chen–Roll–Ross factors as in the case of classical GMM[9].

Before pursuing our estimations, we will eliminate the estimation methods which performed the worst. Table 5 gives the average estimated coefficients and t-statistics of the F&F model obtained by four methods for the VG group. We note that using classical instruments gives poor results in terms of the adjusted R^2. This statistic is only 0.08 for the TSLS using classical instruments and is as low as −0.32 for the GMM combined with classical instruments. We also

Table 5 Estimation of the F&F model by OLS, TSLS-hm and two IV classical methods for the 11 Indexes of the VG group*

	OLS	TSLS-hm	TSLS clas.	GMM clas. nit
coefficient				
c	0.33	0.35	0.13	0.07
$R_m - R_f$	0.20	0.17	0.30	0.26
SMB	0.15	0.18	0.15	0.14
HML	0.04	0.00	0.20	0.26
UMD	0.06	0.05	0.18	0.24
t-stat				
c	3.27	2.68	1.11	1.23
$R_m - R_f$	9.55	4.82	2.82	3.04
SMB	6.03	3.72	1.22	1.03
HML	2.17	1.24	1.34	1.57
UMD	1.89	1.49	1.26	1.74
R^2 adj	0.55	0.51	0.08	−0.32

* The estimation methods used in this table are: 1) OLS: ordinary least squares; 2) TSLS clas., which is a classical two-stage least squares using as instruments lagged values of the explanatory variables and the Chen-Roll-Ross economic and financial factors (classical instruments); 3) TSLS-hm, which in addition to the instruments listed-for the TSLS clas. uses higher moments of the explanatory variables lagged one period; 4) GMM clas. nit, a non-iterated GMM using classical instruments.

note in Table 5 that the factor loadings of the market premium and of HML and UMD are very high in the classical methods compared to the results obtained with the OLS method or the TSLS using higher moments as instruments, therefore, the methods using classical instruments are discarded.

We also eliminate from our estimation methods the iterated versions of the GMM. Indeed, the adjusted R^2 of the iterated GMM is generally low compared to OLS or non-iterated forms of GMM and according to Chan and Faff (2005), there is an issue about the reliability of the iterated GMM. The comparison between iterated and two-step estimation does not reveal anything of material concern.

Table 6 presents the estimated F&F model for the composite VG and HFR indexes. We perform these estimations with OLS and our two preferred methods for correcting specification errors: the TSLS and non-iterated GMM[10] both using higher moments as instruments. These estimations reveal that there is a close relationship between the two composite indexes. The constants of the two indexes, which is Jensen's alpha are very close in the OLS estimation

Table 6 Regressions of the composite indexes of VG and HFRI groups, 1995–2005*

	OLS		TSLS-hm		GMM-hm nit	
	VG	HFRI	VG	HFRI	VG	HFRI
coefficient						
c	0.40	0.44	0.38	0.41	0.36	0.41
$R_m - R_f$	0.35	0.40	0.34	0.42	0.32	0.42
SMB	0.22	0.20	0.21	0.19	0.21	0.20
HML	−0.01	0.03	0.00	0.03	−0.02	0.03
UMD	0.06	0.04	0.09	0.06	0.08	0.06
t-stat						
c	4.06	5.56	3.23	4.57	6.03	7.60
$R_m - R_f$	14.03	19.43	7.52	11.57	15.70	32.33
SMB	8.32	9.72	4.89	5.79	6.91	9.64
HML	−0.38	1.02	−0.09	0.88	−0.86	2.28
UMD	2.54	3.07	2.13	2.61	7.29	7.45
R^2 adj	0.79	0.86	0.78	0.85	0.78	0.85
DW	1.32	1.27	1.33	1.34	1.33	1.37
J-stat					0.15	0.17
p-value(J-stat)					0.95	0.87

* If the p-value of the J-stat is higher than 0.05 in the GMM estimations, we cannot reject the test of the over-identifying restrictions at the 5% level of significance. The instruments seem then relevant. It is the case here.

although it is somewhat higher for the HFR composite index. Annualised, the alpha exceeds 5% for both indexes, which is quite high for exceptional return and is highly significant at the 5% level.

The betas of the two composite indexes are moderate in the OLS regressions: 0.35 for the VG group and 0.40 for the HFRI group. These betas are substantially smaller than the beta of the market portfolio (which is one by definition). As noted earlier, the standard deviations of the returns of the two hedge funds composite indexes are half the standard deviation of the market portfolio returns over the estimation period and that gives way to betas substantially below one for the two composite indexes. But, as we will see, the betas of the strategies differ greatly among themselves.

Table 6 reveals that the relative importance of the factors loadings of SMB, HML and UMD are quite similar for the two composite indexes in the OLS regressions. The coefficient of SMB is 0.22 for the VG index and 0.20 for the HFR index, two very close coefficients. The factor loading of UMD is approximately the same for the two indexes. Although significant, its incidence is much lower on the composite indexes. Finally, the coefficient of HML is very low and not significant for the two indexes. In summary, the OLS estimated models of the HFRI and VG composite indexes are quite similar.

According to Table 6, there seems to be no specification errors at the level of aggregation of the composite indexes. Let us notice that the TSLS methods are equivalent to a Hausman test of the form:

$$R_{pt} - R_{ft} = \alpha^* + \beta_1^*(R_{mt} - R_{ft}) + \beta_2^* SMB_t + \beta_3^* HML_t + \beta_4^* UMD_t + \sum_{i=1}^{4} \varphi_i \hat{w}_{it} + \varepsilon_t^* \quad (21)$$

In this equation, the $\hat{w}_i$ are the residuals of the regression of each endogenous variable[11] of the F&F model on the set of instruments. The resulting $\hat{\beta}_i^*$ obtained by performing an OLS on equation (21) is identical to the coefficients associated to a TSLS using the same set of instruments. The $\hat{\varphi}_i$ are measures of the spread between $\hat{\beta}_i^*$ and the corresponding coefficient computed by estimating the F&F model by an OLS. If $\hat{\varphi}_i > 0$, that indicates that specification errors overstate the loading of the corresponding factor. And if $\hat{\varphi}_i < 0$, that indicates that specification errors understate the loading of the corresponding factor. The $\hat{\varphi}_i$ might thus be viewed as factor correcting the exposure of a fund to the corresponding risk factor[12].

This test reveals no specification errors in the estimation of the Fama and French model at the level of the composite indexes. The coefficients estimated by the TSLS are very similar to those of the OLS method. And the coefficients estimated by GMM are also very close to those of the OLS estimation. There is perhaps a slight decrease in Jensen's alpha after the correction of specification errors performed by the IV methods which suggests an overstatement of the absolute performance of the funds.

We can derive that the level of aggregation of the data hides specification errors. We can disaggregate a little by performing estimations on the 11 indexes of each database and by averaging the results. Table 7 reports these estimations and we note that, the level of aggregation has an impact on the specification errors. The impact of the risk premium seems overstated for the VG group and

Table 7 Regressions of the 11 indexes of VG and HFRI groups, 1995–2005*

	OLS		TSLS-hm		GMM-hm nit	
	VG	HFRI	VG	HFRI	VG	HFRI
coefficient						
c	0.33	0.41	0.35	0.37	0.36	0.39
$R_m - R_f$	0.20	0.23	0.17	0.22	0.17	0.21
SMB	0.15	0.13	0.18	0.17	0.17	0.17
HML	0.04	0.11	0.00	0.09	0.00	0.08
UMD	0.06	0.04	0.05	0.06	0.06	0.06
t-stat						
c	3.20	3.41	2.63	2.73	6.43	5.49
$R_m - R_f$	9.14	11.17	4.58	6.31	11.23	15.39
SMB	5.90	5.73	3.61	3.67	8.43	8.15
HML	2.33	2.39	1.35	1.77	3.84	3.88
UMD	1.83	2.36	1.43	2.04	5.46	5.80
R^2 adj	0.55	0.57	0.51	0.53	0.50	0.52
DW	1.47	1.63	1.53	1.72	1.53	1.72
J-stat					0.15	0.15
p-value (J-stat)					0.90	0.90

*If the p-value of the J-stat is higher than 0.05 in the GMM estimations, we cannot reject the test of the over-identifying restrictions at the 5% level of significance. The instruments seem then relevant. It is the case here.

the SMB's, understated for both groups when we compare the IV methods with the OLS one.

Analysis of individual strategies

Table 8 and 9 give more information about the impact of aggregation on specification errors. Table 8 gives the spread between the estimated coefficients of the Fama and French model applied to the VG group for the OLS and higher moment TSLS. Table 9 does the same thing for the HFR group.

We notice that there may be substantial differences between coefficients corrected and not corrected for specification errors and that was not apparent at the level of aggregation of the composite indexes. In Tables 8 and 9, we put in bold the spreads superior to 0.05 and we filled with gray the cells of the coefficients which are significant in the OLS regressions. We note that for the VG group, there were four major revisions for the constant, three major revisions for the loading of the market risk premium and three major

Table 8 Spread between the OLS and TSLS-hm estimated coefficients for each strategy, VG group

	c	R_m-R_f	SMB	HML	UMD
AG VG	**0.14**	**−0.12**	0.01	−0.07	−0.05
CONV VG	**−0.07**	0.05	0.04	0.02	0.02
DIS VG	0.00	0.04	−0.05	0.02	−0.02
ED VG	0.03	0.02	−0.02	−0.02	−0.04
EM VG	**0.14**	0.04	**−0.23**	−0.03	−0.10
EQMN VG	0.00	0.03	0.00	−0.01	−0.02
FINC VG	−0.03	**0.07**	−0.03	−0.01	0.00
LS VG	0.00	−0.03	**0.07**	0.01	0.00
MACRO VG	−0.03	0.05	**−0.11**	**0.11**	0.00
MT VG	**−0.13**	0.05	0.03	0.07	**0.07**
SHORT VG	**−0.36**	**0.12**	−0.03	**0.29**	**0.24**
CI VG	0.02	0.00	0.01	−0.01	−0.03
Average	−0.03	0.03	−0.03	0.03	0.01

Table 9 Spread between the OLS and TSLS-hm estimated coefficients for each strategy, HFR group

	c	R_m-R_f	SMB	HML	UMD
AG HFRI	**0.09**	−0.05	0.02	−0.03	−0.05
CONV HFRI	−0.04	0.04	0.04	−0.01	0.02
DIS HFRI	**0.09**	−0.04	−0.03	−0.03	−0.04
ED HFRI	0.05	−0.02	−0.04	−0.01	−0.03
EM HFRI	**0.35**	0.03	**−0.23**	0.05	−0.04
EQMN HFRI	0.02	−0.03	−0.01	−0.02	0.01
FINC HFRI 3067	**0.06**	−0.01	**−0.08**	−0.02	−0.02
LS HFRI	0.01	−0.02	**0.07**	0.00	−0.01
MACRO HFRI	0.02	0.01	**−0.09**	**0.07**	−0.03
MT HFRI	**−0.08**	**0.06**	0.04	**0.08**	−0.01
SHORT HFRI	**−0.16**	**0.15**	**−0.07**	**0.17**	0.00
CI HFRI	0.03	−0.03	0.01	−0.01	−0.02
Average	0.04	0.01	−0.03	0.02	−0.02

revisions for the coefficient of SMB. For the HFR group, there were five major revisions for the constant, two major revisions for the loading of the market risk premium and five major revisions for the coefficient of SMB. For both groups, there were few revisions of the loadings of UMD and we do not consider the loadings of HML because they are not enough significant.

Table 13 Estimation of the conditional Fama and French model on the composite index of the VG Group using the dividend yield of S&P 500 as public information for α

Dependent Variable: CIVG
Method: Least squares
Date: 07/22/06 Time: 21:22
Sample (adjusted): 85 199
Included observations: 115 after adjustments

Variable	Coefficient	Std. error	t-Statistic	Prob.
C	0.844393	0.374134	2.256925	0.0260
R_m-R_f	0.125650	0.072127	1.742077	0.0844
SMB	0.222512	0.024711	9.004418	0.0000
HML	0.048460	0.033880	1.430322	0.1555
UMD	0.035094	0.016958	2.069394	0.0409
$(R_m-R_f)*R_f(-1)$	−2.878461	1.064689	−2.703570	0.0080
$(R_m-R_f)*R_f(-1)^2$	1.242649	0.353615	3.514134	0.0006
DIVYIELD(−1)	−0.319365	0.218305	−1.462927	0.1464
R-squared	0.833352	Mean dependent var		0.773826
Adjusted R-squared	0.822449	S.D. dependent var		2.260913
S.E. of regression	0.952676	Akaike info criterion		2.807943
Sum squared resid	97.11225	Schwarz criterion		2.998895
Log likelihood	−153.4567	F-statistic		76.43859
Durbin-Watson stat	1.286781	Prob(F-statistic)		0.000000

Source: EViews 5.1

Fama and French model without conditioning information (Appendix 1). That seems to suggest that there was a misspecification in the original Fama and French model due to the conditional character of alpha and beta.

We replace SMB by the dividend yield of the S&P 500 index to find if alpha is robust to the conditional information. The results are reported in Table 13. We observe that the alpha coefficient is increased following the change of the conditioning information. It was previously equal to 0.40 in the original OLS estimation and it is now as high as 0.84. Consequently, it is not necessary true that the alpha decreases following the introduction of public information in the F&F model. The alpha will be responsive to the choice of the unlimited amount of public information available. Therefore, our method using higher moments as instruments to remove specification errors in the Fama and French model seems relevant.

Table 14 Estimated coefficients of equation (26) for the short-selling and composite indices, VG and HFR groups*

	β_0	θ_1	θ_2
CI VG	0.11	1.24	−2.95
	1.64	*3.83*	*−3.00*
CI HFRI	0.21	0.84	−1.65
	3.58	*2.89*	*−1.89*
SHORT VG	−0.55	−2.04	5.17
	−2.88	*−2.10*	*1.81*
SHORT HFRI	−0.43	−2.23	3.62
	−2.27	*−2.30*	*1.23*

*The t-statistic is in italics.

We can now study the dynamics of the alpha and beta in the F&F model by looking at the behaviour of two indexes of the composite and the short-selling indexes defined for each group of hedge funds. The estimated coefficients of equation (26) for each of the indexes appear in Table 14. We notice that the behaviour of short-sellers is the inverse of the one of the composite indexes for each hedge fund group. Both composite indexes react positively to the level of the interest rate and negatively to the square of interest rate. The short-sellers have the opposite behaviour. As the interest rate tends to follow the market trend, suggesting that when the market is on an upwards trend, the betas of the composite indexes increase and those of the short-sellers decrease. When the beta of short-sellers is negative, it implies that short sellers take more risk in an strengthening market, as it is the case for the entire set of hedge funds. Moreover, an increase in the square of the interest rate might signal a deterioration of the market. The estimations in Table 14 indicate that short-sellers bear less risk in this market situation, like the entire set of hedge funds.

Table 15 confirms the negative correlation between the conditional betas of short-sellers in our two groups of hedge funds and the conditional betas of the composite indexes of the two same groups. The correlation between conditional betas of the short-selling index of the VG group and the corresponding composite index is nearly −1 while the correlation between the corresponding statistics is −0.58 in the case of the HFR group. The conditional betas of the two

Table 15 Correlations of the conditional betas of two strategies

	β short VG	β short HFRI	β CI VG	β CI HFRI
β short VG	1.000	0.063	−0.997	−0.852
β short HFRI	0.063	1.000	−0.143	−0.576
β CI VG	−0.997	−0.143	1.000	0.891
β CI HFRI	−0.852	−0.576	0.891	1.000

hedge fund groups' composite indexes are highly elated since their correlation is equal to 0.89 over the estimation period.

Figure 1 displays the dynamics of the conditional betas of the short-selling and composite indexes for both groups of hedge funds during the 1997–2005 period. We omit the years 1995 and 1996 from the graphs because of the excessive fluctuations of betas at the beginning of the estimation process. As in the case of the Kalman filter, there seems to be a training process at the beginning of the estimation period which blurs the behaviour of the beta.

Exhibit 1 shows clearly the very close relationship between the conditional betas of the two composites indexes and the two short-selling indexes. The behaviour of the conditional betas during the market bubble at the start of the millennium is very characteristic. Following the collapse of the stock market in the spring of 2000, the conditional betas of the composite indexes decreased substantially before recovering after the turmoil. This behaviour was more pronounced for the VG than for the HFR group. We observe the same situation with short-sellers, because they reduce their risk as measured by their beta during the crisis and took on more risk thereafter.

We have performed a Hodrick–Prescott (1997) filtering of the conditional beta of the short-selling index of the VG group during the 1997–2005 period. The results appear in Figure 2. We note a large reversal of the upward trend during the market bubble observed at the beginning of the millennium. The cycle of beta was also more pronounced during this time but it was greatly reduced after the market turmoil.

In summary, conditional alphas and betas may improve the specification of the Fama and French model, although it is not clear that the alpha decreases when it is made conditional. Once again this depends on the public information used.

Figure 1 Conditional betas of the short-selling and the composite indexes of VG and HFR groups, 1997–2005

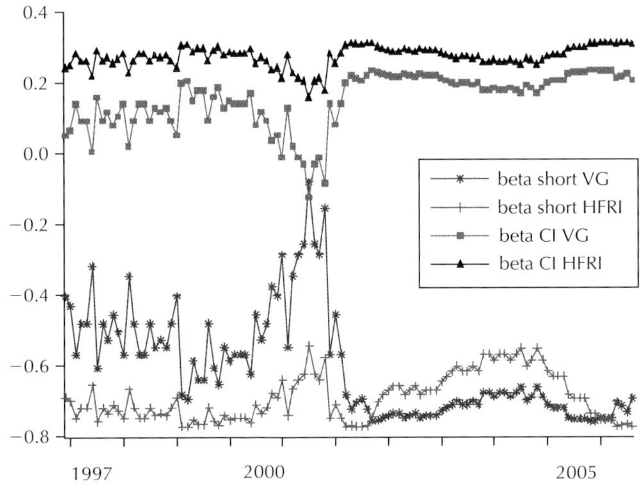

Figure 2 Hodrick-Prescott filtering of the conditional beta of the short-selling index of the VG group

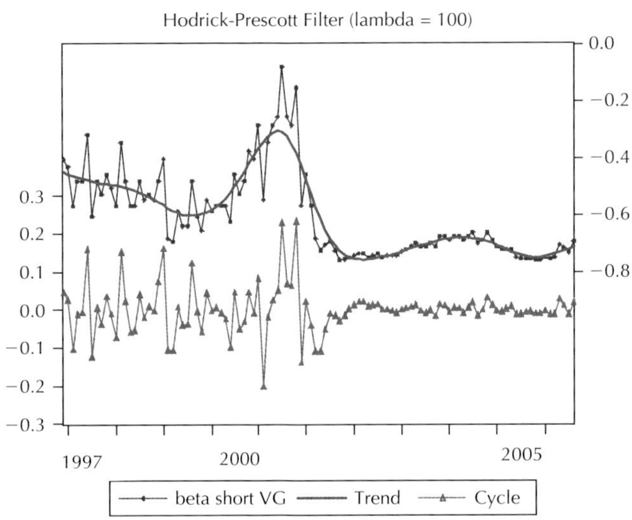

Estimations of the Fama and French model by OLS* (continued)

	c	$R_m - R_f$	SMB	HML	UMD	R^2	DW
LS HFRI	0.51	0.50	0.26	0.00	0.08	0.84	1.50
	4.65	*17.54*	*9.17*	*−0.10*	*3.95*		
MACRO VG	−0.06	0.30	0.20	0.03	0.15	0.34	1.92
	−0.29	*5.41*	*3.29*	*0.34*	*2.60*		
MACRO HFRI	0.24	0.25	0.14	0.16	0.07	0.22	1.82
	1.31	*5.33*	*3.07*	*2.65*	*2.08*		
MT VG	0.42	0.33	0.10	−0.17	0.04	0.61	1.75
	2.61	*8.13*	*2.36*	*−3.18*	*0.93*		
MT HFRI	0.44	0.36	0.06	−0.03	0.06	0.61	2.36
	3.33	*10.68*	*1.70*	*−0.61*	*2.51*		
SHORT VG	0.17	−0.91	−0.42	0.51	0.05	0.85	1.91
	0.68	*−14.67*	*−6.40*	*5.98*	*0.74*		
SHORT HFRI	0.50	−1.00	−0.45	0.43	−0.12	0.84	2.16
	1.89	*−14.41*	*−6.46*	*4.86*	*−2.59*		

* The t-statistics of the coefficients are in italics.

Estimations of the Fama and French model by TSLS using higher moments as instruments

	c	$R_m - R_f$	SMB	HML	UMD	R^2	DW
AG VG	0.31	0.77	0.34	−0.23	0.11	0.85	1.60
	1.52	*9.87*	*4.67*	*−2.49*	*1.53*		
AG HFRI	0.31	0.83	0.42	0.01	0.06	0.91	1.77
	2.26	*14.55*	*8.26*	*0.26*	*1.81*		
CI VG	0.38	0.34	0.21	0.00	0.09	0.78	1.33
	3.23	*7.52*	*4.89*	*−0.09*	*2.13*		
CI HFRI	0.41	0.42	0.19	0.03	0.06	0.85	1.34
	4.57	*11.57*	*5.79*	*0.88*	*2.61*		
CONV VG	0.62	0.01	0.04	0.03	0.00	0.03	0.88
	3.44	*0.25*	*0.79*	*0.54*	*0.00*		
CONV HFRI	0.47	0.04	0.02	0.04	−0.02	0.04	1.04
	4.49	*1.00*	*0.48*	*0.90*	*−0.73*		
DIS VG	0.59	0.10	0.24	0.05	0.03	0.37	1.54
	4.56	*2.02*	*4.95*	*0.91*	*0.73*		
DIS HFRI	0.40	0.28	0.23	0.16	0.05	0.44	1.33
	2.92	*4.95*	*4.54*	*2.82*	*1.45*		
ED VG	0.39	0.25	0.25	0.09	0.12	0.66	1.34
	3.38	*5.46*	*5.78*	*1.69*	*2.89*		
ED HFRI	0.40	0.42	0.27	0.18	0.03	0.76	1.62
	3.71	*9.51*	*6.87*	*4.09*	*0.97*		

Estimations of the Fama and French model by TSLS using higher moments as instruments (continied)

	c	$R_m - R_f$	SMB	HML	UMD	R^2	DW
EM VG	−0.20	0.65	0.62	0.12	0.18	0.43	1.72
	−0.46	*3.80*	*3.83*	*0.61*	*1.10*		
EM HFRI	0.10	0.68	0.63	0.13	0.23	0.48	1.74
	0.27	*4.35*	*3.43*	*0.94*	*2.79*		
EQMN VG	0.47	0.12	0.13	0.03	0.08	0.55	1.08
	5.51	*3.54*	*4.16*	*0.82*	*2.64*		
EQMN HFRI	0.19	0.14	0.04	0.12	0.13	0.47	1.83
	2.38	*4.12*	*1.28*	*3.63*	*6.06*		
FINC VG	0.17	0.07	0.14	0.10	0.07	0.20	1.73
	1.38	*1.48*	*3.16*	*1.79*	*1.68*		
FINC HFRI	0.30	0.16	0.16	0.07	0.02	0.32	1.59
	3.38	*4.23*	*4.85*	*1.86*	*0.72*		
LS VG	0.50	0.46	0.22	−0.05	0.07	0.84	1.30
	3.98	*9.39*	*4.82*	*−0.91*	*1.45*		
LS HFRI	0.50	0.53	0.19	0.00	0.09	0.83	1.55
	3.95	*10.10*	*4.12*	*−0.06*	*2.75*		
MACRO VG	−0.03	0.25	0.30	−0.08	0.15	0.28	1.98
	−0.12	*2.35*	*3.00*	*−0.67*	*1.46*		
MACRO HFRI	0.22	0.24	0.23	0.09	0.10	0.15	1.97
	1.05	*2.72*	*3.00*	*1.07*	*1.84*		
MT VG	0.55	0.27	0.07	−0.25	−0.04	0.60	1.76
	2.85	*3.70*	*1.06*	*−2.84*	*−0.52*		
MT HFRI	0.52	0.30	0.01	−0.11	0.07	0.59	2.36
	3.45	*4.89*	*0.26*	*−1.76*	*1.75*		
SHORT VG	0.53	−1.03	−0.39	0.22	−0.20	0.83	1.94
	1.71	*−8.52*	*−3.47*	*1.54*	*−1.74*		
SHORT HFRI	0.66	−1.14	−0.38	0.26	−0.12	0.82	2.07
	2.14	*−9.01*	*−3.32*	*2.04*	*−1.56*		

Estimations of the Fama and French model by the non-iterated GMM using higher moments as instruments

	c	$R_m - R_f$	SMB	HML	UMD	R^2	DW	J-stat	p-value (J-stat)
AG VG	0.00	0.77	0.33	−0.22	0.11	0.85	1.58	0.15	0.93
	1.02	26.82	11.88	−6.43	5.06				
AG HFRI	0.31	0.83	0.42	0.02	0.07	0.91	1.78	0.16	0.91
	4.80	42.41	17.23	0.94	4.39				
CI VG	0.00	0.32	0.21	−0.02	0.08	0.78	1.33	0.15	0.95
	6.03	15.70	6.91	−0.86	7.29				
CI HFRI	0.41	0.42	0.20	0.03	0.06	0.85	1.37	0.17	0.87
	7.60	32.33	9.64	2.28	7.45				

Having an alternative performance measure like DEA is important because it enables investors to potentially pinpoint the reasons behind a CTA's poor trading efficiency. For institutional investors considering using CTAs, it is critical that a measure provide not only a precise appraisal of the CTA trading efficiency, but also an idea of what the CTAs can be compared with. The single measure of performance, which takes into account the multiple measurements of inputs and outputs to estimate a CTA's efficiency level, is practical because the CTAs themselves are used as benchmarks. Specifically, DEA permits one to evaluate, appraise and rank the trading efficiency of CTAs without using traditional market indices. Among the first studies in DEA to propose the evaluation of CTA classifications followed by the development of the benchmark models were Wilkens and Zhu (2001) and Zhu (2003).

Using data envelopment analysis we investigate the trading efficiency of CTAs and determine whether the ranking ordering produced with the basic DEA model can be used as an alternative measure of performance to the Sharpe ratio.[1] The RTS method is further used to classify CTAs in terms of increasing, decreasing or constant returns-to-scale. Institutional investors, endowments and pension funds can only benefit from this complementary measure when deciding on what CTAs they believe are efficient at trading and maintaining good performance.

If one presumes that CTAs are able to generate larger returns in proportion to their inputs, then they are said to be operating under increasing returns-to-scale. In other words, returns will increase if the CTA increases leverage. Increasing returns-to-scale signifies that increasing the risk of a CTA by 10% would result in increasing the returns by 20%, and vice versa. If an excessive amount of leverage (an input) is employed, then closing a number of positions could result in decreasing returns-to-scale. Decreasing RTS signifies that doubling the inputs will less than double the outputs and increasing RTS means that doubling the inputs will more than double the outputs (see Banker *et al* 2004; Gregoriou and Zhu 2005). A CTA under constant returns-to-scale can scale the inputs and outputs in a linear fashion without increasing or decreasing the fund's efficiency. Under this situation, the CTA can attain a proportional output with a proportional amount of input, in other words, constant RTS specifies that the doubling of inputs will double the outputs. Conversely, when varying returns-to-scale is present, inputs and outputs are not the same; hence, when inputs are increased the outputs can increase or decrease.

The rest of the chapter is organised as follows. The next section presents the literature review. Following that, the data and methodology are discussed. The second to last section presents the results and the final section concludes.

LITERATURE REVIEW

Prior to this study, no detailed trading efficiency analysis of CTAs has been undertaken using DEA. The literature on CTA efficiency is virtually nonexistent, with only a handful of studies touching on the subject (Gregoriou 2003; Diz *et al* 2004; Gregoriou and Chen (in press). Traditionally CTAs trade anywhere from 50–100 futures contracts on various global markets and attempt to minimise their losses as they occur (Vuille and Crisan 2004).

With fewer assets under management, small CTAs will likely trade less frequently and may not be as efficient as large CTAs due to economies of scale. To investigate this Diz (2004) examines the performance of CTAs and concludes that the mean margin-to-equity ratio is not significant when investigating live and dead CTAs. More recent studies on DEA (Gregoriou 2003; Diz *et al* 2004) examine the performance of live CTAs using basic, cross- and super efficiency models during the 1997–2001 period. Both studies conclude that DEA is a valid technique in evaluating the performance of alternative investments.

As further noted in Wilkens and Zhu (2001), hedge funds, managed futures and other actively managed funds have neither a universally accepted performance evaluation methodology nor a consistent classification system. This makes CTA strategies difficult to classify on a quantitative basis for an assortment of reasons including changing CTA risk and skewed return distributions.

Seiford and Zhu (1999) identify three methods of evaluating the RTS nature of decision making units (CTAs in the present case) that have been previously addressed in the DEA literature. There have also been a few theoretical studies in DEA examining RTS by Banker *et al* (1984) and Fare, Grosskopf and Lovell (1994). The RTS estimation has been used by Seiford and Zhu (1999), Zhu (2003) and Banker *et al* (2004) and applied in other areas. A more detailed

Figure 1 RTS regions

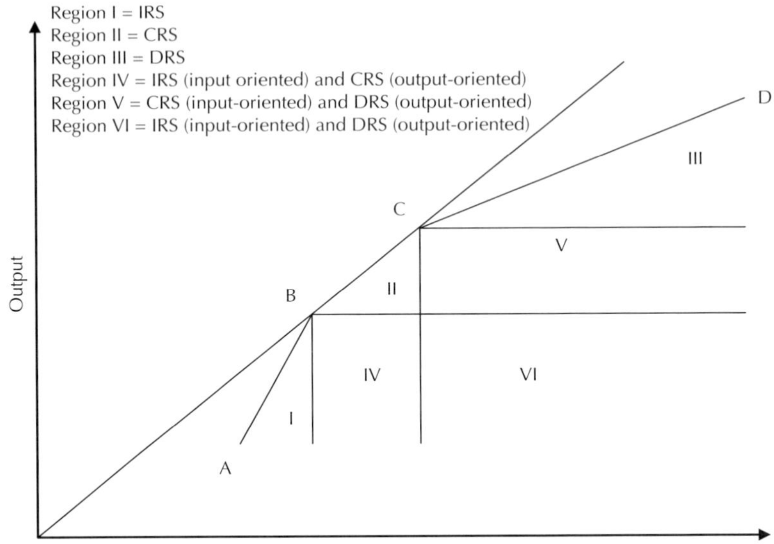

Source: Zhu (2003) and Gregoriou and Zhu (2005)

analysis of RTS estimation can be found in Banker *et al* (2004) and Gregoriou and Zhu (2005).

Wilkens and Zhu (2003) show how an RTS estimation technique in DEA can be used to classify hedge funds using the Centre for International Securities and Derivatives Markets (CISDM) indices. The authors conclude that DEA is a valid technique for classifying hedge funds. One can compare the RTS regions in DEA with the factor analysis technique of Fung and Hsieh (1997), and the general style classification (GSC) system used by Brown and Goetzmann (2003), in which the latter study generates five to eight distinct fund groups. CTA classifications used by database vendors are not very precise and not well defined because the styles are based on information provided by CTAs. As Brown and Goetzmann (2003) note, this may result in incorrect self-classification. RTS can play an important role in manager selection by grouping the individual funds into the appropriate RTS regions. Figure 1 presents the varying returns-to-scale (VRS) model and classifies the VRS frontier with CTAs displaying IRS, CRS and DRS. The six different RTS regions are shown, whereby AB displays

Table 1 Definition of commodity trading advisors classifications

Classification	Definition of investment style
Diversified	Manager trades financial futures/options, currency and forward contracts as well as commodity futures/options Manager limits risk by holding a large number of positions
Currency	Manager trades financial futures/options as well as currency futures/options, forward contracts, and currency, interest rates, stock indexes and precious metals
Financial	Manager specialises in stock index futures and options
Agricultural	Manager specialises in agricultural futures options trading
Stock index	Manager specialises in stock index futures and options

Source: Schneeweis (2003) IDAC.

increasing RTS, BC displays constant RTS and finally CD displays descreasing RTS. Therefore, AB, BC and CD make up the VRS frontier. However, some IRS, CRS and DRS regions are distrinctively determined irrespective of the VRS model used (either input or output oriented) (Zhu 2003).

DATA

The data set consists of the 25 largest live CTAs that reported monthly performance figures net of all management and performance fees to the Barclay Trading Group database. CTAs are tracked from January 1995 to December 2005 and efficiency scores using the basic DEA model are generated. This time frame is selected because using prior years would have resulted in too few CTAs for the analysis and encompasses extreme market events in both bull and bear markets. Furthermore, three CTAs were removed from the analysis due to incomplete data. The definitions of the five CTA classifications are displayed in Table 1.

Because only live funds are examined, there is a possibility that survivorship bias may exist in the data. To address this, the dead CTAs are added and rank last, have the lowest efficiency scores and do not alter the best practice frontier or the rankings of the live CTAs.

METHODOLOGY

DEA lends itself naturally to CTA trading efficiency because of its employment for assessing relative trading efficiency of CTAs using various inputs to produce outputs. In essence, DEA is an ideal method to measure trading efficiency relative to the best performing CTAs. This allows one to identify efficient and non-efficient CTAs and driving factors determining the trading efficiency of CTAs.

The inputs and outputs must correspond to the activities of CTAs for DEA. Four variables are used: two for inputs and two for outputs. The first input, beginning assets under management is used, which represents the amount each CTA has at the start of the investigation period. The second input is, the number of futures contracts traded per million US$ net of all brokerage fees.

For the first output, compound return is used because it identifies CTAs that have performed well during the investigation period. This will further inform us if the CTA has done an efficient job of trading futures contract throughout the examination period. The second output, ending assets under management provides the assets of the CTAs at December 31, 2005. This output permits one to identify which CTAs were able to increase their ending asset under management more efficiently through the use of efficient trading of futures contracts.

An input-oriented variable returns-to-scale model is used to examine the trading efficiency of CTAs. The Banker *et al* (1984) model and the RTS model from Zhu (2003) are applied in the analyses. The notation is adapted from Zhu (2003) for the basic efficiency model. For basic DEA, the ratio of outputs are maximised divided by inputs in Equation 1 which forms the objective function for the particular CTA h_0^*. CTAs are denoted by $j = \{1, 2, \ldots, n\}$ which uses quantities of i inputs with $I = \{1, 2, \ldots. m\}$ to produce quantities of r outputs with $r = \{1, 2, \ldots, s\}$; furthermore, we let x_{ij} be the quantity of input i for j used to produce the quantity y_{rj} of output r. Each CTA uses a variable quantity of m different inputs ($I = 1, 2, \ldots, m$) to generate s different outputs ($r = 1, 2, \ldots, s$). In particular, CTA j uses amount x_{ij} of output i and generates y_{rj} of output r. We then presume $x_{rj} \geq 0$, $y_{rj} \geq 0$ and that each CTA has at least one positive input value and one positive output value. DEA optimisation handles the observed vectors of x_j and y_j as given and selects values of output and input weights for a particular CTA. In Equation 1 a free variable, denoted by u_0, is added in the Banker *et al* (1984) BCC model to allow for variable returns to scale. If an increase in a

CTA's inputs does not produce a proportional change in its outputs then the CTA exhibits variable returns-to-scale. Therefore, as the CTA alters its scale of operations its efficiency will increase or decrease.

Therefore, in an input-oriented BCC model, the formulation minimises the inputs given the outputs. The following optimisation is obtained:

$$h_0^* = \max \frac{\sum_{r=1}^{s} u_r y_{r0} + u_0}{\sum_{i=1}^{m} v_i x_{i0}} \tag{1}$$

subject to:

$$\frac{\sum_{r=1}^{s} u_r y_{rj} + u_0}{\sum_{i=1}^{m} v_i x_{ij}} \leq 1, \quad j = 1, 2, \ldots n \tag{2}$$

where s = number of outputs;
m = number of inputs;
u_r = weight of output r;
v_i = weight of input i;
x_{ij} = amount of i used by CTA;
y_{rj} = amount of r used by CTA;
u_0 = free variable.

Equation 2 is the constraint which imposes that the equivalent weight, when implemented to all CTAs does not allow any CTA to have an efficiency score greater than 1.0. The efficiency score falls between 0 and 1.0 and a CTA is regarded as efficient upon obtaining an efficiency score of 1.0. A best practices frontier is then generated by the efficient CTAs. Therefore, each CTA will select weights to maximise its own self-efficiency with respect to the constraint in Equation 2.

CONCLUSION

This chapter demonstrates that DEA can be used as an alternative selection tool to assist pension funds, institutional investors, FOF managers and high-net worth individuals in selecting CTAs that are the most efficient in trading futures contracts. We believe DEA is a valuable addition to other risk-adjusted measures in that it widens the picture of CTA trading efficiency/performance appraisal. As a relative performance efficiency measure DEA can certainly be used as a validating technique to complement traditional performance analysis as well as monitor the trading efficiency of CTAs. It appears that the largest five (out of six) and efficient CTAs may not be taking on more risk because of the ample management and performance fees they receive. The empirical results support the contention that even when using non-linear returns in a risk-return framework DEA can provide reliable and consistent results.

Investors should determine which RTS methodology best fits their needs by deciding where their fund is located with respect to the RTS regions. Using different inputs and outputs – such as the size of the fund, leverage, the number of trades placed, and so on – will place the fund in different regions. Comparing the Generalised Style Classification groupings and RTS methodology groupings may add further insight into the performance and behaviour of CTAs in bull and bear markets. A manager may use both of these techniques for comparison purposes and to provide a complementary technique for CTA selection.

Future research can include using other DEA models to examine managed futures as well as various CTA indices in different periods.

ACKNOWLEDGEMENTS

Parts of this chapter have been reproduced from the co-editor's previous articles and book on DEA on DEA work in numerous articles and textbooks.

1 A risk-adjusted measure of performance (it is represented by the return of the portfolio minus the risk-free rate divided by the standard deviation).

REFERENCES

Banker, R. D. and R. M. Thrall, 1992, "Estimation of Returns-to-scale Using Data Envelopment Analysis", *European Journal of Operation Research*, **62(1)**, pp 74–84.

Banker, R. D., A. Charnes, and W. W. Cooper, 1984, "Some Models for Estimating Technical and Scale Inefficiencies in Data Envelopment Analysis", *Management Science*, **30(9)**, pp 1078–92.

Banker, R. D., W. W. Cooper, L. M., Seiford, R. M., Thrall, and J. Zhu, 2004, "Returns-to-Scale in different DEA models", *European Journal of Operational Research*, **154(2)**, pp 345–62.

Brown, S. J. and W. M. Goetzmann, 2003, "Hedge Funds With Style", *Journal of Portfolio Management*, **29(2)**, pp 101–12.

Diz, F., 2001, "Are Investors Over-Invested in Equities?" *Derivatives Quarterly*, **7(3)**, pp 59–62.

Diz, F., 2004, "The Effect of Management and Incentive Fees on the Performance of CTAs: A Note", in G. N. Gregoriou, V. N. Karavas, F. S., Lhabitant, and F. Rouah, (eds), *Commodity Trading Advisors: Risk, Performance and Analysis, and Selection*, (New York: John Wiley & Sons Inc), pp 248–58.

Diz, F., G. N. Gregoriou, F., Rouah, and S. Satchell, 2004, "Simple and Cross Efficiency of CTAs Using Data Envelopment Analysis", in G. N. Gregoriou, V. N. Karavas, F. S. Lhabitant, and F. Rouah, (eds), *Commodity Trading Advisors: Risk, Performance and Analysis, and Selection*, (New York: John Wiley & Sons Inc), pp 129–47.

Fare, R., S. Grosskopf, and C. A. K. Lovell, 1994, *Production Frontiers* (Cambridge: Cambridge University Press, UK).

Fung, W. and D. Hsieh, 1997 "Empirical Characteristics of Dynamic Trading Strategies: The Case of Hedge Funds" *Review of Financial Studies*, **10(2)**, pp 275–302.

Gregoriou, G. N., 2003, "Performance Evaluation of Funds of Hedge Funds Using Data Envelopment Analysis", *Journal of Wealth Management*, **5(4)**, pp 88–95.

Gregoriou, G. N. and Y. Chen, 2006, "Evaluation of Commodity Trading Advisors Using Fixed and Variable Benchmark Models", *Annals of Operations Research*, forthcoming.

Gregoriou, G. N. and J. Zhu, 2005 *Data Envelopment Analysis: Evaluating Hedge Funds and CTAs* (Hoboken, NJ: John Wiley and Sons Inc).

Gregoriou, G. N., K. T,. Sedzro and J. Zhu, 2005, "Hedge Fund Performance Appraisal Using Data Envelopment Analysis", *European Journal of Operations Research*, **164(2)**, pp 555–71.

Gregoriou, G. N. and Y. Chen, 2006, "Evaluation of Commodity Trading Advisors using Fixed and Variable Benchmark Models", forthcoming.

Kat, H. M., 2004, "Managed Futures and Hedge Funds: A Match Made in Heaven", *Journal of Investment Management*, **2(1)**, pp 1–9.

Schneeweis, T., 2003, "Benefits of Hedge Funds". *Presentation at the Investment Dealers Association of Canada Conference (IDAC) at St. Andrews*, New Brunswick.

Seiford, L. M. and J. Zhu, 1999, "An Investigation of Returns to Scale in Data Envelopment Analysis", *Omega*, **27(1)**, pp 1–11.

Vuille, S. and C. Crisan, 2004, "A Quantitative Analysis of CTA Funds", Master's Thesis HEC-Lausanne, Switzerland.

Wilkens, K. and J. Zhu, 2001, "Portfolio Evaluation and Benchmark Selection: A Mathematical Programming Approach", *The Journal of Alternative Investments*, **4(1)**, pp 9–20.

Wilkens, K. and J. Zhu, 2003, "Classifying Hedge Funds Using Data Envelopment Analysis", in G. N. Gregoriou, V. N. Karavas and F. Rouah (eds), *Hedge Funds: Strategies, Risk Assessment, and Returns,* (Washington, DC: Beard Books), pp 161–75.

Zhu, J. (2003) *Quantitative Models for Performance Evaluation and Benchmarking* (Norwell, MA: Kluwer Academic Publishers).

6

Absolute Performance and Correlation Persistence of Hedge Funds Returns: an Analysis Using the CISDM Database

Kathryn Wilkens, Donald R. Chambers

CAIAA, Lafayette College

HEDGE FUND RETURN PERSISTENCE

Several past studies find some evidence of persistence in hedge fund returns. Agarwal and Naik (2000) find reasonable evidence, but attribute it more to losers repeating poor performance than hedge fund managers repeating winning performance. Edwards and Caglayan (2001) used a six-factor alpha model with data from 1990 to 1998 and examined persistence over one and two year horizons with both parametric and non-parametric analyses. They found that 27% of winners repeat as winners and 20% of the losers repeated their losing performance.

Malkiel and Saha (2005) wrote a highly publicised article on hedge fund returns concluding that they were lower and riskier than often presumed. Although the chance of a winner repeating was about 50%, much higher than that in Edwards and Caglayan (2001), they concluded that it was a lack of evidence for persistence.

More recently, Guillermo *et al* (2006) correct for look-ahead bias and find evidence of persistence in quarterly hedge fund returns, but find less evidence in annual and bi-annual returns.

DeSouza and Gokcan (2004) also performed parametric and nonparametric analyses of return persistence in hedge fund returns, but suggest that the methodology is flawed for several reasons, and many are highlighted below. They conclude that there is persistence in volatility, but return history is not useful as a predictor of future performance. Similarly, Schneeweis (1998), Herzberg and Mozes (2003) and Kat and Menexe (2003) find little evidence of persistence in mean returns, but only in the volatility of hedge fund returns. Herzberg and Mozes also highlight a finding that returns' correlations to underlying market returns are highly persistent with more risky funds being more correlated to the underlying markets. The prevalence of results indicating volatility persistence in hedge funds in the literature suggest that quantitative analyses of hedge fund return data should focus on risk rather than return. De Souza and Goukan (2004) conclude that the results support the use of a risk budget approach to asset allocation. Lo (2005) also reviews several unique features of hedge fund investing relative to stock and bonds and calls for the use of more advanced quantitative techniques.

Studies of performance persistence in hedge fund returns have mixed results. Each can be criticised for various reasons. As an import example, there is the issue of whether or not the alphas are calculated correctly. Because there is still no commonly accepted definition for hedge fund betas, if alphas are calculated as excess returns beyond the return attributed to beta factors, known biases in database returns need to be addressed. Nevertheless, the literature does not largely support evidence of persistence in hedge fund returns, particularly from "winners".

Some slight evidence is found in favour of persistence, examining yearly returns from 1999 to 2005, and while the excess return from a strategy of investing in previous winners is positive and statistically significant for the aggregate sample, the positive performance varies over years and also by fund type and is generally not significant at the strategy level.

Analyses of persistence in the literature generally involve: (a) nonparametric tests of contingency winner and loser two way contingency tests; and (b) parametric tests involving regressing alphas on selection period alphas. The analysis is more closely associated with the second type of parametric test where it compares returns of a strategy of investing in winners (top third performers) with the overall return. But there is no attempt to separate alphas from beta risk factors because the results would be model dependent. Alexander and Dimitriu (2005) find that the ranking of fund alphas are not consistent across different models. Various models differ, for example, by their inclusion of different beta factors. Further, because we are not looking for superior performance in hedge funds overall, but rather whether persistence in a strategy of investing in top performing funds yields excess returns relative to only the funds within the same universe, we are not as concerned about hedge fund data biases.

One of the reasons for looking at year-on-year persistence rather than monthly or quarterly is that evidence of short-term persistence may not be appropriate for rebalancing decisions due to a host of issues including long lock-up periods, the length of the manager selection process. In addition, several methodological issues can impact results when shorter term returns are used such as smoothing, which may be partly due to illiquidity, and other biases. Annual January to December returns are used to partially address smoothing since December 31 values are audited by most funds and it can be argued that there is less managerial smoothing and more careful pricing.

This is not to say that the impact of risk on return is ignored. In contrast, in finding such little consistent support for performance persistence at the level of unadjusted returns, it is a stronger argument against the use of past returns as a basis for investment decisions than were one to find some level of persistence in risk-adjusted returns. If strong evidence had been found of persistence in raw returns, one would then need to seriously question the specification of excess returns and more carefully consider the impact of risk. In addition, the impact of risk is partially examined by comparing returns between groups with varying degrees of homogeneity.

HEDGE FUND RETURN CORRELATIONS AND THE BENEFITS OF DIVERSIFICATION

One dubious but common criterion for selecting hedge funds is based on the hopes of obtaining superior performance based on past return performance criteria, as discussed above. Another criterion is its low correlation to assets within the portfolio that is being built – hedge funds are not stand-alone investments. When a hedge fund's returns have low correlation with the returns of a portfolio of traditional assets (eg, stocks) the risk/return profile can be significantly improved by adding hedge funds to the portfolio. The low correlations between hedge fund returns and traditional asset returns have long been recognised and substantially documented in the past.

For example, Henker and Martin (1998) illustrate the potential diversification benefits of including CTAs in a multi-asset portfolio using both naive approach and by optimising the portfolio. More recently, Gregoriou and Rouh (2004) find considerable evidence of the diversification benefits of CTAs, particular during negative stock market returns and during extreme market events in general. For CTA returns, Edwards and Liew (1999) note that the low correlations with stock and bond returns during the 1982 to 1996 time periods suggest optimal allocations of 29% and 27% to managed futures in unconstrained and constrained portfolios, respectively. When hedge funds are added to the portfolio, the optimal allocation to hedge funds is 63% in the unconstrained portfolio (while allocations to CTAs are 28%) and in the constrained portfolio the allocations are 8% and 9%, respectively.

However, as more and more assets have been flowing into hedge funds and managed futures, there is evidence that returns of hedge funds are becoming more correlated to the stock market and to each other. Below evidence of increasing correlation coefficients is presented for various hedge fund strategy returns with each other and with a proxy for stock market returns.

DATA AND METHODOLOGY

Return persistence is addressed by comparing mean returns between consecutive time periods. The use of a moving window of data analysis indicates whether return persistence appears to be increasing or decreasing through time. Returns are measured in three ways: (a) raw returns; (b) abnormal returns relative to all hedge funds; and (c) abnormal returns relative to funds within the same classification. The second and third measures of return are used to adjust for risk differentials.

Correlation persistence is addressed by measuring the correlation of returns through time for individual hedge funds and groups of hedge funds. Correlation is measured both between funds and between the funds and the US stock market.

The CISDM Hedge Fund/CTA Database was used with returns through December 2005.

There were 4,504 funds, including commodity pool operators (CPOs), commodity trading advisers (CTAs), fund of funds (FOFs), and Hedge Funds (HF), with data. Of these, there were 3,458 that did not list a currency other than US$ (they listed US$ or listed nothing). In addition, all indexes were removed, leaving 3,421 for the analyses.

Only firms with complete return data over the specified time interval were used. This adds some biases (eg, survival bias) to the database which of course already contains other biases. For the return persistence analysis, we required 84 months of return data from January 1, 1999, to December 31, 2005. This left 993 funds. (For the return persistence analyses funds with identical return data over the specified interval were deleted.) For the correlation (diversification) analysis 72 months of return data were used from 1/00 to 12/05 to have three equal-length time periods leaving 1,202 funds.

ABNORMAL RETURN PERSISTENCE ANALYSIS

One of the most fundamental issues in alternative investments is the extent to which past superior performance (ie, alpha) is correlated with future superior performance.

The potential persistence of superior returns is investigated on an annual basis. Starting with year 1999, all funds are divided into thirds based on total return for 1999: top third, middle third and bottom third. It was found that the equally weighted average monthly return of the top third of the funds (3.9%) outperformed the overall equally weighted monthly average of funds (1.6%) by 2.3% in 1999. These figures are shown in the second to fourth columns of the first data line of Table 1.

In other words, the return of a "perfect foresight" portfolio (investing equally in all funds that generated returns that placed them in the top third of the sample) was computed for 1999. The procedure was then repeated for years 2000–5. While the perfect foresight strategy produced 2.30% higher returns in 1999, the strategy produced 1.51% higher returns in the year 2000 as shown in column 3.

The "perfect foresight" strategy produces an optimal performance level (subject to the constraint that the strategy must be an equally weighted average of one-third of the available funds). Performance of an actual strategy is evaluated by the extent to which it is able to capture any of this ideal advantage.

Table 1 Persistence strategy alphas, all funds

Year	(1)	(2)	(3) =(1)−(2)	(4)	(5) = (4)−(2)	(6) = (5)/(3)
	Top third (%)	All	Perfect foresight alpha (%)	Strategy return (%)	Strategy alpha (%)	Percent of alpha achieved (%)
1999	3.90	1.60	2.30			
2000	2.42	0.91	1.51	0.53	−0.38	−25.00
2001	1.85	0.57	1.27	0.78	0.21	16.30
2002	1.74	0.37	1.36	0.82	0.44	32.40
2003	2.94	1.39	1.54	1.29	−0.10	−6.80
2004	1.54	0.65	0.89	1.12	0.47	52.80
2005	1.57	0.56	1.01	0.95	0.39	38.90
Average	2.01	0.74	1.26	0.92	0.17	18.10

The key question is whether the funds that exhibited "superior" returns in one year continued to generate superior returns in the next year. Therefore the equally weighted average return of the portfolio was computed for the year following the year in which the funds all generated top third performance. In the line labelled year 2000 in the table the return of this "strategy" produced 38 basis points lower monthly return than the strategy of investing equally in all funds. Had the investor used perfect foresight, an increased return of 1.51% was possible. Thus, the persistence strategy achieved −25.00% of the possible return advantage as indicated in the upper right hand corner of the table.

Intuitively it would seem that this indicates that the risk factors that generated high performance in 1999 caused low performance in 2000, and that many funds maintained somewhat stable risk exposures. In other words, the higher performance in 1999 was dominated by "beta" risks rather than "alpha" based returns when the sample is aggregated. This is consistent with the results of Herzberg and Mozes (2003) that find hedge fund returns have a persistent correlation to underlying market factors and relatively risky hedge funds have are less able to hedge against the drops in the underlying market factors.

Yet there is one other year (2003) where, in the aggregate, the strategy of investing in the previous year's top performers yielded a negative excess return ("alpha"). It is noted that 2003 was also a

Table 2 Persistence strategy alphas, by fund type

		CPO	CTA	FofF	HF
# funds	**993**	**131**	**160**	**258**	**444**
	All (%)	**1 (%)**	**2 (%)**	**3 (%)**	**4 (%)**
Year					
2000	−25.00	17.90	−9.60	−39.60	−27.80
2001	16.30	20.70	12.80	36.60	12.10
2002	32.40	4.30	9.70	67.70	44.60
2003	−6.80	−13.00	−29.80	1.30	−6.80
2004	52.80	9.50	6.50	58.50	52.10
2005	38.90	13.20	0.80	46.50	49.60
Average	18.10	8.77	−1.60	28.50	20.63
Alpha2	0.00678*	0.00148	0.001252	0.004845	0.005586

*At the 10% significance level.

turnaround year, like 2000, but smaller in magnitude and differing in direction (from bear to bull rather than from bull to bear). That is, from 1999 to 2000, the overall hedge fund returns declined, but from 2002 to 2003, overall hedge fund returns increased. However, mean reversion may account for this wherein firms that generated high performance in the year 1999 tended to generate low performance in year 2000 when the market dropped, and while the strategy yielded a negative "alpha" in 2003 when the underlying funds dropped, it still represented an increase of 50% from its previous year's "alpha". These observations simply shed light on the difficulty of separating alpha and beta effects when examining raw excess returns in the aggregate.

The final column indicates that return performance persisted in 2001, 2002, 2004 and 2005.

One of the problems with aggregated return analysis is that the higher returns are not adjusted for potential risk differentials. In the next two subsections, the analysis is broken down into fund types and strategies in order to partially control for the differentials.

Table 2 summarises the analogous results broken into the four fund types classified in the CISDM database.[1]

The figures reported in this table are analogous to the final column of the previous table. A second measure of alpha (labelled in

Table 3 Persistence strategy alphas, by strategy

	Conv arb	CTA – sys trend	Em mkt	Eq L/S	Event mult	FofF multi	Sector	NA
# funds	**32** (%)	**133** (%)	**46** (%)	**137** (%)	**33** (%)	**209** (%)	**38** (%)	**134** (%)
Year								
2000	−77.50	4.80	−50.60	−59.10	27.00	−37.50	−29.70	8.00
2001	−3.50	14.20	−18.70	33.90	−38.70	39.50	30.00	25.60
2002	90.30	10.60	57.10	43.60	40.50	69.00	56.20	6.00
2003	23.90	−33.80	48.60	−30.60	−43.60	9.10	46.70	−11.20
2004	80.30	3.60	−5.20	35.80	8.80	51.10	39.80	9.90
2005	48.20	−13.70	49.30	28.60	17.60	44.80	32.00	29.80
Average	26.95	−2.38	13.42	8.70	1.93	29.33	29.17	11.35
Alpha	0.00210	−0.00034	−0.00208	0.00477	0.00434*	0.00454	0.006798	0.00286*

*At the 10% significance level.

the last row of Tables 2 and 3 as "Alpha2") is the excess return (above the sub-class variation risk) found through a parametric regression analysis. While the results indicate that year over year persistence is statistically significant at the most aggregate level, once the alpha is examined at the strategy level the significance disappears.

Table 3 summarises the analogous results for several major strategies: convertible arbitrage, systematic trend-following CTAs, emerging market hedge funds, event/multi-strategy hedge funds, multi-strategy fund of funds, sector-focused hedge funds, and 134 hedge funds that were not given a strategy name (NA).

Two of the subclasses seem to have statistically significant parametric alphas (NA, where no fund strategy was provided, and "Event Multi-Strategy"). However, the parametric alphas are more susceptible to the impact of outliers and are not always consistent with the intuition implied by the percentage of alpha attainable relative to the top third performers.

In summary, one cannot conclude that there is any substantial evidence of performance persistence even when one does not explicitly account for the impact of beta risk and hedge fund data biases. There are no statements of superior performance in hedge funds, only relative performance persistence is examined.

CORRELATION ANALYSIS

To shed light on the stability of diversification potential through time, the correlation coefficient was computed for each fund between that fund's monthly return and the return of an equally weighted portfolio of all funds. This average correlation coefficient was computed for three non-overlapping time intervals of 24 months each as shown in the left hand side of Table 4.

The average correlation of individual fund with the overall sample rose from 0.34 to 0.53 over the 2000–5 interval.

The correlation coefficient for each fund was also computed between that fund's monthly returns and the monthly returns of the S&P 500 (using SPY's total return as a proxy). As shown on the right hand side of Table 4 the average correlations of individual funds with the S&P 500 rose from 0.10 to 0.41 over the 2000–5 interval.

The average correlations summarised in Table 1 are for the entire sample combined. In the next two subsections, the sample

Table 4 Correlation statistics, all funds

		Rho with all funds			Rho with stocks		
	N	**00–01**	**02–03**	**04–05**	**00–01**	**02–03**	**04–05**
All	1202	0.34	0.37	0.53	0.10	0.20	0.41

Table 5 Correlation statistics, by fund type

		Rho with all funds			Rho with stocks			Rho with sub-class		
	N	**00–01**	**02–03**	**04–05**	**00–01**	**02–03**	**04–05**	**00–01**	**02–03**	**04–05**
CPO	142	0.31	0.39	0.58	−0.26	−0.26	0.39	0.65	0.67	0.66
CTA	178	0.24	0.32	0.41	−0.20	−0.14	0.28	0.49	0.49	0.48
FofF	31	0.52	0.50	0.71	0.22	0.35	0.56	0.61	0.63	0.80
HF	571	0.28	0.31	0.46	0.22	0.34	0.38	0.36	0.43	0.49

is broken down into types (eg, CTAs, CPOs, FofFs and HFs) and strategies.

Table 5 reports the correlations analogous to Table 4 but broken into fund type.

In addition to providing sub-classifications, Table 5 introduces another set of averaged correlations in the final columns: the averaged correlation coefficients for all funds of a specific type between that fund's monthly returns and the monthly returns of an equally weighted portfolio of all other funds of the same type.

Table 6 reports the correlations analogous to Table 5 but broken down into fund strategy rather than type.

Only five strategies are summarised since most strategies contained small numbers of observations.

CONCLUSION

Two of the most important issues to hedge fund investors are the extent to which superior performance persists, and the extent of the diversification advantages (ie, the effect on risk).

The analysis of returns over the interval 1999–2005 indicates slight support for the idea that funds with superior performance in one year are more likely to generate superior performance in the

Table 6 Correlation statistics, by strategy

		Rho with all funds			Rho with stocks			Rho with sub-class		
	N	00–01	02–03	04–05	00–01	02–03	04–05	00–01	02–03	04–05
Conv arb	39	0.23	0.34	0.48	0.14	0.26	0.28	0.55	0.70	0.70
CTA/sys trend	146	0.27	0.37	0.46	−0.22	−0.18	0.32	0.55	0.57	0.54
Em mkt	63	0.42	0.35	0.50	0.47	0.47	0.34	0.64	0.62	0.59
Eq L/S	173	0.33	0.35	0.56	0.26	0.47	0.50	0.41	0.56	0.61
FofF multi	244	0.54	0.52	0.73	0.22	0.36	0.58	0.62	0.65	0.82

following year. The analysis also indicates that high total returns can also be attributed to risk differentials.

The analysis of returns over the interval 2000–5 indicates that the potential diversification benefits of hedge fund investing may be declining. Generally, correlation between funds and correlation between funds and the stock market appeared to increase.

1 CPOs typically hire one or more CTAs to manage money deposited in a (public or private) commodity pool. Like mutual funds, public pools are open to the public. Private pools can avoid registration with the CFTC and are generally for high net worth and institutional investors. CTAs may be considered a sub-class of hedge funds.

REFERENCES

Agarwal, V. and N. Y. Naik, 2000, "On Taking the 'Alternative' Route: Risks, Rewards, Style and Performance Persistence of Hedge Funds", *Journal of Alternative Investments*, **2(4)**, pp 6–23.

Alexander, C. and A. Dimitriu, 2005, "Rank Alpha Funds of Hedge Funds", *The Journal of Alternative Investments*, **8(2)**, pp 48–61.

De Souza, C. and S. Gokcan, 2004, "Hedge Fund Investing: A Quantitative Approach to Hedge Fund Manager Selection and De-Selection", *The Journal of Wealth Management*, **6(4)**, pp 52–73.

Edwards, F. R. and M. O. Caglayan, 2001, "Hedge Fund Performance and Manager Skill", *Journal of Futures Markets*, **21(11)**, pp 1003–28.

Edwards, F. R. and J. Liew, 1999, "Hedge Funds versus Managed Futures as Asset Classes," *Journal of Derivatives*, **6(4)**, pp 45–64.

Gregoriou, G. N. and F. Rouah, 2004, "Performance of the Largest CTAs in Negative S&P 500 Months and Extreme Market Events", *The Journal of Wealth Management*, **7(1)**, pp 44–7.

Guillermo B., J Horst, and M. Verbeek, 2006, "Survival, Look-Ahead Bias, and Persistence in Hedge Fund Performance", *Journal of Financial and Quantitative Analysis*, **40(3)**, pp 493–517.

Henker, T. and G. Martin, 1998, "Naïve and Optimal Diversification for Managed Futures," *The Journal of Alternative Investments*, **1(2)**, pp 25–39.

Herzberg, M. M. and H. A. Mozes, 2003, "The Persistence of Hedge Fund Risk: Evidence and Implications for Investors," *The Journal of Alternative Investments*, **6(2)**, pp 22–42.

Kat, H. and F. Menexe, 2003, "Persistence in Hedge Fund Performance: The True Value of a Track Record", *The Journal of Alternative Investments*, **5(4)**, pp 66–72.

Lo, A. W., 2005, *The Dynamics of the Hedge Fund Industry* (Research Foundation of CFA Institute Monograph).

Malkiel, B. and A. Saha, 2005, "Hedge Funds: Risk and Return", *Financial Analysts Journal*, **61(6)**, pp 80–8.

Schneeweis, T., 1998, "Evidence of Superior Performance Persistence in Hedge Funds: An Empirical Comment", *The Journal of Alternative Investments*, **1(2)**, pp 76–80.

7

Return Attribution for Portfolios of Hedge Funds

François-Serge Lhabitant

Kedge Capital, HEC Lausanne and EDHEC

INTRODUCTION

Since Alfred Winslow Jones set up the first hedge fund in 1949, the hedge fund industry has alternated between periods of rapid growth (1966–8, the late 1980s and early 1990s) and periods of severe contraction (1969–70 and 1973–4). But none of these periods are comparable with the frenzy that has seemed to prevail since the beginning of the third millennium. While stocks floundered and reminded us that they were risky investments after all, hedge funds performed well and attracted large amounts of capital, mostly from wealthy individuals and institutional investors walloped by equity markets and discouraged by all-time-low yields.

The preferred investment vehicles for these newcomers were generally funds of hedge funds. In a single simple structure, they offer easy access to a diversified portfolio of selected hedge funds, better liquidity terms than their direct investments, and most of the time, some sort of active asset allocation strategy. Unfortunately, the barriers to entry in the fund of hedge funds universe are low, and the huge impending demand has attracted numerous players of yet unproven quality. Dividing the wheat from the chaff is not easy, as funds of funds provide limited information about the effective quality of their services, eg, the impact of individual manager selection and asset allocation across the various investment styles. How important is the value added, if any, and where is it created? Even the managers of some funds of hedge funds do not have the answers to these simple yet fundamental questions.

How about academics? So far, their focus has been primarily on analysing the sources of performance of long-only fund managers, and little attention has been devoted to funds of hedge funds. This is not really surprising, given (a) the scarcity of data available on hedge funds and the traditional secrecy surrounding them; and (b) the lack of a reference framework to analyse performance results. Indeed, most traditional performance measures are either based on the venerable Capital Asset Pricing Model or implicitly include some normal distribution assumptions. They are therefore not applicable to hedge funds, which are loosely correlated with market indexes and often exhibit return distributions characterised by negative skewness and positive kurtosis. Investors are therefore left naked – they reward portfolio managers by paying performance fees, but have no way to determine whether they added value or not.

Fortunately, the situation is progressively improving. Similarly to what happened to mutual funds in the 1980s, the alternative asset management industry has started an important institutionalisation and industrialisation process. Experience, personal contacts and pure qualitative judgement are progressively being complemented by analytical skills and risk controls. Sophisticated investors considering hedge funds now want to hear about a sound investment process, good risk-adjusted performance, style analysis, benchmarks and even start requesting some form of risk transparency. Strong returns alone are no longer sufficient, as they merge together good, bad and indifferent return contributions from different sources into a single whole. Understanding how the performance was generated is becoming an essential part of sound fund selection and portfolio construction processes. The aim of this chapter is therefore to suggest a simple, yet powerful, framework of performance attribution for funds of hedge funds. Based on the performance attribution model initially suggested by Brinson, Hood and Beebower (1986) – hereafter BHB – for long-only funds, the framework takes into account the typical steps of the decision making process particular to funds of hedge funds.

The structure of the chapter is as follows. The second section surveys the academic literature on performance attribution and discusses the details of the original BHB model for traditional assets. The third section extends this model to the case of hedge fund portfolios by taking into consideration their specificities. It also illustrates the application of the framework to a particular fund of hedge funds. The final section concludes and suggests further extensions.

SINGLE-PERIOD RETURN ATTRIBUTION FOR TRADITIONAL PORTFOLIOS

One of the most popular return attribution approaches was initially developed in February 1972 by a working group of The Society of Investment Analysts (UK), with the aim of calculating the stock selection and asset allocation effects in a balanced (ie, stock and bond) portfolio. For the first time, it introduced the idea of calculating the returns of a "partially restrained fund", ie, a fund invested using theoretical portfolio weights and index returns. This approach is directly analogous to that proposed in the seminal work of BHB.

The Brinson, Hood and Beebower model

The BHB model focuses on a relatively simple single-period problem, namely, disentangling the excess return registered by a portfolio over a given benchmark into three well-identified proportions. These proportions are (a) the portfolio manager skill at picking strongly performing investments (ie, the *selection* contribution); (b) the portfolio manager skill at strategically positioning the fund among investment categories (ie, the *allocation* contribution); and (c) the *interactions* or *joint effects* between selection and allocation effects. It is worth spending a few minutes reviewing the basics of the BHB performance attribution model because they lead quickly to new and interesting territory.

To simplify the presentation, let us assume that the investment universe is divided into a series of N distinct asset classes. The portfolio manager is given a benchmark, which is also represented as a portfolio of the N asset classes. In the benchmark, each asset class j ($j = 1, \ldots, N$) has a weight w_j^B and a return R_j^B, where the latter is typically given by an index. In the analysed portfolio,

Figure 1 Example of the return attribution for one asset class (numbered j)

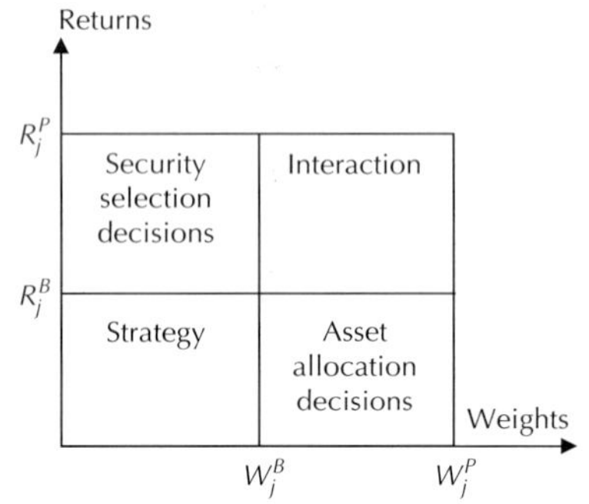

each asset class j ($j = 1, \ldots, N$) has a weight w_j^P and a return R_j^P, where the latter is the return effectively achieved on the asset class.

Active portfolio managers can try to add value by overweighting or underweighting an asset class with respect to the benchmark's weights (ie, $w_j^B \neq w_j^P$), or by selecting assets that are expected to outperform their asset class return (ie, $R_j^B \neq R_j^P$). For a given asset class, the situation can be represented as in Figure 1.

In this example, the portfolio manager over-weighted asset class j ($w_j^P > w_j^B$) and outperformed its benchmark ($R_j^P > R_j^B$). The total return contribution of asset class j to the portfolio return corresponds to the surface of the overall rectangle. It is obtained by multiplying the weight of the strategy in the portfolio (w_j^P) by its effective return (R_j^P), and can be divided in four sources:

- The first area is the *strategic return contribution* of the asset class, that is, the return contribution the portfolio manager would have observed if he had kept the benchmark weights and simply tracked the benchmark return. It is often referred to as the "investment policy" contribution and it is measured as:

$$\text{Strategy}_j = w_j^B R_j^B$$

- The second area is the value added by the *asset allocation decisions* of the portfolio manager, ie, overweighting or underweighting asset class j. It is purely a weighting decision, and the returns used for measuring the impact of asset allocation are those of the asset class in the benchmark.

$$\text{VA Allocation}_j = (w_j^P - w_j^B)\, R_j^B$$

- The third area is the value added by the *security selection decisions* of the portfolio manager, ie, selecting assets in asset class j that outperformed the ones in the benchmark. It is purely a return-based decision, and the weights used to measure the impact of selection decisions are those of the asset class in the benchmark.

$$\text{VA Selection}_j = w_j^B (R_j^P - R_j^B)$$

- Finally, the last area is an *interaction effect*, which combines the joint effect of changing simultaneously the weights and the performance realised *vis-à-vis* the benchmark. In our illustration, there is a positive interaction effect because the portfolio manager over-weighted an asset class that outperformed its benchmark. A similar observation would occur if the manager had underweighted an asset classes that under-performed its benchmark.

$$\text{VA Interaction}_j = (w_j^P - w_j^B)(R_j^P - R_j^B)$$

The total value added by asset class j is the sum of its three components:

$$\text{VA Total}_j = \text{VA Allocation}_j + \text{VA Selection}_j + \text{VA Interaction}_j$$

The interaction component is often confusing – in their original paper, BHB even called it "other", which is not very meaningful. Moreover, it can be quite large if there are large differences in weights and in returns for some asset classes. In practice, since the interaction effect has characteristics of both the selection contribution and allocation contribution, practitioners often associate it with either for simplicity of presentation. The following will include the interaction component in the selection contribution, as will be seen.

Note that the above analysis was made only for one asset class (asset class *j*) in the portfolio. By repeating it for each asset class, and by summing resulting components across asset classes, one can calculate the return contributions at the portfolio level and therefore analyse the total value added – or withdrawn – by passive as well as active management decisions.

The BHB empirical results

One may wonder which of the four above-mentioned components of investment performance has the largest influence in the long run. The answer should obviously influence the way portfolio management activities are to be organised. Should fund managers spend more time on defining their investment, allocating tactically across asset classes, or selecting individual assets? In their seminal paper, BHB analysed the return data of 91 large pension funds over the period 1974 to 1983 and regressed each fund's total return through time on its four respective performance components.[1] They observed that "investment policy dominates investment strategy (market timing and security selection), explaining on average 93.6% of the variation in total plan return" through time and in no case less than 75.5%. Brinson *et al* (1991) updated the original BHB study and found again that investment policy still accounted for more than 90% of return variation. More recently, Blake *et al* (1999) studied UK pension fund performance and once again attributed more than 90% of the time series variation in portfolio returns to investment policy decisions.

These results, which overwhelmingly support the investment policy as the most dominant determinant of portfolio performance, were often misinterpreted in the financial literature. In particular, many industry experts quote BHB to claim that active managers are not able to add any value and, as such, that a substantial portion of all the time, energy and costs spent in managing a portfolio should be focused on the investment policy decision rather than on the stock selection or timing activities. This conclusion may be appealing to some, but it is wrong. None of Brinson *et al*'s studies ever mentioned that 90% or more of *portfolio return* was due to the investment policy. They simply mentioned that *on average*, 90% of the *variation in portfolio returns* could be explained by the investment policy, which is a significantly different proposition. Most people quoting BHB forget the qualifier "on average", the word "variation", or incorrectly interpret the term "variation" as meaning variation of return from plan to plan while it means in reality variance over time. Indeed, the original question addressed by BHB is how much of the variability of returns *over time* is explained by the investment policy. Of course, there are other interesting questions, eg, how much of the variation in returns among funds is explained by differences in investment policies, or what portion of the return level is explained by policy returns, but none of these questions were addressed by BHB.

Of course, a number of authors have also criticised the results and conclusions of the BHB study. As an illustration, Hensel *et al* (1991) stressed the importance of the investor's behaviour and showed that asset allocation could appear more or less important depending on the reference point around which it varies. Indeed, the BHB study does not disentangle the opportunity set from investor behaviour – it is a joint set of what opportunities are being presented by capital markets and what investment activities investors choose to perform. In addition, the data sets used by BHB are subject to caution, as pension funds' portfolio managers generally do not engage into heavy market timing activities or aggressive stock picking bets. The only way the importance of investment policy could have been lower in their results was if the considered pension funds had completely ignored the basic diversification rules and had concentrated their assets in non-diversified portfolios or radically attempted to time the market. However, this attitude would have been in total violation of modern portfolio theory and the ERISA's "prudent expert" rule. Thus, BHB's results may result from the broadly diversified nature and limited active management of pension fund portfolios in the aggregate.

Interestingly, BHB also discussed in a qualitative way the issue of the size of the contributions of investment policy (passive management) and investment strategy (active management) to the level of portfolio return. We quote: "Although investment strategy can result in significant returns, these are dwarfed by the return contribution from investment policy – the selection of asset classes and their normal weights". Later on, BHB revised their conclusion on the significance of strategy returns, but maintained the idea that only investment policy matters: "Individual effects (of active management) varied widely. Clearly the contribution of active management is not statistically different from zero (ie, it is most likely attributable to chance). Active management had no measurable impact on returns." Not surprisingly, these parts of their article are not often quoted in the literature, probably because they are not motivated by impressive quantitative figures.

More recently, Ibbotson and Kaplan (2000) analysed separately the cross-sectional return variation and the inter-temporal return variation of 94 balanced mutual funds and 58 pension funds. They confirmed that more than 90% of return variation *through time* was attributable to strategic asset allocation, but they also obtained that only 40% of the return differences *across funds* was attributable to it. Jahnke (2000) also evidenced that the importance of asset allocation depends on many factors such as the extent to which investors engage in active asset allocation, security selection, expenses and skill. Last, but not least, Statman (2000) endorsed the notion that asset mix policy is critical, because he argues investors are not skilful at market timing or security selection. Obviously, the intention is not to solve these issues in this chapter, and the reader will be referred back to the original texts for further discussion.

EXTENDING THE BHB MODEL FOR HEDGE FUND PORTFOLIOS

For many years, the BHB performance attribution model was successfully used by institutional investors to analyse their portfolios. The simplicity of its arithmetic rules was attractive and fitted well institutional equity and bond portfolios, which are well-defined in terms of investment universe and benchmarks. However, the recent intrusion of hedge funds and funds of hedge funds in portfolios has significantly changed the situation. Indeed, the original BHB model is not directly applicable to hedge funds, unless a series of new definitions are adopted and several adjustments are made. Let us now review them, and illustrate the new performance attribution model by applying it on a specific fund of hedge funds.

Segmentation of the universe and definition of benchmarks

Setting an alternative investment policy cannot be made operational without first segmenting the investment universe into well-identified, mutually exclusive subgroups and defining a benchmark for each subgroup. With traditional assets, subgroups naturally corresponded to asset classes, and benchmarks were typically market capitalisation-weighted total return indexes. With hedge funds, however, subgroups and their reference index are harder to identify. The reasons are two-fold. First, there is no standardised way of breaking down the hedge fund universe, as illustrated by the large differences in the number, definition and granularity of subgroups used by hedge fund databases. Second, choosing a reference index for a particular subgroup is often arbitrary, given the plethora of hedge fund indexes built using different methodologies, underlying sample of funds, biases and ultimately, returns – see Amenc and Martellini (2003a).

A simple solution is to adopt a pragmatic approach based on the available information. Most funds of hedge funds disclose the way they divide the universe in terms of strategies, as well as what is the benchmark for each strategy. In some cases, this will be an internal classification system, while in others they will adopt an external classification.[2] This classification should be the one used to attribute performance, because it reflects the way a portfolio manager views the universe and allocates the assets. In the following, for the sake of illustration, the analysis will be based on the Credit Suisse/Tremont segmentation. That is, we split our investment universe into 10 strategies, namely long-short equity, global macro, convertible arbitrage, fixed income arbitrage, event-driven, market neutral, emerging markets, managed futures, dedicated short and multi-strategies – see Table 1. In addition, cash will be considered as being a tenth "strategy". Each hedge fund strategy is compared to the corresponding Credit Suisse/Tremont Investable Index, and cash is assumed to match the one-month Libor US$ returns.

Once the set of strategies has been identified, one needs to obtain the weights of these strategies in the policy portfolio (benchmark). This is straightforward if the portfolio manager plays the game and agrees to disclose the weights of hedge fund strategies in his long-term allocation. However, some fund of hedge funds managers will only reveal them partially or even not reveal them at all – they pretend to be purely "opportunistic" and have no benchmark weights, or even simply claim that these weights are "proprietary". In such cases, two alternative approaches are available.

Table 1 The Credit Suisse/Tremont segmentation of the hedge fund universe

Category	Strategy
Convertible arbitrage	Invest in the convertible securities of a company. A typical investment is to be long in convertible bond and short in the underlying stock
Dedicated short-bias	Maintain consistent net short (or pure short) exposures to the underlying market
Emerging markets	Equity or fixed income investing in emerging markets around the world
Event-driven	Equity-oriented investing designed to capture price movement generated by an anticipated corporate event (merger, acquisition, distressed securities, etc)
Fixed income arbitrage	Profit from price anomalies between related interest rate securities
Global macro	Leveraged views on overall market direction as influenced by major economic trends and/or events
Long-short equity	Equity-oriented investing on both the long and short sides of the market, with an objective different from being market neutral
Managed futures	Systematic or discretionary trading in listed financial and commodity futures markets and currency markets around the world
Market neutral	Exploit equity market inefficiencies by being simultaneously long and short matched equity portfolios of the same size within a country
Multi-strategies	Dynamically allocate assets across several hedge fund strategies, based on opportunities

- The first alternative is to use an arbitrarily defined set of weights. For instance, for a multi-strategy diversified fund of funds, two obvious benchmark candidates are an equally-weighted or an industry-asset-weighted basket of all the strategies. Most databases provide the necessary information to create such a benchmark. However, one needs to be cautious with such choices as they often rely on hidden assumptions. For instance, using an equally weighted basket of hedge funds as the investment policy implicitly assumes that the fund manager with no view will sell his winners to buy back more losers.
- The second alternative is to rely on the style analysis approach originally developed by Sharpe (1988) and extended by Lhabitant

Figure 2 Weights used in the Credit Suisse/Tremont Index

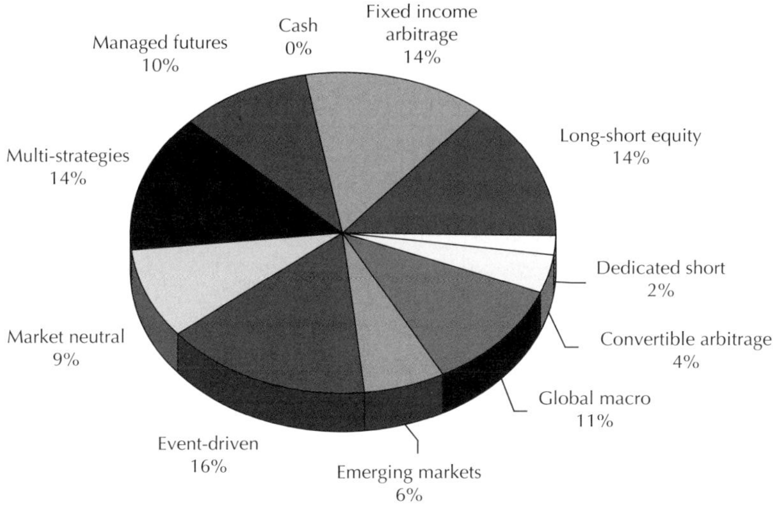

(2001) for hedge funds. Simply stated, style analysis provides the combination of long positions in hedge fund indexes that would have most closely replicated the actual performance of a given portfolio of hedge funds over a specific period of time. This combination of hedge fund indexes can be used to define the policy weights, in the absence of additional information.

In any case, it is essential that one slices the benchmark and the analysed hedge fund portfolio using the same classification. In the present example, the Credit Suisse/Tremont Index has been used as a benchmark, ie, a basket of our ten hedge fund strategies with weights identical to their weights in the Credit Suisse/Tremont Index.

Note that this standardised segmentation provides a baseline for the attribution of hedge fund portfolio performance, but it does not preclude the use of alternative ways of dividing the hedge fund universe, particularly for more specialised or detailed decision-making processes (eg, regional or sector oriented approaches). Let us now review the different components of performance attribution. Note that we no longer think in terms of asset classes, but in terms of hedge fund strategies.

Table 2 Information required for implementing a performance attribution

j	Strategy	w_j^B Benchmark weight (%)	R_j^B Benchmark return (%)	w_j^P Portfolio weight (%)	R_j^P Portfolio return (%)	R_j^* Average hedge fund return (%)
1	Fixed income arbitrage	14	−0.61	21.72	1.66	1.78
2	Long-short equity	14	1.46	17.77	2.97	3.13
3	Dedicated short	2	−3.21			
4	Convertible arbitrage	4	−0.52			
5	Global macro	11	0.07	23.75	3.34	3.64
6	Emerging markets	6	3.09			
7	Event-driven	16	0.96	36.11	0.73	0.48
8	Market neutral	9	0.54			
9	Multi-strategies	14	0.41			
10	Managed futures	10	3.55			
11	Cash	0	0.35	0.66	0.35	0.35
	Total	100	$I = 0.84$	100.00	$R^P = 1.95$	

The analysed portfolio

For the sake of illustration, we have chosen to analyse a fund of hedge funds over one month of its existence. Table 2 shows the information required to implement the performance attribution, namely:

- ❑ The weights of each hedge fund strategy in the benchmark.
- ❑ The return of each hedge fund strategy in the benchmark.
- ❑ The weights of each hedge fund strategy in the analysed portfolio. In practice, most funds of funds provide their investors with information about their beginning-of-period strategy weights on a monthly or quarterly basis, typically under the form of a pie chart on their monthly fact-sheet. In the present case, the fund of hedge funds analysed only invested in five of the ten strategies.
- ❑ The return of each hedge fund strategy in the analysed portfolio (calculated from the returns of individual hedge funds that belong to the strategy).

In addition, we have also calculated the average performance of the funds in the analysed portfolio for each strategy. This will be used to analyse whether the weight given to each fund within a strategy added value or not, as will be seen.

Strategic return contribution

The strategic return contribution of a given strategy is easily measured by multiplying the weight of the strategy in the benchmark by the return of its benchmark index, as we did for traditional asset classes.

$$\text{Strategy}_j = w_j^B R_j^B$$

For instance, the strategic return contribution generated by long-short equity in the example is 14% × 1.46 = 20 basis points. By summing strategy contributions across all strategies, one obtains the benchmark portfolio return.

$$I = \sum_j w_j^B R_j^B$$

In our example, the benchmark portfolio return is 0.84%.

REFERENCES

Amenc, N. and L. Martellini, 2003a, "The Brave New World of Hedge Funds Indices," Working Paper, EDHEC Business School, Valbonne, France.

Amenc, N. and L. Martellini, 2003b, "Evidence of Predictability in Hedge Fund Returns", *Financial Analysts Journal,* **59(5)**, pp 32–46.

Blake D., B. N. Lehmann, and A. Timmermann, 1999, "Asset Allocation Dynamics and Pension fund Performance", *Journal of Business,* **72(4)**, pp 429–61.

Brinson, G. P., L. R. Hood, and G. L. Beebower, 1986, "Determinants of Portfolio Performance", *Financial Analysts Journal,* **42(4)**, pp 39–44.

Brinson, G. P., B. D. Singer, and G. L. Beebower, 1991, "Determinants of Portfolio Performance II: An Update", *Financial Analysts Journal,* **47(3)**, pp 40–8.

Hensel, C. R., D. D. Ezra, and J. H. Ilkiw, 1991, "The Importance of the Asset Allocation Decision", *Financial Analysts Journal,* **47**(4), pp 65–72.

Ibbotson, R. G. and P. D. Kaplan, 2000, "Does Asset Allocation Policy Explain 40, 90, or 100 Percent of Performance?", *Financial Analysts Journal,* **56(1)**, pp 26–33.

Jahnke, W., 1997, "The Asset Allocation Hoax", *Journal of Financial Planning,* **10(1)**, pp 109–13.

Lhabitant, F. S., 2001, "Hedge Funds Investing: A Quantitative Look Inside The Black Box", *The Journal of Financial Transformation,* **1(1)**, pp 82–90.

Sharpe, W. F., 1988, "Determining a Fund's Effective Asset Mix", *Investment Management Review,* November/December, pp 59–69.

Statman, M., 2000, "The 93.6% question of financial advisors", *Journal of Investing,* Spring, pp 16–20.

Part Two

Risk Management

8

Hedge Funds Returns, Higher Moments and Nonlinear Risk

Alain Coën, François-Éric Racicot; Raymond Théoret

University of Quebec, Outaouais; University of Quebec, Montreal

INTRODUCTION

Financial returns, and especially hedge funds returns, are contaminated by errors in variables. If neglected, this problem may completely invalidate the results obtained by estimating financial models, like the CAPM model or that of Fama and French (1992, 1993, 1997). Nevertheless, researchers seldom discard errors in variables in their empirical works, perhaps because the econometric methods related to the correction of the problem of errors in variables are not so advanced as other fields of financial econometrics. Some papers[1] have proposed correction techniques for errors in variables in a CAPM context but these studies are not numerous and much work must be done.

The methods of financial econometrics were traditionally well fitted to estimate financial models which, like the CAPM, postulate a linear relation between return and risk. But this kind of relation is valid only if risk is small or under very special conditions as in Gaussian returns or the quadratic utility function which is not realistic because it implies increasing absolute risk aversion. Prudence of an investor,[2] which is associated to the third derivative of the utility function, and fat tail risk, which is related to the fourth derivative of the utility function, introduce nonlinearities in the relation between return and risk. This chapter repositions the problem of correcting errors in variables in the context of a nonlinear relation between return and risk. Higher order moments and cumulants of returns become very important in this analysis of errors in variables in relation with nonlinear risk.

Following Campbell *et al* (1997), the errors in variables problem in asset pricing models can be addressed in two ways. One (Fama and MacBeth, 1973) is to minimise this problem by grouping stocks into portfolios. The second approach (Shanken, 1992) is to explicitly adjust the standard errors to correct for the biases introduced by the errors in variables. But there is a more recent approach adopted by Kandel and Stambaugh (1995) which uses GLS instead of least squares as an estimator. But, in this approach, the covariance matrix required to weight the observations must be estimated, which might be a problem.

Durbin (1954), Pal (1980) and more recently Racicot (1993) and Dagenais and Dagenais (1997)[3] have proposed an estimation method to correct errors in variables based on cumulants of the error terms of the equations of variables measured with errors. These cumulants serve as instruments to remove errors in variables. This chapter will use a variant of this method to correct the errors in variables problem which might plague the well-known augmented Fama and French model and which is based on higher moments.

As will be shown, the recourse to higher moments to eliminate errors in variables opens the doors to a synthesis between the modern asset pricing theory and the financial econometric treatment of the errors in variables. Surely, Durbin (1954), Pal (1980), Racicot (1993) and Dagenais and Dagenais (1997) did not aim to transpose their technique to asset pricing theory and risk measures. But it is well-admitted now that the first two moments of returns, ie, the mean and the variance, are largely insufficient to measure the risk of a portfolio. Ingersoll (1987), Huang and Litzenberger (1988) or Levy (1992) had mentioned that the paradigm of portfolio selection based on the first two moments of the returns distribution maximises the expected utility of an agent only in either of the two following situations: his utility function is quadratic or the returns distribution is normal. Of course, these two postulates are violated in the real world. Following this "constat", Samuelson (1970), Rubinstein (1973), Kraus and Litzenberger (1976), Friend and Westerfield (1980) and Sears and Wei (1985) have put the foundations of the approach based on higher moments to price financial instruments. These theoretical developments gave birth to the three-moment and the four-moment CAPM.[4]

The theoretical developments related to the use of higher moments as measures of financial risk are linked to other sections of risk theory, but there is yet to be a synthesis. The theory of stochastic dominance[5] has a long past. The increasing orders of stochastic dominance add higher moments of the returns distribution to judge whether a portfolio is superior to another in terms of stochastic dominance. This theory has given rise to new risk measures as the risk of shortfall, which is based on the probability, distribution of returns and transfers of probability mass between high and low wealth states. In the same order of ideas, Scott and Hovarth (1980) have alleged that the odd moments of the returns distribution, like a positive mean and a positive skewness, have positive marginal utility for an investor. The positive even moments, like variance and kurtosis, have for their sake negative marginal utility. These developments constitute the foundations of the modern theory of risk which is in construction.

The aim of this chapter is to test whether a new procedure of correction of errors in variables based on the iterated GMM can give a better explanation of returns in the context of the Fama and French model. Our contribution will be to use as instruments the higher moments of the predetermined regressors[6] in Fama and French's equation. These instruments will not only serve as technical tools but also as measures of risk, that will integrate our estimation method in the modern theory of risk analysis. As will be seen, our procedure is all the more relevant since the regressors (factors) of Fama and French's equation are long–short portfolios which are consequently close to those of hedge funds. Indeed, these portfolios which mimic some "market anomalies" are long in a category of returns (eg, returns of small firms) and short in the opposite category (eg, returns of big firms). Consequently, these portfolios behave like portfolios of options which incorporate many nonlinearities.

Moments higher than two are therefore required to take these nonlinearities into account. Taleb (1997) even suggests using moments of order higher than four to measure the risk of an option,[7] odd moments being measures of asymmetry and even moments being measures of convexity.[8] The empirical work will show that our choice of instruments is judicious. Really, the correlation of a regressor with moments higher than two is often much more important than the correlation with classical inferior moments.

This chapter is organised as follows. The methodology used to carry out empirical analysis is explained in the next section. First, the theoretical background of the problem caused by errors in variables and of the chosen instruments, which consist in higher moments of the regressors of the model of Fama and French, is discussed. Second, the method of estimation used to correct the problem of errors in variables in the model of Fama and French is presented. The third section describes the data series used in this study and reports the empirical results. A summary and concluding remarks are given in the final section.

METHODOLOGY

The biases caused by errors-in-variables

The errors in variables problem is well-known in the econometric literature but is often overlooked in finance. Assume[9] a one independent variable regression model where observed y and x are measured with errors. The true values of these variables are y^* and x^*. The relations between the observed variables and their true counterparts are:

$$y = y^* + u \tag{1}$$

$$x = x^* + v \tag{2}$$

where u and v are error vectors. These error vectors have zero means and their variances are: $E(uu') = \sigma_u^2 I$ and $E(vv') = \sigma_v^2 I$. The vectors u and v are assumed orthogonal.

The exact linear relationship between the two unobserved variables is:

$$y^* = x^* \beta \tag{3}$$

Because y^* and x^* are unobservable, we substitute Equations 1 and 2 in Equation 3:

$$y = x\beta + \varepsilon \tag{4}$$

where $\varepsilon = v - u\beta$. Consequently, by Equation 2, x is correlated with the error term ε, and this creates a bias. To compute it,

Equation 4 is resolved for $\hat{\beta}$, the estimated value of parameter β, by the method of least squares:

$$\hat{\beta} = (x'x)^{-1}x'y \tag{5}$$

Substituting Equation 4 in Equation 5, we obtain:

$$\hat{\beta} = \beta + (x'x)^{-1}x'e \tag{6}$$

Equation 6 shows that $\hat{\beta}$ is biased, and in large samples, it is not consistent:

$$p\lim \hat{\beta} = \beta\left[1 - \frac{\sigma_u^2}{\sigma_x^2}\right] \tag{7}$$

where $\sigma_x^2 = \sigma_{x^*}^2 + \sigma_u^2$. We can rewrite Expression 7 as:

$$p\lim \hat{\beta} = \beta(1-\lambda) \tag{8}$$

where $\lambda < 1$.

According to Equation 8, the problem of errors in variables tends to underestimate $\hat{\beta}$, the degree of underestimation being conditioned by λ. The more λ is near 1, the more the problem of errors in variables is serious. At the limit, λ is 1 and p lim β = 0. When only y is plagued with errors of measurement in Equation 1, there is no bias because x remains uncorrelated with the innovation of the equation. The problem appears when x is measured with error. That creates a correlation between x and the innovation term and therefore, a bias.

The theory about errors in variables suggests therefore some rules-of-thumb to detect them in a model. The first is that if a coefficient increases significantly in absolute value after correcting the least squares estimation for the problem of errors in variables, there is evidence of an error in the variable to which this coefficient is attached. The second rule-of-thumb is that if a coefficient changes sign significantly after correction, there is also presumption of errors in variables. These rules-of-thumb will be used in the empirical section of this chapter.

The usual method to cure a model of its errors in variables disease is to regress the erroneous variables on instruments and to replace the observed value of the variable by its estimated value. The classical instruments are exogenous variables or predetermined variables, ie, lagged values of exogenous or endogenous variables. But the choice of instrumental variables is a real one. These variables must have a good correlation with the erroneous variable but must be unrelated to the innovation of the estimated model. This problem is especially important in the context of the F&F model, where we must find instruments for differences of returns. Indeed, these returns are quite difficult to explain.

The choice of instrumental variables to estimate the augmented Fama and French (F&F) model

The augmented F&F (1992, 1993 and 1997) model is a purely empirical model which may be written as:

$$R_{pt} - R_{ft} = \alpha + \beta_1 (R_{mt} - R_{ft}) + \beta_2 SMB_t + \beta_3 HML_t + \beta_4 UMD_t + \varepsilon_t \quad \textbf{(9)}$$

with:

$R_{pt} - R_{ft}$: the excess return of a portfolio, R_{ft} being the risk-free return;

$R_{mt} - R_{ft}$: the market risk premium;

SMB: a portfolio which mimics the "small firm anomaly", which is long in the returns of selected small firms and short in the returns of selected big firms;

HML: a portfolio which mimics the "income stock anomaly", which is long in returns of stocks of selected firms having a high (book value/market value) ratio (income stocks) and short in selected stocks having a low (book value/market value) ratio (growth stocks);

UMD: a portfolio which mimics the "momentum anomaly", which is long in returns of selected stocks having a persistent upper trend and short in stocks having a persistent downwards trend.

To explain the return of a stock or of a portfolio of stocks, the F&F model adds to the sole factor retained by the CAPM, the market risk premium, three other factors which are supposed to represent market anomalies: the small firm anomaly, the book value to market value anomaly and the momentum anomaly.[10]

We postulate that the three mimicking portfolios *SMB*, *HML* and *UMD* are measured with errors. They are thus correlated with the innovation term in Equation 9 and the estimators of the parameters of this equation obtained by ordinary least squares (OLS) are consequently biased and not consistent. To purge these coefficients from these biases, we must regress in a first pass the independent variables on instrumental variables. The estimated method used in this chapter will be explained below. The problem lays in the choice of these instruments.

As we said before, it is difficult to find valuable instruments for the excess returns of the mimicking portfolios. Being long in some stocks and short in others, their cash flows are similar to those of hedge funds. Higher moments of returns, like asymmetry and kurtosis, might have a great influence on these returns. This suggests the use of higher moments of the variables on the RHS of Equation 9 as instrumental variables. An econometric theory is in construction on this subject. Following Durbin (1954) and Pal (1980), Dagenais and Dagenais (1997) showed that higher moments[11] of independent variables of a regression might be valid instruments to remove errors-in-variables. But instead of defining higher moments as in these papers, we will adopt a method more akin to asset pricing theory which defines higher moments of returns by powers of these returns.

The method of asset pricing based on higher moments is not new. Rubinstein (1973) and Kraus and Litzenberger (1976) put the foundations of the three-moment and four-moment CAPM. The three-moment CAPM integrated asymmetry of returns in the analysis while the four-moment CAPM added kurtosis.

Some authors, like Kraus and Litzenberger (1976), use a general utility function to derive the moment-CAPM. Others use a Taylor expansion of the utility function which, following Samuelson (1970) and Rubinstein (1973), express utility in terms of the higher moments of returns.

Let us assume that the expected utility of wealth, $E[U(W)]$, is a function of the n first moments of the distribution of wealth:

$$E[U(W)] = \varphi[\bar{W}, \sigma_W, skew_W, kur_W, \ldots, sm_{nW}] \qquad \textbf{(10)}$$

with $\bar{W}$ the expected value of wealth; σ_w, the volatility of wealth; $skew_W$, its skewness; kur_W, its kurtosis and sm_{nW}, the nth moment of the distribution of wealth. Moments of order 5 and more are incorporated because we know that they might be important to explain the returns of long-short portfolios like mimicking portfolios which are the foundation of the F&F model.

The expected utility of end-of-period wealth is maximised over the one period horizon subject to the constraint of initial wealth, which is:

$$a_0 + \sum_{i=1}^{n} a_i = w_0 \tag{11}$$

According to Equation 11, the initial wealth w_0 is allocated between the risk-free asset a_0 and n other risky assets designated by a_i. To maximise the utility of end-of-period wealth subject to equation 11, the usual Lagrangian is formed:

$$L = E[U(W)] - \phi\left(a_0 - \sum_{i=1}^{n} a_i - w_0\right) \tag{12}$$

Taking the first-order conditions for a maximum, we have:

$$\frac{\partial L}{\partial a_0} = \varphi_{\bar{W}} \times \frac{\partial \bar{W}}{\partial a_0} - \lambda = 0 \tag{13}$$

$$\frac{\partial L}{\partial a_{i,i\neq 0}} = \varphi_{\bar{W}} \times \frac{\partial E(w)}{\partial a_i} + \varphi_{\sigma_W} \times \frac{\partial \sigma_W}{\partial a_i} + \varphi_{skew_W} \times \frac{\partial skew_W}{\partial a_i} + \varphi_{kur_W} \times \frac{\partial kur_W}{\partial a_i} + \cdots + \varphi_{sm_{nW}} \frac{\partial sm_{nW}}{\partial a_n} - \lambda = 0 \tag{14}$$

with

$$\varphi_x = \frac{\partial E[U(X)]}{\partial x}$$

End-of-period expected wealth is equal to:

$$\bar{W} = (1 + R_0)a_0 + \sum_{i=1}^{n} [(1 + E(R_i))a_i] \tag{15}$$

We thus have:

$$\frac{\partial \bar{W}}{\partial a_0} = 1 + R_0 \tag{16}$$

$$\frac{\partial \bar{W}}{\partial a_i} = 1 + E(R_i) \tag{17}$$

We can therefore express the moments of wealth in terms of the moments of returns of the portfolio as:

$$\sigma_W = \sum_i a_i \beta_{ip} \sigma_p \tag{18}$$

$$skew_W = \sum_i a_i \gamma_{ip} skew_p \tag{19}$$

$$kur_W = \sum_i a_i \theta_{ip} kur_p \tag{20}$$

$$sm_{nW} = \sum_i a_i \omega_{ip} sm_{np} \tag{21}$$

with $\sigma_p = \sqrt{E(R_p - \bar{R}_p)^2}$, the volatility of the return of the risk assets;

$$\beta_{ip} = \frac{E[(R_i - \bar{R}_i)(R_p - \bar{R}_p)]}{\sigma_p^2}$$

the beta of risk asset i with the investor's portfolio of risk assets:

$$skew_p = \sqrt[3]{E[(R_P - \bar{R}_p)^3]}$$

the asymmetry of the return of the portfolio and

$$\gamma_{ip} = \frac{E[(R_i - \bar{R}_i)(R_p - \bar{R}_p)^2]}{sk_p^3}$$

the gamma of risk asset i with the investor's portfolio of risk assets. It is easy to generate all the other variables by following this design.

Equating Equations 13 and 14 to delete ϕ and taking into account Equations 18 to 21, we arrive at an expression for $E(R_i)$ in terms of the moments of the distribution of the return of an investor's portfolio:

$$E(R_i) - R_0 = -\left(\frac{\varphi_{\sigma_W}}{\varphi_{\bar{W}}}\right)\beta_{ip}\sigma_p - \left(\frac{\varphi_{skew_W}}{\varphi_{\bar{W}}}\right)\gamma_{ip}skew_p - \left(\frac{\varphi_{kur_W}}{\varphi_{\bar{W}}}\right)\theta_{ip}kur_p$$
$$- \cdots - \left(\frac{\varphi_{sm_{nW}}}{\varphi_{\bar{W}}}\right)\omega_{ip}sm_{np} \qquad \textbf{(22)}$$

with $\varphi_{moment}/\varphi_{\bar{W}}$ being an investor's marginal rate of substitution between expected wealth and a specific moment. According to Scott and Hovarth (1980), these marginal rates of substitution are positive for odd moments, like mean and positive asymmetry, and negative for even moments, like variance and kurtosis. From Equation 22, odd moments have, *ceteris paribus*, a negative impact on expected return from the point of view of investors. Even moments have a positive impact because they represent risk.

Moving from Equation 22 to the condition of market equilibrium for $E(R_i)$ requires making, according to Kraus and Litzenberger (1976), the strong assumption of homogeneous expectations for investors. Following this assumption, Equation 22 becomes, assuming that p is the market portfolio:

$$E(R_i) - R_0 = \left[\frac{d\bar{W}}{d\sigma_W}\right]\sigma_m\beta_{im} + \left[\frac{d\bar{W}}{dskew_W}\right]skew_m\gamma_{im}$$
$$+ \left[\frac{d\bar{W}}{dkur_w}\right]kur_m\theta_{im} + \cdots + \left[\frac{d\bar{W}}{dsm_{nW}}\right]sm_{nm}\omega_{in} \qquad \textbf{(23)}$$

The terms in brackets in Expression 23 are the slopes of the efficient frontiers whose arguments are expected wealth and the respective moment. Finally, the n-moment CAPM is obtained:

$$E(R_i) - R_f = \psi_1\beta_{im} + \psi_2\gamma_{im} + \psi_3\theta_{im} + \cdots + \psi_n sm_{nm} \qquad \textbf{(24)}$$

We might use directly Expression (24) to define the instruments for removing errors-in-variables by the methods of higher moments in the F&F model. Suppose we want to correct the mimicking portfolio *SMB* for errors-in-variables. In the first pass of the regressions, this variable would be regressed on the co-moments of the lagged excess return of the market portfolio. The variable *SMB* corrected for errors-in-variables would be:

$$\hat{SMB}_t = \kappa_0 + \kappa_1 \beta_{im,t-1} + \kappa_2 \gamma_{im,t-1} + \kappa_3 \theta_{im,t-1} + \cdots + \kappa_n sm_{nm,t-1} \quad \mathbf{(25)}$$

In fact, the co-moments of the mimicking portfolios would also have to be introduced. This approach would be laborious and would require computing rolling windows of co-moments.[12] But there is a procedure for simplifying Equation 25. Kraus and Lintzenberger (1976)[13] have shown that a three-moment CAPM is consistent with the following quadratic form:

$$R_i - R_0 = \alpha_0 + \alpha_1 (R_m - R_0) + \alpha_2 (R_m - R_0)^2 \quad \mathbf{(26)}$$

and consequently a n-moment CAPM can be written as:

$$\begin{aligned} R_i - R_0 = {} & \alpha_0 + \alpha_1 (R_m - R_0) + \alpha_2 (R_m - R_0)^2 \\ & + \alpha_3 (R_m - R_0)^3 + \cdots + \alpha_{n-1} (R_m - R_0)^{n-1} \end{aligned} \quad \mathbf{(27)}$$

A test on α_2 is a test on skewness preferences in asset pricing and a test on α_3, a test on kurtosis preferences, and so on. The higher moments are consequently powers of returns in this approach. We therefore use a financial theory, the *n*-moment CAPM, to give an object to the method of Dagenais and Dagenais (1997) for correcting errors-in-variables. Let us return to the variable *SMB*, which we want to correct for the problem of errors-in-variables. In the first pass of the regression, this variable will be regressed on:

$$\hat{SMB}_t = f(F_{it-1}, F_{it-1}^2, F_{it-1}^3, \ldots, F_{it-1}^5, \ldots) \quad \mathbf{(28)}$$

where F_i are the variables in the RHS of Fama and French's equation (Equation 9) including *SMB*. They stand for the higher moments of these variables. F_{it-1}^2 stands for the skewness of factor F_i; F_{it-1}^3, for its kurtosis, and so on.

The variables appearing on the RHS of Equation 28 will serve as instrumental variables in an iterated GMM procedure to estimate the F&F model, as explained in the next section. The moments conditions of the GMM estimator will preserve orthogonality between the regressors of the F&F equation and the innovation of this equation.

The iterated GMM procedure

We want to estimate the F&F model, that is:

$$R_{pt} - R_{ft} = \alpha + \beta_1(R_{mt} - R_{ft}) + \beta_2 SMB_t + \beta_3 HML_t + \beta_4 UMD_t + \varepsilon_t \quad \textbf{(29)}$$

by the method of iterated GMM. The benchmark is the OLS procedure because it is the usual method to estimate this model.

The instruments used in this regression are given by Equation 28. These are the first lagged value of each regressor in Equation 29 which are expressed up to the fifth power. These variables represent the higher moments of the factors of risk in the equation of F&F. We call them: "risk instruments". These instruments are consequently $(R_{mt-1}-R_{ft-1})$, $(R_{mt-1}-R_{ft-1})^2$, …, $(R_{mt-1}-R_{ft-1})^5$; (SMB_{t-1}), $(SMB_{t-1})^2$, …, $(SMB_{t-1})^5$; (HML_{t-1}), $(HML_{t-1})^2$, …, $(HML_{t-1})^5$; (UMD_{t-1}), $(UMD_{t-1})^2$, …, $UMD_{t-1})^5$. To these instrumental variables, we add other macroeconomic and financial variables to explain returns. These variables will be specified in the next section.

A moment condition is defined for each of these instrumental variables. These moments conditions specify that each instrumental variable must be orthogonal to the innovation term in Equation 29. Let $\boldsymbol{Z}$ be the matrix of instrumental variables. The orthogonality condition is:

$$E(Z'\varepsilon) = 0 \quad \textbf{(30)}$$

with $\varepsilon = h(Y, X, \theta)$ θ being the vector of parameters to estimate.

These moments conditions are approximated by their empirical counterpart, the sample moments, that is:

$$\frac{1}{N}\sum_{i=1}^{N} Z_i\varepsilon_i = G(Y, X, Z; \theta) \quad \textbf{(31)}$$

To estimate the vector of parameters, we must weight the moments by a matrix, which will be defined later. By finding the vector θ which minimizes the following function:

$$\arg\min_{\theta} G'(Y, X, Z; \theta)\ A\ G(Y, X, Z; \theta) \quad \textbf{(32)}$$

we obtain the GMM estimator $\hat{\theta}$ of the vector of parameters θ. In this equation, $\boldsymbol{A}$ is the weighting matrix.

According to the GMM method, $\boldsymbol{A}$ is the inverse of the covariance matrix of the sample moments. This is equivalent to put less weight on the moments conditions that are more imprecise. That seems quite reasonable. This matrix $\boldsymbol{A}$ weights the higher moments of the regressors appearing in Equation 29. Instead of computing the higher moments in conformity with the method of Dagenais and Dagenais (1997), we let the matrix $\boldsymbol{A}$ weighting optimally these higher moments. That is an advantage of the iterated GMM method which computes the optimal covariance matrix between the moments, the higher moments of the regressors in our case.

There are *"grosso modo"* two methods to compute the weighting matrix $\boldsymbol{A}$. Let: $\hat{A} = \hat{\Phi}^{-1}$, where $\hat{\Phi}$ is the estimated covariance matrix of the moments conditions. This computed matrix might be the White matrix or the HAC[14] matrix. The White matrix is the following:

$$\hat{\Phi}_{White} = \hat{\Gamma}_0 = \frac{1}{T-k}\sum_{t=1}^{T} G_t' G_t \tag{33}$$

where T is the number of observations and k, the number of regressors. $\boldsymbol{G}$ is defined by Equation 31. As we can see, the White matrix is not iterated.

This chapter uses the HAC matrix to compute the matrix of weights, which is more flexible than the White matrix. The following iteration algorithm computes the optimal covariance matrix of the moments:

$$\hat{\Phi}_{HAC} = \hat{\Gamma}_0 + \left[\sum_{j=1}^{T-1} \kappa(j,q)(\hat{\Gamma}_j + \hat{\Gamma}_j')\right] \tag{34}$$

where κ is the kernel and q, the bandwidth. The White matrix is the seed value of this algorithm.

The kernel weights the covariance so that $\hat{\Phi}$ is positive semi-definite. EViews provides two choices for the kernel: the Bartlett and the quadratic spectral. The latter is used in our estimations because, contrary to the Bartlett kernel, it is smooth and not truncated. It is equal to:

$$\kappa(j,q)=\frac{25}{12(\pi x)^2}\left[\frac{\sin\left(\frac{6\pi x}{5}\right)}{\frac{6\pi x}{5}}-\cos\left(\frac{6\pi x}{5}\right)\right] \quad (35)$$

where $x = j/q$.

Without entering into details, let us say that there are two methods to compute the bandwidth in EViews: the Andrews method and the Variable-Newey-West method. For our estimations, we chose the Andrews method to compute the bandwidth q in Equation 35 because it seems to converge more quickly towards the solution. This method assumes that the sample moments follow an autoregressive process of order 1 (AR(1)).[15]

EMPIRICAL RESULTS AND ANALYSIS

The sample of hedge funds returns comprises the monthly returns of 20 Greenwich-Van US American hedge funds indexes classified by categories or groups of categories. Appendix 1 gives the enumeration of these funds with their chosen symbol. The observation period begins in January 1995 and ends in November 2005, for a total of 131 observations. The risk factors which appear in the Fama and French equation – that is the market premium and the three mimicking portfolios: *SMB*, *HML* and *UMD* – are for their part drawn from French's website.[16]

We can get a first glance at the sample of hedge funds by looking at Table 1, which gives the descriptive statistics of the average fund. At 8.4%, the mean annualized return of this sample is quite high and its standard deviation is relatively moderate. But it is well-known that standard deviation is an acceptable measure of risk only if risk is small or under very special conditions. Otherwise, we must consider the higher moments of the distributions of excess returns. The skewness of the mean fund is not very different from zero but the mean level of kurtosis, at 6.5, is quite high, the level of kurtosis associated with a normal distribution being 3. Obviously, a large number of equity oriented hedge funds strategies exhibit payoffs which resemble those of a short position in a put option on the market index,[17]

Table 1 Descriptive statistics of the sample of 20 hedge funds returns

	Average	Std. dev.
Mean yield	0.007	0.003
Median yield	0.008	0.004
Maximum yield	0.118	0.060
Minimum yield	−0.088	0.049
Skewness	0.272	0.819
Kurtosis	6.532	2.640
Jarque-Bera	160.20	582.35
Probability	0.07	0.30
Number of funds with kurtosis>3	19	
Number of funds with non-gaussian yields	17	

*: the statistics are averages over the 20 funds.
The standard deviation is computed over the 20 funds.

and therefore bears significant left-tail risk, risk that is ignored by the commonly used mean-variance framework. That means that rare events are more frequent than in a normal distribution and non-linearities of payoffs are very present. Incidentally, there are 19 funds over 20 which have a level of kurtosis exceeding 3 and 17 which have non-Gaussian returns according to the Jarque–Bera test.

We assume that the factors appearing on the RHS of Equation 29 contain errors in variables. Consequently, we search instruments for the four regressors of Equation 29: the market risk premium and the three other risk factors: *SMB*, *HML* and *UMD*. In the methodological section, we justify the recourse to the higher moments of the predetermined variables of these factors. Let us validate these instruments.

Table 2 gives the correlations of the F&F factors with themselves and their chosen instruments from January 1995 to November 2005. Besides the instruments discussed before, we add other macroeconomic variables: the monthly and annual American inflation rate, *IPC_MENS* and *IPC_ANN*, and the monthly and annual growth rate of the American industrial production, *PROD_MENS* and *PROD_ANN*.

According to Table 2, the F&F factors are more or less correlated with classic instruments like the first lag of the factor or with the macroeconomic variables. On the side of the macroeconomic variables, we observe that their correlation with the risk factors located

Table 2 Correlation between the four factors and their instruments

	RM_RF	HML	UMD	SMB
RM_RF	1.00			
HML	−0.29	1.00		
UMD	−0.22	−0.62	1.00	
SMB	0.22	−0.38	0.04	1.00
RM_RF(−1)	0.03	0.15	−0.11	0.19
$RM\_RF(-1)^2$	0.09	−0.03	−0.06	0.08
$RM\_RF(-1)^3$	−0.07	0.10	−0.02	0.10
$RM\_RF(-1)^4$	0.11	−0.05	−0.04	0.02
$RM\_RF(-1)^5$	−0.10	0.08	0.01	0.04
HML(−1)	−0.15	0.11	0.01	0.06
$HML(-1)^2$	−0.05	0.17	−0.01	−0.23
$HML(-1)^3$	−0.14	−0.06	0.09	0.17
$HML(-1)^4$	0.01	0.19	−0.10	−0.28
$HML(-1)^5$	−0.12	−0.11	0.11	0.24
UMD(−1)	0.03	−0.07	−0.07	−0.15
$UMD(-1)^2$	−0.18	0.17	0.07	−0.08
$UMD(-1)^3$	0.19	−0.01	−0.22	−0.06
$UMD(-1)^4$	−0.20	0.16	0.16	−0.12
$UMD(-1)^5$	0.21	−0.05	−0.22	−0.01
SMB(−1)	0.07	−0.05	0.12	−0.02
$SMB(-1)^2$	0.00	0.20	−0.10	−0.18
$SMB(-1)^3$	0.12	0.03	0.01	−0.17
$SMB(-1)^4$	0.04	0.24	−0.15	−0.29
$SMB(-1)^5$	0.13	0.06	−0.06	−0.22
IPC_ANN	−0.03	0.09	−0.03	0.00
IPC_MENS	−0.11	−0.01	0.05	−0.06
PROD_ANN	0.11	−0.11	0.04	−0.24
PROD_MENS	−0.03	−0.07	0.01	−0.06

at the head of the columns is quite low. Only the annual growth of the industrial production has a moderate correlation with three of these factors.[18]

On the side of the risk factors of Equation 29, we noticed before that there are many nonlinearities in these mimicking portfolios, which are similar to portfolios of hedge funds. We also noticed before that these nonlinearities might be captured by the higher moments of these factors. Corroborating this assumption, we observe in Table 2 that the risk factors are generally more correlated or cross-correlated with the higher moments of the first lag of a risk factor than to the first lag itself. For example, the market risk premium is more related to the higher moments of *UMD*(−1) than to *UMD*(−1) itself. Indeed, the correlation between *RM_RF* and *UMD*(−1) is quite low: 0.03, but it is equal to 0.21 for $UMD(-1)^5$, that is the higher moment of $UMD(-1)$ of order 5. The same is true for the factor SMB and the higher moments of $SMB(-1)$. Consequently, higher moments of lagged variables may constitute quite good instruments.

We used six instrumental variables methods to correct the errors in variables problem that may contaminate the factors. These six instrumental variables (IV) methods are: (a) standard two-stage least squares (TSLS) with instruments including macro-variables and simple predetermined (lagged) values of the regressors; (b) higher moments with two-stage least squares adding to the instruments of standard TSLS the higher moments of the first lag of the regressors up to the fifth order (power). We also added as instrument the first lag (and its powers) of the general return index of the hedge funds of the sample; (c) non-iterated standard GMM including the same instruments as standard TSLS; (d) iterated standard GMM; (e) non-iterated higher moments GMM including the same instruments as the higher moments TSLS; (f) iterated higher moments GMM. For these regressions, the OLS method is the benchmark, for which the estimated coefficients are biased because of the presence of errors-in-variables. The other methods are techniques for correcting the errors in variables biases. The preceding section stated the criteria to detect an errors in variables problem. Let us put these criteria into action.

Before discussing the results, it must be noticed that the instrumental methods have a lower adjusted R^2 than the OLS method, and that is normal. But it will be a source of concern if the adjusted R^2 decreases greatly after correcting for the errors in variables problem. After all, the estimated factors are used instead of the observed ones to remove the errors-in-variables problem. Inappropriate instruments might result in low R^2, but this is not the case. The adjusted R^2 of the estimations by our preferred method is to correct the errors in variables problem, which, as will be seen, is the iterated higher moments GMM, which are generally quite comparable with those of the OLS method. That is reassuring.

Tables 3 and 4 give a first grasp of the estimations. These tables contain the total count of significant coefficients for $\alpha = 5\%$ and the mean level of the t statistics computed over the 20 funds for each estimation method. The IV methods, other than the two iterated GMM, appear not to be performing for correcting the errors

Table 3 Count of significant coefficients for the constant and the four factors in each of the estimations methods*

	Constant	RM-RF	SMB	UMD	HML	Line total
OLS (benchmark)	14	18	17	10	3	62
Standard TSLS	8	14	9	5	4	40
Higher moments TSLS	14	14	16	5	2	51
Non iterated standard GMM	7	16	10	6	4	43
Iterated standard GMM	7	16	14	7	4	48
Non iterated higher moments GMM	15	19	17	18	14	83
Iterated higher moments GMM	17	19	18	19	10	83

*For a variable, the table gives the number of significant coefficients for $\alpha = 5\%$.
There are 20 yield indexes of hedge funds in the sample. The estimation is from January 1995 to November 2005.
GMM: generalized method of moments; OLS: ordinary least squares; TSLS: two-stage least squares.

Table 4 Average level of the *t* statistics for the constant and the four factors in each of the estimation methods*

	Constant	RM-RF	SMB	UMD	HML	Line average
OLS (benchmark)	3.23	9.12	6.03	2.31	1.81	4.50
Standard TSLS	1.90	3.57	1.65	1.28	1.25	1.93
Higher moments TSLS	2.70	4.84	3.58	1.48	1.14	2.75
Non iterated standard GMM	1.83	3.98	1.96	1.45	1.27	2.10
Iterated standard GMM	1.77	4.20	2.57	1.74	1.48	2.35
Non iterated higher moments GMM	5.69	8.50	7.69	5.11	3.91	6.18
Iterated higher moments GMM	11.20	14.21	10.94	7.80	4.91	9.81

*The average is computed for a sample of 20 hedge funds indexes.

in variables problem in the model of F&F, except perhaps the higher moments two-stage least squares. This last method has a total count of 51 significant coefficients, which is lower than the 62 obtained by the OLS method. The mean level of the *t* statistics obtained by this method (2.75) is much lower than the corresponding statistics of the OLS method (4.50). The results of the non-iterated standard GMM are quite disappointing, a method being often used in the past to correct for the errors-in-variables problem.

Table 5 Mean level of the estimated coefficients for the constant and the four factors in each of the estimation methods

	Constant	RM-RF	SMB	UMD	HML
OLS (benchmark)	0.004	0.254	0.196	0.047	0.069
Standard TSLS	0.004	0.249	0.170	0.078	0.038
Higher moments TSLS	0.005	0.228	0.198	0.058	0.001

One notices that, in general, the IV methods other than the higher moments GMM, iterated or not, do not perform well to remove errors in variables from the OLS regression. They often make the two factors *SMB* and *UMD* insignificant which are nevertheless often significant in the OLS regression. The variable *HML* constitutes an exception, being generally more significant in the IV methods, But, as will be seen, this variable makes problems and consequently, it seems to suffer from a high errors in variables disease.

This is not the case with the higher moments GMM, iterated or not. As we can see in Tables 3 and 4, the regressors are more significant in these methods than in the OLS one. There is a total of 83 significant coefficients in each of the two higher moments GMM estimations and 62 in the OLS one. The level of the t statistics averaged over the 20 funds is 9.81 for the iterated higher moments GMM and 6.18 for the non-iterated one, which is much higher than the corresponding statistics for the OLS method, that is, 4.50. On this ground, the iterated higher moments GMM looks preferable to its non-iterated version.

Table 5 gives the mean levels of the estimated coefficients averaged over the 20 funds for each estimation method. We conclude that the iterated higher moments GMM method generally makes the coefficients of *SMB* and *UMD* more important and more significant when expressed in absolute terms than in the OLS run. The OLS regressions then tend to underestimate the relative importance of these factors whatever the fund, which is one criterion to identify the presence of errors in variables. Consequently, there seems to be not negligible errors in variables in these two factors and the iterated higher moments GMM method seems to do a good job in removing these errors.

Other criteria were stated to identify the presence of errors in variables in the preceding section. It was said that when the sign of a variable changes significantly, when we move from the OLS regression to an IV method, there will be a presumption of errors in variables. As may be observed in Table 5, the mean level of the estimated coefficient of *HML* is equal to 0.069 in the OLS regression and −0.006 in the iterated higher moments GMM regression. Correcting for the problem of errors in variables changes the sign of *HML* and makes it more significant. According to one of the criteria, there is therefore evidence of an important error in variables problem on the side of the variable *HML*.

The iterated higher moments GMM method gives less weight to the market premium than the OLS. For hedge funds, the traditional beta is generally quite low. For our sample, its mean level is 0.25 for the OLS regression and 0.21 for the iterated higher moments GMM. The mimicking portfolio represented by *SMB* is, among the two others, the portfolio that has the most important estimated sensitivity coefficient. At 0.208, this sensitivity coefficient is very close to the mean level of beta, which is 0.212.

Because the F&F model is a purely empirical one, there is no theory on the signs of the four factors of this model, except perhaps for the market index whose coefficient is generally positive according to the CAPM. But if we consider the three mimicking portfolios *SMB*, *HML* and *UMD* as factors of risk, it is reasonable to expect a positive sign for the estimated coefficients of these factors. A fund can short a factor of risk, as it might short the market index. A hedge fund which makes short selling will have a negative beta. Another which short sells the mimicking portfolio *SMB*, say, will have a negative coefficient for this factor. But this behaviour seems to be the exception rather than the rule. Risk factors in returns equations might generally be preceded by positive signs.

Table 6 gives information on this subject for the sample. For the iterated higher moments GMM method and over the 20 funds, 17 have a positive constant (alpha); 16 have a positive coefficient for the variable *UMD* and 18 have a positive sign for the variable *SMB*. That comforts us in our expectations of considering the mimicking portfolios as risk factors. The proportion of positive constants for the factor *HML*, at 60%, is lower but, as we said, this factor is plagued by an important errors-in-variables problem.

Let us examine another financial consequence of the presence of errors in variables in the F&F model. The constant of this model is

Table 6 Count of positive signs for the constant and the four factors for each of the estimation methods

	Constant	RM-RF	SMB	UMD	HML
OLS (benchmark)	19	19	19	17	17
Standard TSLS	18	17	19	17	13
Higher moments TSLS	20	18	18	17	14
Non-iterated standard GMM	19	17	18	15	15
Iterated standard GMM	16	17	19	17	16
Non-iterated higher moments GMM	15	19	14	18	17
Iterated higher moments GMM	17	17	18	16	12

generally designated by alpha in asset pricing models. We know that alpha is very important in stock picking strategies. Stocks with significant positive alphas must be bought and stock with negative alphas must be shorted. We can see in the preceding tables that the alphas obtained by the iterated higher moments GMM method remained generally positive in regard of the OLS method, becoming even more significant. This result is quite encouraging because it suggests that the estimation of alpha is robust to the problem of errors-in-variables. It also indicates that the hedge funds analysed here have exceptional positive returns over the period of study after taking account of risk.

This chapter introduced nonlinearities in the F&F model by considering as instruments the higher moments of the predetermined variables of this model. The objective was to discard the errors in variables problem. There are other ways to introduce nonlinearities in the F&F model. In the following paragraphs, two of these methods are briefly considered: (a) introducing higher moments directly in Fama and French's model, as many authors do; (b) making variables the coefficients of regression.

To illustrate the first method, let us consider the market timers hedge funds group of our sample. Market timing is usually introduced in the market model by squaring the risk premium. In the context of the F&F model, we may also consider the square of the variable of momentum, that is *UMD*. The OLS estimation of the F&F model with these two added variables gives the result appearing in Table 7.

The variable measuring market timing, that is (*RM_RF^2*), has a positive significant coefficient, which indicates successful market

Table 7 Estimation of the F&F model for the group of market timers with squared variables

Dependent Variable: USMT_RF
Method: Least squares
Date: 02/21/06 Time: 14:08
Sample (adjusted): 13 143
Included observations: 131 after adjustments

Variable	Coefficient	Std. error	*t*-Statistic	Prob.
C	−0.002170	0.002055	−1.056131	0.2930
RM_RF	0.387028	0.042950	9.011071	0.0000
HML	−0.187976	0.057098	−3.292138	0.0013
UMD	0.058470	0.042831	1.365132	0.1747
SMB	0.065525	0.048546	1.349751	0.1796
RM_RF^2	2.349037	0.521227	4.506744	0.0000
UMD^2	0.468703	0.225355	2.079845	0.0396
R-squared	0.654369	Mean dependent var	0.007156	
Adjusted R-squared	0.637645	S.D. dependent var	0.027989	
S.E. of regression	0.016848	Akaike info criterion	−5.277196	
Sum squared resid	0.035199	Schwarz criterion	−5.123560	
Log likelihood	352.6563	*F*-statistic	39.12737	
Durbin-Watson stat	2.108243	Prob(*F*-statistic)	0.00000	

Source: EViews, version 5.1

timing by these hedge funds. The variable *UMD* squared is also significant while its level is not. This model is very superior to the simple market model, as evidenced by Table 8.

This procedure to introduce nonlinearities in the F&F model does not solve the problem of errors in variables. An avenue of research would be to combine the iterated higher moments GMM with a regression similar to that of Table 7.

The coefficients in the F&F model are fixed. This is a source of rigidity because we know that the sensitivity of the returns of hedge funds to risk factors is variable. To illustrate this point, let us consider the group of short sellers of the sample. These funds have a negative beta which varies with the trend of the market. To test for the variability of beta, the Kalman filter can be used. Omitting the *UMD* factor, the observation equation would be:

$$usshs\_rf_t = \beta_0 + \beta_1(t)(RM\_RF)_t + \beta_2 HML_t + \beta_3 SMB_t + \varepsilon_t \quad \textbf{(36)}$$

Table 8 Simple market model for the market timers

Dependent variable: USMT_RF
Method: Least squares
Date: 02/21/06 Time: 14:10
Sample (adjusted): 13 143
Included observations: 131 after adjustments

Variable	Coefficient	Std. error	*t*-statistic	Prob.
C	0.004356	0.001917	2.273009	0.0247
RM_RF	0.395265	0.042157	9.376123	0.0000
R-squared	0.405288	Mean dependent var	0.007156	
Adjusted *R*-squared	0.400678	S.D. dependent var	0.027989	
S.E. of regression	0.021668	Akaike info criterion	−4.810826	
Sum squared resid	0.060565	Schwarz criterion	−4.766930	
Log likelihood	317.1091	*F*-statistic	87.91168	
Durbin-Watson stat	1.908643	Prob(*F*-statistic)	0.000000	

Source: EViews, version 5.1

with *usshs_rf*, the excess return of short sellers and *RM_RF*, the market risk premium. The state equation is a simple autoregression of the risk premium beta:

$$\beta_1(t) = \beta_1(t-1) + \xi_t \tag{37}$$

In Figure 1, we can follow the evolution of the beta of short sellers estimated by the Kalman filter in regard to the market trend. As we notice, the beta of the short sellers remains negative over the observation period but it is highly variable. It follows the market trend with a lag. As the market deteriorates, the beta increases in absolute value. It decreases in absolute value when the market strengthens. This is a typical behaviour for the beta of a short seller.

Therefore, another improvement to the previous regressions would be to introduce variable coefficients in the process of correcting the errors in variables problem.

SUMMARY AND CONCLUSIONS

The higher moments iterated GMM method seems to be performing quite well in removing errors in variables which may plague the

Figure 1 The variability of the beta of short sellers vs market trend

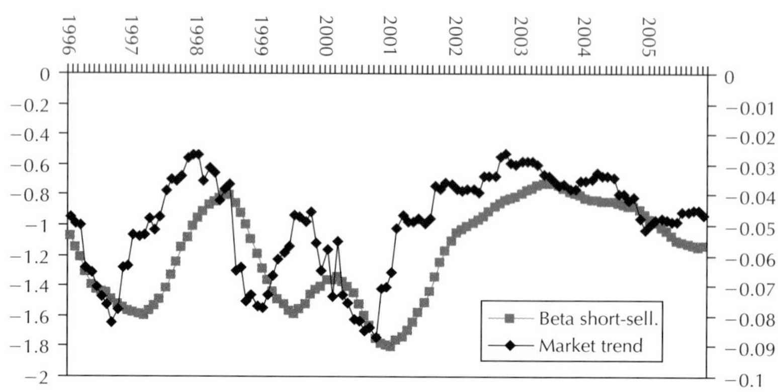

estimation of the F&F model. In general, we notice that the OLS method, viewed as a benchmark, tends to underestimate, in absolute value, the global influence of the three factors: *SMB*, *HML* and *UMD*, which is in accord with the econometric theory of errors in variables. The variable *HML* seems to be particularly contaminated by the disease of errors in variables, having a very different impact before and after correction of the problem of errors in variables. Changes of signs are frequent. Therefore, accounting data, which serve to compute *HML*, seem to lack precision. Obviously, the errors of variable syndrome is not an artefact. The estimated alphas, which are related to stock picking activities, are also generally more important and more significant after correcting for errors in variables.

This study has precisely used higher moments of the distribution of the returns of the mimicking portfolios as instruments to purge the F&F model from its errors in variables. That these instruments are highly related to the risk factors is perfectly normal because the returns of the mimicking portfolios incorporate many nonlinearities. These nonlinearities cannot be captured by a classical CAPM or APT model which postulates a linear relation between the returns to be explained and their risk factors. The Fama and French model is also linear. But the risk factors *SMB*, *HML* and *UMD* take care of the presence of nonlinearities. The good relation between these factors and the chosen instruments in this article, which are the higher moments of those variables, tends to demonstrate these points.

There are by now many articles which put in question the F&F model.[19] This chapter is instead an argument in favour of the model. The three factors of the F&F model have their place in the explanation of risk, because they package the many nonlinearities that are present in the distribution of returns. They are not market anomalies as they were considered in the past. They are instead the "reservoirs" of moments and co-moments risks.

The study also sheds light on the idiosyncratic behaviour of hedge funds. The beta of hedge funds is not generally high, not exceeding 0.25. The short sellers are an exception on this front, having a mean beta of −1. For hedge funds, the three factors: *SMB*, *HML* and *UMD* are really factors of risk, their signs being mostly significantly positive in the regressions between the funds returns and those factors. Nevertheless, the impact of *HML* on hedge funds returns remains problematic, this factor being corrupted by a severe errors-in-variables disease. The incidence of the mimicking portfolio *UMD* is mostly positive but its impact is low. After the market risk premium, it is the factor *SMB* which exerts the most prominent positive impact on the returns of hedge funds. This factor allows one to identify rich and cheap securities, which is one of the most important dimensions of the hedge funds industry.

One avenue of future research will be to use cumulants[20] instead of higher moments to define the instruments. In finance, we generally use moments to quantify risks but cumulants are quite promising on this matter. In his studies, Dagenais used cumulants and not higher moments. Another avenue is to introduce these cumulants directly in the F&F equation instead of treating them as instruments. The future seems quite promising for risk analysis.

APPENDIX 1
List of funds of the study

- ❑ *USEMN*: Equity market neutral
- ❑ *USED*: Event driven
- ❑ *USDS*: Distressed securities
- ❑ *USSS*: Special situations
- ❑ *USMMNA*: Market neutral arbitrage

- *USSHS*: Short selling index
- *USVA*: Value index
- *USF*: Futures index
- *USMACRO*: Macro
- *USMT*: Market timing
- *USDTG*: Directional trading group
- *USMNG*: Market neutral group
- *USLSG*: Long short group
- *USAG*: Aggressive growth
- *USOI*: Opportunity index
- *USSPECG*: Special strategies
- *USEM*: Emerging markets
- *USINC*: Fixed income`
- *USMSI*: Multi-strategy index
- *USHF*: Hedge funds index

1 The first study on the treatment of errors in variables in the context of asset pricing models was done by Fama and Macbeth (1973). Other papers on this subject are those of: Shanken (1992), Ferson and Locke (1998) and Pastor and Stambaugh (1999).

2 Prudence means "aversion to downside risk" in finance, which seems to be a universal virtue.

3 See also: Dagenais (1994) and Racicot (2003).

4 On the three-moment and four-moment CAPM, see: L'Habitant (2004), chap. 8; Harvey and Siddique (2000); Lim (1989); Kraus and Litzenberger (1976) and Rubinstein (1973).

5 See the survey of Levy (1992) on stochastic dominance.

6 That is lagged regressors.

7 For example, the fifth moment is the asymmetry sensitivity of the fourth one. The seventh moment is the sign of the convexity changes as the underlying asset moves up or down. For Taleb, moments higher than four are especially important for compound options. See: Taleb (1997), pp 202–4.

8 For example, kurtosis measures negative convexity, which is bad from the point of view of a risk averter.

9 This presentation follows quite closely Judge *et al* (1985).

10 The original F&F model contained only the first two anomalies. The momentum anomaly, which is due to Carhart (1997) and Jegadesh and Titman (1993), was introduced subsequently, to form the augmented Fama and French model.

11 The reader will excuse us for confounding at this stage higher moments and cumulants for the sake of the presentation. We will come back to the distinction between the two concepts later.

12 As reported in the next section, we will let the method chosen to estimate the model, the iterated GMM, weights optimally the moments instead of weighting them a priori in an ad hoc fashion.

13 See also L'Habitant (2004) on this point, chapter 8. Sometimes, the higher order moments are expressed in deviations from the mean. According to this formulation, the four-moment CAPM would be: $E(R_i) - R_0 = \beta_1[E(R_m) - R_0] + \beta_2[R_m - E(R_m)]^2 + \beta_3[R_m - E(R_m)]^3$.

14 HAC is the acronym of: heteroscedasticity and autocorrelation consistent covariance matrix.

15 For more details on the technical aspects of the GMM estimation method in EViews, see the *EViews User's Guide*, version 5.1.

16 The French's website is: http://mba.tuck.dartmouth.edu/pages/faculty/ken.french/data_library.html

17 A short put option carries the risk of rare but large losses.

18 We notice that the correlation between *SMB* and the annual growth of industrial production is quite high, being equal to −0.24. This correlation suggests that the *SMB* factor would have a positive impact on returns in recessions.

19 For example, Chung *et al* (2001) observed that *SMB* and *HML* become insignificant or less significant when moments or co-moments are taken into account. F&F factors might simply be good proxies for the higher moments of the return distribution. But our regression technique, which considers co-moments as instruments, suggests that they capture these co-moments but also other influences.

20 On this subject, see: Malevergne and Sornette (2005).

REFERENCES

Artzner, P., F. Delbaen, J. M. Eber, and D. Heath, 1999, "Coherent Measures of Risk", *Mathematical Finance*, **9(3)**, pp 203–28.

Bertsimas, D., G. J. Lauprete, and A. Samarov, 2004, "Shortfall as a Risk Measure: Properties, Optimization and Applications", *Journal of Economic Dynamics and Control*, **28(7)**, pp 1353–81.

Campbell, J. Y., A. W. Lo, and C. MacKinlay, 1997, *The Econometrics of Financial Markets* (Princeton: Princeton University Press).

Carhart, M. M., 1997, "On Persistence in Mutual Fund Performance", *Journal of Finance*, **52(1)**, pp 57–82.

Chung, Y. P., H. Johnson, and M. J. Schill, (2001), "Asset Pricing when Returns are Nonnormal: Fama French Factors vs. Higher Order Systematic Co-moments", Working Paper.

Dagenais, M. G., 1994, "Parameter Estimation in Regression Models with Errors in the Variables and Autocorrelated Disturbances", *Journal of Econometrics*, **64(1–2)**, pp 145–63.

Dagenais, M. G. and D. L. Dagenais, 1997, "Higher Moment Estimators for Linear Regression Models with Errors in the Variables", *Journal of Econometrics*, **76(1–2)**, pp 193–221.

Durbin, J., (1954), "Errors in Variables", *International Statistical Review*, **22(1/3)**, pp 23–32.

Fama, E. F. and K. R. French, 1992, "The Cross-section of Expected Stock Returns", *Journal of Finance*, **47(2)**, pp 427–65.

Fama, E.F. and K.R. French, 1993, "Common Risk Factors in the Returns on Stocks and Bonds", *Journal of Financial Economics*, **33(1)**, pp 3–56.

Fama, E. F. and K. R. French, 1997, "Industry Costs of Equity", *Journal of Financial Economics*, **43(2)**, pp 153–93.

Fama, E. F. and J. D. MacBeth, 1973, "Risk, Return, and Equilibrium: Empirical Tests", *Journal of Political Economy*, **81(3)**, pp 607–36.

Ferson, W. E. and D. H. Locke, 1998, "Estimating the Cost of Capital Through Time: An Analysis of the Sources of Error", *Management Science*, **44(4)**, pp 485–500.

Friend, I. and R. Westerfield, 1981, "Co-skewness and Capital Asset Pricing", *Journal of Finance*, **35(1)**, pp 897–914.

Harvey, C. R. and A. Siddique, 2000, "Conditional Skewness in Asset Pricing Tests", *Journal of Finance*, **55(3)**, pp 1263–95.

Huang, C. F. and R. H. Litzenberger, 1988, *Foundations for Financial Economics* (New York, Englewood Cliffs, NJ: Prentice Hall).

Ingersoll, J., 1987, *Theory of Financial Decision Making* (Lanham, MD: Rowman and Littlefield Publishers).

Jegadeesh, N. and S. Titman, 1993, "Returns to Buying Winners and Selling Losers: Implications for Stock Market Efficiency", *Journal of Finance*, **48(1)**, pp 65–91.

Judge, G. G., W. E. Griffiths, R. C. Hill, H. Lütkepohl, and T. C. Lee, 1985, *The Theory and Practice of Econometrics* (New York: Wiley).

Kandel S. and R. Stambaugh, 1995, "Portfolio Inefficiency and the Cross-Section of Expected Returns", *Journal of Finance*, **50(1)**, pp 157–84.

Kraus, A. and R. Litzenberger, 1976, "Skewness Preference and the Valuation of Risk Assets", *Journal of Finance*, **31(4)**, pp 1085–100.

Leibowitz, M. L. and R. D. Henriksson, 1989, "Portfolio Optimization with Shortfall Constraints: A Confidence-limit Approach to Maintaining Downside Risk", *Financial Analysts Journal*, **March–April**, pp 34–41.

Levy, H., 1992, "Stochastic Dominance and Expected Utility: Survey and Analysis", *Management Science*, **38(4)**, pp 555–74.

L'Habitant, F. S., 2004, *Hedge Funds: Quantitative Insights* (New York: John Wiley & Sons).

Lim, K.-G., 1989, "A New Test of the Three-Moment Capital Asset Pricing Model", *Journal of Financial and Quantitative Analysis*, **24(2)**, pp 205–16.

Malevergne, Y. and Sornette, D., 2005, "Higher Moments Portfolio Theory, Capitalizing on Behavioral Anomalies of Stock Markets", *Journal of Portfolio Management*, **31(1)**, pp 49–55.

Pal, M., 1980, "Consistent Moment Estimators of Regression Coefficients in the Presence of Errors in Variables", *Journal of Econometrics*, **14(3)**, pp 349–64.

Pastor L. and R. Stambaugh, 1999, "Costs of Equity Capital and Model Mispricing", *Journal of Finance*, **54(1)**, pp 67-121.

Racicot, F.-É., 2003, *Trois essais sur l'analyse des données économiques et financières, Ph.D. thesis*, chap.3, University of Quebec (Montreal).

Racicot, F-.É., 1993, *Estimation et tests en présence d'erreurs de mesure sur les variables explicatives*, M.Sc. thesis (Economics), University of Montreal.

Rubinstein, M., 1973, "The Fundamental Theorem of Parameter-preference Security Valuation", *Journal of Financial and Quantitative Analysis*, **8(1)**, pp 61–9.

Samuelson, P. A., 1970, "The Fundamental Approximation Theorem of Portfolio Analysis in Terms of Means, Variances and Higher Moments", *Review of Economic Studies*, **37(4)**, pp 537–42.

Scott, R. C. and P. A. Hovarth, 1980, "On the Direction of Preference for Moments of Higher Order than the Variance", *Journal of Finance*, **35(4)**, pp 915–19.

Sears, R. S. and K. C. J. Wei, 1985, "Asset Pricing, Higher Moments, and the Market Risk Premium: A Note", *Journal of Finance*, **40(4),** pp 1251–3.

Shanken, J., 1992, "On the Estimation of Beta-Pricing Models", *Review of Financial Studies*, **5(1),** pp 1–33

Taleb, N., 1997, *Dynamic Hedging* (New York: John Wiley).

9

Operational Risk Management Approaches and Concepts: Lessons Drawn from a Fund of Hedge Funds Provider

Pierre-Yves Moix, Bernard Bachmann

RMF Investment Management

OPERATIONAL RISKS IN THE HEDGE FUND INDUSTRY

Recent developments in the hedge fund industry indicate that what was once a "cottage industry" is now maturing to meet the requirements of institutional investing. As investors grow more familiar with alternative investments they are showing increased interest in operational issues and in how hedge funds and funds of hedge funds manage operational risks.

This chapter seeks to show *why* this interest is legitimate and examines how investors or funds of hedge funds may want to *approach* operational risks. It also looks at some of the issues that need to be considered when assessing operational risks and outlines some of the core *concepts* in operational risk management.

The conclusions suggest that in an increasingly institutionalised industry, fundamental operational risk management approaches have a clear advantage over basic approaches but are considerably more resource intensive to implement.

The costs of operational risk management might outweigh the benefits in some cases but fundamental approaches become a necessity where there is a higher level of fiduciary duty. Additionally, fundamental operational risk management not only allows investors to identify operational risks but creates an opportunity to work with hedge fund managers to improve their control environment and operational set-up.

This proactive element in fundamental operational risk management allows for investment in managers which other investors might choose to avoid. This is particularly beneficial for early stage investments and allocation to new alternative strategies, both of which traditionally carry substantial operational risks. The fundamental approach to operational risk management is thus a key competitive advantage in the detection of new alpha sources and capacity creation.

Why operational risks matter

As discussed in Moix and Scholz (2003), we distinguish between two generic types of risks: strategy risks and structural risks:

- ❑ Structural risks arise from the structure, operations and management of a hedge fund business. They entail, but are not limited to, operational risks, ie, the risks of loss resulting from inadequate or failed internal *processes*, *people* and *systems* or from *external events*.[1] Thus, operational risk management is the process of identifying and mitigating operational risks.
- ❑ Strategy risks are inherent in the investment strategy and its execution. The investment strategy determines how the manager invests, which markets and instruments are traded, and which opportunity and return sources are targeted. These risks are usually market risks, liquidity risks, and credit risks.

Table 1 summarises key strategy risks with respect to the main hedge fund styles and strategies.

The following should be noted:

- ❑ The diversity of risk sources in hedge fund investments outweighs the risks inherent in a traditional mutual fund. Moreover, the degrees of freedom given to hedge fund managers – ie, the use of leverage and derivatives, short selling and dynamic trading strategies – increases the complexity of the associated strategy risks.
- ❑ The strategy risks faced by hedge funds require a high level of operational expertise that used to be a key competency of large investment banks, not asset managers. In this context, strategy risks appear to be strongly linked to structural risk sources.

Table 1 Key financial risk sources by strategy

Style	Strategy	Key financial risk sources
Equity hedged	Long/short equities	Stocks, event risk, idiosyncratic risk
Event driven	Merger arbitrage	Broken deals, time until deal completion, regulatory environment, idiosyncratic risk
	Distressed securities	Default rates and losses, recovery rates, liquidity, legal environment, idiosyncratic risk
	Special situations	Default rates and losses, recovery rates, liquidity, legal environment, idiosyncratic risk
Relative value	Convertible bond arbitrage	Volatility, credit spreads, liquidity, new emissions, idiosyncratic risk
	Fixed income arbitrage	Volatility within yield curve, liquidity, credit spreads
	Market neutral/ statistical arbitrage	Volatility, bid-ask spreads, trading volume, trendless markets, model risk
Global macro	Emerging markets, currency, commodities	Country risk, political conflicts, FX, interest rates
Managed futures	Discretionary, systematic	Stocks, commodities, interest rates, currencies, model risk

- While hedge fund strategies require operational know-how beyond the complexity of long-only mutual funds, the operational expertise necessary to execute the different investment strategies also varies across styles and regions due to the nature of the instruments used and differences in regulatory oversight.

Given the fiduciary duty of institutional investors and the partial portfolio transparency given to these investors, it is particularly critical to proactively assess whether managers have the necessary operational expertise to take the strategy risks inherent to their trading strategy.

Empirical evidence of the importance of operational risks

The perception of hedge funds is sometimes biased by the reporting of major failures, which have made hedge funds seem more risky than traditional investments. The Hennessee Group has been publishing attrition rates since 1999, as outlined in Figure 1.

The average attrition rate is less than 5%. Though some experts were warning in 2004 that the industry hype could lead to an

management approach should seek to identify: (a) the controls governing investment transactions; (b) the controls on governing financial reporting; and (c) the controls on verifying financial reporting.

The third section will examine the efficacy of this approach by drawing lessons from publicly available hedge fund failures. What we would like to stress at this point is that the most basic form of operational risk assessment concentrates on the controls that mitigate operational risk instead of identifying the source of operational risk. This is a purely passive approach, the outcome of which is a high-level assessment of the current operational set-up of a hedge fund manager. Because there is no analysis of the sources of operational risks, deficiencies have to be taken as a given with limited potential for improvements to the manager's control environment.

Fundamental operational risk management

In contrast to basic operational risk management approaches, fundamental concepts attempt to look beyond the level of investors' governance that mitigates operational risk. The focal point is placed on the hedge fund's value chain, the investment process.

For example, the analysis would not begin by asking "what are the controls around producing or verifying financial reporting?" Instead the analysis begins with an understanding of the financial reporting *process*, identifying the *people* involved, acknowledging the *systems* used and detecting the dangers of *external events*. Figure 2 outlines the differentiation between the two approaches.

Figure 2 Basic *versus* fundamental approaches

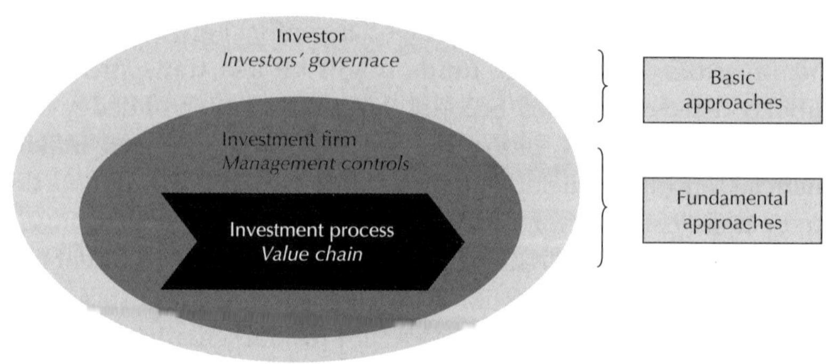

Drawing conclusions about operational risk sources is a delicate task because these are qualitative issues requiring judgement. The objective of a fundamental operational risk assessment is to make qualitative conclusions on operational risk sources that are comparable across contexts and to reduce judgemental elements to a minimum. In contrast, basic operational risk management approaches identify elements of governance at the investor level. These conclusions are less qualitative than fundamental aspects and frequently can be answered with an affirmative or negative answer.

There is a fine line between identifying the controls at an investor level (basic approach) and understanding the sources of operational risks arising from processes, people, systems and external events at the value chain level (fundamental approach). It is mostly conceptual – starting bottom up instead of top down. This is why we will have to turn to the next section to clarify further implications. For now it is important to emphasise that fundamental approaches intend to get to the source of the operational risk, while basic approaches direct their attention to a higher level – the level of investors' governance and controls that mitigates operational risks.

OPERATIONAL RISK MANAGEMENT CONCEPTS

This section intends to add content to the two approaches outlined above by answering the questions: (a) what are the *basic* controls that mitigate the conflict of interest between investor and hedge fund manager; and (b) what are the elements of a framework on which *fundamental* operational risk management procedures should be based?

Basic operational due diligence concepts

As a hedge fund investor with only four questions to ask; what is the absolute minimum of information required to come to an investment conclusion? To some investors this might seem like opening Pandora's Box so we must phrase our answers carefully. Hedge fund failures, eg, the case of Bayou Hedge Fund,[4] can provide some insight.

Naturally, the story is complex and there is an evolutionary element to understanding how these events occurred. Nevertheless, four major deviations from standard corporate governance, summarised in Table 3, can be identified:

Table 3 Governance deficiencies and potential remedies for Bayou

Deficiencies	Description	Potential remedies
Affiliated administrator	Bayou did not use a third party administrator to value investors' accounts. Monthly net-asset values (NAV), historical track records and assets-under-management (AuM) were self-administered	Using independent third party administrators – most preferably with good valuation expertise. Valuation is based on a predefined valuation policy
Affiliated prime broker	Bayou's trades were allegedly made through Bayou Securities, a registered broker/dealer. The broker/dealer had only one primary client – the Bayou fund. This makes it relatively easy to misrepresent month-end pricing	Not allowing trades to be executed via affiliated prime brokers – at least, if affiliation is required, demanding clear disclosure of affiliation, strong segregation of duties and no influence on valuation
Affiliated auditors	The audit firm shared office space with Bayou, and the firms had related ownership interests in the firm. The audit firm was not regulated	Require independent third party auditors that are overseen by a regulatory body
Limited power of attorney	Bayou had poor controls around cash wirings, ie, money could be moved without the oversight of a respected third party. No external signatures were required	Require cash wiring procedures to include at least on of the dual signatures from an independent third party (eg, administrators) based on predefined counterparty lists

Remarkably, these deficiencies are highly correlated with the Capco study's conclusions and in addition the proposed remedies provide a fine answer to the questions outlined in the last section on *basic operational risk management*. If cash is there to stay and if the only means is to be invested in an asset that is valued by an independent third party and verified by another independent third party – in a perfect world – there is little to worry about.

Fundamental operational risk management concepts

The Germans say trust is good, but control is better – but what are the controls when trust is not good enough? The following sections will try to outline what we think applies to fundamental instead of basic operational risk management concepts by: (a) sketching out the *cornerstones* of a fundamental operational risk management framework; and (b) describing the *tools* to implement such a framework.

Assessing aspects of governance and the segregation of duties between departments, or drawing conclusions about the adequacy of systems, processes and people require qualitative analysis based on judgement. The actual risk exposure is difficult to quantify,[5] this is why we suggest approaching the problem from two angles. First, by slicing and dicing the problem into smaller objects of interest before making an assessment makes it less judgemental and easier to make comparisons across styles and regions. Second, using an analytical framework on which to base a fundamental operational risk assessment offers more utility than an ad hoc approach to an organisation.

Building such a framework to assess operational issues can result in variety of solutions and will depend on the context. What we suggest in the following example is that investors need to apply a consistent methodology.

Cornerstones of a fundamental operational risk framework

The first step in building a framework relies on the opening comments when operational risk was defined as *the risk of financial loss arising from processes, people, systems and external events.*[6]

The second crucial element in building a framework lies in identifying the sources of operational risks in hedge funds. This requires an understanding of what hedge funds actually do when they pursue their investment strategies. Consequently this step defines the scope of the operational risk assessment approach. Figure 3 provides an overview of operational risk sources summarised by four topics: (a) business management; (b) functional responsibilities; (c) operations and controlling; and (d) outsourcing. Each topic includes subtopics for illustrative purposes.

The specific content of these topics obviously can differ depending on the context of the manager and the objective of the investor. Thus, it is believed that the key topics on operational risk sources remain the same:

(1) *Governance structures*: What are the processes and controls around running a business as an entrepreneur in contrast to running a proprietary desk?

Figure 4 OpRM tools by phases

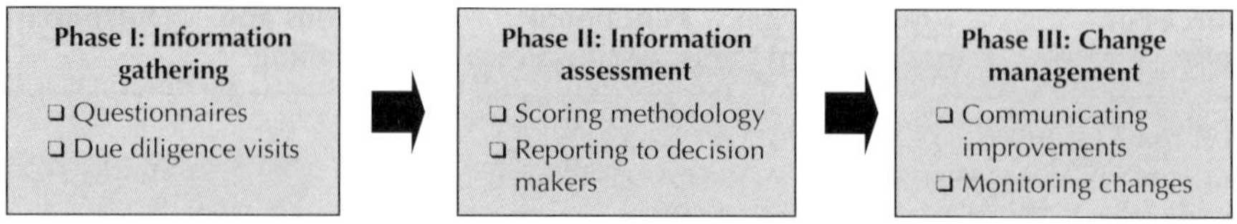

Fundamental operational risk management tools

Fundamental operational risk management tools are the instruments that put the framework into action. Implementing a fundamental operational risk management concept can be separated into three phases: (a) the *information gathering* phase; (b) the *information assessment and reporting* phase; and (c) the *change management* phase. Figure 4 includes a summary of tools grouped by phases.

In phase I, it has become an industry standard to work with questionnaires and to perform onsite due diligence visits. The following should be noted:

❑ *Questionnaires*: Recognised organisations, AIMA[10] for example, publish best-practice guidelines for hedge fund questionnaires. Occasionally, seasoned hedge fund managers provide investors with standardised documents that are based on the AIMA guidelines. While they are a good starting point, the information in the questionnaire will not necessarily correspond with the structure of the framework discussed above; a reason why the operational questionnaire may have to be tailored accordingly.

  There are several lessons that can be drawn from the responses, too. First, there is the level of actual information on operational matters, which is the primary intent of phase I. The content will demand clarifications and identify areas of concerns, but the responses offer other conclusions, too. On the one hand, there is the quality of the answers which provide an insight into the understanding a responsible person has for operational matters. On the other hand, the process itself is a good indicator of the organisational efficiency of a hedge fund, ie, how smoothly a questionnaire is returned provides some insight into how well, or poorly, a fund is organized.

❑ *Due diligence visits*: In an initial investment phase, it will probably be necessary to make an onsite visit prior to the investment.

In some cases multiple visits might be required, eg, in the case of a start-up hedge fund where operations are sketched-out, but not active. The onsite visit has two objectives, to:

(a) clarify the comments in the questionnaire, eg, what is the exact role of the CFO or risk management because different managers will label roles similarly, but assign different responsibilities to them; and
(b) verify the information obtained, eg, to sit down with a responsible controller and review his process in detail, because intent and reality might differ.

Verification of information should target the level of processes and inherent controls instead of examining results (eg, recalculating NAV), unless samples can be selected randomly. This is where fundamental operational risk management resembles basic operational risk management approaches at a different level of control.

In phase II, the assessment phase, the information gathered has to be evaluated. Organisational set-ups are diverse and comparisons across funds are problematic. This is why the information gathering process should be well structured. It provides the foundation for the application of systematic management tools, like scoring methodologies, rating/benchmarking concepts and standardised reporting and recommendation forms.

❑ *Scoring methodology and benchmarking*: Applying a scoring methodology to the operational assessment lies at the centre of a framework based approach because it allows investors to summarise and assess the information gathered in the questionnaires and during the onsite visits. The matrix reduces complexity by slicing and dicing the fund's operations, while the structured questionnaire and the onsite visit contain the content to "fill the boxes". Hence, it applies a quantitative measure to a qualitative problem and lays the foundation for comparison across styles, region and time. Table 6 has reproduced Table 4 and included scores for illustrative purposes.[11] The following should be noted:

(a) the matrix presented above contains a "natural" weighting of important control elements, so called killer criteria, because topics are overlapping;[12]

OpR dimensions

Table 6 Operational risk assessment matrix – including scores

Sources of OpR	**Business management**			**Functional responsibilities**			**Operations and controlling**			**Outsourcing**	
OpR dimensions											
Processes	3	3	5	3	4	5	3	4	2	3	4
People	3	4	5	3	3	5	3	4	5	3	2
Systems	3	4	5	3	4	5	3	4	2	3	4
External events	0	0	2	0	0	2	0	0	0	0	1

(b) checklists and a database of background information – like fund administrators, prime brokers, systems and service providers – help build expectations – this is a prerequisite for identifying benchmarks and applying scores; and

(c) the scoring/benchmarking methodology has an iterative aspect. The experience gained from analysing a large sample of hedge fund managers increases the quality of the assessment over time and provides additional information to build expectations.

❑ *Reporting to key decision makers*: In most cases, the specialists assessing operational risks are not the key decision makers. Hence, reporting back to an investment committee is an essential part of the risk management process. Documentation and reporting standards are a function of the investment mandate. Non-institutional mandates might allow ad hoc standards, but more formal processes are favoured for institutional mandates. A formalised process should include:

(a) documenting the process and the observations made during the fundamental assessment to provide investors with an audit trail to meet their level of fiduciary duty;

(b) structuring and summarising the key advantages and disadvantages of the operational set-up; and

(c) standardising the language for the ordinary, while diverging from standard phrases when significant issues are identified. A centralised database, including the final assessment report and all other documents received, round the concept off.

The advantage of standardised reporting is that it makes it easier to direct attention in the context of information overflow. Additionally, a central database enables information sharing across departmental responsibilities and overcomes the problem of managing interfaces – one of the disadvantages of centralisation.[13]

In phase III, the change management phase, fundamental operational risk management approaches turn the information flow around. Instead of describing and assessing the hedge fund manager (information inflow), the risk manager communicates process improvement recommendations to the hedge fund manager and monitors changes over time (information outflow):

- *Communicating recommendations*: The fundamental operational risk assessment will most probably highlight structural deficiencies. Some issues might lead to a decision not to invest. Most other issues will be less dramatic and can probably be resolved through procedural improvement. These conclusions provide a basis to close the circle by feeding information back to the manager to enhance controls. In this context, OpRM is close to consulting and incubator strategies.
- *Monitoring changes*: Once process improvements have been recommended it is necessary to follow-up with the hedge fund manager to ensure that implementation is taken seriously. Most probably this will require revisiting the location. Moreover, the systematic monitoring of key indicators like asset flows, staff turnover, client structure, etc will provide early warning signs of operational issues.

The intensity of interaction will depend on the type of hedge fund manger. In general, the experienced manager (eg, "hedge fund dissident") is less likely to need or want to be consulted. A start-up fund (eg, "former proprietary trader for an investment bank"), however, generally requires closer guidance and will appreciate the feedback on his operational set-up and comparison to his competitors. In contrast to basic operational risk management concepts, fundamental approaches provide a valuable data pool on operational issues across hedge fund styles, regions and life cycles.

CONCLUSIONS

Operational risks appear to matter more when investing in hedge funds than it does in traditional investment decisions. Empirical research indicates that operational issues are a dominant source of hedge fund failures. This is why there is good reason for investors to show an interest for operational risks in hedge fund investments and the hedge fund industry has accepted this circumstance.

Investor interest in operational risks should vary according to (a) the hedge fund's strategy, (b) the hedge fund manager's origin and (c) the investors' investment mandate. Executing hedge fund strategies requires expertise, but some strategies are more complex than others. Furthermore, some managers are fairly fresh to the fund business, while others have several years' experience from a previous hedge fund. Finally, some investors will state a clear risk mandate, while others concentrate entirely on return objectives. *How* investors should approach operational risks and *what* they should be looking for will differ depending on these factors.

The chapter has outlined two ways of approaching operational risk management. *Basic operational risk management* approaches identify and assess the controls that mitigate operational risks at the investors' governance level, while *fundamental operational risk management* approaches focus on the investment processes and inherent controls to identify the sources of operational risk.

We have tried to sketch out what might be considered to be basic operational risk management and fundamental operational risk management *concepts*:

- ❑ Basic concepts are founded on a corporate governance background that traditionally drives the discussion on public listed companies. We have dared to suggest a list of minimal controls that should be assessed by learning from Bayou.
- ❑ Fundamental concepts are framework based. We have outlined the cornerstones of a framework by building an assessment matrix. Furthermore, some tools have been added to support the implementation of the framework based assessment process.

We conclude that fundamental approaches, in contrast to basic concepts, provide a unique data source for formulating recommendations for improving operational processes by comparing funds across styles, regions and time. This gives fundamental approaches a clear benefit over basic approaches particularly when one recognises that poor growth management is the primary source of hedge fund failures. Fundamental approaches help to actively identify potential improvements to communicating and monitoring processes, while basic approaches are limited to a binary "go/no-go" investment decision. Hence, basic approaches limit the investor's potential investment universe. Fundamental approaches, in contrast, allow for investment into early-stage hedge funds or new alternative strategies where operational risks are most prevalent, because operational risks are managed in a proactive and dynamic way.

This advantage does not come for free. Fundamental approaches require significant resources. Teams have to be hired, processes have to be built and experience has to be gained. This might lead investors to conclude that the costs outweigh the benefits and therefore choose to apply basic assessments.

While this rationale might apply to certain investors, regulated investors such as insurance companies or pension funds have to adhere to higher levels of fiduciary duties. In this case, cost-benefit calculations have to include reputation and regulatory concerns.

This is where fund of hedge funds providers enter the arena. Typically, fund of hedge fund providers add value to the investment process by maintaining a strong relationship with individual hedge fund managers and providing expertise in selecting superior hedge fund strategies (due diligence), by structuring investment products with unique risk-return opportunities while enhancing overall portfolio diversification (portfolio management) and/or by managing risk exposures and providing transparency (risk management).

A fund of hedge fund provider's business model is based on scale. It is concluded that operational risk management can add value to the investment process by enhancing the due diligence and the risk management process, subject to investing in fundamental operational risk management know how. Clearly, this indicates that operational risk management expertise appears to be a source of both *economies of scale* and *economies of scope* for fund of hedge funds providers.

So, when trust is good, but control is better, we recommend operational risk management and when "ticking the box" is not good enough, fundamental approaches are the answer. The question of *make-or-buy* is a matter of scale. In the case of a *buy*, fund of hedge funds providers may add value.

1 Basel (2001a)

2 For further details and background refer to the following www.hennesseegroup.com and http://www.hedgefundintelligence.com/eh/reports/2005_05/overview.htm

3 For further details refer to www.crestmontresearch.com

4 The Bayou Hedge Fund Group was closed in 2005 after an investigation by the SEC. A confession by the CFO Marinho helped to bring down the full scope of the fraud scheme. For further details and the background of the Bayou fraud scheme refer to the Bloomberg Journal (November 2005), the SEC comments under http://www.sec.gov/litigation.shtml or for a summary see http://www.fundstreet.org/research/

5 This is also why the literature around implementing Basle II focuses primarily around quantifying losses from operational risks.

6 Basel (2001a).

7 Each of these topics will have further subtopics as included in Figure 2 for illustrative purposes. For documentation purposes these subtopics were not included in Table 4, ie, the class "Business Management" consists of the three sub-categories (1.1) Governance, polices and procedures, (1.2) Organisational structure and human resources and (1.3) Infrastructure, IT and business continuity.

8 www.coso.org

9 www.isaca.org

10 www.aima.org

11 The scoring methodology in the matrix applies a benchmarking score from 1–5 (5 equals benchmark, 3 average and 1 very below average) for the dimensions *process, people* and *systems*. For *external events* a bonus/penalty score from −2 to +2 is employed. Referring back to the comments on IT management above, the illustrative example claims that this is a benchmark hedge fund with respect to IT receiving maximum points for all dimensions of operational risk.

12 For example, if the fund is self-administered, the fund will receive low scores for "outsourcing to administrator" and for the fund's poor corporate governance structure. Additionally, mid- and back-office oversight, pricing and valuation controls, as well as accounting are questionable. All in all, the matrix will apply a poor total score and treat self-administration as a "killer criteria".

13 As discussed above, the advantage of centralisation is specialisation and independence. A disadvantage of centralisation is that different departments have to coordinate information and interfaces between responsibilities. By sharing information in a centralised database, the disadvantages of centralisation can be overcome.

REFERENCES

AIMR, 1999, *AIMR's Standard of Practice Handbook.*

Anson, M., 2002, *Handbook of Alternative Assets* (New York: Wiley Finance).

Basel Committee on Banking Supervision, 2001a, "The New Basel Capital Accord: An Explanatory Note", Report to the Bank for International Settlements, January.

Basel Committee on Banking Supervision, 2001b, "Sound Practices for the Management and Supervision of Operational Risks", Report to the Bank for International Settlements, January.

Barra Strategic Consulting Group, 2001, *Funds of Hedge Funds: Rethinking Resource Requirements.*

Capco, 2003, "Understanding and Mitigating Operational Risk in Hedge Fund Investments", Research and Working Paper.

Moix, Pierre-Yves and Stefan Scholz, 2003, *Risk Control Strategies: The Manager's Perspective* (London: Euromoney Books).

Moix, Pierre-Yves and Bernard Bachmann, 2006, "A practical perspective on operational risk management", in Conrad Meyer and Dieter Pfaff, *Finanz- und Rechnungswesen, Jahrbuch 2006,* Publisher.

Osterloh, Margrit and Jetta Frost, 1996, *Prozessmanagement als Kernkompetenz,* Gabe Verlag.

10

Hedge Funds, Corporate Governance and the Separation of Ownership and Control

Paul U. Ali

University of Melbourne

INTRODUCTION

Hedge funds routinely resort to securities loans, short sales and equity derivatives to establish portfolio positions and implement equity-based investment strategies. In this regard, hedge funds are no different to the other professional investors that proliferate in the global equity markets. Yet, however, the use by hedge funds of these instruments has been singled out for attention by regulators and commentators who are concerned that the instruments may have been abused by hedge funds to exert unfair influence over the affairs of corporations and disenfranchise other shareholders.

These concerns have arisen in situations where hedge funds (and, no doubt, other professional investors) have used the above instruments to create "naked voting rights" in corporations, often by combining an outright acquisition of voting shares with the divestiture of the economic ownership of the issuing corporation represented by those shares. This decoupling or contrived separation of voting power from economic ownership has ignited a debate over whether the right to vote should be tied to economic ownership.

The singling out of hedge funds for increased scrutiny in relation to their dealings in the economic incidents of voting shares seems to be driven by two factors – and the importance attached to these two factors has overshadowed the fact that while many hedge funds are significant users of securities loans, short sales and equity derivatives, the use of those instruments is by no means confined to hedge funds. Indeed, it is possible to argue that calls, in general, for the imposition of a greater regulatory burden on hedge funds or the truncation of the trading activities of hedge funds are largely attributable to those two factors. Hedge funds are commonly viewed, first, as highly secretive investment vehicles that are almost exclusively the province of the very rich and, second, as wielding considerable financial power that, unlike other major investors, they are prepared to exercise in aggressive or even unethical ways in the pursuit of their investment objectives.

These two factors present a highly skewed, and largely inaccurate, view of hedge funds.[1] Admittedly, hedge funds are lightly regulated compared with many other collective investment vehicles but that is attributable to their use of the "qualified institutional buyer"-style exceptions available to all institutional or wholesale investment vehicles under the securities laws of the major markets in which hedge funds operate (as opposed to being attributable to some inherent desire for secrecy). In addition, hedge funds have increasingly become institutionalised, with institutional investors, not high net worth individuals, dominating the market for hedge funds. In some markets, hedge funds have also become subject to a high degree of retailisation through the public offer of interests in funds of hedge funds to retail investors. Those funds of hedge funds are subject to the same registration and disclosure rules as any other collective investment vehicle in which retail investors can invest. Moreover, the aggregate value of assets under management by hedge funds, although large, remains small relative to the value of assets under management by mutual funds. Finally, what distinguishes hedge funds from other collective investment vehicles, such as mutual funds, is not that they are more aggressive (let alone unethical) but that they are subject to fewer formal constraints (in their investment mandates, for instance) as regards their investment strategies, the classes of assets they can invest in and their use of leverage and derivatives.

The focus on hedge funds as the users of securities loans, short sales and equity derivatives is thus misplaced. What, instead, is required is a consideration of whether the use of these instruments to create naked voting rights should be curtailed by regulation.

And, in this context, it is arguable that, with the exception of the way in which custodians and brokers account for the votes of shares that have been lent out under securities loans, the instruments in question are functioning exactly as they were designed to do. Securities loans ensure that shares are available on a temporary basis to borrowers, short sales facilitate the taking of short positions in shares, and equity derivatives make possible the disaggregation or replication of the economic incidents of shares.

This chapter discusses how naked voting rights can be created and whether shareholders who have divested themselves of economic exposure to the corporations in which they hold shares should be denied the ability to vote their shares. The chapter concludes with some comments on institutional investors who invest in hedge funds (and other collective investment vehicles) that make use of naked voting rights.

EQUITY DERIVATIVES AND NAKED VOTING RIGHTS

Although naked voting rights are controversial, the discrete steps involved in their creation are neither exotic nor controversial. The first step – the acquisition of voting shares – is predicated upon two factors common to all transactions in voting shares.

First, voting rights are coupled with title to voting shares. A voting share can be characterised as a bundle of legally enforceable rights against the corporation that has issued the shares. The bundle of rights encompasses cashflow rights as well as control rights, being the right to receive notice of general meetings of the corporation, the right to attend such meetings, and the right to vote on matters put to the members of the corporation at such meetings, whether in person or by proxy. These control rights can only be exercised persons holding title to the voting shares, directly by the legal owner or indirectly by the beneficial owner of the shares. An investor is the legal owner of voting shares where the investor's name is recorded in the corporation's register of shareholders or members as holding the relevant number of shares.

It is not, however, common practice for professional investors, such as hedge funds, to hold legal title to shares or other securities. Instead, voting shares are normally held indirectly via an intermediary. The shares are held in "street name", with a custodian or broker holding legal title to the shares and, accordingly, being recorded in the register of the corporation as a member of that corporation. This interposition of a custodian between the shares and the actual investor effects a segregation of beneficial title from legal title, with the bare legal title remaining with the custodian but beneficial title (which comprises all of the risks and benefits associated with the shares, including the right to cast the votes attaching to the shares) passing to the custodian's client, the investor. It is thus the client, not the custodian (despite being the legal owner of the shares), that enjoys the voting rights attached to the shares. The custodian is legally obligated to pass on to its client all information, including notices of meetings, received from the issuing corporation and to cast the votes attaching to the shares in the manner directed by its client.[2]

The second factor is the "record date". This is the time fixed by the issuing corporation, ranging from 48 hours to a month prior to the relevant meeting, to determine eligibility to attend and vote at the meetings of the corporation. For hedge funds and other professional investors who hold only beneficial title to shares, eligibility to vote depends also upon how the custodian internally allocates amongst its various clients the rights attaching to the shares to which it holds legal title. The internal allocation of voting rights is also complicated by the fact that custodians typically hold shares in a single omnibus account (rather than in separate accounts for individual clients), that there may be a further party interposed between the custodian and the shares (eg, where the custodian is a master or global custodian and the first tier of beneficial title is held by a local sub-custodian) or between the custodian and the hedge fund, and that hedge funds and other professional investors may hold voting shares in a single corporation through more than one custodian. The determination of eligibility and the allocation of voting rights are further complicated by the fact that the voting shares may have been lent out by the custodian under a securities loan.

Accordingly, like any other investor who wishes to vote at a general meeting of a corporation, a hedge fund that intends to create naked voting rights in respect of that corporation's shares must, as a first step, acquire title to the shares prior to the relevant record date.

The next step in the creation of naked voting rights involves the laying off or hedging of the hedge fund's economic exposure to the issuing corporation. This can readily be achieved through the use of equity derivatives, for example by the hedge fund entering into an equity swap (under which the total return on the voting shares is swapped by the hedge fund for a fixed or floating non-equity rate), the purchase of a put option over the shares or the sale of single share futures.[3]

The coupling of an acquisition of voting shares with equity derivatives can thus be employed to effect a separation of the right to cast the votes attaching to those shares from all or a substantial portion of the economic exposure to the issuing corporation represented by the shares. A hedge fund (or other professional investor) that has undertaken these steps retains bare title to shares net of economic exposure, in analogous fashion to the custodian or broker that holds the shares for the hedge fund, but, unlike that custodian or broker, remains able to direct how the votes attached to the shares can be cast. The hedge fund can, in common with other shareholders of the corporation, vote at the relevant general meeting of the corporation but without – and this is the contentious point – having an economic stake in the future of the corporation. The hedge fund can, consequently, vote its shares in a manner reflecting not its interest as a shareholder (ie, as a residual claimant on the cashflow and capital of the corporation) but in accordance with some extraneous motive.

BACK-TO-BACK SALES AND NAKED VOTING RIGHTS

Naked voting rights can also be created by manipulating the record date through the use of back-to-back sales, with the first leg of the transaction completed prior to the record date and the second leg completed immediately after that date. This can take the form of a securities loan or the independent purchase and sale of the shares. Due to its holding of title to the voting shares at the record date, the hedge fund will continue to enjoy the right to cast the votes attached to those shares even though at the time the meeting of the corporation is held the hedge fund may no longer hold title to the shares. Unlike the method described for creating naked voting rights in the previous paragraph, a hedge fund that participates in a back-to-back sale of voting shares bears short term economic exposure to the issuing corporation. However, depending upon the timing of the second leg of the transaction, this exposure may be only overnight or intra-day.

SECURITIES LOANS AND NAKED VOTING RIGHTS

A third method for creating naked voting rights relies upon the inefficiencies inherent in the holding of shares via intermediaries and, more particularly, the way in which the votes attaching to shares that are the subject of securities loans are accounted for by some custodians and brokers.[4] Securities loans involve the outright transfer of voting shares and other securities for short-term periods, typically to facilitate short sales or otherwise cover short positions.[5] During the term of the loan, dividends and other cashflows generated on the underlying shares are remitted by the borrower to the lender in the form of "manufactured dividends" and, on the termination of the loan, equivalent shares are returned to the lender. Thus, the key right that is transferred during the term of the loan is the right to vote the shares.[6] Securities loans can, consequently, be used to create naked voting rights in the same manner as back-to-back sales of voting shares.

While securities loans and short sales are an integral feature of equity markets, the treatment of the votes attaching to the underlying shares is a matter of considerable controversy. In the case of a securities loan, the borrower acquires title to the shares being lent and, accordingly, on the inception of the loan the lender's entitlement to vote the shares ceases with the borrower acquiring that right together with the other rights embodied in the shares. This would not be problematic if the lender was the absolute owner of the shares or the loan was effected by a custodian or broker with the knowledge of the beneficial owner of the shares. However, the lending of shares and other securities is mostly done by custodians and brokers pursuant to pro-forma or blanket consents from their clients, meaning that the client will not normally know that particular shares have been lent and cannot be voted.

This particular issue can be resolved through the recall of shares. The terms on which the shares are lent will, in line with industry practice, permit the shares to be recalled by the lender for the purposes of voting. While it is the client who decides whether to vote its shares and, consequently, whether the shares that have been lent need to be recalled in order to re-instate the client's voting rights, the custodian may have a strong economic disincentive to recall the shares (due to the fee-income received from the lending of the shares).

In practice, it seems that the conflict between the client's desire to vote its shares and the custodian's desire to generate fee-income from securities loans has been resolved by the custodian permitting both the client and the borrower to vote the shares.[7] This is accomplished by the custodian allocating to the two parties the necessary extra votes from other shares in the same corporation held by the custodian and which have not been voted by their beneficial owners.

This allocation of votes from unvoted shares to shares that have been lent generates a duplicate set of naked votes unattached to either title to shares or economic exposure to the issuing corporation. There is, moreover, not just the potential for a single iteration of naked voting rights but also for multiple iterations, for example where shares held by a custodian for a client are lent to a short seller and the custodian that holds the shares for the purchaser, in turn, lends the shares to a second short seller. It is possible that the votes attaching to the shares could be voted in their entirety by three different parties, namely the first-mentioned client, the purchaser of the shares from the first short seller and the purchaser of the shares from the second short seller.[8]

In fact, a hedge fund that chooses to create naked voting rights by coupling an acquisition of shares with a short sale of shares could find itself in the enviable position of being able to "double up" its voting rights while having divested itself via the short sale of economic exposure to the issuing corporation.

VOTING RIGHTS AND ECONOMIC OWNERSHIP

Voting rights are coupled with title to voting shares, and title itself normally represents the ownership by the shareholder of a residual claim against the cashflows and capital of the issuing corporation. The holding of a residual claim gives shareholders an economic incentive to monitor the management of the corporation, and conferring upon shareholders voting rights proportionate to their residual claim or economic stake in the corporation is viewed as the optimum means of matching that economic incentive with voting power.[9] This relationship between voting rights and economic ownership of corporations is reflected in the "one share, one vote" principle that is the norm for listed corporations.

However, title alone does not necessarily signify economic ownership of the issuing corporation. As has been seen above, situations can be contrived where an investor retains title to shares net of any economic exposure to the issuing corporation yet continues to enjoy the right to vote the shares. Nor does the retention of title have to be anything more than transient. Naked voting rights can also be created by back-to-back sales of voting shares on either side of a record date. Further, the practice of custodians and brokers allocating unexercised votes from one group of beneficial owners to a second group desirous of voting but whose shares have lent out (and in respect of which title has passed) has created a situation where the naked voting rights conferred upon the latter are linked to neither title nor economic exposure.

The use of securities loans, short sales and equity derivatives to create naked voting rights leads to the issue of whether eligibility to vote should be confined to those shareholders with an economic stake in the issuing corporation. One proposal that has been mooted is that the voting power of individual shareholders should be restricted to a level commensurate with their net long economic exposure to the issuing corporation, meaning that shareholders who have divested themselves of their economic ownership of the corporation through, eg, short positions should not be entitled to vote their shares.[10]

The purpose of this proposal is to restore shareholders to a situation in which voting power corresponds to economic ownership of corporations. There are, however, considerable practical difficulties with measuring with any degree of exactitude the economic ownership of individual shareholders and thus applying such a voting qualification consistently across a corporation's shareholders. In addition, such a rule would capture not only the deliberate creation of naked voting rights but would also extend to all situations where the shareholders had hedged their positions, whether partially or wholly (as well as indirectly via short equity index positions), had partially off-setting economic exposure to the issuing corporation through participating in different equity strategies in which the shares are a component, and even where the off-setting position had been assumed as a proxy for some other risk (where, eg, the hedging of equity price risk is used as a proxy for the hedging of credit risk in relation to the issuing corporation).

Moreover, basing eligibility to vote on economic ownership assumes that the holders of naked voting rights, due to their not having an economic stake in the corporation, will vote in their own self-interest and in a manner inimical to the collective interests of the shareholders who continue to have an economic stake in the corporation. This assumes that there is some degree of homogeneity of interest amongst the latter shareholders, an erroneous assumption. The courts in the major common law jurisdictions have long recognised that, even amongst shareholders with an economic stake in the corporation, shareholders are free to vote their shares entirely in their own self-interest and that their individual interests may be diametrically opposed.[11]

Furthermore, confining the right to vote to shareholders with an economic stake in the issuing corporation is not only a matter of denying the voting rights that are normally a legal incident of title to shares but also raises the issue of how long one must be a shareholder of the issuing corporation in order to vote. The use of a record date by corporations is essentially a balancing of the benefits to the corporation of being able to establish with certainty, the persons who, out of a fluctuating body of shareholders, are entitled to vote at general meetings against the risk that the record date can be manipulated. Nonetheless, shareholders who have used back-to-back sales or securities loans to strip away their economic exposure are, like other shareholders entitled to vote at the relevant general meeting, holders of title to voting shares at the record date. To deprive the former of their right to vote is in effect to impose a temporal requirement for the holding of shares on shareholders. This necessarily involves the arbitrary determination of what is a sufficiently non-transient holding of shares for the purposes of retention of voting rights.

The third method of creating naked voting rights identified above differs from the first two methods in that voting rights are conferred upon a party who, due to its shares having been lent out by its custodian or broker, no longer holds title to shares. This is not a case of a person having title to shares at the record date divesting itself of economic exposure to the issuing corporation. Instead, the naked voting rights have arisen because it is more expedient for some custodians and brokers to reallocate unexercised votes to clients wishing to vote their shares rather than recalling the shares that have been lent out or denying all shares that have been lent out the right to vote.

Finally as noted above, linking eligibility to vote to economic ownership means decoupling the right to vote from title. This raises the issue (something that is beyond the scope of this brief chapter) of whether the right to vote should be extended to non-shareholders who have an economic stake in the issuing corporation corresponding to the net long economic position of those shareholders who are permitted to vote.

CONCLUDING REMARKS – INSTITUTIONAL INVESTORS IN HEDGE FUNDS

The chief investors in hedge funds are now institutional investors such as mutual funds, pension funds, life insurance companies, family offices, and charitable endowments and foundations. These investors – because they are investing on behalf of their own investors and clients, not on their own account – are subject to a duty to act prudently when investing the funds entrusted to them. That duty of prudence, the "prudent investor rule", applies to all institutional investors in the UK and the USA as well as in other markets such as Australia whose laws are derived from English law.

An institutional investor, in determining whether an allocation of funds to a hedge fund constitutes a prudent investment, must, as a minimum, understand the hedge fund's investment strategy, the mechanisms employed by the hedge fund to execute that strategy and be in a position to monitor the actual execution of that strategy.[12] The majority of hedge funds follow arbitrage or relative value strategies where their returns are derived from changes in the pricing relationships between different securities and, for these hedge funds, there is less or little incentive to resort to naked voting rights to influence investment outcomes. That, however, is not necessarily the case for hedge funds that follow opportunistic or event-driven strategies, particularly where the hedge fund is seeking to profit from a change of control transaction, restructuring or other contentious events in the life cycle of a corporation. The creation of naked voting rights and, in particular, the multiplication of voting rights that is possible in relation to securities loans may be of assistance to the hedge fund in realising its investment objectives.

It is conceivable that, due to the increased regulatory scrutiny of naked voting rights and the publicity that has accompanied allegations of their use in contested change of control transactions[13] a court might interpret the prudent investor rule as requiring an institutional investor to ascertain the extent to which naked voting rights form part of the strategy of the hedge funds in which it has invested. Moreover, for institutional investors that are listed corporations, self-interest (or even self-preservation) may warrant a greater understanding of naked voting rights. Such an institutional investor might find that it is itself the target of the exercise of naked voting rights in circumstances where the creation of those rights has, in fact, been partially financed by the institutional investor's own investment in a hedge fund.

ACKNOWLEDGEMENTS

This research was supported by a grant from the Australian Research Council (DP0557673).

1 See Ali *et al* (2003).

2 In practice, while beneficial title to the voting shares will be held by the hedge fund, control over the voting and disposition of the shares will usually be controlled by a separate entity, the hedge fund manager: see Stapledon and Bates (2000) and Ali *et al* (2003).

3 The issues raised in this chapter are distinct from those normally associated with equity swaps. A common feature of many takeover bids is the entry by the bidder into a cash-settled equity swap, with the bidder's swap counterparty hedging its exposure under the swap by acquiring shares in the target. This raises the prospect of the bidder and swap counterparty "acting in concert" – the hedge shares are removed from the "free float", thus potentially influencing the success or failure of the bid, and the parties may have entered into the swap on the tacit understanding that, on the unwinding of the swap and the associated hedge position, the bidder will acquire the hedge shares. On a separate matter, the purchase of the put option can be financed by sale of a covered call option over the shares, creating a cashless or zero-cost collar. This has the advantage of enabling the investor to retain some limited upside in respect of the voting shares.

4 See Stapledon and Bates (2000) and Martin and Partnoy (2005).

5 See Securities Borrowing and Lending Code of Guidance, C.7.3 (Securities Lending and Repo Committee, Bank of England, December 2004).

6 See Christopherson *et al* (2004), Hu and Black (2006a), and Hu and Black (2006b). In the UK, the market consensus is that securities loans should not be implemented solely for the purpose of acquiring votes: Securities Borrowing and Lending Code of Guidance, C.7.4.

7 See Martin and Partnoy (2005).

8 See Drummond (2006).

9 See Black and Kraakman (1996).

10 See Martin and Partnoy (2005).

11 For example: "There is, if I may say so, no obligation on a shareholder of a company to give his vote merely with a view to what other persons may consider the interests of the company at large. He has a right, if he thinks fit, to give his vote from motives or promptings of what he considers his own individual interest" (*Pender v Lushington* (1877) 6 Ch D 70, at pp 75–6 (per Jessel MR)).

12 See Ali *et al* (2003). Equivalent duties also apply to the managers of the hedge funds in which these institutional investors have invested.

13 See Drummond (2006).

REFERENCES

Ali, P. U., G. P. Stapledon, and M. Gold, 2003, *Corporate Governance and Investment Fiduciaries* (Sydney: Thomson Legal & Regulatory).

Black, B. and R. Kraakman, 1996, "A Self-Enforcing Model of Corporate Law", *Harvard Law Review*, **109**, pp 1911–81.

Christopherson, S. E. K., C. C. Geczy, D. K. Musto, and A. V. Reed, 2004, "How and Why do Investors Trade Votes, and What Does it Mean?", Working Paper 2004s-23, CIRANO.

Drummond, B., 2006, "Corporate Voting Charade", *Bloomberg Markets*, **15(4)**, pp 96–104.

Hu, H. T. C. and B. Black, 2006a, "Empty Voting and Hidden Ownership: Taxonomy, Implications, and Reforms", Law and Economics Working Paper No 70, University of Texas School of Law.

Hu, H. T. C. and B. Black, 2006b, "Hedge Funds, Insiders, and Decoupling of Economic and Voting Ownership in Public Companies", Law and Economics Working Paper No 53, University of Texas School of Law.

Martin, S. and F. Partnoy, 2005, "Encumbered Shares", *University of Illinois Law Review*, **3**, pp 775–813.

Stapledon, G. P. and J. J. Bates, 2000, "Unpacking the 'Interest-Holders' in a Share: Reducing the Costs of Voting", *Company Financial and Insolvency Law Review*, pp 293–329.

11

Value-at-Risk Predictions of Hedge Fund Portfolios: A Comparison of Alternative Approaches

Oliver A. Schwindler

HF-Analytics, Bamberg University

INTRODUCTION

Given the growing need for managing hedge fund risk, risk prediction plays an important role in the management of hedge fund portfolios. In this study, we compare the out-of-sample performance of three different approaches to estimate Value-at-Risk (VAR) for hedge fund portfolios. We compare on the one hand VAR models based on moments of the empirical distribution and on the other hand a model based on extreme value theory (EVT). The first group of models covers an approach based on a thin-tailed normal distribution and an approach based on the Cornish-Fisher (CF) expansion which controls for skewness and kurtosis. We choose for the EVT approach a generalised Pareto distribution (GPD) model. The main difficulty common to all these VAR models is the estimation of the required quantile of the loss distribution, since there is no analytical representation of this distribution. The VAR numbers calculated by the different VAR models are compared to the actual losses. Due to the private nature of hedge funds, they escape much of the regulation that forces more transparency on the published data. Hedge funds have fewer restrictions on the use of leverage, short-selling, and derivatives than more regulated investment vehicles. This allows for greater flexibility regarding asset classes, trading styles, markets, level of transparency and liquidity. Moreover, hedge funds hold long and short positions, use leverage through borrowing or derivatives, exploit arbitrage opportunities and can have significant asymmetric exposures to several markets or risk factors at the same time. Especially after the collapse of Long Term Capital Management (LTCM) in August 1998, the importance of sound risk management has been emphasised for hedge funds.[1] Recently, there has been an increased focus on the determination of capital requirements for hedge funds. These trends have led to the development of various risk-measurement techniques for hedge fund portfolios and funds of hedge funds. As hedge funds trade in multiple asset classes, a uniform applicable measure for risk is needed. VAR fulfills this requirements and has therefore emerged as the most prominent measure of downside market risk. It has gained increasing acceptance among hedge funds and funds of hedge funds over the past years.[2]

This increased focus on risk management and transparency of hedge funds has motivated academic and practitioner-oriented research in the area of hedge funds risk exposures. The early studies from Fung and Hsieh (1997), who extended Sharpe's (1992) asset class factor model to include more diversified hedge fund strategies, and Liang (1999) suffer from the usage of the traditional mean-variance framework. Brooks and Kat (2002) show that the distributions of monthly hedge fund index returns exhibit statistically significant skewness, kurtosis and autocorrelation of different orders. Moreover, they demonstrate that although hedge fund indices are highly attractive in mean-variance terms, this is much less the case when skewness, kurtosis and autocorrelation are taken into account. Agarwal and Naik (2004) use a mean-conditional VAR framework, and demonstrate the extend to which the mean-variance framework underestimates the tail risk. Favre and Galeano (2002) suggest the VAR based on the CF expansion for portfolio optimisation of funds of hedge funds. In a recent study Jorion (2000) investigates LTCM's VAR and estimates the amount of capital that would have been necessary to support it's risk profile. Based on his analyses he argues that LTCM severely underestimated its risk due to its reliance on short-term history and risk concentration. Gupta and Liang (2005) use the EVT to estimate VAR thresholds, and infer capital adequacy from these VARs for individual hedge funds.

Based on these findings, we analyse both a VAR model based on the normal distribution and a VAR model based on the CF expansion.

Additionally, we choose a VAR model based on EVT, as previous literature indicates that this methodology provides a better prediction of catastrophic market risk during volatile periods.[3] This is due to the fact that instead of using the whole distribution the VAR measure based on EVT utilises only the distribution of extreme returns. For the analysis of the forecasts of all three approaches, we use a nonadaptive model, which does not utilise a sliding window and instead uses all the available data up to the day on which the forecasts are generated. This approach is preferable as estimates from the extreme value theory require more data for out-of-sample forecasts. This can be attributed to the fact, that extreme events are rare, especially in the short data history of hedge fund returns. The forecasted VAR thresholds calculated by a specific model are compared to the actual VAR threshold of the empirical distribution using Theil's Inequality Coefficient (TIC), heteroscedasticity-adjusted mean absolute errors (HMAE) and root mean square errors (HRMSE) in order to analyse the quality of the forecasts.

This chapter is organised as follows. We present in the next section the different VAR models used in this study and then describe the hedge fund index returns data. The subsequent section provides the empirical findings, on which the conclusion in the last section is based on.

VALUE-AT-RISK MODELS

Let $R_t = \ln(P_t/P_{t-1})$ be the returns at time t where P_t is the price of an asset (or portfolio) at time t. The $\text{VAR}_t(\alpha)$ at the $(1 - \alpha)$ percentile is defined by

$$Pr(R_t \leq VAR_t(\alpha)) = \alpha \tag{1}$$

which calculates the probability that returns at time t will be less than (or equal to) $\text{VAR}_t(\alpha)$, α percent of the time.

In discrete time, log-returns are described by the following return process:

$$\ln P_{t+\Delta} - \ln P_t = R_t = \mu\Delta t + \sigma\varepsilon\sqrt{\Delta t} \tag{2}$$

where Δt is the length of the time interval in which the discrete time data is recorded. $\Delta W_t = \varepsilon\sqrt{\Delta t}$ is the Wiener process with zero mean and variance of Δt since ε is a random variable drawn from the standard normal distribution ($\varepsilon \sim N(0, 1)$). Equation (2) implies by assuming $\Delta t = 1$ that $\varepsilon = (R - \mu)/\sigma$. The critical step in calculating VAR measures is the estimation of the threshold, which defines what variation in returns R_t is considered to be extreme. Let $\Im$ be the threshold, equation (1) is then given by

$$Pr(R_t < \Im) = Pr\left(\varepsilon \leq a = \frac{\Im - \mu}{\sigma}\right) = \alpha \qquad \textbf{(3)}$$

where $Pr(\cdot)$ is the underlying probability distribution, μ and σ are the mean and standard deviation of R_t, respectively. In the traditional parametric VAR model with a normal distribution the threshold $\Im_{Normal}$ is calculated by

$$\Im_{Normal}(\alpha) = \mu - z(\alpha) \times \sigma \qquad \textbf{(4)}$$

where μ and σ are the estimated mean and standard deviation of the empirical distribution and $z(\alpha)$ is the critical value from the normal distribution for the probability $(1 - \alpha)$.

As Brooks and Kat (2002) show, hedge fund returns are skewed and fat-tailed, their distributions can not be solely described by their means and standard deviations. As this would lead to an underestimation of the underlying risk, incorporating more parameters characterising the distribution of the returns can be done by estimating VAR using the Cornish-Fisher (CF) expansion provided by Cornish and Fisher (1937). The CF expansion adjusts the critical value $z(\alpha)$ for the skewness and kurtosis of the empirical distribution. The threshold $\Im_{CF}$ is then given by

$$\Im_{CF}(\alpha) = \mu + \Omega(\alpha) \times \sigma. \qquad \textbf{(5)}$$

$\Omega(\alpha)$ is the adjusted critical value and is calculated by

$$\Omega(\alpha) = z(\alpha) + \frac{1}{6}(z(\alpha)^2 - 1)S + \frac{1}{24}(z(\alpha)^3 - 3z(\alpha))K - \frac{1}{36}(2z(\alpha)^3 - 5z(\alpha))S^2 \qquad \textbf{(6)}$$

where S is the skewness and K is the excess kurtosis of the empirical distribution. The equations (5) and (6) indicate that the CF expansion allows to compute VAR measures for asymmetric and leptokurtic distributions as kurtosis and skewness are included. Note that, if the return distribution is normal, S and K are equal to zero, implying that $\Omega(\alpha) = z(\alpha)$.

As presented in Table 1, skewness and excess kurtosis statistics of hedge fund returns are found to be significant different from zero at the 1% level, we expect the VAR threshold obtained from the CF expansion to be more accurate than the threshold estimated by the normal distribution. The EVT provides another alternative for estimating VAR. We choose the peaks-over-threshold (POT) approach because it is the most sophisticated method in practice. An overview of EVT is briefly given in the Appendix.[4] To keep things simple, we follow the usual convention in extreme value theory by discussing only the case of upper extremes. The corresponding results for lower extremes are easily deducted by simply transforming the returns R_t into $-R_t$, by which maximum becomes minimum and vice versa. The POT method focuses on the distribution of exceedances over a predetermined high threshold u. We denote y the excess return beyond the threshold as $y = R - u$. The distribution of y is called the conditional excess distribution. For a high threshold u Këllezi and Gilli (2000) show that, the conditional excess distribution can be approximated by the generalised Pareto distribution (GPD)

$$G_{\xi,\sigma}(y) = 1 - \left(1 + \xi \frac{y}{\sigma}\right)^{-1/\xi} \quad \text{if } \xi \neq 0. \tag{7}$$

Lhabitant (2003) shows that the GPD yields the following VAR threshold

$$\Im_{EVT}(\alpha) = u + \frac{\hat{\sigma}}{\hat{\xi}}\left(\left(\alpha \frac{n}{n_u}\right)^{-\hat{\xi}} - 1\right) \tag{8}$$

where u denotes the predetermined threshold, n_u and n are the number of extremes and the number of total data points, respectively. Once the scale ($\hat{\sigma}$) and shape ($\hat{\xi}$) parameters of the GPD are

Table 1 Hedge fund index return data: January 1990–December 2005 (n = 192)

HFRI index	Mean	Std. Dev	Worst	Best	Skewness	Kurtosis	JB	P	T	L
Funds weighted composite	1.12	1.97	−8.70	7.65	−0.61***	5.91***	79.61***	1.899*	1.657	3.143
Convertible arbitrage	0.80	1.02	−3.19	3.33	−1.10***	4.88***	69.83***	1.929**	1.753	3.383*
Distressed securities	1.19	1.73	−8.50	7.06	−0.64***	8.55***	276.27***	1.714	2.264***	3.880***
Emerging markets (total)	1.31	4.21	−21.02	14.80	−0.84***	7.02***	160.93***	1.844	1.806	3.329*
Equity hedge	1.36	2.54	−7.65	10.88	0.18	4.35***	17.20***	1.789	1.707	3.053
Equity market neutral	0.74	0.90	−1.67	3.59	0.18	3.37	2.44	1.944**	1.797	3.493**
Equity non hedge	1.33	4.05	−13.34	10.74	−0.49***	3.57*	10.99**	1.617	2.019**	3.265
Event driven	1.15	1.88	−8.90	5.13	−1.29***	7.61***	236.14***	1.880*	2.278***	4.284***
Fixed income (total)	0.84	0.98	−3.27	5.34	−0.27*	7.96***	212.29***	1.717	2.405***	4.129***
Fixed income arbitrage	0.67	1.21	−6.45	4.70	−1.71***	13.49***	1028.33***	2.145***	1.910*	4.097***
Fixed income high yield	0.78	1.79	−7.16	9.54	−0.77***	9.85***	418.96***	1.862*	2.586***	4.816***
Macro	1.25	2.38	−6.40	7.88	0.35 * *	3.58*	7.19**	1.780	2.129***	3.792***
Market timing	1.04	1.95	−3.28	5.96	0.06	2.43*	2.61	1.601	1.632	2.613
Merger arbitrage	0.81	1.23	−6.46	2.90	−2.56***	13.92***	1224.29***	1.813	2.132***	3.865***
Relative value arbitrage	0.94	1.04	−5.80	5.72	−0.83***	13.23***	909.79***	1.763	1.668	2.940
Short selling	0.32	6.04	−21.21	22.84	0.14	4.57***	22.31***	1.775	1.917*	3.403**
Statistical arbitrage	0.69	1.12	−2.71	4.46	−0.06	3.47	2.26	1.601	1.901	3.043
Fund of Funds	0.80	1.60	−7.47	6.85	−0.25	7.14***	148.92***	1.924*	2.141***	4.119***

Skewness is tested using the test proposed by D'Agostino (1970) for normality and kurtosis is tested using the test proposed by Anscombe and Glynn (1983) for normality. For testing the hypothesis of normally distributed returns, we use the Jarque–Bera (JB) test. The test statistic is defined by $JB = n[(S^2/6) + (K - 3)^2/24]$, where n denotes the number of observations, S the skewness and K the kurtosis. The test statistic is asymptotically χ^2 distributed, however as Jarque and Bera (1980) note for moderate sample sizes finite-sample critical values should be used. We therefore simulated the significance points with a Monte Carlo Simulation. The simulated critical values for the 10%, 5% and 1% level of significance are 4.05, 5.69 and 11.92.

P, T and L are the test statistics of the tests for peakedness (P), fat tails (T) and leptokurtosis (L) proposed by Schmid and Trede (2003). The finite-sample significance points are taken from Schmid and Trede (2003). *, **, *** denote the 10%, 5% and 1% level of significance, respectively.

estimated one can calculate the VAR threshold, $\Im_{EVT}$, based on the considered confidence level α.

HEDGE FUND DATA

The hedge fund indices used in this study were obtained from Hedge Fund Research, Inc. (HFR), which is one of the best-known and largest hedge fund database currently available. There are several reasons behind choosing HFR indices. First, they do not adjust historical returns used for the calculation of their indices for closed or liquidated funds, therefore mitigating the known survivorship bias.[5] Second, HFR indices have a critical large number of constituents, which gives a better representation for return distributions of individual hedge fund strategies. Finally, HFR indices are equally weighted, which mitigates concentration in a few hedge funds with large assets under management. The database contains monthly returns from January 1990 to December 2005 for 16 hedge fund strategy indices, reflecting the monthly net of fee returns. Additionally, we use the monthly returns for the Fund Weighted Composite Index and the Fund of Funds Composite Index.

Table 1 presents the descriptive statistics for the 18 hedge fund indices. More specifically, the table reports the means, standard deviations, skewness, kurtosis, the Jarque–Bera (JB) statistics as well as the worst and the best monthly return for each index. Eleven indices display significant negative skewness, whereas for the Macro index a significant positive skewness has been calculated. Almost all hedge fund indices exhibit excess kurtosis, except the indices for Equity Market Neutral and Statistical Arbitrage strategies. Given the ongoing discussion about what exactly kurtosis measures,[6] we additionally report the test statistics of the tests for peakedness (P), fat tails (T) and leptokurtosis (L) proposed by Schmid and Trede (2003). These tests are based on quantiles and can account for peakedness and tail behavior separately. As kurtosis depends on both peakedness near the center and tail weight (see Johnson and Kotz (1985)) these tests will provide a more detailed picture of the empirical distribution, especially of the tails. The tests reveal that a high kurtosis statistic stems from the peakedness or the tail of the distribution as only one of these test statistics is statistically significant. However, leptokurtosis can be documented for 12 hedge fund indices. To sum up, these results indicate that the risk profile of hedge funds cannot be accurately described by the mean and standard deviation alone.

EMPIRICAL RESULTS

The VAR measures for the normal distribution, $\Im_{Normal}$, and the VAR measure with the Cornish-Fisher expansion, $\Im_{CF}$ are obtained using equations (4) and (5), respectively. As shown in equation (8), the VAR threshold for the extreme value approach, $\Im_{EVT}$, depends on the estimated location (μ), scale (σ), shape (ξ) parameters of the GPD, and the loss probability level (α).[7] We use the 8% left tail of the empirical return distribution for the maximum likelihood estimation of the mentioned parameters.[8]

We use a nonadaptive model, which uses all data available up to the day on which the forecast is generated, for the prediction of the VAR thresholds. However, the hit ratio of a nonadaptive model is highly influenced by the choice of the length of the initial period used for the first forecast. Since an increase in the initial forecast period decreases the evaluation period this in turn decreases automatically the hit ratio as the relative number of violations of the VAR threshold decreases. On the other side, a short initial forecast period can produce unstable and volatile VAR predictions.[9]

As Figure 1 shows, the 5% VAR forecasts are indeed highly unstable in the first half of the evaluation period.[10] Therefore, we take the first 96 monthly data points for the initial VAR forecast to ensure stable quantile estimates. Figure 1 also shows that the CF expansion is very sensitive to outliers due to the usage of skewness and kurtosis for the VAR calculation.[11] As a result of this, during the period from August 1998 until September 1998, where almost all hedge fund strategies suffered their heaviest losses, the VAR thresholds of the CF expansion increase considerably.

To analyse the accuracy of the three different VAR models, we use the TIC, HMAE and the HRMSE. The TIC, which always lies between zero and one, where zero indicates a perfect fit, is calculated by:[12]

$$TIC = \frac{\sqrt{\frac{1}{n}\sum_{i=1}^{n}(\Im_{actual,i} - \Im_{estimated,i})^2}}{\sqrt{\frac{1}{n}\sum_{i=1}^{n}(\Im_{actual,i})^2} + \sqrt{\frac{1}{n}\sum_{i=1}^{n}(\Im_{estimated,i})^2}}. \quad \textbf{(9)}$$

However, TIC only computes the total variation in $\Im_{actual,i}$ explained by $\Im_{Normal}$, $\Im_{CF}$ and $\Im_{EVT}$. Although it provides the direction and the

Figure 1 Monthly downside returns and 5% VAR forecasts

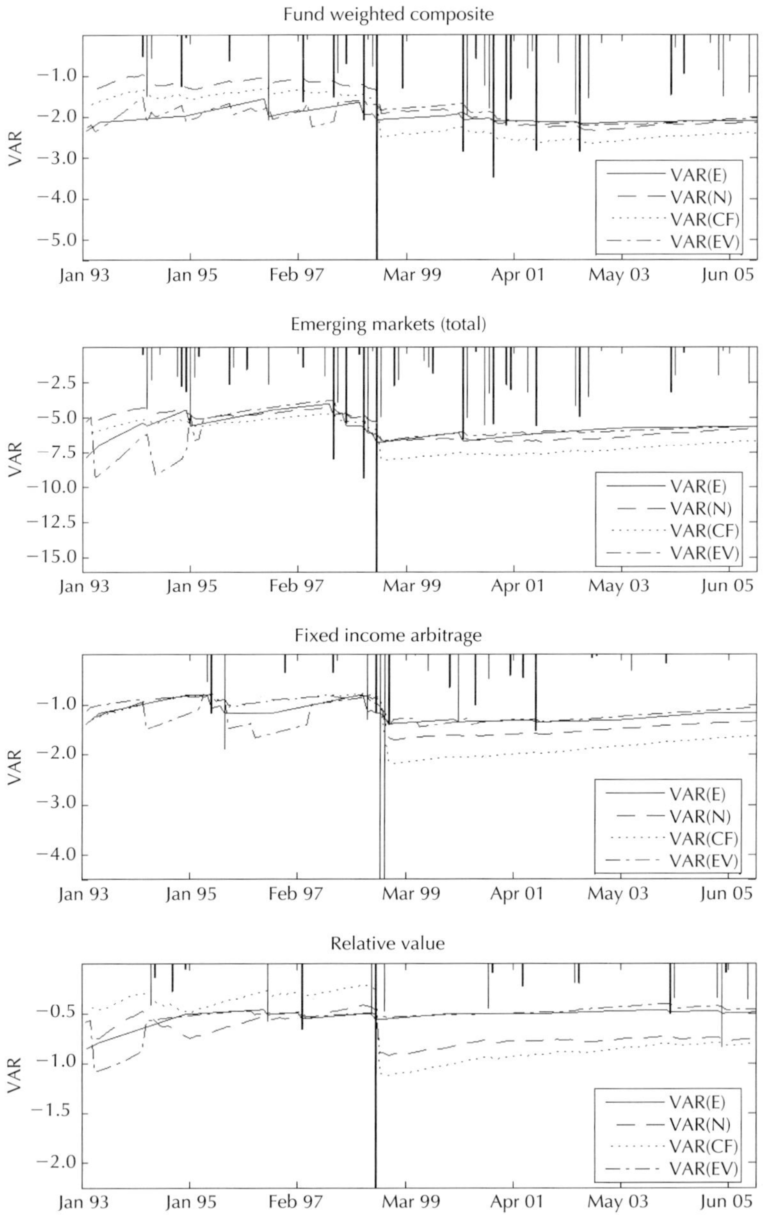

magnitude of the relationship between the actual and the estimated VAR threshold, it does not measure how far away the estimated threshold is from the actual. To compute directly the deviation between $\Im_{actual,i}$ and $\Im_{estimated,i}$ we use the HMAE and the HRMSE, proposed by Anderson, Bollerslev and Lange (1999), which are heteroskedasticity adjusted statistics and calculated by

$$HMAE = \frac{1}{n}\sum_{i=1}^{n}\left|1-\frac{\Im_{actual,i}}{\Im_{estimated,i}}\right| \qquad \textbf{(10)}$$

$$HRMSE = \sqrt{\frac{1}{n}\sum_{i=1}^{n}\left(1-\frac{\Im_{actual,i}}{\Im_{estimated,i}}\right)^2}. \qquad \textbf{(11)}$$

Tables 2, 3 and 4 report the values for the TIC, HMAE and the HRMSE for the 5%, 2.5% and the 1% VAR threshold over the evaluation period from January 1997 to December 2005 (n = 96). The numbers in parentheses are the rankings between the three competing models for each evaluation criteria. For the 5% VAR threshold the average TIC turns out to be 7.13% for the EVT, 8.68% for the normal distribution and 10.93% for the CF expansion. The average mean absolute (percentage) error turns out to be 10.96% for the EVT, 21.35% for the normal density and 15.97% for the CF expansion. Similarly, the average root mean square (percentage) error is found to be 14.85% for the EVT, 18.19% for the normal distribution and 34.91% for the CF expansion. These results indicate that the EVT performs much better than the normal distribution and the CF expansion in estimating the 5% VAR. More precisely, the EVT provides for equity hedge, fixed income arbitrage, relative value arbitrage, event driven, convertible arbitrage and merger arbitrage strategies the best estimate for the 5% VAR. However, it should be noted that EVT is not always the best method for estimating the 5% quantile, as the CF expansions provides for equity market neutral, macro and fixed income high yield strategies the best forecast. Moreover, the normal distribution provides the best results for statistical arbitrage and distressed strategies.

For the 2.5% VAR threshold the average TIC turns out to be 7.16% for the EVT, 12.14% for the CF expansion and 14.82% for the normal distribution. The average HMAE turns out to be 13.43% for

Table 2 Relative Performance of alternative approaches to estimating 5% VAR threshold

HFRI index	TIC			HMAE			HRMSE		
	$\Im_{Normal}$ (%)	$\Im_{CF}$ (%)	$\Im_{EVT}$ (%)	$\Im_{Normal}$ (%)	$\Im_{CF}$ (%)	$\Im_{EVT}$ (%)	$\Im_{Normal}$ (%)	$\Im_{CF}$ (%)	$\Im_{EVT}$ (%)
Funds weighted composite	4.54 (2)	8.69 (3)	3.56 (1)	7.57 (2)	16.07 (3)	5.66 (1)	13.05 (2)	16.43 (3)	8.25 (1)
Convertible arbitrage	26.16 (3)	10.49 (2)	7.76 (1)	67.64 (3)	18.68 (2)	8.01 (1)	72.08 (3)	23.18 (1)	34.51 (2)
Distressed securities	6.13 (1)	11.11 (3)	7.98 (2)	11.02 (1)	19.48 (3)	15.19 (2)	12.71 (1)	20.84 (3)	17.58 (2)
Emerging markets (total)	3.72 (2)	9.69 (3)	1.68 (1)	6.32 (2)	17.22 (3)	2.45 (1)	7.79 (2)	17.55 (3)	3.56 (1)
Equity hedge	4.50 (3)	4.41 (2)	2.38 (1)	7.85 (2)	7.91 (3)	4.22 (1)	8.40 (2)	8.71 (3)	5.55 (1)
Equity market neutral	5.36 (2)	4.77 (1)	13.08 (3)	9.08 (2)	8.30 (1)	22.20 (3)	11.73 (2)	10.39 (1)	23.94 (3)
Equity non hedge	7.16 (3)	3.26 (1)	3.62 (2)	13.54 (3)	6.03 (1)	6.85 (2)	14.89 (3)	6.63 (1)	8.72 (2)
Event driven	10.16 (2)	20.26 (3)	5.60 (1)	17.29 (2)	32.22 (3)	9.68 (1)	19.30 (2)	34.36 (3)	10.89 (1)
Fixed income (total)	4.18 (1)	6.06 (2)	22.08 (3)	7.31 (1)	67.34 (3)	24.21 (2)	13.92 (1)	285.13 (3)	36.33 (2)
Fixed income arbitrage	8.72 (2)	19.10 (3)	2.92 (1)	15.61 (2)	31.08 (3)	5.15 (1)	16.42 (2)	31.65 (3)	6.82 (1)
Fixed income high yield	11.02 (2)	8.73 (1)	15.97 (3)	17.69 (2)	15.12 (1)	26.51 (3)	22.66 (2)	17.87 (1)	28.15 (3)
Macro	6.70 (2)	6.07 (1)	8.47 (3)	12.60 (2)	10.99 (1)	14.01 (3)	13.56 (2)	12.21 (1)	17.66 (3)
Market timing	2.99 (2)	2.67 (1)	3.90 (3)	5.05 (2)	4.44 (1)	5.38 (3)	6.05 (2)	5.44 (1)	7.26 (3)
Merger arbitrage	20.86 (2)	37.62 (3)	9.86 (1)	33.64 (2)	54.21 (3)	15.82 (1)	34.67 (2)	54.63 (3)	17.66 (1)
Relative value arbitrage	21.93 (2)	29.31 (3)	3.19 (1)	35.12 (2)	49.35 (3)	5.37 (1)	35.44 (2)	52.98 (3)	7.19 (1)
Short selling	2.32 (3)	2.20 (2)	2.07 (1)	3.36 (2)	3.40 (3)	2.92 (1)	4.46 (3)	4.26 (2)	4.11 (1)
Statistical arbitrage	3.64 (1)	4.51 (2)	8.04 (3)	6.58 (1)	8.77 (2)	13.62 (3)	8.56 (1)	11.60 (2)	15.93 (3)
Fund of Funds	6.25 (2)	7.83 (3)	6.18 (1)	10.13 (2)	13.85 (3)	9.94 (1)	11.76 (1)	14.57 (3)	13.24 (2)
Average	8.68 (2)	10.93 (3)	7.13 (1)	15.97 (2)	21.35 (3)	10.96 (1)	18.19 (2)	34.91 (3)	14.85 (1)

The numbers in parentheses are the rankings between the three competing models for each evaluation criteria. The TIC, given in equation (9), computes the total variation in $\Im_{actual,i}$ explained by $\Im_{Normal}$, $\Im_{CF}$ and $\Im_{EVT}$. The HMAE and HRMSE are used to compute directly the deviation between $\Im_{actual,i}$ and $\Im_{estimated,i}$. These two evaluation statistics given in equations (10) and (11) follow the statistical tradition of reporting statistics based on the deviation between actual and estimated value, while adjusting for heteroscedasticity in the forecast error. The evaluation period for the mentioned evaluation criteria is from January 1997 to December 2005 (n = 96).

Table 3 Relative performance of alternative approaches to estimating 2.5% VAR threshold

HFRI index	**TIC**			**HMAE**			**HRMSE**		
	$\Im_{Normal}$ (%)	$\Im_{CF}$ (%)	$\Im_{EVT}$ (%)	$\Im_{Normal}$ (%)	$\Im_{CF}$ (%)	$\Im_{EVT}$ (%)	$\Im_{Normal}$ (%)	$\Im_{CF}$ (%)	$\Im_{EVT}$ (%)
Funds weighted composite	4.09 (2)	16.56 (3)	3.97 (1)	6.68 (2)	26.20 (3)	6.17 (1)	9.51 (2)	27.96 (3)	8.21 (1)
Convertible arbitrage	28.50 (3)	8.66 (2)	8.23 (1)	75.99 (3)	13.49 (2)	11.04 (1)	79.60 (3)	18.29 (1)	38.33 (2)
Distressed securities	14.68 (3)	10.01 (2)	7.80 (1)	31.91 (3)	19.39 (2)	15.70 (1)	6.37 (3)	4.50 (2)	4.16 (1)
Emerging markets (total)	8.24 2)	12.02 (3)	5.15 (1)	13.70 (2)	21.21 (3)	9.28 (1)	18.28 (2)	22.13 (3)	11.03 (1)
Equity hedge	3.48 (1)	4.50 (2)	5.23 (3)	6.40 (1)	6.51 (2)	9.35 (3)	7.18 (1)	9.42 (2)	10.79 (3)
Equity market neutral	16.28 (3)	14.38 (2)	4.20 (1)	37.79 (3)	32.48 (2)	7.38 (1)	40.6 (3)	33.85 (2)	14.44 (1)
Equity non hedge	12.14 (3)	3.54 (2)	3.47 (1)	27.36 (3)	6.59 (2)	5.75 (1)	27.98 (3)	7.64 (1)	8.03 (2)
Event driven	25.65 (3)	4.77 (1)	14.42 (2)	68.04 (3)	7.65 (1)	32.13 (2)	70.23 (3)	11.73 (1)	36.06 (2)
Fixed income (total)	25.27 (3)	7.17 (1)	11.00 (2)	64.66 (3)	15.67 (1)	21.11 (2)	67.48 (3)	22.57 (1)	28.55 (2)
Fixed income arbitrage	12.76 (2)	21.01 (3)	12.28 (1)	17.02 (2)	33.66 (3)	16.95 (1)	27.36 (1)	35.95 (3)	27.77 (2)
Fixed income high yield	31.45 (3)	13.92 (2)	3.59 (1)	91.21 (3)	31.40 (2)	6.31 (1)	91.56 (3)	32.13 (2)	8.11 (1)
Macro	3.19 (1)	4.95 (3)	3.47 (2)	6.22 (1)	9.91 (3)	6.28 (2)	6.69 (1)	10.77 (3)	7.38 (2)
Market timing	2.97 (3)	2.11 (2)	1.95 (1)	4.99 (3)	3.62 (2)	3.22 (1)	6.37 (3)	4.50 (2)	4.16 (1)
Merger arbitrage	39.15 (3)	15.85 (1)	28.11 (2)	113.23 (3)	28.00 (1)	65.66 (2)	124.65 (3)	34.80 (1)	77.95 (2)
Relative value arbitrage	21.75 (2)	52.62 (3)	6.67 (1)	34.67 (2)	66.32 (3)	10.67 (1)	35.67 (2)	67.58 (3)	12.85 (1)
Short selling	5.40 (3)	2.87 (1)	2.89 (2)	9.44 (3)	4.40 (2)	3.41 (1)	11.07 (3)	6.14 (2)	5.89 (1)
Statistical arbitrage	8.88 (3)	6.62 (2)	4.04 (1)	16.28 (3)	12.11 (2)	7.20 (1)	17.92 (3)	13.71 (2)	9.25 (1)
Fund of Funds	3.04 (2)	16.87 (3)	2.57 (1)	4.90 (2)	28.75 (3)	4.13(1)	7.41 (2)	28.89 (3)	4.98 (1)
Average	14.82 (3)	12.14 (2)	7.16 (1)	35.03 (3)	20.41 (2)	13.43 (1)	36.44 (3)	21.81 (2)	17.65 (1)

The numbers in parentheses are the rankings between the three competing models for each evaluation criteria. The TIC, given in equation (9), computes the total variation in $\Im_{actual,i}$ explained by $\Im_{Normal}$, $\Im_{CF}$ and $\Im_{EVT}$. The HMAE and HRMSE are used to compute directly the deviation between $\Im_{actual,i}$ and $\Im_{estimated,i}$. These two evaluation statistics given in equations (10) and (11) follow the statistical tradition of reporting statistics based on the deviation between actual and estimated value, while adjusting for heteroscedasticity in the forecast error. The evaluation period for the mentioned evaluation criteria is from January 1997 to December 2005 (n = 96).

Table 4 Relative performance of alternative approaches to estimating 1% VAR threshold

HFRI index	TIC			HMAE			HRMSE		
	$\Im_{Normal}$ (%)	$\Im_{CF}$ (%)	$\Im_{EVT}$ (%)	$\Im_{Normal}$ (%)	$\Im_{CF}$ (%)	$\Im_{EVT}$ (%)	$\Im_{Normal}$ (%)	$\Im_{CF}$ (%)	$\Im_{EVT}$ (%)
Funds weighted composite	32.80 (3)	10.75 (1)	24.45 (2)	84.60 (3)	19.22 (1)	52.24 (2)	98.99 (3)	29.12 (1)	63.62 (2)
Convertible arbitrage	36.55 (3)	11.76 (2)	7.33 (1)	100.00 (3)	26.56 (2)	14.62 (1)	116.36 (2)	26.88 (1)	149.28 (3)
Distressed securities	36.74 (3)	9.01 (1)	17.68 (2)	100.00 (3)	16.30 (1)	35.86 (2)	112.85 (3)	28.24 (1)	42.66 (2)
Emerging markets (total)	32.69 (3)	8.66 (1)	20.11 (2)	91.95 (3)	15.26 (1)	47.71 (2)	95.15 (3)	20.93 (1)	49.15 (2)
Equity hedge	19.86 (3)	11.33 (1)	15.75 (2)	41.23 (3)	19.48 (1)	29.69 (2)	52.62 (3)	27.61 (1)	38.49 (2)
Equity market neutral	12.93 (3)	9.61 (2)	4.71 (1)	29.40 (3)	21.01 (2)	6.25 (1)	33.46 (3)	23.79 (2)	14.54 (1)
Equity non hedge	22.84 (3)	9.98 (2)	9.86 (1)	58.24 (3)	21.15 (2)	20.67 (1)	61.12 (3)	22.64 (2)	22.47 (1)
Event driven	40.37 (3)	9.49 (1)	16.41 (2)	100.00 (3)	17.83 (1)	36.39 (2)	135.84 (3)	21.78 (1)	39.27 (2)
Fixed income (total)	36.52 (3)	6.54 (1)	12.24 (2)	100.00 (3)	13.81 (1)	29.17 (2)	116.30 (3)	20.74 (1)	37.80 (2)
Fixed income arbitrage	44.76 (3)	8.64 (1)	24.90 (2)	200.00 (3)	19.58 (1)	65.63 (2)	161.74 (3)	28.45 (1)	69.59 (2)
Fixed income high yield	28.65 (3)	21.87 (2)	2.34 (1)	80.56 (3)	3.90 (2)	3.64 (1)	80.72 (3)	4.35 (1)	5.02 (2)
Macro	10.81 (2)	11.21 (3)	5.99 (1)	19.05 (2)	21.22 (3)	10.14 (1)	23.45 (2)	24.09 (3)	11.95 (1)
Market timing	6.01 (3)	2.11 (1)	3.04 (2)	10.84 (3)	3.16 (1)	4.62 (2)	11.77 (3)	4.82 (1)	7.33 (2)
Merger arbitrage	49.88 (3)	16.90 (1)	16.99 (2)	199.35 (3)	40.21 (1)	41.23 (2)	200.03 (3)	40.83 (1)	42.12 (2)
Relative value arbitrage	44.41 (2)	18.63 (1)	47.21 (3)	128.50 (2)	29.25 (1)	147.82 (3)	148.72 (2)	49.72 (1)	172.66 (2)
Short selling	15.72 (3)	8.52 (1)	9.31 (2)	36.55 (3)	18.29 (1)	20.35 (2)	37.11 (3)	19.85 (1)	22.50 (2)
Statistical arbitrage	7.88 (3)	5.40 (2)	5.38 (1)	16.68 (3)	10.25 (2)	9.38 (1)	17.48 (3)	13.31 (1)	14.02 (2)
Fund of Funds	31.51 (3)	9.55 (1)	21.32 (2)	80.55 (3)	16.69 (1)	46.09 (2)	90.49 (3)	30.46 (1)	54.15 (2)
Average	28.39 (3)	10.55 (1)	14.72 (2)	82.08 (3)	18.51 (1)	34.52 (2)	88.57 (3)	24.31 (1)	47.59 (2)

The numbers in parentheses are the rankings between the three competing models for each evaluation criteria. The TIC, given in equation (9), computes the total variation in $\Im_{actual,i}$ explained by $\Im_{Normal}$, $\Im_{CF}$ and $\Im_{EVT}$. The HMAE and HRMSE are used to compute directly the deviation between $\Im_{actual,i}$ and $\Im_{estimated,i}$. These two evaluation statistics given in equations (10) and (11) follow the statistical tradition of reporting statistics based on the deviation between actual and estimated value, while adjusting for heteroscedasticity in the forecast error. The evaluation period for the mentioned evaluation criteria is from January 1997 to December 2005 (n = 96).

actual VAR threshold for the individual hedge fund indices over the evaluation period from January 1997 to December 2005. A ratio above one indicates that the VAR model overestimated the actual quantile, whereas a ratio below one indicates that the model underestimated the actual VAR threshold. For the 5% VAR threshold all three models overestimated on average the actual quantile,[15] whereas for the 1% threshold all models underestimated on average the actual quantile. For the 2.5% quantile both the VAR model based on the normal distribution and on EVT underestimated on average the actual VAR threshold, whereas the VAR model based on the CF overestimated on average the actual quantile. These results confirm the previous findings with the TIC, HMAE and the HRMSE. Another important figure for evaluating the forecast quality of a VAR model is the violation ratio. A violation occurs when a realised return is greater than the estimated VAR threshold. The violation ratio is defined as the total number of violations, divided by the total number of one-period forecasts. If the model is correct, the expected violation ratio is the tail area for each quantile. Table 6 displays the violation ratios for the left tail of the monthly returns. It can be seen that the violation ratios vary substantially between both hedge fund strategies and VAR models. For example the normal distribution and the CF expansion have a violation ratio of 0.64% for merger arbitrage and event driven strategies well below the aimed level of 5%. Whereas both models have violation ratios for equity market neutral and short selling strategies above the aimed level of 5%. The EVT model has a violation ratio of 1.92% for merger arbitrage and event driven strategies and 5.13% for equity market neutral strategies. Similar findings can be also documented for the 2.5% and the 1% VAR threshold.

CONCLUSION

We provide an empirical analysis of the out-of-sample performance of the normal distribution, the CF expansion and the EVT in computing VAR thresholds for hedge fund index returns. The violation ratio and alternative performance measures - TIC, HMAE and HRMSE – are used to assess the accuracy and performance of these VAR models. The results indicate that all three models, on average, overestimate the actual VAR threshold at the 5% level. The results for the 2.5% threshold are mixed. The CF expansion, on average,

Table 6 VAR violation ratios for the left tail of monthly returns

HFRI index	5% VAR			2.5% VAR			1% VAR		
	$\Im_{Normal}$ (%)	$\Im_{CF}$ (%)	$\Im_{EVT}$ (%)	$\Im_{Normal}$ (%)	$\Im_{CF}$ (%)	$\Im_{EVT}$ (%)	$\Im_{Normal}$ (%)	$\Im_{CF}$ (%)	$\Im_{EVT}$ (%)
Funds weighted composite	5.77	4.49	3.21	3.21	1.92	1.28	0.64	0.64	0.64
Convertible arbitrage	3.21	2.56	2.56	2.56	1.92	1.92	1.92	1.92	1.92
Distressed securities	1.92	1.92	2.56	1.28	0.64	1.28	1.28	0.64	0.64
Emerging markets (total)	5.13	3.85	4.49	1.92	1.92	1.92	1.92	1.28	0.64
Equity hedge	3.85	3.85	3.85	1.92	1.92	1.92	1.28	0.64	0.64
Equity market neutral	5.13	5.77	5.13	3.21	3.21	3.21	2.56	1.92	1.28
Equity non hedge	3.21	2.56	2.56	1.92	1.92	1.92	1.92	0.64	0.64
Event driven	0.64	0.64	1.92	0.64	0.64	0.64	0.64	0.64	0.64
Fixed income (total)	2.56	4.49	3.85	2.56	2.56	2.56	1.92	1.28	1.92
Fixed income arbitrage	3.85	3.85	4.49	2.56	2.56	1.92	1.92	1.28	1.28
Fixed income high yield	1.28	1.28	0.64	1.28	0.64	0.64	0.64	0.64	0.64
Macro	3.85	3.85	1.92	2.56	2.56	1.28	0.64	0.64	0.64
Market timing	4.49	4.49	2.56	1.92	2.56	2.56	0.64	1.28	1.28
Merger arbitrage	0.64	0.64	1.92	0.64	0.64	0.64	0.64	0.64	0.64
Relative value arbitrage	2.56	3.21	2.56	0.64	1.28	1.28	0.64	0.64	0.64
Short selling	5.77	5.13	5.77	3.21	1.92	2.56	1.28	1.28	1.28
Statistical arbitrage	4.49	5.77	6.41	2.56	3.85	3.85	0.64	1.28	3.21
Fund of Funds	6.41	5.77	5.13	3.85	3.21	3.21	2.56	1.92	1.92

The evaluation period is from January 1997 until December 2005 (n = 96).

overestimates the actual quantile whereas the normal distribution and EVT, on average, underestimate the actual VAR threshold. All three models, on average, underestimate the actual VAR threshold at the 1% level. For the 2.5% and the 1% level a model based on the CF expansion or EVT should be preferred over a model based on the normal distribution, given the relative low estimation errors in Table 3 and 4. However, for the 5% level the results are mixed. In this case, the forecasting performance depends on the chosen hedge fund strategy. For some hedge fund strategies the actual violation ratios of the VAR models deviate substantially from their aimed levels.

These results suggest that the market risk of a portfolio of hedge funds should not be managed only with the information obtained from the VAR threshold. The risk manager should also look at additional risk measures like the Conditional VAR[16] (CVAR). Additionally, the portfolio should be stressed with a set of different scenarios,[17] to get an impression how the portfolio could behave in an extreme market environment.

APPENDIX: OVERVIEW OF EXTREME VALUE THEORY

Extreme value theory (EVT) deals with the distribution of extreme returns and focuses, compared to the VAR models based on the normal distribution or based on the CF expansion, only on the tails of the return distribution. Generally, there are two related ways of identifying extreme returns in real data. The first approach is called the *block maxima* method and considers the maximum return in successive periods, for example months or years. These selected observations constitute the extreme events, also called block (or per period) maxima. The second approach focuses on the returns in the sample that exceed a given high threshold and is therefore called *peaks over threshold* (POT) method. EVT provides two classes of extreme value distributions (EVD) which are used to model the distribution of the identified extreme returns. The first class, called the generalised extreme value (GEV) distribution proposed by Jenkinson (1955), relies on the limit law for sample maxima derived by Fisher and Tippett (1928) and encompasses the three standard EVDs: Frechet, Gumbel and Weibull. The second class, called the generalised Pareto distribution (GPD) introduced by Pickands (1975), nests the Pareto, uniform and exponential distributions and is used for modeling the conditional excess distribution of the POT approach.

Distribution of maxima

Let $\{R_t\}_{t=1}^{m}$ be a sequence of returns with sample size m and denote the maximum of the first $n < m$ observations of R by $M_n = \max(R_1, R_2, \ldots, R_n)$. Following the Fisher and Tippett (1928) theorem, M_n is normalised with a location parameter, μ_n, and a scale parameter, σ_n, in such a way that $x = (M_n - \mu_n)/\sigma_n \xrightarrow{d} H(x)$. Jenkinson (1955) provides a one-parameter presentation of the GEV distribution, which is given for $1 + \xi x > 0$ by,

$$H_\xi(x) = \begin{cases} e^{-(1+\xi x)^{-1/\xi}} & \text{if } \xi \neq 0 \\ e^{-e^{-x}} & \text{if } \xi = 0 \end{cases} \quad \textbf{(12)}$$

where ξ is the shape parameter, which reflects the weight of the tail. The Frechet distribution ($\xi > 0$) is fat tailed as its tail is slowly decreasing, the Gumbel distribution ($\xi = 0$) is thin tailed as its tail is rapidly decreasing, and the Weibull distribution ($\xi < 0$) has no tail – after a certain point there are no extremes. The most frequently employed estimation method is the maximum likelihood method, which provides efficient parameter estimates of the GEV distribution.[18] A crucial advantage of the maximum likelihood method is its asymptotic theory, which provides simple approximations for standard errors and confidence intervals.

Distribution of exceedances

An alternative approach is to consider the distribution of exceedances over a certain threshold u. Let Y be the excess returns beyond the threshold, $Y = R - u$. Denote the number of exceedances of u by

$$N_u = \text{card}\{i : i = 1, \ldots, n, R_i < u\} \quad \textbf{(13)}$$

and the corresponding excesses by $Y_1, Y_2, \ldots, Y_{N_u}$. Let F_u be the *conditional excess distribution function,* ie, the probability that a return R exceeds the threshold u by at most an amount y given that

R exceeds the threshold u. For $y \geq 0$ the conditional excess distribution function of R is given by

$$F_u(y) = P(R - u \leq y \mid R > u) = P(Y \leq y \mid R > u). \quad \textbf{(14)}$$

Let F_R be the cumulative distribution function (CDF) of R. For $y \geq 0$, F_u can be written in terms of F_R:

$$F_u(y) = \frac{F_R(u+y) - F_R(u)}{1 - F_R(u)} = \frac{F_R(r) - F_R(u)}{1 - F_R(u)}. \quad \textbf{(15)}$$

However, equation (15) is of little use in practice, since we will not know F_R in most of the cases. Fortunately, extreme value theory provides a second fundamental theorem that will help us approximate F_u. Balkema and de Haan (1974) and Pickands (1975) show that, for a large threshold u, $F_u(y)$ is well approximated by

$$F_u(y) \approx G_{\xi,\sigma}(y) \qquad u \to \infty$$

where the generalised Parteo distribution is given by

$$G_{\xi,\sigma}(y) = \begin{cases} 1 - (1 + \xi \frac{y}{\sigma})^{-1/\xi} & \text{if } \xi \neq 0 \\ 1 - e^{-y/\sigma} & \text{if } \xi = 0 \end{cases} \quad \textbf{(16)}$$

with $y \geq 0$ if $\xi \geq 0$, and $y \in [0, -\sigma/\xi]$ if $\xi < 0$. ξ is called the shape parameter and σ the scale parameter. The GPD embeds a number of other distributions. When $\xi > 0$, it takes the form of the ordinary Parteo distribution, which has a polynomially decreasing tail. For $\xi = 0$, the GPD corresponds to the exponential distribution as the tail decreases exponentially and when $\xi < 0$ the distribution is short tailed (uniform). The case $\xi > 0$ is the most relevant for risk management since it results in a heavy-tailed distribution. As for the GEV, the maximum likelihood method is the most frequently used estimation method to estimate the values of the parameters σ and ξ from the series of excesses.[19]

As Longin and Solnik (2001) point out the selection of the threshold u plays a central role in estimating the parameters of the GPD. In threshold selection, we face a trade off between bias and variance.[20] If we choose a high threshold, the number of observations is small and the outcome of this are inefficient parameter estimates with large standard errors. However, choosing a low threshold leads to biased parameter estimates, as observations from the center of the distribution are included in the estimation process. Unfortunately, no automatic algorithm with satisfactory performance for the selection of the threshold u is available.[21] In practice this is done by graphical methods such as the QQ-plot, the Hill-plot or the sample mean excess plot.

1 See The President's Working Group on Financial Markets (1999).

2 For an alternative method of measuring the loss potential of hedge fund strategies, see López de Prado and Peijan (2004).

3 As McNeil and Frey (2000), Longin (2000) and Bali (2003) show that VAR measures based on the normal density may provide acceptable estimates of the maximum likely loss under normal market conditions, they fail, in contrast to VAR models based on EVT, to account for extremely volatile periods.

4 For a comprehensive and accessible overview of the subject, the interested reader is referred to Embrechts, Klüppelberg and Mikosch (2003), Reiss and Thomas (2001), McNeil, Frey and Embrechts (2005) and Coles (2001).

5 Survivorship bias comes from the fact that data vendors collect only survived funds and an upward bias occurs when we evaluate performance of all funds based on survived funds only. For a detailed analysis of the survivorship bias in hedge fund data see Brown, Goetzmann and Ibbotson (1992), Brown, Goetzmann and Ibbotson (1999), Fung and Hsieh (2000) and Liang (2000).

6 For a detailed discussion of the concept and the interpretation of kurtosis see Darlington (1970), Hildebrand (1971), Ruppert (1987) and Balanda and MacGillivray (1988).

7 For estimating the μ, σ and ξ parameters, we employ the EVIM toolbox of Gençay, Selçuk and Ulugülyağci (2001).

8 Note that previous studies on EVT use the 2.5% and the 5% left tail of the empirical distribution to obtain the excess over a high threshold. However, the existing literature generally uses daily datasets with large numbers of observations. Since we have only monthly returns we have to use a moderately lower threshold for the estimation of the parameters for the EVT model.

9 As Gençay, Selçuk and Ulugülyagci (2003) point out a VAR model should produce relative stable quantile forecasts since adjusting the implemented capital frequently is costly to implement.

10 The figures for the other hedge fund indices are not significantly different to those presented. To save space we do not document them. However, they are available upon request from the author.

11 This outlier sensitivity is due the fact that both skewness and kurtosis are very sensitive to outliers.

12 For a detailed description of Theil's Inequality Coefficient see Theil (1966).

13 These findings for the 1% VAR are in line with that of Bali and Gokcan (2004).

14 Note that these hedge fund strategies have normal distributed return distributions.

15 It should be noted that for Convertible Arbitrage and Equity Non Hedge strategies the VAR model based on the normal distribution excessively underestimates the actual VAR threshold.

16 The Conditional VAR is the expected loss exceeding the VAR threshold. This measure is sometimes also call the Mean Excess Loss, Mean Shortfall, or Tail VAR. For a detailed overview of CVAR see Artzner, Delbaen, Eber and Heath (1999).

17 For an introduction to stress testing see Jorion (2001), Christoffersen (2003) or Aragonés, Blanco and Dowd (2001). A coherent framework for stress testing can be found in Berkowitz (2000).

18 The literature discusses both parametric and nonparametric approaches for estimating the parameters μn, σn and ξ of the GEV distribution. Two parametric techniques are commonly used: the maximum likelihood method (see Hosking (1985) and Hosking and Wood (1985)) and the regression method (see Gumbel (1958) and Longin (1996)). Another parametric estimation procedure that also has attracted a lot of interest is the method of moments: for the probability-weighted moments see Hosking and Wood (1985) and for its subsequent development into the theory of L-moments see Hosking (1990). The nonparametric approaches which are based on the direct estimation of the shape parameter ξ have been developed by Pickands (1975), Hill (1975) and Dekkers and De Haan (1989).

19 The literature discusses different approaches for estimating the parameters σ and ξ of the GPD. For the maximum likelihood method see Smith (1987), for the method-of-moments and the method of probability-weighted moments see Hosking and Wallis (1987), for the elemental percentile method see Castillo and Hadi (1997) and for the exponential regressions see Matthys and Beirlant (2003).

20 For a detailed discussion of this problem see Embrechts, Klüppelberg and Mikosch (2003).

21 The issues on determining the fraction of data belonging to the tail is treated for example by Danielsson, de Haand, Pengd and de Vries (2001), Danielsson, de Vries (1997) and Dupuis (1998).

REFERENCES

Agarwal, V. and N. Y. Naik, 2004, "Risks and Portfolio Decisions Involving Hedge Funds", *Review of Financial Studies*, **17(1)**, pp 63–98.

Anderson, T. G., T. Bollerslev, and S. Lange, 1999, "Forecasting Financial Market Volatility: Sampling Frequency vis-a-vis Forecast Horizon", *Journal of Empirical Finance*, **6(5)**, pp 457–77.

Anscombe, F. J. and W. J. Glynn, 1983, "Distribution of the Kurtosis Statistic for Normal Samples", *Biometrika*, **70(1)**, pp 227–34.

Aragonés, J. R., C. Blanco, and K. Dowd, 2001, "Incorporating Stress tests into Market Risk Modeling", *Derivatives Quarterly*, **7(3)**, pp 44–9.

Artzner, P., F. Delbaen, J. Eber, and D. Heath, 1999, "Coherent Measures of Risk", *Mathematical Finance*, **9(3)**, pp 203–28.

Balanda, K. P. and H. L. MacGillivray, 1988, "Kurtosis: A Critical Review", *The American Statistician*, **42(2)**, pp 111–19.

Bali, T. G., 2003, "An Extreme Value Approach to estimating Volatility and Value at Risk", *Journal of Business*, **76(1)**, pp 83–108.

Balkema, A. A. and L. de Haan, 1974, "Residual Life Time at Great Age", *Annals of Probability*, **2(5)**, pp 792–804.

Berkowitz, J., 2000, "A Coherent Framework for Stress Testing", *Journal of Risk*, **2(2)**, pp 1–11.

Brooks, C. and H. M. Kat, 2002, "The Statistical Properties of Hedge Fund Index Returns and their Implications for Investors", *Journal of Alternative Investments*, **5(2)**, pp 26–44.

Brown, S. J., W. Goetzmann, and R. G. Ibbotson, 1992, "Survivorship Bias in Performance Studies", *Review of Financial Studies*, **5(4)**, pp 553–80.

Brown, S. J., W. N. Goetzmann, and R. G. Ibbotson, 1999, "Offshore Hedge Funds: Survival and Performance, 1989–95", *Journal of Business*, **72(1)**, pp 91–117.

Castillo, E. and A. S. Hadi, 1997, "Fitting the Generalized Pareto Distribution to Data", *Journal of the American Statistical Association*, **92(440)**, pp 1609–20.

Christoffersen, P., 2003, *Elements of Financial Risk Management* (Amsterdam: Academic Press).

Coles, S., 2001, *An Introduction to Statistical Modeling of Extreme Values* (London: Springer).

Cornish, E. A. and R. A. Fisher, 1937, "Moments and Cumulants in the Specification of Distributions", *Review of the International Statistical Institute*, **5**, pp 307–20.

Danielsson J. and C. G. de Vries, 1997, "Beyond the Sample: Extreme Quantile and Probability Estimation", London School of Economics, *Working Paper.*

Danielsson, J., L. de Haand, L. Pengd, and C. G. de Vries, 2001, "Using a Bootstrap Method to Choose the Sample Fraction in Tail Index Estimation", *Journal of Multivariate Analysis*, **76(2)**, pp 226–48.

Darlington, R. B., 1970, "Is Kurtosis Really 'Peakedness'?", *The American Statistician*, **24(2)**, pp 19–22.

Dekkers, A. L. M. and L. De Haan, 1989, "On the Estimation of the Extreme-Value Index and Large Quantile Estimation", *Annals of Statistic*, **17(4)**, pp 1795–832.

Dupuis, D. J., 1998, "Exceedances over High Thresholds: A Guide to Threshold Selection", *Extremes*, **1(3)**, pp 251–61.

D'Agostino, R. B., 1970, "Transformation to Normality of the Null Distribution of g1", *Biometrika*, **57**, pp 679–81.

Embrechts, P., C. Klüppelberg, and T. Mikosch, 2003, *Modelling Extremal Events for Insurance and Finance* (Berlin: Springer).

Favre, L. and J. Galeano, 2002, "Mean-modified Value-at-Risk Optimization with Hedge Funds", *Journal of Alternative Investments*, **5(2)**, pp 21–5.

Fisher, R. A. and L. H. C. Tippett, 1928, "Limiting Forms of the Frequency Distribution of Largest or Smallest Member of a Sample", *Proceedings of the Cambridge Philosophical Society*, **24**, pp 180–90.

Fung, W. and D. A. Hsieh, 1997, "Empirical Characteristics of Dynamic Trading Strategies: The Case of Hedge Funds", *Review of Financial Studies*, **10(2)**, pp 275–302.

Fung, W. and D. A. Hsieh, 2000, "Performance Characteristics of Hedge Funds and Commodity Funds: Natural vs. Spurious Biases", *Journal of Financial and Quantitative Analysis*, **35(3)**, pp 291–307.

Gençay, R., F. Selçuk, and A. Ulügulyağci, 2001, "EVIM: A Software Package for Extreme Value Analysis in Matlab", *Studies in Nonlinear Dynamics and Econometrics*, **5(3)**, pp 213–39.

Gençay, R., F. Selçuk, and A. Ulügulyağci, 2003, "High Volatility, Thick Tails and Extreme Value Theory in Value-at-Risk Estimation", *Insurance: Mathematics and Economics*, **33(2)**, pp 337–56.

Gumbel, E. J., 1958, *Statistics of Extremes* (New York: Columbia University Press).

Gupta, A. and B. Liang, 2005, "Do Hedge Funds Have Enough Capital? A Value-at-Risk Approach", *Journal of Financial Economics*, **77(1)**, pp 219–53.

Hildebrand, D. K., 1971, "Kurtosis Measures Bimodality?", *The American Statistician*, **25(1)**, pp 42–43.

Hill, B. M., 1975, "A Simple General Approach to Inference About the Tail of a Distribution", *Annals of Statistic*, **3(5)**, pp 1163–74.

Hosking, J. R. M., 1985, "Maximum-Likelihood Estimation of the Parameters of the Generalized Extreme-Value Distribution", *Applied Statistics*, **34(3)**, pp 301–10.

Hosking, J. R. M., 1990, "L-Moments: Analysis and Estimation of Distributions Using Linear Combinations of Order Statistics", *Journal of the Royal Statistical Society, Series B*, **52(1)**, pp 105–24.

Hosking, J. R. M. and J. R. Wallis, 1987, "Parameter and Quantile Estimation for Generalized Pareto Distribution", *Technometrics*, **29**, pp 339–49.

Hosking, J. R. M. J. R. Wallis and E. F. Wood, 1985, "Estimation of Generalized Extreme-Value Distribution by the Method of Probability-Weighted Moments", *Technometrics*, **27**, pp 251–61.

Jarque, C. M. and A. K. Bera, 1980, "Efficient Tests for Normality, Homoscedasticity and Serial Independence of Regression Residuals", *Economic Letters*, **6(3)**, pp 255–59.

Jenkinson, A. F., 1955, "The Frequency Distribution of Annual Maximum (or Minimum) Values of Meteorological Elements", *Quarterly Journal of the Royal Meteorology Society*, **87**, pp 145–58.

Johnson, N. L. and S. Kotz, 1985, *Encyclopedia of Statistical Sciences (Vol. 5)* (New York: John Wiley).

Jorion, P., 2000, "Risk Management Lessons from Long-Term Capital Management", *European Financial Management*, **6(3)**, pp 277–300.

Jorion, P., 2001, *Value at Risk* (New York: McGraw-Hill).

Këllezi, E. and M. Gilli, 2000, "Extreme Value Theory for Tail-Related Risk Measures", University of Geneva, *Working Paper*.

Lhabitant, F., 2003, "Hedge Funds: A Look Beyond the Sample", in Gregoriou, G. N., V. N. Karavas and F. Rouah (eds.), *Hedge Funds: Strategies, Risk Assessment, and Returns*, pp 209–34, (Whashington: Beard Books).

Liang, B., 1999, "On the Performance of Hedge Funds", *Financial Analysts Journal*, **55(4)**, pp 72–85.

Liang, B., 2000, "Hedge Funds: The Living and the Dead", *Journal of Financial and Quantitative Analysis*, **35(3)**, pp 309–27.

Longin, F. M., 1996, "The Asymptotic Distribution of Extreme Stock Market Returns", *Journal of Business*, **69(3)**, pp 383–408.

Longin, F. M., 2000, "From Value at Risk to Stress Testing: The Extreme Value Approach", *Journal of Banking and Finance*, **24(7)**, pp 1097–130.

Longin, F. and B. Solnik, 2001, "Extreme Correlation of International Equity Markets", *Journal of Finance*, **56(2)**, pp 649–76.

López de Prado, M. M. and A. Peijan, 2004, "Measuring Loss Potential of Hedge Fund Strategies", *Journal of Alternative Investments*, **7(1)**, pp 7–31.

Matthys, G. and J. Beirlant, 2003, "Estimating the Extreme Value Index and High Quantiles with Exponential Regression", *Statistica Sinica*, **13(3)**, pp 853–80.

McNeil, A. J. and R. Frey, 2000, "Estimation of Tail-Related Risk Measures for Heteroscedastic Financial Time Series: An Extreme Value Approach", *Journal of Empirical Finance*, **7(3–4)**, pp 271–300.

McNeil, A. J., R. Frey, and P. Embrechts, 2005, *Quantitative Risk Management* (New Jersey: Princeton University Press).

Pickands, J., 1975, "Statistical Inference Using Extreme Value Order Statistics", *Annals of Statistic*, **3(1)**, pp 119–31.

President's Working Group on Financial Markets, 1999, "Hedge Funds, Leverage, and the Lessons of Long-Term Capital Management".

Reiss, R. and M. Thomas, 2001, *Statistical Analysis of Extreme Values from Insurance, Finance, Hydrology and Other Fields* (Basel: Birkhäuser).

Ruppert, D., 1987, "What is Kurtosis?", *The American Statistician*, **41(1)**, pp 1–5.

Schmid, F. and M. Trede, 2003, "Simple Tests for Peakedness, Fat Tails and Leptokurtosis based on Quantiles", *Computational Statistics & Data Analysis*, **43(1)**, pp 1–12.

Sharpe, W. F., 1992, "Asset Allocation Management Style and Performance Measurement", *Journal of Portfolio Management*, **18(2)**, pp 7–19.

Smith, R. L., 1987, "Estimating Tails of Probability Distributions", *Annals of Statistic*, 15(3), pp 1174–207.

Theil, H., 1966, *Applied Economic Forecasting* (Amsterdam: North-Holland).

12

Managed Accounts or the Price of Liquid and Transparent Hedge Fund and CTA Investing

Florian Haberfelner; Dieter G. Kaiser; Karin Kisling

Benchmark Capital Management GmbH; Benchmark Alternative Strategies GmbH; Benchmark Capital Management GmbH

INTRODUCTION

Investing in hedge funds and CTAs used to be compared with investing in a black box. The ongoing institutionalisation has effectively changed the hedge fund industry in recent years. An ever increasing number of hedge funds show some portfolio transparency to their investors with respect to risk exposure and some even offer complete transparency. However, a greater majority of hedge funds demand prolonged notice and lock-up periods. The managed accounts approach is seen as an alternative to investing into an existing fund structure for banks and institutional investors. Here the hedge fund manager is acting on the basis of a trading adviser agreement whereby the manager's strategy is replicated on an account kept in the name of the investor. Managed accounts stem from the investors' need to weaken such properties of hedge fund investing as illiquidity, lacking regulation, and non-transparency and thus aim to minimise the operational risks. Managed accounts often provide transaction and portfolio transparency due to an electronic connection with the prime broker. This enables the investor to control the hedge fund regarding compliance with the investment guidelines (like maximum leverage, asset classes, asset regions, forbidden illiquid investments). The managed accounts investor is also capable of influencing all involved parties (eg, prime broker, custodian and auditor) and legal agreements (eg, prime brokerage agreement and ISDA swap agreements). In Germany managed accounts are very popular among investors since this is a way of efficiently handling the tax reporting required by investment law by directly booking all portfolio positions.

In addition, managed accounts allow the investor to interfere at any time to liquidate all positions within a short time frame assuming sufficient liquidity in the market. The transparency of the portfolio enables an independent position valuation by the administrator and furthermore serves as the basis of effective and active risk management. The permanent flow of information and the continuous access to the accounts is very attractive for the issuer issuing structured products with the underlying hedge fund. These properties allow for optimised hedging and precise risk control when dealing with capital guarantee products, including options. The providers of investable hedge fund indexes (eg, FTSE, MSCI, DOW Jones and S&P) mainly fall back on managed account platforms when selecting index constituents due to higher liquidity and better transparency. According to Pilz (2003) the challenges faced when founding managed accounts, like transaction volume or resources needed, should not be underestimated. For example, if a statistical arbitrage fund is replicated on a managed account, one has to deal with thousands of daily transactions implying increased settlement efforts. The valuation methods are developed by the managed account manager and the valuation interval is usually on a daily basis thereby causing difficulties and tremendous efforts if the manager does not trade liquid instruments or OTC contracts on a daily basis. If there is no thorough valuation, the question arises whether the portfolio transparency and the short valuation interval are meaningful. The requirements faced by the investor with respect to managing position information for a hedge fund portfolio are often underestimated. A sophisticated risk measurement system usually is about US$100,000 which does not include costs of implementation and maintenance.

Following Giraud (2005) the managed accounts concept exists in the following forms:

- *Standard Custodial Arrangements*: The assets are kept in a dedicated account managed by the hedge fund manager.

- *Prime Brokerage Custody*: The assets are kept in a dedicated account managed by the manager in the name of the fund. The prime broker may serve as an independent risk control and valuation authority.
- *Basic Managed Accounts*: The assets are kept in the books of the custodian in the name of the investor and the manager is given the right to manage this account within his mandate. Here the bank only serves as an independent valuation authority.
- *Managed Account Platforms*: The assets are kept in separate dedicated accounts in the investor's name and the bank or the respective platform manager takes care of back office, valuation and risk control tasks. The platform itself may engage in prime brokerage contracts.

This chapter focuses on managed account platforms. The article is structured as follows. The second section develops a managed account model and thereupon derives four hypotheses. The third section introduces the database. The fourth section tests the four hypotheses using different quantitative analysis tools. The final section states the results and derives some conclusions.

THE MANAGED ACCOUNT MODEL

Managed account platforms are often confronted with the fact that the choice of managers who are willing to execute their strategy on a transparent account (for the investor or at least for a third party) is limited. Some of the reasons for a hedge fund to opt for a managed account may include:

- outsourcing of marketing capacities towards the managed account platform;
- opening up an additional customer target group valuating transparency;
- additional external valuation and risk control authorities; and
- the manager's area of expertise covers liquid instruments which may be easily replicated within the managed account approach.

At the same time the increasing institutionalisation of the hedge fund industry has led to transparency which is frequently seen as a symbol of quality with respect to the trading approach and trading activities. Portfolio transparency may be interpreted as a function

sensitive information concerning his transactions shall not become public. This is what the second hypothesis is based upon.

Hypothesis 2: Compared with the hedge fund universe, managed accounts mainly reflect directional strategies.

It is assumed that the amount of capital in managed accounts by arbitrage-driven non-directional strategies is less than those of directional strategies. At the same time it is obvious that managed account providers will show efforts to lead successful funds to their platforms and therefore mainly fall back to known names with representative performance numbers to minimise the risk of selecting below average funds. Thus, it can be assumed that on managed account platforms only a few small, unknown and young funds following niche strategies are found. This justifies the third hypothesis.

Hypothesis 3: Managed accounts are managed mainly by known hedge funds.

At the same time, managed accounts offer a previously unknown level of flexibility regarding tactical asset allocation in the field of hedge funds. The allocation within a managed account solution may be adjusted on a weekly basis in most cases, also allowing for a weekly net inventory value reporting. This is not the case with established fund structures. In general fund of hedge funds accept subscriptions and redemptions only at specific times and most certainly not for every trading day. According to an investigation of Hedge Fund Research (2004), 78.90% of hedge funds accept monthly subscriptions but only 46.36% accept monthly redemptions. Additionally, there are individual notice periods which have to be met on every valuation day. The notice period for subscriptions (five trading days) is far less than that of redemptions (about 30 to 35 trading days). In the hedge fund domain it is usual for orders to state a certain amount of capital as opposed to orders based on specified number of shares, since net asset values of single hedge funds (and thus also NAVs of fund of hedge funds) are often produced with a delay of four weeks. Only then investors will know how many shares they will actually receive. When taking this into account, managed accounts offer a genuine liquidity advantage with respect to traditional hedge fund structures. In general, restrictive subscription and redemption terms result in lower cash reserves and reduced settlement features. Hence, the performance of hedge funds accepting illiquidity in their trading strategy and transferring it on to the investor should be higher than those not doing so. Hence, investors holding illiquid positions in traditional funds should be compensated with a liquidity premium compared to investors in managed accounts. This results in the fourth hypothesis.

Hypothesis 4: Managed account investors do not collect a liquidity premium.

Based on all four hypotheses we conclude that – when proven correct – the investment universe of an institutional investor using a managed account platform should differ strongly from the investment universe he would face using traditional hedge fund investments.

DATA BASIS

In order to derive some statements concerning composition, performance and directional type of managed accounts compared to the broad hedge fund universe, we worked with two comparative universes. First, we deal with a managed account universe composed of several platforms and second, with a renowned hedge fund database. Performance time series of managed account platforms are only available for a comparatively short period of time. Only 10 accounts in the universe in use have already existed prior to the year 2000. Consequently, the observation period for the analysis executed had to be chosen comparably short, covering January 2003 to January 2006. Thus it was ensured that the managed account universe was comprised of at least 100 hedge funds at any point in time during the period in question.

The analysis summarises the performance time series of five managed account platforms, one of which was set up in 1998, three in 2002 and one in 2004. The smallest platform in Table 1 contains 32, the biggest platform contains 166 whereas on all platforms the mean was 66.8 and the median, 39 managed account single funds. Altogether 334 hedge funds managed as managed accounts were available and these were used to construct a managed account

Table 1 Description of five managed account platforms of the data basis

	Mean	Median	Min	Max	Std Dev
Number of managed accounts	66.80	39	32	166	56.58
Assets under custody (in US$ billion)	5.22	1.80	0.4	21	8.86
Fund age (months)	26.39	25.77	19.97	37.16	6.74
Minimum investment (in US$ thousand)	420	250	100	1000	354.61
Platform fees (p.a.)	0.82	0.85	0.5	1	0.21
Management fees (p.a.)	1.48	1.49	1.36	1.55	0.08
Performance fees (p.a.)	20.42	20	19.9	21.5	0.70
Closed funds (%)	4.41	4.31	2.78	6.25	1.69
Defunct funds (%)	11.17	9.31	6.63	19.44	5.85

universe. In the case funds overlap, ie show up on more than one platform, the fund with the longer history was kept in the universe. When there was an anonymous fund name or name of the fund company was missing, a possible overlap was investigated using correlation analysis. If there was a correlation of 0.9 or higher, the respective unknown fund was eliminated from the universe. Hence, there remained a universe of 259 managed accounts.

On the single hedge fund level there are three funds represented in four managed account platforms (Manager: Graham Capital Management, Sparx Asset Management, Winton Capital Management), six funds represented in three platforms (Argent Funds Group, Aspect Capital, Bridgewater Associates, Campbell & Company, Okumus Capital, Para Advisors) and 54 represented in two managed account platforms. The largest overlaps exist within the strategies global macro and long/short equity as illustrated in Table 2. All managed accounts in the universe are denominated in US$ and their performance history is net of all fees. Due to the enormous number of funds and the tremendous assets under management (US$25 billion) it is assumed that the managed account universe reaches a high level of representativity.

For the comparative universe, Eurekahedge is used and is adjusted in the following way: When a fund was found in several classes, only the US$ class was considered in the hedge fund universe. Therefore, there was a comparative universe of more than 2,600 hedge funds. The return time series of all hedge funds

Table 2 Managed accounts not considered in the universe sorted by platform and peer group

	MAP 1	MAP 2	MAP 3	MAP 4	MAP 5	Total
CA		2	1	1	3	7
ED	1	3	1	3	4	12
FI				1	1	2
MF/GM		7	6	9	3	25
LS	3	5	6	6	5	25
MN		3		1		4
Total	4	20	14	21	16	75

denominated in a currency other than in US$ were adjusted by the difference in interest and were thereby transformed on a US$ hedged basis. Since the calculations were based on the actual constituents of the database, the appearance of survivorship bias was unavoidable. The same also holds true for the managed account platforms, so the results should be comparable. We observe 6% closed funds in the Eurekahedge database which could be a hint that funds seeking fresh capital might be overrepresented (self-reporting bias).

For the peer group analysis hedge funds and managed accounts were divided into the following strategies: Equity market neutral (EM), long/short equity (LS), managed futures/global macro (GM), convertible arbitrage (CA), fixed income arbitrage (FI) and event driven (ED). When the classification or the strategy description was not sufficient, they were integrated depending on the correlation with the Edhec indexes. In case a fund could not be integrated properly (correlation < 0.9), it was classified as "other" and therefore only made it into the results of the respective overall universe (COM). The same was done for peer groups which could not be considered due to a lack of examples in the managed account platforms (multi strategy for instance). Whether the universe in use is representative for the entire hedge fund universe was evaluated executing an OLS regression analysis against the Edhec strategy indexes. The Edhec indexes were chosen since according to Lhabitant (2004) they show the highest degree of representativity of the entire hedge fund universe. All following investigations only use funds and managed accounts with performance data of at least 12 months.

Table 3 Results of a regression analysis of hedge fund peer group indexes *vs* Edhec indexes

	MN	LS	GM	FI	CA	ED	COM
Correlation	0.76	0.99	0.98	0.69	0.92	0.97	0.95
R^2 of the regression (%)	57.87	97.14	95.76	48.16	84.10	94.63	89.97
p-Value (*F*-statistic) (%)	0.00	0.00	0.00	0.00	0.00	0.00	0.00
Alpha (%)	0.14	0.15	0.11	0.45	0.45	0.30	0.20
p-Value of alpha (%)	4.30	0.89	11.18	0.00	0.00	0.00	1.98
Beta	0.67	1.04	0.92	0.68	0.84	0.99	1.17
p-Value of beta (%)	0.00	0.00	0.00	0.00	0.00	0.00	0.00

The results show that all regressions are statistically significant. The *p*-value (*F*-statistic) for all branches is $<0.1\%$. For a majority of strategies, the correlations are above 0.9, whereas the – significant – betas usually lie between 0.8 and 1.2. The peer groups equity market neutral and fixed income arbitrage show the least degree of representativity regarding the entire hedge fund universe with correlations of 0.76 and 0.69 and betas are 0.67 and 0.68 respectively.

RESULTS

When comparing the number of funds in the various managed accounts with those in the various hedge fund databases, hypothesis one is confirmed. The considered MA platforms contain altogether 334 hedge funds and 259 without overlaps. The high degree of overlaps (22.45%) between the single MA platforms underlines as well that the managed accounts represent only a small part of the entire hedge fund universe. By comparison, the Eurekahedge database only produces overlaps of about one tenth.

To verify the second hypothesis – managed accounts mainly reflect directional strategies – a peer group comparison analysis of managed accounts *vs* the Eurekahedge universe by number of funds is performed. Table 4 shows that there are substantial differences. Obvious differences can be seen within the sub-strategies' long/short equity (−10.66%), convertible arbitrage (8.12%) and event driven (8.19%). The strategy managed futures/global macro (1.95%) shows the smallest divergence. The main strategies of the MA platforms are long/short equity (33.20%) and managed futures/global macro (20.46%). However, the percentage of non-

Table 4 Strategy allocations

	Managed accounts		Eurekahedge		MA-EH
	Percentage	**Number**	**Percentage**	**Number**	**Percentage**
Equity market neutral	6.18	16	4.04	108	2.14
Long-short equity	33.20	86	43.87	1,173	−10.66
Managed futures/ global macro	20.46	53	18.51	495	1.95
Fixed income arbitrage	9.27	24	7.29	195	1.97
Convertible arbitrage	10.81	28	2.69	72	8.12
Event driven	16.60	43	8.41	225	8.19
Other	3.47	9	15.18	406	−11.71
Total	1	259	1	2,674	

Table 5 Percentage of funds featuring a significant dependence towards a market index (error probability 5%)

	Managed accounts (%)	Eurekahedge (%)
MSCI world index	43.72	50.90
S&P 500 index	36.74	44.04
JPM GGB index	12.56	16.77
CRB commodities	7.91	10.43

directional strategies, especially equity market neutral (6.18%), convertible arbitrage (10.81%) and event driven (16.60%) is higher than expected. Especially compared with the Eurekahedge universe, the percentage of directional strategies there is higher and that of non-directional strategies lower.

This is a sign that the second hypothesis cannot be accepted. As already suggested on pp **000–0**, when classifying single funds the respective statement regarding their directional style should only be interpreted as a tendency. Hence, we attempted to quantify it implementing a correlation and regression analysis. The MSCI World, the S&P 500, the JPMorgan Global Government Bond Index and the CRB All Commodities Spot Index were chosen as market indexes. First, correlations and regressions were conducted for every fund and every managed account on an individual basis. Afterwards the median of the results of the respective peer group

Table 6 Correlation results

	Managed accounts (%)							Eurekahedge (%)						
	MN	LS	GM	FI	CA	ED	COM	MN	LS	GM	FI	CA	ED	COM
MSCI world	9.32	34.61	25.77	21.54	19.50	42.78	29.59	11.48	39.66	22.59	15.23	23.49	41.93	31.66
S&P 500	3.96	29.34	24.42	16.21	10.67	37.31	24.72	8.38	34.30	19.68	11.26	17.75	38.31	27.04
JPM GGB	−2.20	8.59	16.44	15.03	21.37	20.36	13.29	7.41	10.63	17.96	16.59	20.57	19.49	14.09
CRB index	13.96	4.94	8.24	11.52	27.52	16.46	11.67	6.73	10.51	14.57	12.08	28.15	11.31	12.36

Table 7 Regression results

	Managed accounts							Eurekahedge						
	MN	LS	GM	FI	CA	ED	COM	MN	LS	GM	FI	CA	ED	COM
MSCI world index														
R^2 of the regression (%)	7.20	25.22	8.11	3.77	4.10	19.77	11.37	4.12	21.46	7.13	4.38	5.01	18.60	12.71
p-Value (*F*-statistic) (%)	12.67	1.25	13.31	28.70	29.58	2.16	9.28	28.26	0.84	12.03	26.93	21.61	1.51	4.53
Alpha (%)	0.28	0.24	−0.12	0.36	−0.08	0.16	0.14	0.29	0.50	0.17	0.57	0.31	0.74	0.44
p-Value of alpha (%)	19.51	34.13	53.28	32.42	44.94	23.43	36.73	23.87	21.27	44.53	1.30	21.96	1.47	19.08
Beta	0.07	0.30	0.31	0.05	0.10	0.17	0.17	0.03	0.42	0.27	0.04	0.09	0.23	0.24
p-Value of beta (%)	12.67	1.25	13.31	28.70	29.58	2.16	9.28	28.26	0.84	12.03	26.93	21.61	1.51	4.53
S&P 500 index														
R^2 of the regression (%)	4.35	20.16	6.85	5.42	2.51	14.40	8.03	3.44	15.92	6.29	3.22	3.23	15.89	9.42
p-Value (*F*-statistic) (%)	22.77	3.78	15.06	37.06	40.23	3.25	14.39	33.53	2.79	17.59	31.05	30.71	2.76	9.31
Alpha (%)	0.38	0.39	−0.05	0.31	0.04	0.24	0.19	0.34	0.67	0.28	0.63	0.41	0.87	0.56
p-Value of alpha (%)	16.38	25.50	57.76	17.75	49.46	11.46	33.19	19.82	11.24	39.87	0.79	14.15	0.66	11.16
Beta	0.05	0.27	0.35	0.04	0.05	0.16	0.16	0.03	0.39	0.26	0.03	0.08	0.21	0.23
p-Value of beta (%)	22.77	3.78	15.06	37.06	40.23	3.25	14.39	33.53	2.79	17.59	31.05	30.71	2.76	9.31
JPM GGB index														
R^2 of the regression (%)	3.63	2.38	3.97	6.55	4.88	4.59	3.72	2.14	2.55	5.56	5.28	6.38	5.02	3.69
p-Value (*F*-statistic) (%)	35.64	47.31	30.90	20.70	21.81	25.30	34.47	44.63	37.33	18.78	22.88	17.07	22.18	29.94
Alpha (%)	0.41	0.63	0.08	0.35	−0.01	0.34	0.33	0.36	1.00	0.34	0.65	0.33	1.08	0.75
p-Value of alpha (%)	14.13	12.41	46.53	12.33	49.37	5.20	23.78	18.57	3.65	34.02	0.29	11.12	0.23	5.02
Beta	−0.01	0.12	0.25	0.09	0.12	0.11	0.11	0.03	0.14	0.31	0.08	0.16	0.18	0.15
p-Value of beta (%)	35.64	47.31	30.90	20.70	21.81	25.30	34.47	44.63	37.33	18.78	22.88	17.07	22.18	29.94
CRB commodities														
R^2 of the regression (%)	1.66	1.75	2.75	4.79	9.25	3.10	2.83	1.74	1.76	2.49	2.79	8.60	2.49	2.24
p-Value (*F*-statistic) (%)	44.72	51.93	46.05	34.55	10.57	48.00	42.31	48.08	48.25	38.06	38.63	10.26	42.30	41.64
Alpha (%)	0.29	0.66	0.08	0.31	−0.05	0.36	0.30	0.35	1.01	0.34	0.62	0.28	1.06	0.75
p-Value of alpha (%)	8.93	13.66	55.35	33.08	45.05	4.42	22.90	15.61	4.14	36.36	0.33	16.89	0.27	5.72
Beta	0.05	0.06	0.14	0.07	0.17	0.09	0.10	0.03	0.12	0.21	0.05	0.18	0.10	0.11
p-Value of beta (%)	44.72	51.93	46.05	34.55	10.57	48.00	42.31	48.08	48.25	38.06	38.63	10.26	42.30	41.64

Table 8 Overlaps of managed account platforms with the Eurekahedge database

	MAP 1		MAP 2		MAP 3		MAP 4		MAP 5		Total (without overlap)	
	Total	**Eureka (%)**	**Total**	**Eureka (%)**	**Total**	**Eureka (%)**	**Total**	**Eureka (%)**	**Total**	**Eureka (%)**	**Total**	**Eureka (%)**
Convertible arbitrage	14	57.14	4	100.00	6	0.00	5	60.00	6	66.67	28	53.57
Event driven	26	73.08	8	37.50	5	40.00	10	20.00	6	66.67	43	55.81
Fixed income arbitrage	16	25.00	3	33.33	0	0.00	4	50.00	3	100.00	24	37.50
Global macro	40	57.50	8	75.00	6	0.00	18	44.44	6	83.33	53	54.72
Long/short equity	61	40.98	11	72.73	10	50.00	19	47.37	10	70.00	86	43.02
Market neutral	9	11.11	5	80.00	0	0.00	5	60.00	1	0.00	16	31.25
Total											250	47.60

was calculated and displayed in Tables 6 and 7. The results show a surprisingly homogeneous directional style of the managed accounts and the hedge funds and not – as expected – a higher directional value of the managed accounts.

The correlations for both universes are on a similar level for every strategy. Exceptions are the correlations of the strategies long/short equity and event driven with the MSCI World and the S&P 500 which however are not statistically significant due to a lack of a sufficient number of observations. With respect to the MSCI World, the regressions of both universes for the classes' long/short equity and event driven are significant with an error probability of less than 5%. The respective betas are 0.3 (LS) and 0.17 (ED) in the managed account universe and 0.42 (LS) and 0.23 (ED) in the Eurekahedge universe. Only long/short equity and event driven show a significant dependence towards the S&P 500. Here there are betas of 0.27 (LS) and 0.16 (ED) for managed accounts and 0.39 (LS) and 0.21 (ED) for hedge funds.

None of the peer group medians show a statistically significant dependence towards one of the market indexes. Among the medians of the respective total universe, only the Eurekahedge universe is significant against the MSCI World with an error probability of less than 5%. Even if the results for both universes are quite similar, a close look reveals a stronger directional drift of the Eurekahedge universe. This is backed up by Table 5. It shows the percentage of those funds of the respective universe featuring a significant regression result at a 95% confidence level towards one of the market indexes used. Hence, one is unable to find any results backing up hypothesis 2 which must be rejected.

The third hypothesis claims that renown hedge funds dominate managed account platforms. To back up this hypothesis it is assumed that a large part of public databases consist of known hedge funds. Hence the reputation of a hedge fund is modelled via its existence in the Eurekahedge database. It can be noticed that the adjusted managed account universe (without the overlaps of single funds between the platforms) is made up of known hedge funds to a degree of 47.60%. Considering the strategies convertible arbitrage (55.6%), event driven (55.8%) and global macro/managed futures (54.7%), the overlaps concerning the Eurekahedge database are above average. The strategy equity market neutral shows the lowest degree of overlap (31.3%). At the single strategy level it is noticeable that the degree of overlap ranges from 11% up to 83% (samples of less than five are not considered to be significant). Regarding the results, among the 75 excluded funds 57 (76%) are part of the Eurekahedge universe, not forgetting that there is no universal hedge fund database in existence. Liang (2000) shows for example that the overlap of the Hedge Fund Research and TASS databases only amounted to between 28.6% and 40.0%. Therefore, if we were to include other databases are included in the research, one would reach a higher degree of accuracy. Taking this into account the third hypothesis is considered – managed account platforms mainly consist of known hedge funds – to be confirmed.

We now investigate the size of funds in the managed account universe as well as in the Eurekahedge universe since a close connection is assumed between the reputation of a fund and its capital under management. Table 9 shows that the funds in managed account platforms are more than twice as large in size compared with the average hedge fund. There are various academic studies covering the impact of fund size on the performance – the results are very heterogeneous. Gregoriou and Rouah (2002) as well as Koh *et al* (2003) do not find evidence of a significant influence whereas Brorsen and Harri (2004) as well as Ammann and Moerth (2005) conclude that hedge fund returns decline with growing market capitalisation and it therefore is advisable for hedge funds to decline fresh capital in order to maintain their performance. De Souza and Gokcan (2003) use a regression of the TASS database that the assets under management have a positive influence on the performance of a hedge fund. Amenc *et al* (2003) find evidence that the average alpha of large funds exceeds the average alpha of small funds. According to Getmansky (2004) there is a positive and concave relationship between current performance and past fund size.

Comparing the liquidity of managed accounts and established fund structures we are able to confirm the assumption that managed account investors dispose of a high degree of flexibility concerning tactical asset allocation. Since the Eurekahedge database has no data about the liquidity of single funds, the Hedge Fund Intelligence database (HFI) is used as a comparison tool. The period of notice of MAs is weekly in 68.0% of all cases but with

Table 9 Size of the funds in the Eurekahedge and managed account universes

	Median	Min	Max	Mean	Std Dev
Eurekahedge total (in Mio US$)	43	0.01	7167	162.68	381.61
MA funds in Eureka (in Mio US$)	110	3	5359	322.40	624.51

Table 10 Notice periods of managed account platforms and comparison funds

	MA (%)	HFI (%)
Weekly	68.0	
Monthly	32.0	39.37
Quarterly		26.58
Yearly		2.61
n.a.		30.05

funds of the HFI database it turns out to be monthly (39.37%) or even quarterly (26.58%).

The higher level of liquidity presumably goes along with a lower liquidity premium. To find evidence for this hypothesis, we consider the average returns between funds in MA platforms and the Eurekahedge index. A positive return difference is assumed to be equivalent to a liquidity premium. The results presented in Table 11 consist of single fund calculations and peer group averages and universe (COM) averages, respectively. The peer group results show that on average the returns of the Eurekahedge are higher but the respective volatility is higher as well. The percentage of positive months also is higher for all peer groups of the hedge fund universe. All but one of the peer groups of the managed account universe displays a negative skew and it is positive for all peer groups of the comparative universe. On the other hand, the kurtosis of all but one peer group of the Eurekahedge database is higher.

The difference in average returns really is striking when you consider its dimension. The results show that in the time period

Table 11 Descriptive statistics, risk and performance measures

	Managed accounts							Eurekahedge						
	MN	LS	GM	FI	CA	ED	COM	MN	LS	GM	FI	CA	ED	COM
Descriptive statistics[a]														
Average return (p.m.) (%)	0.37	0.53	0.31	0.37	0.09	0.54	0.41	0.46	1.28	0.72	0.78	0.67	1.40	1.04
Average return (p.a.) (%)	4.49	6.59	3.83	4.56	1.05	6.67	5.02	5.64	16.51	8.98	9.78	8.38	18.22	13.21
Volatility (%)	3.97	7.78	13.32	4.60	4.51	5.07	7.73	5.68	11.15	13.51	4.77	5.89	7.94	10.11
Best month (%)	2.90	4.90	8.05	2.11	2.88	3.44	4.68	4.10	8.89	9.86	4.22	4.63	7.08	8.04
Worst month (%)	−2.20	−3.75	−6.73	−1.57	−2.63	−2.81	−3.78	−3.06	−5.09	−7.30	−2.21	−2.93	−3.06	−4.82
Positive months (%)	60.04	64.33	52.31	69.22	56.33	68.31	61.28	64.07	67.16	58.78	79.38	66.60	77.03	67.45
Skewness	−0.10	−0.08	0.13	−0.12	−0.12	−0.15	−0.05	0.14	0.21	0.19	0.18	0.06	0.28	0.21
Kurtosis	0.55	0.41	0.34	0.58	0.58	1.59	0.64	2.07	1.17	1.27	2.46	0.87	1.36	1.43
Jarque-Bera p-Value (%)	52.91	50.36	46.79	47.37	50.94	35.42	47.39	36.79	43.97	41.31	26.33	38.65	33.55	39.77
Risk measures[a]														
Mtl. Standard deviation (%)	1.15	2.25	3.84	1.33	1.30	1.46	2.23	1.64	3.22	3.90	1.38	1.70	2.29	2.92
Mtl. Downside deviation (%) (MAR=2%)	0.69	1.40	2.53	0.85	0.97	0.87	1.43	0.97	1.55	2.35	0.65	0.90	0.89	1.49
Maximum drawdown (%)	−4.39	−7.34	−14.82	−2.46	−7.72	−4.16	−7.74	−5.96	−8.44	−14.50	−3.65	−6.64	−4.58	−8.59
VaR (p.m.; 99%) (%)	−2.30	−4.69	−8.63	−2.72	−2.94	−2.87	−4.78	−3.36	−6.21	−8.35	−2.42	−3.28	−3.93	−5.75
CF–VaR (p.m.; 99%) (%)	−2.26	−4.76	−8.04	−3.01	−3.07	−3.20	−4.77	−3.25	−5.10	−7.75	−2.16	−3.12	−3.14	−4.88
Assym. Indicator[b]	1.07	1.59	1.34	1.69	0.87	1.85	1.37	1.15	1.79	1.49	1.47	1.12	2.75	1.71
Performance measures[b]														
Sharpe Ratio (r = 2%)	0.38	0.84	0.03	0.73	−0.17	0.86	0.37	0.55	1.24	0.45	1.66	0.63	1.97	1.08
Sortino Ratio (MAR = 2%)	0.61	1.55	−0.07	1.34	−0.28	1.54	0.54	0.82	2.65	0.65	3.23	1.00	5.49	2.15
Calmar Ratio	1.04	1.63	0.14	2.83	0.15	1.76	0.88	1.09	2.13	0.70	3.03	0.96	4.61	1.86
Omega (MAR = 0.25% p.m.)	1.09	1.69	0.94	1.38	0.74	1.43	1.10	1.31	2.36	1.27	2.97	1.37	4.46	2.02

[a]The results are representing the mean for the results calculated for the individual funds.
[b]The results are representing the median for the results calculated for the individual funds.

observed, managed accounts produced less than half of the return of the broad hedge fund universe. Equity market neutral is yet the best performing peer group compared with the Eurekahedge (4.49% *vs* 5.64%). There are especially large return gaps in the strategies event driven (11.55%) and long/short equity (9.92%). One must not neglect a possible survivorship bias of the Eurekahedge database, but even if we assume a historically extreme survivorship bias of 4.41% as detected by Malkiel and Saha (2005) in Eurekahedge and 0% in managed accounts, there still is an excess return of the Eurekahedge universe compared with the managed account universe, except for the strategy equity market neutral. If in this context we consider the selection bias of hedge fund indexes as a negative distortion of the sample condition as discovered and calculated to be 1.4% per annum by Fung and Hsieh (2000), the underperformance of managed accounts would increase again. According to Ackermann, McEnally and Ravenscraft (1999) survivorship and self-selection bias would neutralise themselves almost completely.

Several investigations concerning the correlation between risk adjusted performance of hedge funds and long capital lock up periods back up the result that there is indeed a high positive correlation. Schneeweis *et al* (2001) as well as De Souza and Gokcan (2003) conclude that there are signs that lock up periods do have a positive influence on the performance that hedge funds. Kaiser and Kisling (2005) conclude that with equity based hedge fund strategies extended lock up periods go hand in hand with higher risk adjusted performance. Kaiser and Kisling (2006) find evidence of a positive correlation between extended capital lock up periods, higher Sharpe ratios and higher management and performance fees. Aragon (2004) concludes his investigations stating that yearly hedge fund returns with capital lock up periods exceed those without by about 4%. Agarwal *et al* (2004) find that for hedge funds, on average, with a decent track record there is less capital inflow if there is a capital lock up period. The results coincide with the observation of Liang (1998) that hedge funds with a large number of assets under management, long capital lock up periods and short track records outperform other hedge funds.

However, the assumption that a return difference only indicates a liquidity premium is controversial. Additionally, comparing the volatilities with their return counterparts it is obvious that the risk of all Eurekahedge index strategies exceeds that of the MA platforms. A higher return might thus solely be the consequence of higher risk. We take this factor into consideration by using the Sharpe ratio. Table 11 shows the noticeable differences. Thus, the statement that the Eurekahedge investments possess a higher liquidity premium cannot be rejected. Regarding the Sharpe ratios, the biggest differences are with the non-directional strategies, such as, event driven (1.1), fixed income arbitrage (0.93) and convertible arbitrage (0.8). This proves Hypothesis 4.

Better insight into the risk properties of both comparative universes is given by Panel 2 of Table 11, where selected risk measures for each peer group are displayed. The results show the average of the single fund results. The risk measures indicate less risk in managed account investments and thus back-up the statement concerning volatility. In line with volatility, the standard deviation of all peer groups of the Eurekahedge universe is higher. The same holds for the absolute (analytically determined) value-at-risk. The results of the downside deviation are well balanced, and half of the peer groups show a higher risk for the Eurekahedge funds. For four of the six peer groups this also holds for the maximum drawdown. The Cornish–Fisher adjusted VaR including their skewness and kurtosis extension is higher for exactly half of the Eurekahedge peer groups.

In Panel 3 of Table 11 both universes are compared by using the Sharpe ratio and various other performance measures. Now the crucial measure is the median of the single fund returns instead of the mean. Our reasoning is that a single fund with a risk measure close to zero may cause a substantial distortion for the respective performance measure and therefore for the average of the peer group as well. The following parameters are used: the Sortino ratio which uses the downside deviation for risk adjustment; the Calmar ratio which uses maximum drawdown; and Keating and Shadwick's Omega (2002). No matter which performance measure is considered, the results are identical. All performance measures of each single peer group clearly show a better performance for the Eurekahedge universe. The slightly better risk measures of the managed account universe could not compensate for the lower returns in the investigation period.

CONCLUSION

The popularity of investing in hedge funds and CTAs via managed accounts is based upon various advantages such as position transparency, external risk management and an increased liquidity brought about by this form of investment. This empirical study is the first to find evidence that these advantages coincide with high opportunity costs. First, the investment universe accessible to investors via managed account platforms is clearly smaller than the entire hedge fund universe. Hence, after identifying and removing the overlaps, it is found that only 259 hedge funds are accessible on five renowned managed account platforms whereas considering the entire hedge fund universe, we are looking at 6,000 to 10,000 single hedge funds. The assumption that mainly directional hedge fund strategies are replicated on managed account platforms could not be confirmed. At the same time, evidence is found that hedge funds on different managed account platforms predominantly belong to large target funds of renowned hedge fund management companies. Finally, we show empirically that in the observation period managed account returns turned out to be only about half of the broad hedge fund universe returns. The only peer group whose returns turned out to be competitive compared with the Eurekahedge universe is the equity market neutral strategy. We observed especially large return gaps (liquidity premiums) with the strategies event driven (11.55%) and long/short equity (9.92%). Even after a survivorship bias adjustment of these returns a substantial excess return of the Eurekahedge universe compared with the managed account universe remains.

Should the investor decide to pay this price, then the feeling of security conveyed by a managed account is undisputed since it is constantly under surveillance by an external risk management. The risk management systems implemented by these platforms undoubtedly are of great value for the investor. All these benefits notwithstanding, the investor should not neglect the risk inherent in the platform itself. The platform's very nature concentrates third party risks. As can be observed in the current case of the platform provider Plusfunds, it is highly advisable to investigate managed account platforms with respect to counterparty risk prior to any engagement. The platform provider Plusfunds, for example, got into trouble after the bankruptcy of its exclusive broker Refco in October 2005. The results of the empirical study should encourage investors to thoroughly question whether the advantages of investing into hedge funds or CTAs via managed accounts outweigh the less obvious disadvantages like the missed opportunity to collect liquidity premiums.

REFERENCES

Ackermann, C., R. McEnally, and D. Ravenscraft, 1999, "The Performance of Hedge Funds: Risk, Return, and Incentives", *Journal of Finance*, **54(3)**, pp 833–74.

Agarwal, V. and N. Y. Naik, 2000, "Multi-period Performance Persistence Analysis of Hedge Funds", *Journal of Financial and Quantitative Analysis*, **35(3)**, pp 327–42.

Agarwal, V., N. D. Daniel, and N. Y. Naik, 2004, "Flows, Performance, and Managerial Incentives in Hedge Funds", Working Paper, Georgia State University.

Amenc, N., S. Curtis, and L. Martellini, 2003, "The Alpha and the Omega of Hedge Fund Performance Measurement", Working Paper, Edhec Business School, February.

Amenc, N., P. Malaise, L. Martellini, and M. Vaissié, 2004, "Fund of Hedge Fund Reporting – A Return-Based Approach to Fund of Hedge Fund Reporting", Discussion Paper, Edhec Business School.

Ammann, M. and P. Moerth, 2005, "Impact of Fund Size on Hedge Fund Performance", *Journal of Asset Management*, **6(3)**, pp 219–38.

Aragon, G. O., 2004, "Share Restrictions and Asset Pricing: Evidence from the Hedge Fund Industry", Working Paper, The Wallace E. Carroll School of Management, Boston College.

Brorsen, B. W. and A. Harri, 2004, "Performance Persistence and the Source of Returns for Hedge Funds", *Applied Financial Economics*, **14(2)**, pp 131–41.

De Souza, C. and S. Gokcan, 2003, "How Some Hedge Fund Characteristics Impact Performance", *AIMA Journal*, September.

Fung, W. and D. A. Hsieh, 2000, "Performance Characteristics of Hedge Funds and Commodity Funds: Natural vs Spurious Biases", *Journal of Financial and Quantitative Analysis*, **35(3)**, pp 291–308.

Getmansky, M., 2004, "The Life Cycle of Hedge Funds: Fund Flows, Size and Performance", Working Paper, MIT Sloan School of Management.

Giraud, J. R., 2005, "Mitigating Hedge Funds' Operational Risks – Benefits and Limitations of Managed Account Platforms", Working Paper, Edhec Business School, June.

Gregoriou, G. N. and F. Rouah, 2002, "Large versus Small Hedge Funds: Does Size Affect Performance?", *Journal of Alternative Investments*, **5(5)**, pp 75–7.

Hedge Fund Research, 2004, HFR Industry Report Q2 2004.

Jaeger, L., 2006, "Aktives Risikomanagement und Transparenz in einem Hedgefonds-Portfolio", in M. Busack and D. G. Kaiser (eds), *Handbuch Alternative Investments*, Band 1, Gabler Verlag, Wiesbaden, pp 393–426.

Kaiser, D. G., 2004, *Hedgefonds – Entmystifizierung einer Anlageklasse – Strukturen, Chancen Risiken*, Wiesbaden: Gabler Verlag.

Kaiser, D. G. and K. Kisling, 2005, "Der Einfluss von Kapitalbindungsfristen auf die Sharpe Ratio aktienbasierter Hedgefonds-Strategien", *Absolut | report*, **28**, pp 26–33.

Kaiser, D. G. and K. Kisling, 2006, "Einflussfaktoren der risikoadjustierten Wertentwicklung von Hedgefonds", in M. Busack and D. G. Kaiser (eds), *Handbuch Alternative Investments*, Band 1, Wiesbaden: Gabler Verlag, pp 299–318.

Keating, C. and W. Shadwick, 2002, "Omega: A Universal Performance Measure", *Journal of Performance Measurement*, **6(2)**, pp 59–84.

Koh, F., W. Koh, and M. Teo, 2003, "Asian Hedge Funds: Return Persistence, Style, and Fund Characteristics", Working Paper, Singapore Management University.

Liang, B., 1998, "On the Performance of Hedge Funds", Working Paper, Case Western Reserve University.

Lhabitant, F. S., 2004, "Testing the Representativity of Pure Style Indices", Working Paper, Edhec Business School.

Malkiel, B. G. and A. Saha, 2005, "Hedge Funds: Risk and Return", Working Paper, Princeton University.

Pilz, A., 2003, "In Quest of Transparency", *AIMA Journal*, June.

Sharpe, W. F., 1992, "Asset Allocation: Management Style and Performance Measurement", *Journal of Portfolio Management*, **18(2)**, pp 7–19.

Schneeweis, T., H. Kazemi, and G. Martin, 2001, "Understanding Hedge Fund Performance: Research Results and Rules of Thumb for the Institutional Investor", Working Paper, Center for International Securities and Derivatives Markets (CISDM), Isenberg School of Management, University of Massachussets.

13

Hedge Funds Investing in Emerging Markets

Mehmet Orhan; Turker Tekten

Economics Department, Fatih University; Standard Bank

INTRODUCTION

The term "hedge fund" can be traced back to 1949 when Alfred Winslow Jones coined the term to describe investment companies which hedged their risk by buying undervalued stocks and selling overvalued ones (see Caldwell 1995; Fung and Hsieh 1999; Do *et al* 2005). Over the last decade the number of hedge funds has been growing exponentially. Hedge funds today are more oriented towards making more profit than eliminating or mitigating risk. When A. W. Jones established the first hedge fund in the USA he used leverage and short selling simultaneously. He categorised the sources of risk in stock investments into two: the risk from mistakenly selected stocks to invest upon, and the risk of a change in the market. Jones had collected a bundle of stocks to hedge against a drop in the market. He bought what he considered were undervalued stocks and short sold what he thought were overvalued. This was a strategy that hedged his fund against risk to some extent, more than half a century ago. He held short positions to benefit if the market went down, and could profit regardless of the market conditions.

Hedge funds are investment vehicles that use leverage and derivatives while providing absolute returns for wealthy individuals and institutions, but are not subject to the same regulations as mutual funds. Thus, they are free to speculate in equity, debt and currency markets around the world. Similar to mutual funds, there are a variety of different hedge fund classifications. Naturally, each hedge fund strategy is different from one another because returns they generate and volatility behaviour vary.

Many hedge funds make use of price discrepancies or arbitrage to take advantage of market imbalances to profit from price inefficiencies. Typically the global macro classification, has a large appetite for investing in emerging markets where economic policies often display instability resulting in high inflation rates and changing growth rates. These opportunities are usually triggered by government policies that lead to macroeconomic shocks to economies as well as some international conditions. Since many of these activities have not much to do with the general trend in a market, hedge funds benefit from actions that are uncorrelated to the general trend of the markets.

Hedge funds investing in emerging markets represent about one twentieth or 373 out of a total of 8,611 hedge funds. In 2005, total assets of hedge funds in emerging markets was US$44.5546 billion which constitute 4.03% of all hedge funds (with the total of US$1.1 trillion). Hedge funds have important roles for emerging markets because they provide liquidity when traditional capital is sceptical about investing in specific emerging market countries due to high risk. Therefore, emerging markets are vulnerable to short-term speculative hedge funds, and with the lack of regulation and absence of market stability, hedge funds may in some cases produce extreme high returns.

This chapter concentrates on hedge funds investing in emerging markets. The next section presents the behaviour of hedge fund returns for different strategies. Strategies of hedge fund returns with VAR and Modified VAR are compared in the third section. The fourth section analyses some time series aspects of returns and estimates alpha and beta of hedge funds investing in emerging markets. The final section concludes.

BEHAVIOUR OF HEDGE FUND RETURNS

Comparison of hedge fund strategies

Different hedge funds investing in emerging markets are analysed. The dataset used in this analysis is from Eurekahedge net of all fees and the examination period is from 1 December 1999–31 May 2006. The data includes 77 observations belonging to 313 hedge funds however, a few monthly observations in some strategies are missing and are discarded. It is understood that there may be a survivorship problem in the study and data providers follow different methods to eliminate this bias. Furthermore, the number of hedge funds investing in emerging markets is small when compared with other strategies.

Hedge funds allocating at least 90% of their assets to emerging markets are included. Emerging markets include emerging Europe, Latin America, Russia, Asia (ex-Japan, Australia and New Zealand), Middle East, Africa and the Caribbean, according to Eurekahedge. We make use of indices to generate the return series. The indices are developed for hedge funds investing in emerging markets for the following strategies:

(1) Arbitrage (ARB);
(2) CTA/Managed futures (CTA);
(3) Distressed debt (DIS);
(4) Event driven (EVE);
(5) Fixed income (FIX);
(6) Long/short equities (LSE);
(7) Macro (MAC);
(8) Multi-strategy (MUL);
(9) Relative value (REL).

Abbreviations in parentheses represent the strategies in the remaining part of the text, tables and charts.

We define strategy s (s runs over all nine strategies listed above, $s = 1,2, \ldots,9$) at time t ($t = 1,2, \ldots,T$ where T is the last month of observations) over the indices as:

$$R_{t,s} = \frac{I_{t,s} - I_{(t-1),s}}{I_{(t-1),s}} \tag{1}$$

Here t starts from the second observation due to differencing, I is the index for strategy s at time t. One observation is dropped while generating the return series from the index series because of differencing. The exact number of observations along with a summary of descriptive statistics are reported in Table 1.

Here, "N" is the number of months, "Min." is the minimum observation over the time period and "Max." is the maximum. "Mean" is the sample average of returns over the specified time period and "St. Dev." is the square root of the sample variance. We report the figures for skewness (S_R) and kurtosis (K_R) of the return series that are defined as:

Table 1 Summary statistics of strategy returns in emerging markets (in percentages)

Strategy	N	Min.	Max.	Mean	St. Dev.	Skewness	Kurtosis
ARB (9)[a]	76	−1.36	4.67	1.04	0.85	0.76	3.87
CTA (3)	77	−11.18	36.60	1.33	5.98	2.87	15.71
DIS (17)	77	−2.32	6.77	1.44	1.58	0.56	1.67
EVE (7)	76	−2.31	27.30	2.32	4.01	4.06	21.57
FIX (23)	77	−2.85	5.36	1.21	1.51	0.20	1.50
LSE (141)	77	−7.08	9.82	1.46	3.72	−0.48	−0.09
MAC (14)	76	−3.47	4.86	1.16	1.53	−0.02	0.41
MUL (88)	77	−1.96	4.78	1.53	1.57	−0.33	−0.37
REL (11)	76	−7.68	11.71	1.57	3.63	−0.30	0.55
HFE (320)	77	−3.67	5.90	1.52	2.27	−0.50	−0.28

[a]Numbers in parentheses are the number of hedge funds following strategies.

$$S_R = \frac{N}{(N-1)(N-2)} \sum_t \left(\frac{R_t - \mu_R}{\sigma_R} \right)^3 \tag{2}$$

$$K_R = \left[\frac{N(N+1)}{(N-1)(N-2)(N-3)} \sum_t \left(\frac{R_t - \mu_R}{\sigma_R} \right)^4 \right] - \left[\frac{3(N-1)^2}{(N-2)(N-3)} \right] \tag{3}$$

where μ_R is the population mean of the return series, and σ_R is the standard deviation of the same series. The skewness is the ratio of the third moment around the population mean to the cube of the standard deviation and kurtosis is the ratio of the fourth moment around the population mean to the square of the second moment.

According to these figures the event driven (EVE) strategy offers the highest average return (2.32%) but with the second highest standard deviation (4.01%). All other strategies have similar means (range is 0.53%) but the CTA strategy has the highest standard deviation. Hedge fund management should accept this high risk in exchange for the 1.33% mean return. The same comment is valid for LSE and REL, but these two strategies have slightly higher average returns. According to the minimum return statistics CTA is the worst strategy (−11.18%) followed by REL (−7.68), and LSE (−7.08). The order is similar for the maximum returns, (for CTA it is 36.60%, for EVE it is 27.30%, and for REL 11.71%).

The statistic "coefficient of variation" is defined for comparisons where mean and standard deviation are considered together. It is the ratio of standard deviation to mean. If one adopts the coefficient of variation as the comparison criterion, the worst two strategies appear as CTA and LSE with coefficients of variations 4.50 and 2.55. The best strategy according to this criterion is ARB with a coefficient of variation equal to 0.82. Prudent hedge fund managers should prefer the arbitrage strategies to avoid risk but their returns will be limited, on average.

The last line of the table reports the statistics for hedge fund investments regardless of strategies followed. The mean return for all hedge funds over the specified period is 1.52% with a standard deviation of 2.27%.

The same statistics are reported for the identical strategies applied to global markets instead of emerging markets in Table 2 to compare hedge fund returns. Eurekahedge database includes a total of 2303 live hedge funds. The comparison of Tables 1 and 2 reveals that the average returns of global markets are less than these returns of emerging markets, but the standard deviations are smaller for the global markets for all hedge fund strategies. The strategy with the highest average return is the DIS global, whereas the smallest average return belongs to ARB strategy (Table 2). Furthermore, the range of the average return figures is smaller in the global than in the emerging markets category.

Table 2 Summary statistics of strategy returns in global markets (in percentages)

Strategy	*N*	Min.	Max.	Mean	St. Dev.	Skewness	Kurtosis
ARB (155)	77	−1.01	2.69	0.74	0.65	0.26	0.80
CTA (304)	77	−4.13	8.54	1.03	2.49	0.35	0.31
DIS (51)	77	−2.53	4.55	1.30	1.42	−0.32	0.19
EVE (98)	77	−2.93	4.19	1.02	1.45	−0.46	0.49
FIX (144)	77	−0.92	3.15	0.88	0.71	0.48	1.23
LSE (1,058)	77	−2.78	9.47	0.99	2.05	0.67	2.60
MAC (143)	77	−2.10	4.55	0.88	1.33	0.44	0.15
MUL (267)	77	−1.38	4.16	1.07	1.09	0.03	−0.04
REL (83)	77	−2.73	5.05	1.06	1.46	−0.03	0.35
HFG (2,303)	77	−1.61	5.59	0.99	1.34	0.42	0.79

Figure 1 Histograms of HF Returns based on different strategies

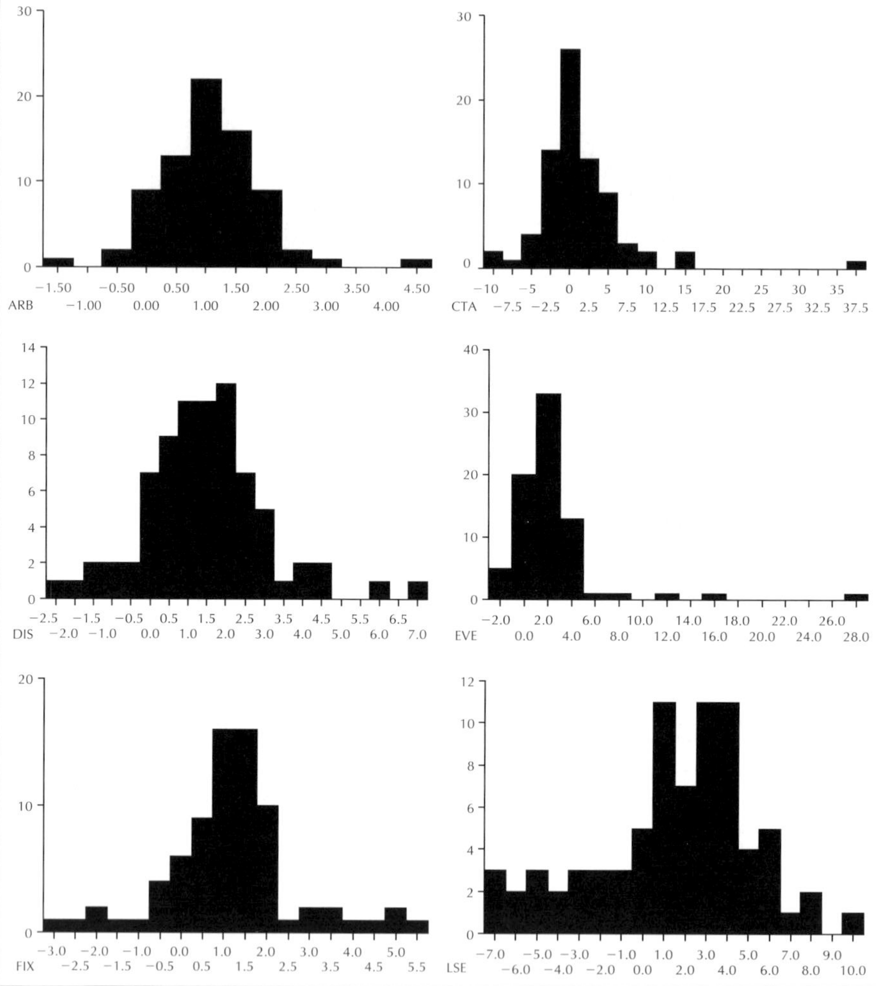

Normality tests

Although some descriptive statistics shed light on hedge fund returns, their use for inference is limited. Therefore, they are tested for the empirical distributions' closeness to normality. First the histograms of the strategies are displayed in Figure 1.

Histograms of ARB, and CTA resemble the normal density however there are a few outliers. Histograms of DIS, LSE, MUL and REL strategies look quite different to the normal density. In general,

Figure 1 (continued)

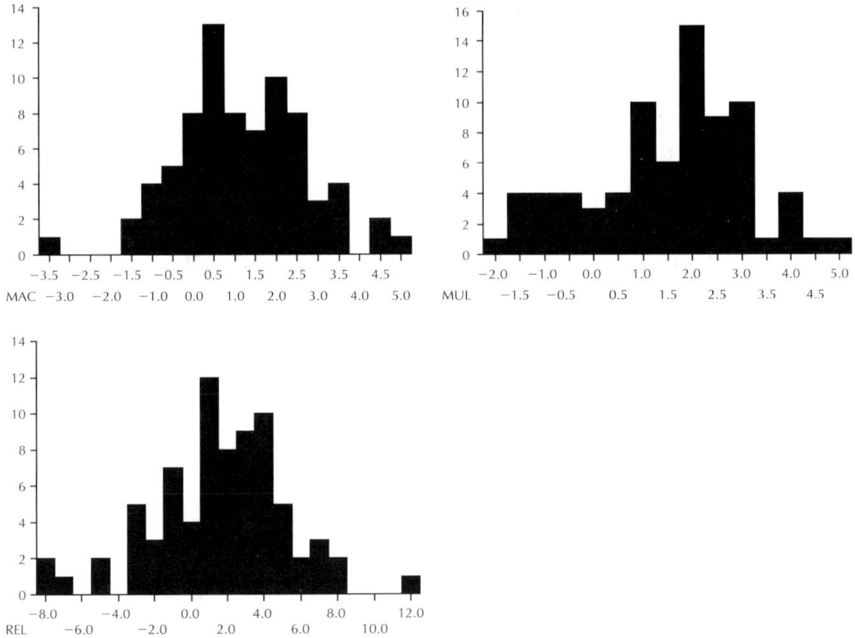

no single strategy looks normally distributed, but upon casual inspection it is not sufficient to conclude that strategy returns are not normally distributed. To be certain a Jarque–Bera Test is performed for normality. The Test statistic, JB, is based on skewness and kurtosis, and is defined as:

$$JB = N\left[\frac{S^2}{6} + \frac{(K-3)^2}{24}\right] \tag{4}$$

where S is skewness and K is kurtosis defined in Equations (2) and (3). The null hypothesis of the Test claims the normality of the distribution. The JB statistics and their p-values are presented to formally conclude the normality of returns for strategies in Table 3.

Test statistics reveal that none of the series are normally distributed, expressed by p-values which are very close to zero. One can detect the outliers in the series, remove them and re-test for normality with the remaining series. This procedure can be repeated

Table 3 Jarque–Bera statistics of returns

Strategy	Skewness	Kurtosis	J-B statistic	*p*-value
ARB	0.76	6.54	47.00	0.000
CTA	2.87	15.71	624.00	0.000
DIS	0.56	1.67	9.70	0.007
EVE	4.06	21.57	1300.80	0.000
FIX	0.20	1.50	7.73	0.020
LSE	−0.48	−0.09	33.59	0.000
MAC	−0.02	0.41	21.25	0.000
MUL	−0.33	−0.37	37.83	0.000
REL	−0.30	0.55	20.15	0.000
HFE	−0.50	−0.28	37.72	0.000

until normality is attained but this is beyond the scope of this study. In addition, the removal of outliers is not necessarily the correct procedure since these points carry some characteristics of the strategies and are not the consequences of mistakes in observing or recording the observations.

Correlation between strategies

The strategies of hedge funds investing in emerging markets along with their returns may have some linear association expressed by the correlation coefficients. There are several prominent formulae to calculate correlation coefficients and we prefer Pearson's product moment coefficient of correlation, ρ. This correlation coefficient between strategies X and Y is defined as:

$$\rho = \frac{\sum_t (X_t - \mu_x)(Y_t - \mu_Y)}{\sqrt{\sum_t (X_t - \mu_x)^2 \sum_t (Y_t - \mu_Y)^2}} \quad \textbf{(5)}$$

The correlation coefficients matrix displays all possible correlation coefficients in Table 4. Numbers in parentheses are reported to make a firmer conclusion about the correlation between returns of different strategies. Some of the coefficients are high indicating that some strategy pairs are highly correlated. There are no negative correlation coefficients recorded which means all returns are moving in the same directions as long as their monthly performances are considered.

According to the figures ARB is highly correlated to FIX, DIS, LSE, and MUL, whereas CTA has somewhat weaker correlations with MAC attaining the highest correlation coefficient with 0.379.

Table 4 Correlation coefficients of investment strategies (numbers in parentheses are significance levels)

	ARB	CTA	DIS	EVE	FIX	LSE	MAC	MUL	REL
ARB	1.000	0.061	0.600	0.281	0.603	0.554	0.427	0.502	0.392
		(0.601)	(0.000)	(0.014)	(0.000)	(0.000)	(0.000)	(0.000)	(0.000)
CTA		1.000	0.018	0.056	0.152	0.296	0.379	0.348	0.190
			(0.876)	(0.628)	(0.186)	(0.009)	(0.001)	(0.002)	(0.101)
DIS			1.000	0.377	0.699	0.562	0.313	0.452	0.478
				(0.001)	(0.000)	(0.000)	(0.006)	(0.000)	(0.000)
EVE				1.000	0.210	0.166	0.028	0.120	0.151
					(0.068)	(0.152)	(0.809)	(0.302)	(0.194)
FIX					1.000	0.703	0.499	0.642	0.481
						(0.000)	(0.000)	(0.000)	(0.000)
LSE						1.000	0.645	0.854	0.682
							(0.000)	(0.000)	(0.000)
MAC							1.000	0.674	0.443
								(0.000)	(0.000)
MUL								1.000	0.554
									(0.000)
REL									1.000

DIS is highly correlated to FIX and LSE and the least correlated of all strategies is EVE where the highest correlation coefficient is listed as 0.210 (with FIX).

RISK MEASURES

The most important comparison criterion for hedge fund returns of different strategies is their risk behaviour. This section evaluates the risks of strategies with Value-at-Risk (VAR) analysis. There are three methods of VAR calculations: Historical, Variance-Covariance, and Monte Carlo Simulation. The historical method is adopted since the other two require assumptions that are very difficult to fulfil. The Variance–Covariance method assumes the normality of returns and the previous section has concluded that none of the series is normally distributed. The Monte Carlo Simulation requires some assumptions over the data generation processes of the model, however, the exact model specification is not known which requires substantial work with assumptions.

The key implication of the historical method is "history repeats itself". The method has three basic components: confidence level, maximum loss, and time interval, though emphasis to time intervals is not given because monthly data are used for all series. The maximum loss possible is stated with some confidence and historical data of the strategy are used for this purpose. All returns of all strategies are sorted in ascending order. Minimum α% of the returns are flagged for 100 (1 − α)% confidence levels.

VAR figures for strategies are the maximum flagged returns in absolute value. The absolute values are expressed since these returns are generally negative, ie losses. The returns are the maximum loss in the coming months, since historical returns are assumed to repeat in the future. One may be subject to higher losses in coming periods and the historical method is inferior in this regard. It is also customary to use 90%, 95%, and 99% confidence levels. The same is followed in the present study, and we further include 93% and 97% for a more detailed illustration of VAR in Table 5.

The most prudent managers are assumed to prefer 99% confidence level. The riskiest strategies are the following: CTA with a maximum loss of 11.18% followed by REL (7.68%) and LSE (7.08%), HFE and MAC with maximum losses over 3%, FIX, DIS, and EVE with maximum losses between 2% and 3%. The best performers in terms of their risk content are ARB and MUL where ARB has the lowest maximum loss of 1.36%.

The order changes when confidence levels are altered and decreased to 97%. CTA, REL, and LSE are the worst three followed by HFE and FIX. All the remaining strategies have maximum losses less than 2% and the strategy with the lowest losses is ARB with

Table 5 VAR figures for different strategies

	99%	97%	95%	93%	90%
ARB	−1.36	−0.37	−0.21	−0.16	−0.04
CTA	−11.18	−8.98	−5.90	−4.76	−3.75
DIS	−2.32	−1.69	−1.42	−0.92	−0.39
EVE	−2.31	−1.79	−1.46	−1.23	−0.63
FIX	−2.85	−2.24	−1.79	−1.15	−0.46
LSE	−7.08	−6.58	−6.21	−5.46	−4.64
MAC	−3.47	−1.59	−1.21	−1.04	−0.90
MUL	−1.96	−1.73	−1.45	−1.18	−0.90
REL	−7.68	−7.50	−5.53	−4.29	−3.09
HFE	−3.67	−3.40	−3.14	−2.63	−1.84

Table 6 Modified VAR figures for different strategies

	99%	97%	95%	93%	90%
ARB	−1.41	−0.80	−0.52	−0.31	−0.09
CTA	−24.52	−14.84	−10.93	−8.24	−5.65
DIS	−2.71	−1.83	−1.40	−1.07	−0.71
EVE	−11.54	−7.99	−6.16	−4.73	−3.19
FIX	−2.51	−1.73	−1.36	−1.07	−0.76
LSE	−5.56	−4.66	−4.14	−3.69	−3.16
MAC	−2.38	−1.69	−1.35	−1.08	−0.80
MUL	−1.68	−1.17	−0.90	−0.68	−0.43
REL	−5.96	−4.73	−4.09	−3.56	−2.98
HFE	−2.72	−2.19	−1.88	−1.61	−1.30

0.37%. LSE, CTA, and REL are the worst and change their order in other confidence levels. At 90% confidence level LSE is the worst and CTA and REL follow.

Since VAR figures reported in the table have the shortcoming of ignoring the skewness and kurtosis of the series, the modified VAR originated by Favre and Galeano (2002) is included. The modified VAR, MVAR, is calculated with:

$$MVAR = \mu - \left(z + \frac{1}{6}(z^2 - 1)S + \frac{1}{24}(z^3 - 3z)K' - \frac{1}{36}(2z^3 - 5z)S^2 \right)\sigma \quad \textbf{(6)}$$

where μ and σ are mean and standard deviation of the series. S, and K' are skewness and excess kurtosis (kurtosis over 3.00). The confidence level is adjusted with different values of z which is the z-critical value to be found from standard normal distribution table.

According to modified VAR figures the riskiest strategies are CTA followed by EVE and REL at the 99% confidence level. But for 90% confidence level the third riskiest strategy becomes LSE rather than REL. The least risky strategy is ARB at all confidence levels followed by MUL.

BEHAVIOURS OF RETURNS THROUGH TIME

The graphs of hedge fund returns for visual inspection are displayed in Figure 2 for a period of approximately six years. The strategy returns appear as if no trend exists. Note that the scales for different returns are calibrated differently to fit the points into cells

are the best, linear, unbiased estimators. If stationarity does not exist as a result of the violation of any one of the three assumptions stated above, one has to find the best estimator under given assumptions because OLS is proven be worse.

One has to be very careful if time series in hand is non-stationary because the behaviour of the series will be changing continuously and investors have to be prepared for sudden changes. Therefore, the first step in dealing with any time series data is testing for stationarity of the series. Technically, non-stationary series include the unit root. That is, a series, X_t, evolving over time as: $X_t = a + b X_{t-1} + u_t$ has the unit root if b is greater than or equal to the unity. Assume that $b = 2$; this implies that anticipated values of X_t will be larger than the previous ones causing the series to explode, ie, the series is non-stationary. Dickey and Fuller (1979) develop the Augmented Dickey–Fuller Test to detect the unit root and to check for stationarity. The null hypothesis of this Test claims that there is a unit root in the series.

The Test results are reported in Table 7. According to these results all series prove to be stationary even at 0.1% significance level. The critical values for 1%, 5% and 10% significance levels are almost the same for all series (differences in N lead to negligible changes in results), and are −3.52, −2.90 and −2.59, respectively. Note that all ADF Test statistics are much smaller than even the critical value for 1% significance level.

Table 7 Augmented Dickey-Fuller Test results for stationarity

Series	Test statistic	R^2	*F*-statistic
ARB	−6.18	0.48	21.45
CTA	−5.37	0.52	23.35
DIS	−5.69	0.44	18.22
EVE	−6.35	0.48	21.59
FIX	−7.45	0.59	32.77
LSE	−5.13	0.42	16.49
MAC	−4.32	0.59	32.50
MUL	−4.39	0.40	15.37
REL	−4.64	0.46	19.25
HFE	−5.57	0.43	17.63

Table 8 Augmented Dickey-Fuller Test results for stationarity

Series	Test statistic	R^2	*F*-statistic
$(R_{EMHFR} - R_f)$	−5.33	0.42	16.68
$(R_{EMR} - R_f)$	−5.32	0.45	19.24

Estimation of alpha and beta

A version of the Capital Asset Pricing Model (CAPM) is used to estimate the numerical values of α and β from the regression:

$$(R_{EMHFR} - R_f) = \alpha + \beta(R_{EMR} - R_f) + \varepsilon \tag{7}$$

In this regression equation, R_{EMHRF} is the emerging markets hedge fund return, R_f is the risk-free return, and R_{EMR} is the market return for emerging markets. ε is the disturbance term satisfying classical assumptions.

The hedge fund return series introduced in Section 2, page 3 is used for R_{EMHRF}, R_f is the monthly return of the US Treasury-bill, and R_{EMR} is the Morgan-Stanley hedge fund index for emerging markets.

One has to make sure that variables in the regression equation are stationary so the regression is not spurious. The unit roots of series on LHS and RHS of regression Equation (7) are tested for with the Augmented Dickey–Fuller Test. Results displayed in Table 8 prove that both series do not have unit roots and are stationary.

The critical values for 1%, 5% and 10% significance levels are −3.52, −2.90, and −2.59, respectively.

Note that all ADF Test statistics are much smaller than even the critical value for 1% significance level.

The regression results are presented in Table 9 which reveal that both alpha and beta are highly significant. The coefficient of determination is 90% and high *F*-statistic with a *p*-value very close to zero confirms the robustness of the model. Finally, the Durbin–Watson (DW) statistic proves that there is no autocorrelation.

Beta is close to one and alpha is positive and significant. A positive and significant alpha implies hedge fund managers trading in emerging markets have superior performance over emerging market returns, but only by 0.4%.

Table 9 Regression results to estimate alpha and beta

Variable	Coefficient	St. Error	*t*-statistic	Prob.
Constant	0.400	0.090	4.456	0.000
$(R_{EMR} - R_f)$	1.050	0.040	26.093	0.000
R^2	0.900	AIC	2.234	
Ad. R^2	0.899	SC	2.295	
DW statistic	1.983	*F*-statistic	680.1	

CONCLUSIONS

The mean for hedge fund returns investing in emerging markets over the last 76 months (approximately six years) is 1.52% which is 0.53% greater than the average of hedge fund returns invested globally (the mean return is reported 0.99% in the bottom line of Table 2). But in order to benefit from this excess return, hedge fund managers investing in emerging markets must be more careful because the standard deviation of hedge fund investments in emerging markets (2.27) is significantly larger than that of investments in global markets (1.34).

ACKNOWLEDGMENT

We are thankful to Dieter G. Kaiser and Prof. Greg N. Gregoriou for their kind and helpful comments and efforts.

REFERENCES

Baba, N. and H. Goko, 2006, "Survival Analysis of Hedge Funds", *Bank of Japan Working Series,* No: 06-E-05.

Caldwell, T., 1995, "Introduction: The Model for Superiors Performance" in J. Ledermann and R. A. Klein (eds) *Hedge Funds* (New York: Irvin Professional Publishing), pp 1–17.

Dickey, D. A. and W. A. Fuller, 1979, "Distribution of the Estimators for Autoregressive Time Series with a Unit Root", *Journal of the American Statistical Association,* **74,** pp 427–31.

Do, V., R. Faff, and J. Wickramanayake, 2005, "An Empirical Analysis of Hedge Fund Performance: The Case of Australian Hedge Funds Industry", *Journal of Multinational Financial Management,* **15,** pp 377–93.

Favre, L. and J.-A. Galeano, 2002, "Mean–Modified Value-at-Risk Optimization with Hedge Funds", *Journal of Alternative Investment,* **5,** pp 21–5.

Fung, W. and D. A. Hsieh, 1999, "A Primer on Hedge Funds", *Journal of Empirical Finance,* **6,** pp 309–31.

Part Three

Portfolio Management

14

Optimising Hedge Fund Portfolios with Omega Functions

Jean-François Bacmann, Ursula Bosshard

RMF Investment Management

INTRODUCTION

The measurement of risk embedded in hedge fund investments has recently raised strong interest in the financial community. Indeed, hedge fund returns are not normally distributed: they exhibit skewed and leptokurtic behaviour (see among others: Schmidhuber and Moix, 2001; Brooks and Kat, 2002). In this context, the risk of hedge funds cannot be solely captured by the standard deviation, but is in essence much more complex. Such findings have strong implications on asset allocation techniques in the hedge fund world. As argued by Fung and Hsieh (1999) the traditional mean-variance framework is no longer valid and should be avoided. Moreover, risk-averse investors exhibit preferences with respect to the higher moments of the return distribution (see eg, Scott and Horvath, 1980; Pratt and Zeckhauser, 1987). They tend to like positive skewness and to dislike high levels of kurtosis. Such behaviour has a strong impact on the selection of optimal portfolios built with hedge funds.

Instead of assuming a quadratic utility, different families of utility functions have been considered to capture the effects of higher moments. Leland (1999) shows how to modify the Beta of the CAPM in order to capture the asymmetric distribution effects in the context of a power utility function. More recently, Sharma (2004a,b) introduced the AIRAP measure defined as the certain equivalent return linked to the same type of utility function in the context of performance measurement. However, power utility functions focus on a limited domain of wealth in order to ensure their definition. Some other researchers suggest using a Taylor series expansion of a general utility function linking the expected utility to the different moments of the distribution (see Berenyi, 2002). Yet this approach is limited by the convergence of the Taylor expansion, which depends on the utility function, and the choice of the truncation which determines the quality of the approximation. The main drawback of this approach lies in the estimation of the higher moments. In particular, the existence of the fourth moment is not guaranteed as already pointed out by Dacorogna *et al* (2001).

While theoretically sounded, utility functions are not really used in practice as it is difficult to identify the correct one corresponding to the relevant investor. Therefore, some recent research focuses solely on the first four moments of the return distribution without referring explicitly to a utility function. Signer and Favre (2002) and McFall Lamm (2003) argue in favour of the delta-gamma approximation via the Cornish–Fisher expansion. In this context, the Value-at-Risk derived from a normal distribution is corrected to take the skewness and the kurtosis into account. The quality of the approximation relies strongly on the size of the dataset which is rather small in the context of hedge funds. More recently, Davies *et al* (2003) proposed a Polynomial Goal Programming optimisation in the mean-variance-skewness-kurtosis framework. Their approach also faces the problem of the approximation being exacerbated by the optimisation framework and by the definition of a set of three parameters designed to model substitution effects between the different moments on an ad-hoc basis.

Recently, the omega function, introduced by Keating and Shadwick (2002) has been advocated to judge the performance of financial assets as it incorporates the information about. Bacmann and Pache (2004) investigate the properties of omega when building optimal portfolios of hedge funds. In particular, they show that the composition of these portfolios strongly depends on the choice of a threshold and therefore does not take all higher moments into account. This chapter goes one step further by synthesising the information content of the omega function in one single metric. This new measure is consistent with the Sharpe ratio when returns are normally distributed, and incorporates asymmetric tail behaviour preferences under general return distributions. Moreover, it only requires the existence of the first two moments of the distribution. Intuitively, the asymmetric Sharpe ratio penalises a distribution for having a negative fat tail and rewards it for having a positive fat tail. This new measure is applied in the context of portfolio optimisation with hedge fund styles. We analyse the out-of-sample performance of the optimal asset allocation obtained with the new measure. For that purpose, reallocations are performed on a rolling basis. The subsequent performance and risk characteristics are compared among several alternatives (eg, Sharpe ratio, Sortino ratio, Stutzer index, etc).

The chapter is organised as follows. The next section presents the omega function and the asymmetric Sharpe ratio. The following section discusses the hedge fund data sample and the measures traditionally used to optimise portfolios. The optimal in-sample allocations obtained via several risk-adjusted performance measures are examined in the fourth section. The following section compares the different methods in a dynamic allocation framework. The final section concludes the chapter.

THE SHARPE RATIO ADJUSTED FOR ASYMMETRY

This section introduces a new risk-adjusted measure designed to take the asymmetric behaviour of hedge fund returns into account. It is defined as a combination of the Sharpe ratio and a transformation of the omega function. The omega function, designed by Keating and Shadwick (2002), captures all the moments of a return distribution. For that purpose, it splits the return space into two sub-parts according to a threshold. The returns below this threshold are considered as losses while the returns above the threshold are viewed as gains. More specifically, omega provides a risk-reward measure for which returns are weighted by their probability of occurrence. The mathematical formulation of the function is the following:

$$\Omega(r) = \frac{I_2(r)}{I_1(r)}$$

where

$$I_1(r) = \int_a^r F(x)\,\mathrm{d}x$$

and

$$I_2(r) = \int_r^b (1 - F(x))\,dx$$

F is the cumulative distribution function of the returns defined on the interval $[a, b]$ and r is the return level regarded as the loss threshold.

As noted by Keating and Shadwick (2002), the omega function is equivalent to the return distribution.[1] Thus, all the higher moments are encoded in the omega function. Omega is a smooth monotone decreasing function from $[a, b]$ to $[0, +\infty]$. When the threshold is chosen as the mean of the distribution, the omega function is equal to one whatever the distribution is. In practice, the omega function at a given threshold can be easily estimated as

$$\Omega(r) = \frac{\sum_i \max(0, R_i - r)}{\sum_i \max(0, r - R_i)}$$

The omega function possesses several appealing mathematical properties which are detailed in Cascon *et al* (2002). In particular, if a distribution function is symmetric about its mean, the associated omega function also exhibits symmetric behaviour. More precisely, F is symmetric about its mean μ if and only if $\Omega_F(\mu - r) = \Omega_F^{-1}(\mu + r)$ for all $r > 0$. F is said to exhibit positive (respectively negative) asymmetry about μ for a given positive r if $\Omega_F(\mu - r) > \Omega_F^{-1}(\mu + r)$ (resp. $\Omega_F(\mu - r) < \Omega_F^{-1}(\mu + r)$).

Next, a general asymmetric indicator is computed over the omega function using the symmetric property. For that purpose, n equally spaced thresholds $[r_1, r_2, \ldots, r_n]$ are considered, so that $r_1 = 0$ and $r_n = \min(\mu - a; b - \mu)$. The asymmetric indicator is then estimated as:

$$AsymInd = \frac{1}{n} \sum_{i=1}^{n} \Omega_F(\mu - r_i)\Omega_F(\mu + r_i)$$

It is easy to show that the asymmetric indicator is equal to one for symmetric distributions, smaller than one for negatively asymmetric distributions and greater than one for positively asymmetric distributions. Moreover, as for the omega function, the asymmetric indicator does not require the existence of the moments whose order is greater than one. In other words it is more general than the skewness and incorporates the effects of higher moments.

The asymmetric indicator does not depend on the mean or on the standard deviation of the distribution. Let us define ϕ as $\phi(r) = (r - \mu)/\sigma$ and H as the induced centred reduced distribution, $H = F \circ \phi^{-1}$. Following property 3 of Theorem 1 in Cascon *et al* (2002), $\Omega_F(\mu + r) = \Omega_H(\phi(\mu + r)) = \Omega_H(r/\sigma)$. The asymmetric indicator can be expressed as:

$$AsymInd = \frac{1}{n}\sum_{i=1}^{n} \Omega_H(-r_i/\sigma)\Omega_H(r_i/\sigma) = \frac{1}{n}\sum_{i=1}^{n} \Omega_H(-r_i^*)\Omega_H(r_i^*)$$

As a consequence, it is equivalent to computing the asymmetric indicator using the empirical distribution or its centred reduced equivalent. As the thresholds span the range of the distribution definition, the asymmetric indicator is independent from the mean and the standard deviation.

We define the asymmetric Sharpe ratio as:

$$AsymSharpe = \frac{\frac{1}{T}\sum_{t=1}^{T} R_t}{\sigma(R)} * AsymInd^{\gamma}$$

where γ is a substitution parameter between the standard deviation and the asymmetry.

The asymmetric Sharpe ratio reduces to the traditional Sharpe ratio when the returns are normally distributed. When the return distribution exhibits positive (negative) asymmetry, the Asym Sharpe figure is greater (lower) than the Sharpe ratio. As argued by Leland (1999), optimal strategies are preference dependent and no measure will correctly rank all distributions regardless of the preferences of the investor. Therefore, the parameter γ is introduced which is related to the preference of the investor with respect to asymmetric behaviour. The higher the coefficient, the more the investor is looking for positive asymmetry at the expense of the standard deviation. When γ is set to 0, the investor is not affected by higher moments and behaves as in the case of quadratic utility.

DATA SET AND SET-UP OF THE EXPERIMENTS

Hedge fund indexes are particularly suitable for studying the impact of higher moments on optimal asset allocation problems.

These indexes may exhibit strong deviations from normal distribution, like negative skewness and high kurtosis for arbitrage strategies. Moreover, the hedge fund world is rather heterogeneous: global macro strategies and managed futures have positive skewness and small kurtosis. This diversity is the reason why studying optimal hedge fund allocation adds value when evaluating the asymmetric Sharpe ratio.

In order to assess the usefulness of the asymmetric Sharpe ratio, hedge fund indexes are employed, provided by Hedge Fund Research, Inc (HFR). The monthly HFR indexes represent the equally weighted returns, net of fees, of the component hedge funds. They are computed on a monthly basis from a database comprising more than 3,700 funds. To represent the hedge fund investment universe, 11 non-overlapping HFRI strategy indexes are selected: HFRI Equity Hedge Index, HFRI Equity Non-Hedge Index, HFRI Equity Market Neutral Index, HFRI Relative Value Index, HFRI Convertible Arbitrage Index, HFRI Fixed Income Arbitrage Index, HFRI Event Driven Index, HFRI Distressed Securities Index, HFRI Merger Arbitrage Index, HFRI Macro Index and HFRI Emerging Markets Index. Further, the Stark 300 Trader Index is added to the dataset in order to represent an investment in CTAs. All the data consist of monthly returns between January 1990 and December 2003.

Table 1 reports the basic statistics of the indexes over the period. As hedge funds are claiming to provide absolute returns, the returns of all the indexes are defined in excess of Libor 1-month US$. According to the Jarque–Bera test at 95%, normality was not rejected for two indexes out of 12, the HFRI Equity Market Neutral Index and the HFRI Macro Index. Nine indexes exhibited negative skewness and high kurtosis levels (see eg, HFRI Fixed Income Arbitrage Index). Moreover, the three best strategies according to the Sharpe ratio, HFRI Relative Value Arbitrage Index, HFRI Convertible Arbitrage Index, and HFRI Distressed Securities Index, showed strong departure from normality characterised by a negative skewness and a high kurtosis. This probably implies that optimal portfolios designed according to the Sharpe ratio will exhibit negative skewness and high kurtosis.

Table 1 also displays the values obtained for the asymmetric indicator. It is interesting to note its relation to the skewness. Indeed, the

Table 1 Sample statistics of the different style indexes (January 1990–December 2003)

	HFRI equity hedge index	HFRI equity non-hedge index	HFRI equity market neutral index	HFRI relative value arbitrage index	HFRI convertible arbitrage index	HFRI fixed income: arbitrage index
Annual mean (%)	12.64	11.90	4.66	7.43	6.26	3.69
Annual standard deviation (%)	9.04	14.59	3.10	3.68	3.42	4.52
Annual sharpe	1.40	0.82	1.50	2.02	1.83	0.82
Asymmetric ind.	1.30	0.54	1.19	0.61	0.35	0.42
Skewness	0.08	−0.56	0.06	−1.03	−1.32	−1.72
Kurtosis	4.31	3.55	3.48	14.68	5.93	12.28
JB stat	**12.34**	**10.87**	**1.74**	990.01	**109.59**	**689.29**

	HFRI event-driven index	HFRI distressed securities index	HFRI merger arbitrage index	HFRI macro index	HFRI emerging markets (total)	Stark 300 trader index
Annual mean (%)	9.67	9.96	5.71	11.51	10.66	5.37
Annual standard deviation (%)	6.77	6.35	4.32	8.64	15.38	11.71
Annual sharpe	1.43	1.57	1.32	1.33	0.69	0.46
Asymmetric ind.	0.48	0.64	0.40	1.23	0.51	2.99
Skewness	−1.43	−0.73	−3.09	0.25	−0.83	0.79
Kurtosis	7.95	8.23	17.41	3.36	6.68	5.97
JB stat	**230.58**	**207.76**	**1730.82**	2.71	**114.79**	**79.87**

Notes: The returns of the hedge fund styles are defined in excess of the Libor 1 month US$. The JB Stat designates the Jarque Bera statistic. Bold value indicates that the null hypothesis of normally distributed returns is rejected at the 5% level.

asymmetric indicators above one are achieved for the positively skewed indexes. Conversely, the indicators below one are linked to the negatively skewed indexes. This shows that the asymmetric indicator is clearly related to the asymmetry in the distribution. The relationship between the asymmetric indicator and the kurtosis is less evident. In our view, the asymmetry is a more important determinant of the asset allocation. For example, the Stark 300 Trader presents a relatively high kurtosis of 5.97. However, this value is caused by large positive returns. In such a context, the existence of high kurtosis should be beneficial to the investor.

Comparing the Sharpe ratio adjusted for higher moments to the traditional Sharpe ratio is not sufficient. Indeed, several methods have been developed to account for non-normal distributions. Thus, we also consider and detail several other alternatives. As a first benchmark, we use the Cornish–Fisher expansion of the standard deviation as proposed by Signer and Favre (2002) and more recently by Lee and Lee (2004). The standard deviation in the expression of the Sharpe ratio is substituted by the risk measure σz_{CF}. The parameter z_{CF} is a function of the first three cumulants and is expressed as:

$$z_{CF} = z_c + \frac{1}{6}(z_c^2 - 1)S + \frac{1}{24}(z_c^3 - 3z_c)K - \frac{1}{36}(2z_c^3 - 5z_c)S^2$$

where z_c is the critical value of the standard normal distribution corresponding to a chosen significance level (eg, -2.33 at 99%), S is the skewness of the return distribution, and K is its excess kurtosis.

The second benchmark is related to the downside deviation. As a lower partial moment measure, the downside deviation has the advantage of not increasing with a greater upside potential of the return distribution. The asymmetry is a desirable property in order to take the investor's aversion to returns below a certain loss threshold into account. Sortino and Price (1994) propose a performance ratio similar to the Sharpe ratio where the standard deviation is replaced by the downside deviation. Recently, Bacmann and Pache (2004) show empirically that the Sortino ratio is able to capture at least partially the higher moments effects related to hedge fund returns.

In a recent chapter, Sharma (2004a) derives a new measure, called AIRAP, as the implied certain equivalent associated with a power utility function. He shows that this measure accounts for higher moments and leverage effects previously found in hedge fund returns. In order to compare the results of an AIRAP based measure and the previously defined performance ratio, the AIRAP based Sharpe ratio, also known as MSRAIRAP, is used in the remainder of the chapter. Sharma (2004a) introduces this ratio as a Sharpe ratio where the standard deviation is substituted by the risk premium derived from a power utility function. Still, the constant relative risk aversion parameter has to be fixed. Following Sharma (2004a), the parameter is set at 4 in order to be conservative.

The last measure is defined according to the work of Stutzer (2000). The so-called Stutzer index does not rely explicitly on a utility function but on a behavioural hypothesis. It assumes that investors aim to minimise the probability that the excess returns over a given threshold will be negative over a long-term horizon. When the portfolio has a positive expected excess return, the probability defined above will decay to zero at an exponential decay rate as the time horizon increases. The maximum possible decay rate is defined as the Stutzer index. When returns are normally distributed, the Stutzer index is equal to half of the squared Sharpe ratio. As shown by Bacmann and Scholz (2003), the Stutzer index penalises investments presenting a negative skewness and high kurtosis. Moreover, it can be easily implemented in an optimisation framework as described by Stutzer (2000) and Bacmann and Pache (2004).

IN-SAMPLE RESULTS

This section presents the asset allocations obtained when maximising the previously defined performance measures. For that purpose, we use several levels of γ, the substitution parameter between standard deviation and the asymmetry. All the computations are done with returns in excess of Libor 1-month US$. As a consequence, 0% is used as a threshold for the maximisation of the Sortino ratio and the Stutzer index. This implies that the minimum acceptable rate of return is set as the Libor rate for the Sortino ratio. Other threshold choices may lead to different optimal allocations and different characteristics in terms of higher moments, as shown by Bacmann and Pache (2004). However, we consider that any other choice would be arbitrary and would lack objectivity.

We start by optimising the different measures using the full data sample, between January 1990 and December 2003. Table 2 shows the composition of the optimal portfolios obtained with the different performance measures. Eight out of 12 hedge fund indexes appear in at least one optimal portfolio. The four indexes left aside display high standard deviation and/or negative skewness. None of the optimised performance measures lead to extremely concentrated portfolios. Each optimal portfolio contains between five to eight hedge fund indexes. Moreover, the maximum weight achieved in each optimal portfolio is below 42%.

Analysing the weight invested in negatively skewed styles gives an indication of how a performance measure is incorporating higher moments. More specifically, the asymmetric Sharpe ratio invests only 2.85% in negatively skewed styles, whereas at the other end the Sharpe ratio invests 64.63%. In between, the Sortino ratio invests 42.66% in negatively skewed styles which clearly shows that the Sortino ratio is able to capture higher moments at least partially.[2] Moreover, the preference parameter defined in the asymmetric Sharpe ratio formula plays an important role. Panel B of Table 2 presents the different optimal portfolios. The weight invested in negatively skewed strategies seems to be a direct function of the parameter chosen. This weight ranges from 10.22% with a preference parameter set to 0.75 to 46.74% with a parameter set to 0.1.

Table 3 displays the sample statistics of the optimal portfolios obtained with the different methodologies. The portfolios are optimised over the full time period and the sample statistics are computed on the full time period, the first half (January 1990–December 1996) and the second half (January 1997–December 2003). The optimal portfolio obtained with the asymmetric Sharpe ratio displays the best mean return, the highest standard deviation and the highest positive skewness. This picture is consistent in both sub-periods. The Sharpe ratio presents the most negative skewness. This is to be expected as the optimal portfolio derived from the Sharpe ratio invests in the most negatively skewed strategies. In fact, this negative number stems mainly from the second half which incorporates the Russian crisis event. In the first period, few hedge fund styles exhibit negative skewness. Figure 1 provides the comparison of the different

Table 2 Weights of the optimal portfolios obtained with the different performance measures

	HFRI equity hedge index (%)	HFRI equity market neutral index (%)	HFRI relative value arbitrage index (%)	HFRI convertible arbitrage index (%)	HFRI fixed income: arbitrage index (%)	HFRI merger arbitrage index (%)	HFRI macro index (%)	Stark 300 trader index (%)
Panel A: Comparison of the different methods								
Asymmetric Sharpe $\gamma = 1$	26.77	40.24	0.00	0.00	2.85	0.00	5.32	24.82
Sharpe	0.00	27.06	31.47	20.94	6.05	8.17	0.00	6.30
Modified Sharpe	20.70	40.93	0.00	11.51	8.50	0.70	0.00	17.65
Sortino ratio	11.89	30.87	12.94	17.14	8.94	3.64	0.01	14.58
MSRAIRAP	0.00	32.30	18.38	21.08	12.30	10.31	0.00	5.63
Stutzer	4.86	31.34	18.25	24.36	7.06	2.02	0.00	12.12
Panel B: Impact of the substitution parameter on the optimal portfolio								
Asymmetric Sharpe $\gamma = 0.1$	7.10	31.17	5.96	28.18	8.97	3.63	0.00	14.99
Asymmetric Sharpe $\gamma = 0.25$	8.86	41.64	0.00	25.18	2.71	0.00	1.54	20.06
Asymmetric Sharpe $\gamma = 0.5$	16.73	41.34	0.00	13.65	0.00	0.00	7.65	20.63
Asymmetric Sharpe $\gamma = 0.75$	18.70	41.65	0.00	10.22	0.00	0.00	8.41	21.02

Asym. Sharpe designates the asymmetric Sharpe ratio. Mod. Sharpe designates the modified Sharpe ratio, according to the Cornish-Fisher expansion. MSRAIRAP is the modified Sharpe ratio linked to the AIRAP measure introduced by Sharma (2004a).

Table 3 In sample statistics of the optimal portfolios

	Asymmetric Sharpe $\gamma = 1$	Sharpe	Modified Sharpe	Sortino	MSRAIRAP	Stutzer
Full time period: 01/1990–12/2003						
Annual mean (%)	7.27	5.90	6.50	6.26	5.49	5.94
Annual standard deviation (%)	4.46	2.29	3.44	2.83	2.17	2.50
Annual downside deviation (%)	1.57	1.11	1.13	1.00	1.04	0.98
Skewness	1.03	−1.25	0.91	0.41	−1.06	−0.04
Kurtosis	5.12	9.14	4.78	4.24	7.64	4.25
Time period: 01/1990–12/1996						
Annual mean (%)	9.13	7.15	8.03	7.65	6.79	7.11
Annual standard deviation (%)	4.46	2.15	3.35	2.76	1.97	2.47
Annual downside deviation (%)	1.30	0.59	0.85	0.64	0.53	0.66
Skewness	1.32	−0.11	1.22	0.83	−0.09	0.43
Kurtosis	7.13	2.57	6.58	4.71	2.58	3.56
Time period: 01/1997–12/2003						
Annual mean (%)	5.42	4.65	4.98	4.86	4.19	4.77
Annual standard deviation (%)	4.43	2.38	3.49	2.85	2.31	2.50
Annual downside deviation (%)	1.79	1.46	1.36	1.25	1.38	1.22
Skewness	0.82	−2.12	0.75	0.09	−1.62	−0.48
Kurtosis	3.35	13.39	3.51	3.80	10.01	4.78

The returns of the hedge fund styles are defined in excess of the Libor 1 month US$. Optimal portfolios are computed over the full time period (01/1990–12/2003).

methods by depicting the evolution of an investment of 1,000 in December 1989. The optimal portfolio obtained with the asymmetric Sharpe ratio performs better overall than all the others. In other words, the good performance of the asymmetric Sharpe ratio is not limited to a single period. This implies that the August 1998 crisis is not the sole cause of the difference between the methods.

The high standard deviation of the portfolio maximising the asymmetric Sharpe ratio is mainly due to the large positive fat tail

Figure 1 VAMI chart of the different optimal portfolios – in sample results

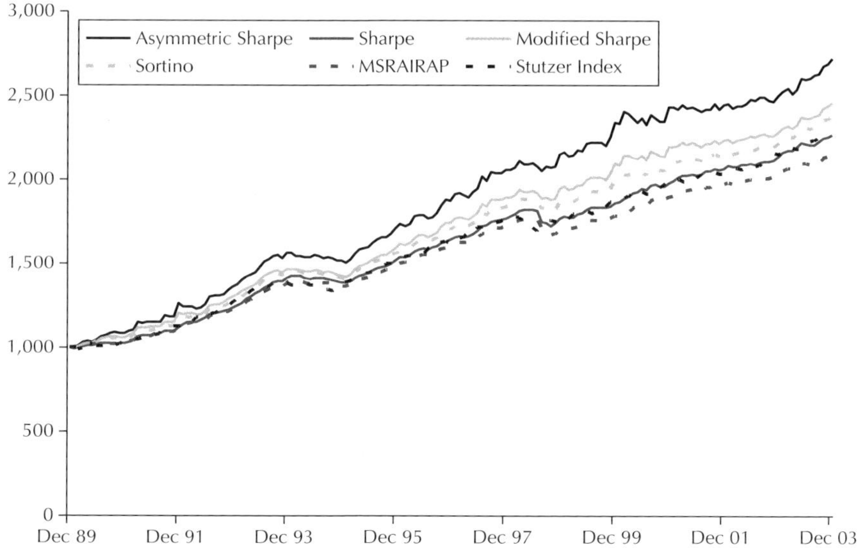

The graph represents the evolution of an investment of 1,000 during the period January 1990 to December 2003.

of the portfolio return distribution. Figure 2 depicts the omega functions of the four main optimal portfolios (Asymmetric Sharpe, Sharpe, Modified Sharpe, Sortino). On the negative side, the optimal portfolio obtained with the asymmetric Sharpe ratio presents the thinnest tail. The modified Sharpe ratio also generates a portfolio whose negative tail is similar to the one of the asymmetric Sharpe ratio. However, it does not perform as well as the one obtained with the asymmetric Sharpe ratio in the positive tail. The optimal portfolios derived with the Sharpe ratio and the Sortino ratio exhibit slightly more risk on the downside and less gain on the upside. However, the omega function of the Sortino optimal portfolio dominates the one of the Sharpe optimal portfolio at all thresholds, which indicates a second order stochastic dominance. In conclusion, the omega function of the asymmetric Sharpe optimal portfolio confirms the superior distributional properties of this investment and shows that the standard deviation is not a sufficient rating criterion.

We also analyse the impact of the preference parameter on the in-sample statistics. In the standard version of the asymmetric

Figure 3 Omega functions of optimal portfolios – in sample results

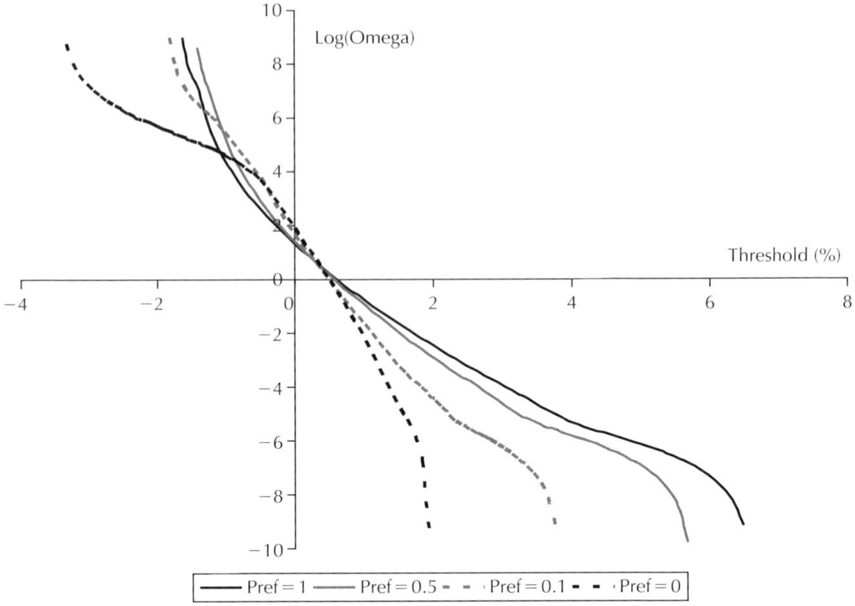

The graph provides the comparison of the omega functions computed on the track record of optimal portfolios on the period January 1990 to December 2003. 'Pref' refers to the preference parameter defined in the asymmetric Sharpe ratio.

allocation is computed using at least 60 observations. The portfolios are then held for one-month, six-month or 12-month intervals during which their out-of-sample monthly returns are recorded. At the end of the investment interval, the optimisation is repeated using the additional returns available. The following alternative is considered: either a rolling window of 60 months or an increasing window starting in January 1990. The former solution may be able to cope with changing parameters of the distributions. However, it is less sensitive to higher moments. Indeed, some extreme realisations like August 1998 have a strong impact on the return distribution of arbitrage styles. In the context of rolling windows, the omission of strong negative events may dramatically change the skewness statistics whereas it is intrinsically negative. This is why we favour the increasing window methodology and only report the results based on it.

Table 5 Out of sample statistics of the optimal portfolios

	Asymmetric Sharpe $\gamma = 1$	Sharpe	Modified Sharpe	Sortino	MSRAIRAP	Stutzer
1 month horizon						
Annual mean (%)	5.45	4.79	4.61	4.61	4.52	4.59
Annual standard deviation (%)	3.77	2.45	3.61	3.11	2.32	2.89
Annual downside deviation (%)	1.66	1.41	1.80	1.56	1.37	1.57
Asymmetric ind.	3.68	0.52	1.30	0.95	0.46	0.68
Skewness	0.38	−1.41	0.19	0.01	−1.47	−0.54
Kurtosis	2.99	9.02	3.86	4.63	8.68	5.85
6 months horizon						
Annual mean (%)	5.06	4.72	4.57	4.32	4.51	4.39
Annual standard deviation (%)	3.66	2.39	3.72	3.09	2.27	2.83
Annual downside deviation (%)	1.69	1.37	1.98	1.64	1.32	1.56
Asymmetric ind.	2.07	0.62	0.88	0.79	0.55	0.66
Skewness	0.25	−1.51	−0.09	−0.23	−1.53	−0.66
Kurtosis	2.73	9.93	3.86	4.78	9.21	6.00
12 months horizon						
Annual mean (%)	5.29	4.64	4.48	4.27	4.51	4.32
Annual standard deviation (%)	3.86	2.44	3.82	3.17	2.29	2.90
Annual downside deviation (%)	1.74	1.39	2.06	1.70	1.33	1.61
Asymmetric ind.	3.05	0.59	0.93	0.81	0.57	0.69
Skewness	0.34	−1.39	−0.05	−0.21	−1.50	−0.63
Kurtosis	2.87	9.10	3.89	4.70	8.91	5.79

The returns of the hedge fund styles are defined in excess of the Libor 1 month US$ between January 1995 and December 2003.

Table 5 reports the out-of-sample statistics for the different optimal portfolios depending on the investment horizon. Compared with the in-sample statistics, the mean return and the skewness are reduced. The best returns are still provided with the asymmetric Sharpe optimal portfolio. It is also the only methodology which provides a positive skewness regardless of the investment horizon. The optimal portfolio maximising the modified Sharpe ratio and the Sortino ratio are also exhibiting positive skewness albeit smaller on a one-month horizon basis. As shown by the kurtosis values, the asymmetric Sharpe optimal portfolio is not presenting any fat tail. All the other methods exhibit higher kurtosis, the maximum being reached by the Sharpe optimal portfolio.

Figure 4 presents the comparison of the different methods by depicting the evolution of an investment of 1,000 in December 1994. As in Figure 1, the optimal portfolio corresponding to the asymmetric Sharpe ratio dominates the other optimal portfolios. Moreover, this ratio is less affected by the August 1998 event, as its observed drop is smaller than for the other methods. However, the price paid for avoiding negative skewness is higher volatility, especially compared with the standard Sharpe ratio. Finally, the Sharpe ratio dominates all the other methods as a result of the bear market starting in 2000.

Figure 5 depicts the omega functions of the out-of-sample returns with monthly rebalancing. As already found for the in-sample omega functions, the asymmetric Sharpe ratio dominates the other methods in the positive and the negative tail. Surprisingly, the difference in the positive tail is significantly reduced compared with the in-sample results. Still, the Sharpe ratio has a positive thin tail. The negative tail of the asymmetric Sharpe ratio is less pronounced than for the other methods. In this context, the difference from the other optimal portfolios is bigger than in the in-sample case. Moreover, the Sortino ratio presents a better omega function than the Modified Sharpe ratio at low thresholds. Finally, evidence is found of second order stochastic dominance of the asymmetric Sharpe ratio over the Modified Sharpe ratio.

Table 6 analyses the impact of the preference parameter on the out-of-sample characteristics of the optimal portfolio. In particular, the skewness decreases with the preference parameter whereas the kurtosis increases with this parameter. This indicates that fat tail

Figure 4 VAMI chart of optimal portfolios – out of sample results

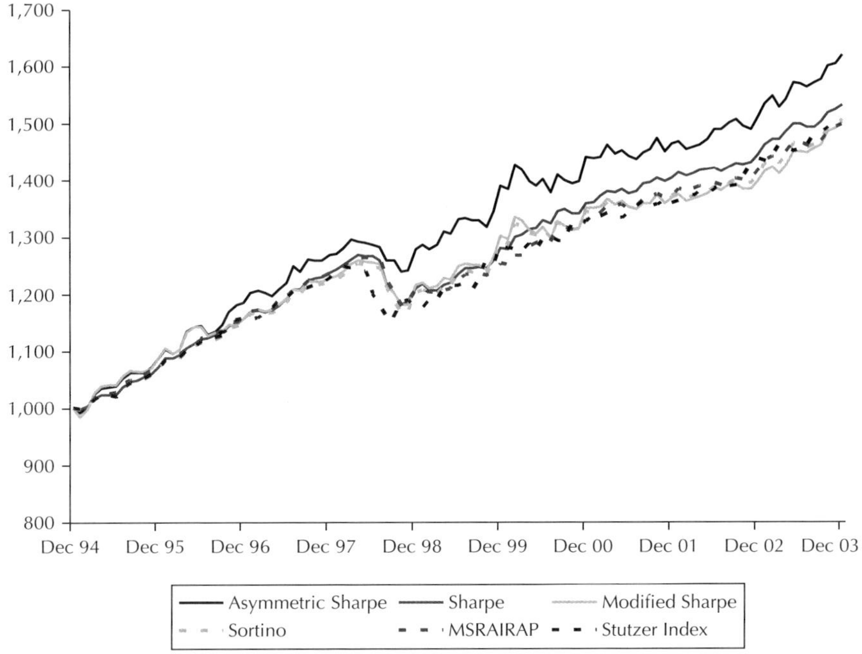

The graph represents the evolution of an investment of 1,000 during the period January 1990 to December 2003. The first optimal portfolios are computed with the first 60 monthly returns. The optimal weights are then used to obtain the out-of-sample return of the following month. The time period is then increased by a month, the procedure reiterated and the portfolios rebalanced.

risk can be reduced by modifying the preference parameter. Figure 6 depicts the different omega functions linked to the preference parameters. The choice of the preference parameter is important for reducing downside risk. It has only a marginal impact on the upside potential. The negative tail of the Sharpe ratio is similar to one corresponding to a preference parameter set to 0.1. However, its upside potential is far better than the Sharpe ratio.

CONCLUSION

The asymmetric distribution of hedge fund styles, which results from the implementation of complex strategies, calls for new methods taking this important characteristic into account in order to build optimal portfolios. In particular, arbitrage styles present low

Figure 5 Omega functions of optimal portfolios – out of sample results

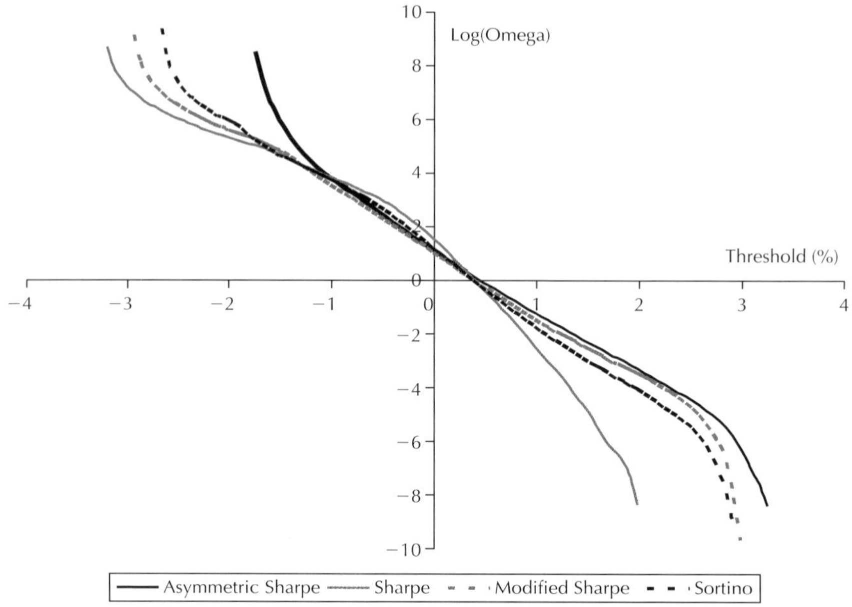

The graph provides the comparison of the omega functions computed on an out-of-sample basis. The first optimal portfolios are computed with the first 60 monthly returns. The optimal weights are then used to obtain the out-of-sample return of the following month. The time period is then increased by a month, the procedure reiterated and the portfolios rebalanced.

volatility and negative skewness whereas managed futures have higher volatility with positive asymmetry. As a consequence, hedge fund portfolio construction based on the mean-variance framework does not permit an adequate risk control of the optimal portfolios. The empirical results clearly show that mean-variance over-allocates to the low volatile styles linked to highly negative skewness. In this context, investors are likely to face unwanted and unavoidable fat tail risk.

In order to solve this problem and to control the fat tail risk, a new measure is proposed, namely the asymmetric Sharpe ratio. This measure is defined as a metric computed with the omega function of a given investment. It penalises an investment for having a fat negative tail and rewards it for having a fat positive tail. Moreover, when returns are normally distributed, the measure corresponds with the Sharpe ratio. A preference parameter is also introduced which captures the substitution effect between the

able 6 Out of sample statistics of the optimal portfolios

	Asymmetric Sharpe $\gamma = 1$	Asymmetric Sharpe $\gamma = 0.75$	Asymmetric Sharpe $\gamma = 0.5$	Asymmetric Sharpe $\gamma = 0.25$	Asymmetric Sharpe $\gamma = 0.1$	Asymmetric Sharpe $\gamma = 0$
1 month horizon						
Annual mean (%)	5.45	5.12	4.84	4.78	4.58	4.79
Annual standard deviation (%)	3.77	3.53	3.35	3.33	3.16	2.45
Annual downside deviation (%)	1.66	1.58	1.60	1.62	1.70	1.41
Asymmetric ind.	3.68	2.88	1.25	1.16	0.80	0.52
Skewness	0.38	0.33	0.20	0.15	−0.31	−1.41
Kurtosis	2.99	3.00	3.84	4.01	5.57	9.02
6 months horizon						
Annual mean (%)	5.06	5.12	4.13	4.29	4.37	4.72
Annual standard deviation (%)	3.66	3.71	3.60	3.46	3.07	2.39
Annual downside deviation (%)	1.69	1.71	2.07	1.90	1.67	1.37
Asymmetric ind.	2.07	2.19	0.71	0.77	0.72	0.62
Skewness	0.25	0.29	−0.35	−0.22	−0.43	−1.51
Kurtosis	2.73	2.94	4.66	4.44	5.86	9.93
12 months horizon						
Annual mean (%)	5.29	5.07	4.32	4.28	4.31	4.64
Annual standard deviation (%)	3.86	3.60	3.79	3.51	3.21	2.44
Annual downside deviation (%)	1.74	1.63	2.09	1.94	1.76	1.39
Asymmetric ind.	3.05	2.27	0.86	0.78	0.81	0.59
Skewness	0.34	0.28	−0.08	−0.18	−0.29	−1.39
Kurtosis	2.87	2.82	4.28	4.41	5.50	9.10

The returns of the hedge fund styles are defined in excess of the Libor 1 month US$ between January 1995 and December 2003.

Figure 6 Omega functions of optimal portfolios – out of sample results

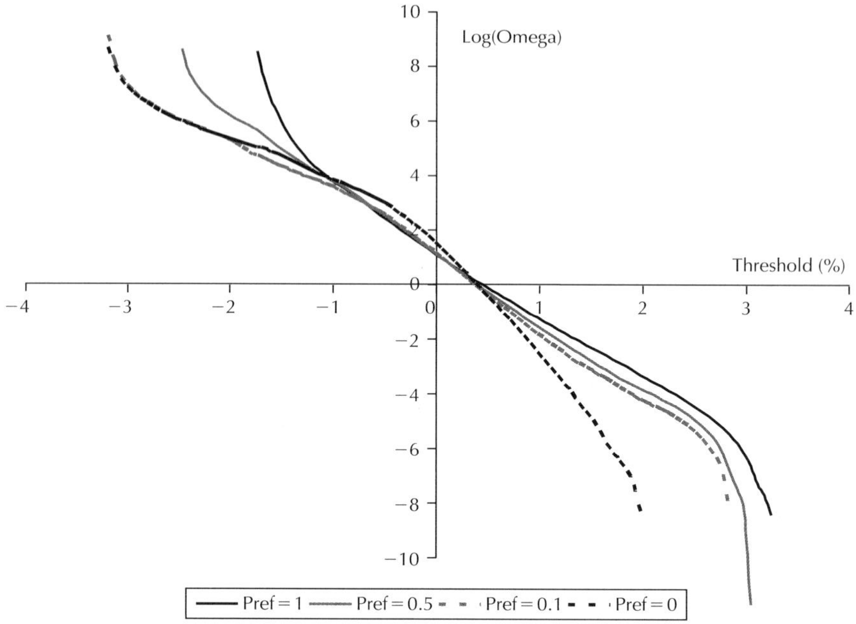

The graph provides the comparison of the omega functions computed on an out-of-sample basis. The first optimal portfolios are computed with the first 60 monthly returns. The optimal weights are then used to obtain the out-of-sample return of the following month. The time period is then increased by a month, the procedure reiterated and the portfolios rebalanced. 'Pref' refers to the preference parameter defined in the asymmetric Sharpe ratio.

asymmetric behaviour and the variance of the distribution. In other words, this parameter indicates whether the investor has more preference towards positively skewed investments or less volatile ones. We compare the statistics of optimal portfolios derived with different measures like the Sharpe ratio, the Sortino ratio, the modified Sharpe ratio, etc. The asymmetric Sharpe ratio displays the best properties in- and out-of-sample: its downside risk is reduced compared with the alternatives and its mean return is significantly higher than for the other methods. Finally, we study the impact of the preference parameter on the optimal allocation decision and show that the sample statistics of the generated optimal portfolio can be controlled using this parameter.

ACKNOWLEDGEMENTS

We thank Stefan Scholz, Michel Dubois, Con Keating, Anthony Ledford, and Pierre Jeanneret for in-depth comments and suggestions. All errors remain ours.

1 The logarithm of the omega function is particularly suitable to visualise the distribution (see eg, Bacmann and Scholz, 2004).

2 It should be noted that the way the Sortino ratio incorporates higher moments is linked to the choice of the threshold (see eg, Bacmann and Pache, 2004).

REFERENCES

Amenc, N. and L. Martellini, 2002, "Portfolio Optimization and Hedge Fund Style Allocation Decisions", *Journal of Alternative Investment*, **5(2)**, pp 7–20.

Bacmann, J. F. and S. Pache, 2004, "Optimal Hedge Fund Style Allocation under Higher Moments", in B. Schachter (ed.), *Intelligent Hedge Fund Investing* (London: Risk Books).

Bacmann, J. F. and S. Scholz, 2003, "Alternative Performance Measures for Hedge Funds", *AIMA Journal*, pp 26–28, June.

Bacmann, J. F. and S. Scholz, 2004, "Adding Hedge Funds to Traditional Investments", *AIMA Journal*, pp 34–36, June.

Berenyi, Z., 2002, "Measuring Hedge Fund Risk with Multi-moment Risk Measures", Working paper (University of Munich).

Bernardo, A. and O. Ledoit, 2000, "Gain, Loss and Asset Pricing", *Journal of Political Economy*, **108(1)**, pp 144–72.

Brooks, C. and H. Kat, 2002, "The Statistical Properties of Hedge Fund Index Returns and Their Implications for Investors", *Journal of Alternative Investments*, **5(2)**, pp 26–44.

Cascon, A., C. Keating, and F. Shadwick, 2002, "The Mathematics of the Omega Measure", Working paper (The Finance Development Centre).

Dacorogna, M., U. Müller, O. Pictet, and C. De Vries, 2001, "The Distribution of Extremal Foreign Exchange Rate Returns in Extremely Large Data Sets", *Extremes*, **4(2)**, pp 105–127.

Davies, R., H. Kat, and S. Lu, 2003, "Fund of Hedge Funds Portfolio Selection: A Multiple Objective Approach", Working paper (City University London).

Fung, W. and D. Hsieh, 1999, "Is Mean-Variance Analysis Applicable to Hedge Funds?", *Economic Letters*, **62**, pp 53–8.

Keating, C. and F. Shadwick, 2002, "A Universal Performance Measure", *The Journal of Performance Measurement*, **6(3)**, pp 59–85.

Lee, B. and Y. Lee, 2004, "The Alternative Sharpe Ratio", in B. Schachter (ed.), *Intelligent Hedge Fund Investing* (London: Risk Books).

Leland, H., 1999, "Beyond Mean-Variance: Risk and Performance Measurement in a Nonsymmetrical World", *Financial Analysts Journal*, pp 27–36, (January–February).

McFall Lamm, R., 2003, "Asymmetric Returns and Optimal Hedge Fund Portfolios", *Journal of Alternative Investments*, **6(2)**, pp 9–21.

Mina, J. and A. Ulmer, 1999, "Delta-Gamma Four Ways", Working paper (Riskmetrics Group).

Pratt, J. and R. Zeckhauser, 1987, "Proper Risk Aversion", *Econometrica*, **55(1)**, pp 143–54.

Schmidhuber, C. and P. Y. Moix, 2001, "Fat Tail Risk: the Case for Hedge Funds", *AIMA Newsletter*, (September–December).

Scott, R. and P. Horvath, 1980, "On the Direction of Preference for Moments of Higher Order than the Variance", *Journal of Finance*, **35(4)**, pp 915–19.

Sharma, M., 2004a, "AIRAP Alternative RAPMs for Alternative Investments", *Journal of Investment Management*, **2(4)**, pp 106–129.

Sharma, M., 2004b, "AIRAP Alternative Views on Alternative Investments", in, B. Schachter (ed.), *Intelligent Hedge Fund Investing* (London: Risk Books).

Signer, A. and L. Favre, 2002, "The Difficulties of Measuring the Benefit of Hedge Funds", *Journal of Alternative Investments*, **5(1)**, pp 31–41.

Sortino, F. and L. Price, 1994, "Performance Measurement in a Downside Risk Framework", *Journal of Investing*.

Stutzer, M., 2000, "A Portfolio Performance Index", *Financial Analysts Journal*, **56(3)**, 52–61.

15

Strategy Selection for Hedge Fund and Managed Futures Portfolios using Higher Moments

Lutz Johanning, Juliane Proelss, Artus Ph. Rosenbusch, Denis Schweizer

European Business School

INTRODUCTION

The problem of creating an optimal single hedge fund allocation is increasingly important in today's market. The number of funds of hedge funds is increasing, the heterogeneity of single funds is also increasing (and thus the complexity of the allocation problem), and the net asset flow to funds of hedge funds is decreasing (for more details, see the HFR Year-End 2005 Industry Report). Today's investors are increasingly demanding absolute returns, and meeting that demand is essential to attract new assets. Although funds of hedge funds have existed for over 30 years, until now, there has been no consensus on how to solve the optimal single fund allocation problem.

One important reason for this is that hedge fund returns are not normally distributed, and thus higher moments need to be included. Many researchers have found that higher moments should only be ignored if: (a) the distribution has an insignificant variation; (b) the returns are normally distributed; (c) the derivatives of the investor utility functions are zero for any moments above the second; or (d) investor utility functions are quadratic (see, eg, Chunhachinda, *et al*, 1997; Arditti, 1967 and Samuelson, 1970). Researchers such as Cremers *et al* (2005), Prakash *et al* (2003) and Alexiev (2005) have shown that (a) and (b) are not applicable to hedge fund returns, as they have a significant variation and are not normally distributed and (c) refers to a special case of a model incorporating higher moments.

With regard to (d), however, Hanoch and Levy (1970) show that quadratic utility functions are subject to serious limitations, because they bound the range of possible outcomes and imply increasing absolute risk aversion. As a result, many authors have found theoretical and empirical evidence that quadratic utility functions are insufficient to describe real investor utility functions (see, eg, Kraus and Litzenberger, 1976; Gordon *et al*, 1972; Pedersen and Satchell, 2003). If one believes hedge fund returns are not normally distributed and investors do not have quadratic utility functions, it is necessary to impose unrestricted utility functions, which implies that higher moments must be considered.

Arditti and Levy (1975) point out that the economic importance of including the third moment is widely recognised (eg, Markowitz, 1952; Samuelson, 1970; Harvey *et al* 2004). Little is currently known about the role of fourth and higher moments. Kraus and Litzenberger (1976), for example, find that investors are averse to variance but prefer positive skewness, which is consistent with decreasing absolute risk aversion. They chose to ignore fourth and higher moments in their model, primarily because at that time no behavioural arguments for including them had been made.

On the other hand, many researchers hold the opposite opinion. Fang and Lai (1997), for example, demonstrate that kurtosis is important. They find that investors discern differences in kurtosis and are rewarded with higher expected returns for bearing systematic skewness and kurtosis. Dittmar [2002] argues that the incorporation of kurtosis can be justified by utility-based arguments such as investor risk aversion, as well as intuitive rational arguments that investors are risk-averse to extreme outcomes. Additionally, moments beyond the fourth are hard to interpret intuitively.

Cvitanic *et al* (2005) study the effect of higher moments on the optimal portfolio. They find evidence that ignoring higher moments can lead to significant overinvestment in risky assets, especially in the presence of high volatility. Jondeau and Rockinger (2005) also show that a mean-variance optimisation can lead to large opportunity costs in the presence of heavy non-normality. Based on all of this previous research, it is assumed that moments up to the fourth are relevant for investors and should be incorporated into a portfolio allocation model. Furthermore, as Scott and Horvath (1980, p 916) note, "Investor preference is positive (negative) for positive (negative) values of every odd central moment, and negative for every even central moment."

First, a brief overview is given of several approaches that have attempted to incorporate higher moments. Cvitanic *et al* (2002), for example, analysed the model's risk using an approach based on non-myopic investors with incomplete information to calculate an optimal portfolio allocation. They found that the optimal allocation depends heavily on the framework applied.[1]

There are three conventional frameworks: classic mean-variance (and its extensions), mean-downside deviation, and mean value-at-risk. All are based on a Gaussian distribution. Several extensions have also been proposed to account for the skewness and kurtosis of the real return distributions.

Several researchers have used a modification of the value-at-risk approach to solve the asset allocation problem, with higher moments accounting for non-Gaussian distributions and non-linear correlations (see Favre and Galeano, 2002; Kooli *et al*, 2004; Rengifo and Rombouts, 2004). Favre and Galeano (2002) calculate a mean-modified VAR to build a portfolio that has the lowest probability of losing more than an investor-specific VAR at a defined confidence level.

Kooli *et al*, 2004 estimate a modified VAR using three different approaches: normal VAR, historical VAR, and an adjusted VAR using the Cornish–Fisher expansion. These approaches are intuitive and can incorporate absolute return more easily. However, they only take downside risk into account.

Rengifo and Rombouts (2004) generalise the VAR portfolio optimisation approach suggested by Campbell *et al* (2001), and develop a dynamic, forward-looking framework that accounts for evolution in variance, skewness and kurtosis. Their model uses a VAR constraint obtained using an ARCH-type model. However, it is only applied within a two-stock, two-index setting.

Malevergne and Sornette (2004a, b) emphasise the importance of risk measurement choice in the portfolio optimisation context to derive an efficient frontier. The efficient frontier accounts better for the non-Gaussian properties of the return distribution, especially the fat tails. Malevergne and Sornette (2004c) suggest using

Furthermore, each database has its own system of categorising the heterogeneous investment styles, making comparison across databases difficult.

Summarising hedge fund indices are also subject to selection bias, liquidation bias, and survivorship bias. Researchers such as Fung and Hsieh (2000) have studied the impact of these biases, and have found an average selection bias of about 1.4% per year, and average survivorship bias of 3% per year. However, Ackermann *et al* (1999) find that positive and negative survival-related biases offset each other.

As Davies *et al* (2005) note, a random sampled portfolio is a sufficient proxy as there is no empirical evidence that individual fund of hedge fund managers outperform the market. Thus, it is believed the investment choice offered by the 13 strategy groups are a good proxy for the typical investment opportunities of a multi-strategy fund of hedge fund managers. As long as the flaws of hedge fund indices are kept in mind, it seems to be the best basis for a fund of hedge fund strategy allocation.

Index data from CSFB/Tremont are used because it is one of the largest hedge fund databases. Its data are asset-weighted and rebalanced monthly, which implies that the indices do not under- or overweight top performers or decliners. The subcategories represent a minimum of 85% of assets under management. For further details, see the CSFB/Tremont database.

Table 1 gives more insights into the different monthly return distributions of the strategy groups. Except for managed futures and event driven–risk arbitrage, the hypothesis of normally distributed monthly returns is rejected at the 1% level for all strategies. Higher moments must therefore be taken into account. According to the descriptive statistics, the highest monthly returns for the sample period are realised by global macro, event driven–distressed, and long/short equity.

While global macro and long/short equity exhibit average risk, event driven–distressed exhibits high risk as seen by its low skewness and high kurtosis. It is striking that, except for event driven–risk arbitrage, which has a low risk measure according to the first three moments, all the event driven strategies exhibit the same return characteristics. Hence, it is even more important to distinguish between the three subcategories.

Note also that dedicated short bias and fixed income arbitrage have the lowest mean monthly returns during the observed period. While dedicated short bias has the highest measured variance, the third and fourth moments show favourable characteristics. Fixed income arbitrage has low returns as well as high risk.

INCORPORATING INVESTOR PREFERENCES INTO THE PGP FRAMEWORK

As noted earlier, previous research has focused on the estimation of an optimal portfolio using different sets of preference parameters, α, δ and γ. Although the optimal portfolios obtained through the classic PGP framework are easily interpretable, and the methodology and choice for the preference parameters, α, δ and γ are intuitive, one important factor is missing: how to use those preference parameters to represent the preferences and choices of real-world investors. We aim to derive a reasonable, economically justified set of α, δ and γ to link the classical PGP framework with real investor preferences.

In order to derive estimates for α, β and γ, an optimal portfolio that includes those preferences is first estimated. Following current literature, investors want to maximise returns while minimising losses. Depending on individual risk aversion and market volatility, as well as other less feasible constants, investors are more or less sensitive to the time horizon in which they realise overall negative returns. For economic reasons, it is assumed that investors do not want to lose any money within a one-year horizon. This aversion to overall negative returns independent of a benchmark is described in the literature as the search for absolute returns. Following Favre and Galeano (2002), Kooli *et al* (2004) and Rengifo and Rombouts (2004), we find that VAR is a suitable portfolio optimisation method that incorporates absolute return constraints without neglecting higher moments.

To obtain such a portfolio, we stipulate that the return of a portfolio is a linear combination of different hedge fund strategies to be maximised as follows: VAR should be positive for the 5% quartile, meaning that 95% of the time investors will not lose any money within one year. The weights of the hedge fund strategies sum to 1, and short-selling is not permitted. Contrary to other researchers like Favre and Galeano (2002), we do not assume or estimate a certain distribution of the historical returns to calculate VAR.

Instead, VAR is calculated according to the historical distribution as the best possible estimate for the future distribution of the portfolio. We thus minimise the risk of incurring unnecessary estimation errors of the return distribution.

However, a portfolio with those constraints is not easy to compute. The set of permitted outcomes is coherent, but not polyedric, and possibly not even convex. The optimisation problem thus cannot be solved by a classical LP/QP solver. But since the objective function is not especially complex and the variables are constrained, the optimum can be found using a random, local search technique or a generic method.

Next the optimal portfolio is transposed into the PGP framework and the investor preference parameters that are consistent with the given portfolio determined. In contrast to Lai's (1991) optimisation procedure, which restricts the volatility of the target portfolios to 1, we attempt to construct a PGP portfolio that will be identical to that obtained through the VAR approach.

Having estimated a portfolio incorporating real investor preferences, the only remaining unknowns in the PGP framework are the investor preference parameters, α, δ and γ. The PGP portfolio is standardised by using the volatility of the VAR portfolio to solve this problem. It is now possible to estimate the preference parameters of a PGP portfolio that are identical to the VAR portfolio. In line with previous arguments, the target quantity is coherent but not geometrically trivial. By applying a random or generic optimisation procedure, we can derive estimates for the unknown parameter.

Contrary to findings by such researchers as Davies *et al* (2005) and Chunhachinda *et al* (1997), we find it is unnecessary to estimate different sets of parameters to incorporate investor preferences, eg, for absolute returns. Thus, there is a representative set of real investor preference parameters expressed through the VAR portfolio.

Four-moment PGP framework

This section briefly describes the PGP model and how to obtain the optimal portfolio. More details of the PGP methodology are provided by Prakash *et al* (2003) and Lai (1991). The economy can be described as follows: We consider $n + 1$ assets, which can be decomposed into n hedge fund strategy groups and the risk-free rate. The standard portfolio selection assumptions are used, eg, perfect divisibility of the invested strategies, no taxes, no transaction costs, and perfect markets. The constraints are also imposed that the lending and borrowing rates must be equal and flat, and short-selling is not permitted. The technical assumptions are as follows: The first four moments for returns $\tilde{r}_i$ of the risky assets exist, and the $n \times n$ covariance matrix V of the asset returns $\tilde{r}_i$ is positive definite.

Let

I = the $n \times 1$ identity vector,

X^T = $(x_1, x_2, \ldots, x_n)$ be the transposed portfolio weight vector, where x_i equals the percentage amount invested in risky asset i,

$\tilde{r}_i$ = the mean return of risky asset i,

r_f = the risk-free rate,

$\tilde{R}^T$ = the transposed vector of the mean returns of risky assets $i = 1, \ldots, n$,

σ^*_{VAR} = the standard deviation of the optimal VAR portfolio, and

E = the expectation operator.

The portfolio selection problem for higher moments can now be expressed as a multiple objective programming problem:

$$
\begin{aligned}
&\text{Maximise} && Z_1 = E(X^T\tilde{R}) + x_{n+1} \cdot r_f \\
&\text{Maximise} && Z_3 = E[X^T(\tilde{R} - E[\tilde{R}])/(X^T V X)^{1/2}]^3 \\
&\text{Minimise} && Z_4 = E[X^T(\tilde{R} - E[\tilde{R}])/(X^T V X)^{1/2}]^4 \\
&\text{subject to} && X^T V X = \sigma^*_{\text{VAR}},\ X \geq 0,\ x_{n+1} = 1 - I^T X
\end{aligned}
$$

where Z_1 is the expected return, Z_3 is the skewness, and Z_4 is the kurtosis of the risky portfolio. The standard PGP problem can now be written as follows:

Minimise $Z = (d_1)^a + (d_3)^\delta + (d_4)^\gamma$

subject to

$$
\begin{aligned}
Z_1^* &= E(X^T\tilde{R}) + x_{n+1} \cdot r_f + d_1 \\
Z_3^* &= E[X^T(\tilde{R} - E[\tilde{R}])/(X^T V X)^{1/2}]^3 + d_3 \\
-Z_4^* &= -E[X^T(\tilde{R} - E[\tilde{R}])/(X^T V X)^{1/2}]^4 + d_4 \\
& d_1, d_3, d_4 \geq 0,\ X \geq 0,\ x_{n+1} = 1 - I^T X,\ X^T V X = \sigma^*_{\text{VAR}}
\end{aligned}
$$

Contrary to the classic PGP framework and according to Lai (1991) and others, the variance in our case is not restricted to 1, but rather

PGP optimisations. The parameters derived from this procedure reflect the preferences described through the optimal VAR portfolio, or the demand for absolute return.

EMPIRICAL RESULTS

This section estimates an optimal VAR portfolio according to the procedure previously described. Using the PGP framework, a portfolio is approximated that is close to the previously computed VAR portfolio. The unknown parameters are the preference parameters, α, δ and γ.

Table 2 reports the portfolio weights for the optimal (absolute return) VAR portfolio and the PGP portfolio that minimises the squared distance between the two portfolio weight vectors. The table shows that a PGP optimal portfolio with preference parameters for return, skewness, and kurtosis of $\alpha = 1$, $\delta = 16$ and $\gamma = 0$ will closely replicate the optimal VAR portfolio.

Without introducing restrictions on portfolio weights x_i, the optimal "absolute return" portfolio consists of three different strategies, with Global Macro having the highest allocation. The estimated unrestricted portfolio is consistent with Davies *et al*'s (2005) results. They derived an optimal portfolio for small investors (each strategy portfolio consisted of five funds), with return ($\alpha = 1$) and skewness ($\delta = 1$) preferences consisting mainly of global macro (78%) and long/short equity (10%).

Based on risk/return characteristics, one would expect to see an allocation to event driven–multi-strategy or equity market neutral rather than to global macro or long/short equity. But when taking higher moments into account, the aforementioned strategies are among those with the highest positive skewness and lowest kurtosis. It is therefore surprising that no money is allocated to equity market neutral, which appears to have the most favourable risk characteristics even for higher moments. Instead, more than 25% is allocated to event driven–distressed.

But a closer look reveals two major reasons for this result. The methodology and the assumed preferences are the first reason: Estimating a portfolio for an investor who wishes to maximise absolute return is intuitively tantamount to an investor willing to take moderate risks in order to obtain higher profits. When this

Table 2 Asset allocation across strategy groups for optimal absolute return portfolios for an unrestricted portfolio

	VAR portfolio	PGP portfolio
	Distance VAR/PGP portfolio 0.60	Estimated preference parameters $\alpha = 1$ $\delta = 16$ $\gamma = 0$
Risk and return (per year)		
Mean return (%)	13.39	13.39
Std. Dev. (%)	9.17	9.19
Skewness	0.34	0.33
Kurtosis	3.13	3.15
VAR	−0.08	0.00
Allocation		
Convertible arbitrage (%)	0.00	0.00
Dedicated short bias (%)	0.00	0.00
Event driven–distressed (%)	26.42	26.25
Event driven (%)	0.00	0.00
Event driven–multi-strategy (%)	0.00	0.00
Emerging markets (%)	0.00	0.00
Fixed income arbitrage (%)	0.00	0.00
Managed futures (%)	0.00	0.00
Global macro (%)	45.58	46.07
Long/short equity (%)	28.00	27.69
Multi-strategy (%)	0.00	0.00
Equity market neutral (%)	0.00	0.00
Event driven–risk arbitrage (%)	0.00	0.00

Note: Reported values calculated from monthly index returns from January 1996 to November 2005.

strategy is expressed by moments, the investor will tend to allocate money to strategies with high mean monthly returns, moderate volatility (as a risk measure), positive skewness (as a measure of higher probabilities of positive returns), and low kurtosis (as a measure of aversion to extreme risks). Consequently, equity market neutral will not maximise the expected risk-adjusted return for an absolute return investor. However, that does not fully explain such a high allocation to event driven–distressed, a strategy offering high returns but significant negative skewness and excess kurtosis.

The second reason is the relationship between the assets in a diversified portfolio, which plays an important role in determining the return characteristics. As Davies *et al* (2005) note, the covariance, co-skewness, and co-kurtosis significantly influence capital allocation. For certain strategies, this may imply that any negative impact – exhibited in the moment statistics – is outweighed by favourable properties of the co-moment characteristics. It therefore follows that the optimal absolute return portfolio exhibits a higher mean, lower volatility, higher skewness and lower kurtosis than any of the annualised single strategies while also meeting the non-loss restriction at the 5% quartile.

Obviously, investors who demand absolute returns have the highest preference for returns, as expressed in the PGP framework by an alpha of 1. A weight or alpha of 1 is equivalent to a linear penalisation function with a gradient of 1. This implies that the respective moment is significant, and a further reduction of the distance is always beneficial. The estimation shows that investors with absolute return preferences have a lower preference for skewness than for return ($\gamma = 16$). If the distance to the respective optimum is low enough, it would therefore not be worthwhile to optimise the distance any further. The higher the preference parameter, the faster reducing the distance becomes futile, because the gradient of exponential functions disappears as one approaches zero.

According to the estimation for γ, investors who demand absolute returns have no clear preference regarding kurtosis. This is to be expected, as the VAR portfolio does not fully account for extreme risks (only stress tests can capture such risks). Nevertheless, this phenomenon can also be explained via the tenets of behavioural finance. Kahneman and Tversky (1974) find that investors tend to disregard intangible information. Since extreme risks are not present in daily life, investors tend to repress those risks and they are not reflected in active preferences. Kahneman and Tversky's (1979) prospect theory posits that investors tend to assess returns relative to a reference point. The further the returns are away from the reference point, the less weight investors give them (this is often described as declining marginal (positive or negative) utility). If investors attribute less weight to extreme returns, this implies a gamma of 0.

We confirm the results of Davies *et al* (2005), who find that a fund of fund portfolio should consist of only a few strategies rather than a large diversification. Global macro plays an important role in this fund of hedge fund portfolio. However, many investors demand

Table 3 Asset allocation across strategy groups for optimal absolute return portfolios for a restricted portfolio

	VAR portfolio	PGP portfolio
	Distance VAR/PGP portfolio 3.18	Estimated preference parameters $\alpha = 1$ $\delta = 8$ $\gamma = 0$
Risk and return (per year)		
Mean (%)	13.07	13.06
Std. Dev. (%)	8.61	8.57
Skewness	0.35	0.37
Kurtosis	2.52	2.53
VAR	−0.32	−0.42
Allocation		
Convertible arbitrage (%)	0.00	0.00
Dedicated short bias (%)	0.00	0.00
Event driven–distressed (%)	30.00	30.00
Event driven (%)	5.15	2.97
Event driven–multi-strategy (%)	2.87	4.38
Emerging markets (%)	0.00	0.00
Fixed income arbitrage (%)	0.00	0.00
Managed futures (%)	0.00	0.00
Global macro (%)	30.00	30.00
Long/short equity (%)	30.00	30.00
Multi-strategy (%)	0.85	0.00
Equity market neutral (%)	1.13	2.65
Event driven–risk arbitrage (%)	0.00	0.00

Note: Reported values are calculated from monthly index returns from January 1996 to November 2005.

even more diversification, and the framework allows us to incorporate such a maximum allocation constraint. In order to analyse the implications for portfolio allocation and preference parameters, an optimal portfolio is estimated with a maximum allocation restriction of 30% to one strategy. The results are reported in Table 3.

Because of the allocation restriction, the modified VAR and PGP portfolios exhibit a higher square distance, which slightly affects the allocation to strategies other than those obtained with the unrestricted optimisation. Nevertheless, the maximum allocation difference is about 2%. Because the allocation to global macro can go no higher than 30%, the allocation to the two other strategies, which display favourable risk and return characteristics, rises to 30%. The

1 Cvitanic *et al* (2002) consider the classic CAPM, a CAPM with stale prices, a CAPM with non-linearities, an explicit single-index factor model, and an explicit multi-index factor model to obtain a proxy for alpha. They use the dispersion as a measure for model uncertainty.

2 The Jarque–Bera test statistic is based on skewness (S) and kurtosis (K) for testing whether a series is normally distributed. The test statistic JB is defined as: $JB = n/6(S^2 + (K - 3)^2/4)$, where n is the number of observations. The statistics follow an asymptotic chi-squared distribution with two degrees of freedom (see Bera and Jarque (1981) for more details).

REFERENCES

Ackermann, C., R. McEnally, and D. Ravenscraft, 1999, "The Performance of Hedge Funds: Risk, Return, and Incentives," *Journal of Finance*, **54(3)**, pp 833–74.

Alexiev, J., 2005, "The Impact of Higher Moments on Hedge Fund Risk Exposure," *Journal of Alternative Investments*, **7(4)**, pp 50–65.

Anson, M., H. Ho, and K. Silberstein, 2005, *Hedge Fund Optimization using Higher Order Moments of the Distribution.* Bad Soden, Germany: Uhlenbruch.

Arditti, F. D., 1967, "Risk and the Required Return on Equity," *Journal of Finance*, **22(1)**, pp 19–36.

Arditti, F. D. and H. Levy, 1975, "Portfolio Efficiency Analysis in Three Moments: The Multiperiod Case," *Journal of Finance*, **30(3)**, pp 797–809.

Bera, A. K. and C. M. Jarque, 1981, "Efficient Tests for Normality, Homoscedasticity and Serial Independence of Regression Residuals: Monte Carlo Evidence," *Economics Letters*, **7(4)**, pp 313–18.

Campbell, R., R. Huisman, and K. Koedijk, 2001, "Optimal Portfolio Selection in a Value-at-Risk Framework," *Journal of Banking and Finance*, **25(9)**, pp 1789–1804.

Chunhachinda, P., K. Dandapani, S. Hamid, and A. J. Prakash, 1997, "Portfolio Selection and Skewness: Evidence from International Stock Markets," *Journal of Banking and Finance*, **21(2)**, pp 143–67.

Cremers, J.-H., M. Kritzman, and S. Page, 2005, "Optimal Hedge Fund Allocations," *Journal of Portfolio Management*, **31(3)**, pp 70–81.

Cvitanic, J., A. Lazrak, L. Martellini, and F. Zapatero, 2002, "Optimal Allocation to Hedge Funds: An Empirical Analysis." Unpublished Working Paper, November.

Cvitanic, J., V. Polimenisz, and F. Zapaterox, 2005, "Optimal Portfolio Allocation with Higher Moments," Unpublished Working Paper, December.

Davies, R. J., H. M. Kat, and S. Lu, 2005, "Fund of Hedge Funds Portfolio Selection: A Multiple-Objective Approach." Unpublished Working Paper.

Dittmar, R. F., 2004, "Nonlinear Pricing Kernels, Kurtosis Preference, and Evidence from the Cross Section of Equity Returns," *Journal of Finance*, **57(1)**, pp 369–403.

Fang, H. and T.-Y. Lai, 1997, "Co-Kurtosis and Capital Asset Pricing," *Financial Review*, **32(2)**, pp 292–307.

Favre, L. and J.-A. Galeano, 2002, "Mean-Modified Value-at-Risk Optimization with Hedge Funds," *Journal of Alternative Investments*, **5(2)**, pp 21–25.

Fung, W. and D. A. Hsieh, 2000, "Performance Characteristics of Hedge Funds and Commodity Funds: Natural vs. Spurious Biases," *Journal of Financial and Quantitative Analysis*, **35(3)**, pp 291–307.

Gordon, M. J., G. E. Paradis, and H. C. Rorke, 1972, "Experimental Evidence on Alternative Portfolio Decision Rules," *American Economic Review*, **62(1)**, pp 107–18.

Guidolin, M. and A. Timmermann, 2005, "International Asset Allocation under Regime Switching, Skew and Kurtosis Preferences," Unpublished Working Paper.

Hanoch, G. and H. Levy, 1970, "Efficient Portfolio Selection with Quadratic and Cubic Utility." *Journal of Business*, **43(2)**, pp 181–9.

Harvey, C. R., J. C. Liechty, M. W. Liechty, and P. Müller, 2004, "Portfolio Selection With Higher Moments." Unpublished Working Paper.

Jondeau, E. and M. Rockinger, 2005, "Conditional Asset Allocation under Non-Normality: How Costly is the Mean-Variance Criterion?" Unpublished Working Paper, February.

Jurczenko, E., B. Maille, and P. Merlin, 2005, "Hedge Funds Portfolio Selection with Higher-Order Moments: A Non-Parametric Mean-Variance-Skewness-Kurtosis Efficient Frontier," Unpublished Working Paper, October.

Kahneman, D. and A. Tversky, 1974, "Judgment under Uncertainty: Heuristics and Biases," *Science*, **185(4157)**, pp 1124–31.

Kahneman, D. and A. Tversky, (1979) "Prospect Theory: An Analysis of Decision under Risk," *Econometrica*, **47(2)**, pp 263–91.

Kazemi, H., T. Schneeweis, and R. Gupta, (2003) "Omega as a Performance Measure," Unpublished Working Paper.

Kooli, M., S. P. Amvella, and J.-P. Gueyie, 2004, "Hedge Funds in a Portfolio Context: A Mean-Modified Value at Risk Framework," Unpublished Working Paper, September.

Kraus, A. and R. H. Litzenberger, 1976, "Skewness Preference and the Valuation of Risk Assets," *Journal of Finance*, **31(4)**, pp 1085–100.

Lai, T.-Y., 1991, "Portfolio Selection with Skewness: A Multiple-Objective Approach," *Review of Quantitative Finance and Accounting*, **1**, pp 293–305.

Malevergne, Y. and D. Sornette, 2004a, "High-Order Moments and Cumulants of Multivariate Weibull Asset Returns Distributions: Analytical Theory and Empirical Tests – II." Unpublished Working Paper.

Malevergne, Y. and D. Sornette, 2004b, "Higher-Moment Portfolio Theory: Capitalizing on Behavioral Anomalies of Stock Markets," Unpublished Working Paper.

Malevergne, Y. and D. Sornette, 2004c, "Multivariate Weibull Distributions for Asset Returns – I," *Finance Letters*, **6(2)**, pp 16–32.

Markowitz, H. M., 1952, "Portfolio Selection," *Journal of Finance*, **7(1)**, pp 77–91.

Pedersen, C. S. and S. E. Satchell, 2003, "Utility Functions whose Parameters Depend on Initial Wealth," *Bulletin of Economic Research*, **45(4)**, pp 357–71.

Popova, I., D. Morton, E. Popova, and Y. Jot, 2005, "Optimal Hedge Fund Allocation with Asymmetric Preferences and Distributions," Unpublished Working Paper.

Prakash, A. J., C.-H. Chang, and T. E. Pactwa, 2003, "Selecting a Portfolio with Skewness: Recent Evidence from US, European, and Latin American Equity Markets," *Journal of Banking and Finance*, **27(7)**, pp 1375–90.

Rengifo, E. W. and J. V. K. Rombouts, 2004, "Dynamic Optimal Portfolio Selection in a VaR Framework," Unpublished Working Paper, July.

Sahu, S. K., M. D. Branco, and D. K. Dey, 2003, "A New Class of Multivariate Skew Distributions with Applications to Bayesian Regression Models," *Canadian Journal of Statistics*, **31(2)**, pp 129–50.

Samuelson, P. A., 1970, "The Fundamental Approximation Theorem of Portfolio Analysis in Terms of Means, Variances and Higher Moments," *Review of Economic Studies*, **37(4)**, pp 537–42.

Scott, R. C. and P. A. Horvath, 1980, "On the Direction of Preference for Moments of Higher Order than the Variance," *Journal of Finance*, **35(4)**, pp 915–19.

Sun, Q. and Y. Yan, 2003, "Skewness Persistence with Optimal Portfolio Selection," *Journal of Banking and Finance*, **27(6)**, pp 1111–21.

Terhaar, K., R. Staub, and B. Singer, 2003, "Appropriate Policy Allocation for Alternative Investments," *Journal of Portfolio Management*, **29(3)**, pp 101–10.

16

Hedge Funds: From Diversification to Diworsification

François-Serge Lhabitant

Kedge Capital, HEC Lausanne and EDHEC

INTRODUCTION

Diversification seems to be a long established practice in investments. Yet in the 4th century Rabbi Issac bar Aha gave this following asset allocation advice: "a man should always place his money, a third into land, a third into merchandise, and keep a third on hand". More recently, in his famous article on the St Petersburg Paradox, Daniel Bernoulli argued that risk-averse investors should diversify their portfolios: "it is advisable to divide goods which are exposed to some small danger into several portions rather than to risk them all together." Last but not least, the danger of risking everything in a single investment – putting all your eggs in one basket – is as familiar as childrens fables and has appeared in literature for several centuries. However, despite these repeated recommendations, investors remained primarily focused on return. Risk was only secondary – as summarised by Peter Bernstein, in the old days, "risk was in the gut, not in the numbers". In the defence of these investors, we should acknowledge that they had no adequate theory to quantify the benefits of diversification or to assess its effectiveness in the context of a portfolio.

The situation changed dramatically in 1952 when a young graduate student named Harry Markowitz published his doctoral thesis. Markowitz outlined what came to be known as Modern Portfolio Theory (MPT), ie, a normative theory describing how investors should build optimal portfolios. According to MPT, the key to success, surprisingly, is not in the prediction of individual asset price movements using fundamental or technical analysis. It is rather in finding the optimal way to combine these assets to form a portfolio. In particular, an essential element in the analysis should be the contribution of each security to the risk of the entire portfolio, which might be significantly different from its risk as a standalone investment.

MPT should have revolutionised the investment world. Unfortunately, it was probably too innovative for its time. On the academic side, Markowitz's chapter almost did not earn him his PhD because his review committee had doubts on the economic nature of his research topic. And on the practitioners' side, the adoption of MPT principles by the professional investment community took almost 25 years, primarily because of the limits in terms of computing power. Today, the missing computing power is finally there, and more than fifty years after its invention, MPT is widely applied in the construction of portfolios. Its key underlying principle, diversification, is even sometimes called the "free lunch of finance", because it can reduce the risk of a given portfolio without necessarily reducing its average expected return.

The key question when applying MPT, of course, is how far should one go in terms of diversification, and in particular, how many assets are needed to effectively diversify a portfolio. In theory, adding more assets into a portfolio always provides new diversification opportunities, but in practice, the marginal gain associated with these new opportunities is likely to diminish as the size of the portfolio gets larger. The optimal level of diversification can therefore be determined by a simple marginal analysis; that is, more assets should be added as long as their marginal benefits (risk reduction) exceed their marginal costs (selection, transaction, holding and monitoring costs). Several academic chapters have performed this marginal analysis for equity portfolios, with various results.

Evans and Archer (1968) evidenced that a portfolio with only 10 stocks had about the same amount of risk as that of the market portfolio. Tole (1982) suggested that the optimal number of stocks in a diversified portfolio was between 25 and 40, while Statman (1987) was more in favour of 30 to 40 stocks. This apparent increase in the number of stocks needed to achieve a given level of diversification has been explained by a study made by Campbell *et al* (2001) on all US stocks quoted on the main US exchanges from 1963 to

1997. While the overall volatility of markets and stocks has been stable over the last thirty years, there has been a noticeable increase in the firm-specific risk component of individual stock returns. Indeed, for most US stocks, this component has more than doubled in importance between 1962 and 1997. As a result, more stocks are now needed to diversify optimally an equity portfolio. This was also confirmed by Malkiel (2002), who even suggested that one now needs 200 securities to achieve the same amount of diversification that historically was possible with as few as 20 securities

In this chapter, we have decided to leave the equity universe and focus on the new darlings of the investment world, namely, hedge funds. The popularity of these new investment vehicles has grown exponentially in recent years, as a result of the poor performance of stock markets and the historically low bond yields. However, due to a number of well-publicised collapses and the general opacity of their behaviour, hedge funds have often been branded as far riskier than most conventional modes of investing. Consequently, most investors spread risk amongst many hedge funds rather than amongst one, either directly or via a fund of hedge funds. This raises again the same question: how many hedge funds are needed to achieve an optimally diversified portfolio?

The structure of this chapter is as follows. In the second section, we discuss some of the mathematics of risk diversification, in particular when using risk measures that are not sub-additive and/or return distributions that are non-Gausssian. The third section addresses the question of diversification in hedge funds versus diversification in traditional securities. The fourth section presents and discusses the results of our empirical tests. The fifth section concludes our analysis and opens the road for further research.

THE MATHEMATICS OF DIVERSIFICATION

The mathematics behind portfolio diversification were formalised for the first time by Harry Markowitz in 1952. More than fifty years later, they still influence the practice of portfolio management on its most fundamental level.

Diversification when risk is measured by the variance

When modelling returns, Markowitz used only their first two distributional moments, ie, their mean and their variance. Using the variance as a risk measure allowed him to derive a simple yet analytical formula for the risk of a portfolio P comprising N assets:

$$\sigma_P^2 = \sum_{i=1}^{N}\sum_{j=1}^{N} \rho_{i,j} w_i \sigma_i w_j \sigma_j \tag{1}$$

where σ_P is the volatility of the portfolio, σ_k is the volatility of asset k ($k = 1, \ldots, N$), w_k is the weight of asset k in the portfolio, and $\rho_{i,j}$ is the correlation between the returns of asset i and asset j.

Equation (1) opens the door to portfolio construction algorithms. In particular, it suggests that an investor willing to reduce the variance of his portfolio can essentially take three possible paths: (i) he may select assets with low individual volatility, (ii) he may assign small weights to assets that have a high volatility, or (iii) he may look for assets that have a low correlation with other assets in his portfolio. The third solution is actually the most effective, because the correlation coefficient can be negative. Adding negatively correlated assets into a long-only portfolio therefore *lowers* the overall volatility of the portfolio, even if when these new assets have individually a large weight or a high volatility.

Equation (1) also suggests that the number of assets (N) needed to optimally diversify a portfolio should be a function of the characteristics of the individual assets, and in particular of their respective correlation coefficients. To understand how this works in practice, let us simply consider the special case where all assets have the same volatility (denoted σ), the same correlation coefficient (denoted ρ), and the portfolio is equally weighted. The covariance matrix is an $N \times N$ matrix with σ^2 on the diagonal and $\rho\sigma^2$ elsewhere, and all weights are equal to $1/N$. Equation (1) then becomes:

$$\sigma_P^2 = \sum_{i=1}^{N} w^2\sigma^2 + \sum_{i=1}^{N}\sum_{\substack{j=1 \\ i\neq j}}^{N} \rho w^2 \sigma^2 \tag{2}$$

Substituting the weights gives:

$$\sigma_P^2 = \frac{1}{N^2}\sum_{i=1}^{N} \sigma^2 + \sum_{i=1}^{N}\sum_{\substack{j=1 \\ j\neq i}}^{N} \rho \frac{1}{N^2} \sigma^2 \tag{3}$$

For any given w_i, the sum of all w_j for $j \neq i$ must equal $(1 - w_i)$. Rearranging terms yields:

$$\sigma_P^2 = \frac{1}{N}\sigma^2 + \frac{(N-1)}{N}\rho\sigma^2 \quad \textbf{(4)}$$

Equation (4) shows that the total risk (portfolio variance) of an equally-weight portfolio with N assets can be broken down into two components. The first component is the first term on the right hand side of Equation (4). It is independent of the correlation coefficient and can be eliminated rapidly by increasing the number of assets in the portfolio, as it depends upon $1/N$. The second component is represented by the second term on the right hand side of Equation (4). It cannot be completely eliminated, even when increasing the number of assets in the portfolio, but it converges towards the average covariance among all assets in the portfolio[1]. It can therefore be reduced by a proper asset selection, ie, by selecting assets that are loosely correlated or that have a small volatility.

Equation (4) also suggests two approaches to create a diversified portfolio.

- The naïve diversification approach consists of building an equally-weighted portfolio with a large number of randomly selected assets. Naïve diversification attributes no importance to the relationship between assets – the correlation between the assets is not utilised in the allocation decision. Rather, naïve diversification attempts to free ride on the size effect, as the variance reduction comes primarily from the $1/N$ effect. The simplicity of this approach combined with its effectiveness, has captured the attention of both investors and researchers.
- The MPT approach consists of using the information that we have regarding the future correlation of assets in order to determine the optimal weights. The size of the portfolio is then considered as a fixed, and the variance reduction comes primarily from choosing an adequate weighted mix of correlations. This approach is of course more effective but it requires using a quadratic programming algorithm to optimise the combination of assets based on their standard deviations and correlations.

The choice between the naïve and the MPT approaches to risk diversification is usually driven by the sophistication of the investor, but also by the availability of quality information on the correlation between assets.

Diversification when risk is measured by alternative risk measures
Using the variance as a risk measure is fine as long as one assumes that returns follow a Gaussian distribution. Unfortunately, it is now well known in finance that returns tend to deviate from the Gaussian model and exhibit heavy-tailed and/or possibly asymmetric marginal distributions. In such situations, the appropriateness of the variance as a risk measure is highly questionable. This explains why investors are often considering alternative risk measures in their analysis – for instance the semi-variance, the value at risk, the expected shortfall, etc. Of course, one should wonder what happens to the mathematics of diversification when using these alternative risk measures. The answer is not straightforward and depends primarily on whether the considered risk measure is or not *sub-additive*.

Let us recall that a function $f(\cdot)$ is said to be sub-additive if

$$f(x_1+\cdots+x_N)\leq f(x_1)+\cdots+f(x_N) \tag{5}$$

When $f(\cdot)$ denotes a risk measure, the question of interest is therefore whether aggregating individual risks can or cannot increase the overall risk of a portfolio. With a sub-additive risk measure, the risk of a portfolio will always be smaller than the sum of the stand-alone risks that compose it. But this is no longer systematically true if the risk measure is not sub-additive. In this latter case, diversification could even turn out to be a bad risk management strategy because it results in an increase of the risk of a portfolio.

Intuitively, it seems that being sub-additive should be a basic requirement of any "sensible" risk measure. Unfortunately, the reality is that several popular risk measures are not sub-additive – in particular Value at Risk (VAR) and semi-variance. As an illustration, Table 1 describes ten possible scenarios for two assets. When considering the VAR at an 85% confidence level, it is clear that the sub-additivity property is not verified. Indeed, the risk of *any*

Table 1 VAR is not necessarily sub-additive. In this example, the VAR of the combined investments is larger (in absolute terms) than the sum of individual VARs

Scenario	Loss on $Asset_1$ (US$)	Loss on $Asset_2$ (US$)	Loss on equally weighted portfolio (US$)
1	0	0	0
2	0	0	0
3	0	0	0
4	0	0	0
5	0	0	0
6	0	0	0
7	0	0	0
8	0	0	0
9	0	−1	−0.5
10	−1	0	−0.5
$VAR_{85\%}$	**0**	**0**	**−0.5**

portfolio made of these two assets will be larger than the individual risk of these assets. In such a case, there is actually no incentive at all to diversify, and investors should hold only one of the two assets.

This non sub-additivity makes VAR a problematic criterion for diversification, but also for portfolio optimisation, internal allocation of capital, as well as for the design of VAR-type risk-adjusted compensation schemes – see Artzner, Delbaen, Eber, and Heath (1999). Fortunately, VAR remains sub-additive in the case of normally distributed returns. Variance is also sub-additive, and this property turned out to be essential in Markowitz's MPT, where more diversification can only reduce risk.

A generalisation: the case of stable laws

Markowitz's results on diversification are only valid in the context of return distributions that are entirely described by their mean and variance, such as the Gaussian case. When returns are issued from more complex distributions, the benefits of diversification need to be reassessed on a case by case basis. As an illustration, let us discuss the case of stable laws. Stable laws, which are also called

α-stable, stable Paretian or Levy stable, were introduced by Levy (1925) during his investigations of the behaviour of sums of independent random variables. Unlike normal distributions, which are fully described by their mean and variance, a stable distribution is described by four parameters:

- a location parameter $\mu \in R$.
- a skewness parameter $\beta \in [-1, 1]$. When $\beta = 0$, the distribution is symmetric about μ.
- a scale parameter $\sigma > 0$. Note that this scale parameter is directly related to the traditional volatility measure in the Gaussian case, as $\sigma_{\text{Gaussian}} = \sigma \sqrt{2}$.
- an index of stability $\alpha \in [0, 2]$, also called the tail index, tail exponent or characteristic exponent, which determines the rate at which the tails of the distribution tapers off.

In general, the pth moment of a stable random variable is finite if and only if p is smaller than α. Therefore, when $\alpha > 1$, the mean of the distribution exists and is equal to μ. When $\alpha < 2$, the variance is infinite and the tails are asymptotically equivalent to a Pareto law, ie, they exhibit the behaviour of a power law. And when α approaches 2, the distribution approaches the Gaussian distribution.

Closed form formulas for stable law densities or distributions are known only for three specific distributions, the Gaussian ($\alpha = 2$), the Cauchy ($\alpha = 1$) and the Levy ($\alpha = 0.5$, $\beta = 1$). Consequently, stable laws densities are usually more conveniently described by their characteristic function $\phi(t)$, which is the inverse Fourier transform of their probability density function. One common representation is:

$$\ln \phi(t) = \begin{cases} -\sigma^{\alpha} |t|^{\alpha} \left[1 - i\beta sign(t) \tan \dfrac{\pi\alpha}{2} \right] + i\mu t & \alpha \neq 1 \\ -\sigma |t| \left[1 + i\beta sign(t) \dfrac{2}{\pi} \ln |t| \right] + i\mu t & \alpha = 1 \end{cases} \tag{6}$$

In the following, for the sake of simplicity, we will just discuss the case with $\beta = 0$, ie, symmetric distributions.

Stable distributions have a key property that makes them great candidates for analysing diversification benefits. When a portfolio

P is made of assets whose returns are issued from a stable distribution with a tail index α and scale parameter σ_i, then the return of the portfolios is also stable, with the same tail index and the scale parameter of the portfolio is given by

$$\sigma_P = \left(\sum_{i=1}^{N} w_i^{\alpha} \sigma_i^{\alpha} \right)^{1/\alpha} \quad (7)$$

Fama (1965) and Samuelson (1967) used this property to adapt the portfolio theory of Markowitz (1959) for infinite or undefined variance distributions of rates of return. In particular, when one uses equal weights ($w_i = 1/N$), we can distinguish three possible cases:

- When $1 < \alpha \leq 2$, the portfolio risk, as measured by the scaling parameter σ_P, decreases as the number N of assets in the portfolio increases.
- When $\alpha = 1$, there is no diversification effect, as the portfolio risk, as measured by the scaling parameter σ_P, does not change as the number N of assets in the portfolio increases.
- When $0 < \alpha < 1$, neither the mean nor the variance of the rates of return of the assets in the portfolio exist. In such a case, increasing the number of assets in the portfolio may actually increase the portfolio risk.

This short illustration clearly shows that (i) diversification may also work beyond the Gaussian case, despite the fact that these stable distributions have undefined variances in some of the cases considered ($1 < \alpha \leq 2$); and (ii) diversification will not work at all for some return distributions. These two results should be kept in mind when creating hedge fund portfolios, as individual hedge fund's returns tend to be non-normally distributed.

DIVERSIFICATION IN THE CASE OF HEDGE FUND PORTFOLIOS

Let us now come back to the main topic of our chapter, ie, the case of hedge fund diversification. We are regularly surprised to see some fund of hedge funds that invest in more than a hundred individual hedge funds, and they justify this by the desire of their manager to diversify his portfolio. In our opinion, there is something fundamentally wrong in this approach.

The first point to remember when building a portfolio of hedge funds is that their managers are primarily paid to take specific risks and hedge out market risk. Someone may argue that this goes against all fundamental principles of modern portfolio theory. That person would be right, but if we follow his argument, in a perfect world, hedge funds should not exist. In reality, hedge funds exist and their managers take on specific risk because they are convinced that markets are inefficient and that their skills, non-regulated structure, privileged access to some deal flow, better execution or simply experience allows them to exploit this inefficiency. And hedge fund investors support this idea, as they agree to pay stratospheric management and performance fees to get access to the specific risks (and returns) produced by these managers. As a result, there should exist a fundamental difference between buying shares of a company and buying shares of a hedge fund. In the former case, the specific risk exposure is theoretically accessible for free, easily diversifiable and should not be rewarded by the market. In the latter case, specific risk exposure is expensive to access but well rewarded. Note that it is also easily diversifiable, but after having paid high costs to acquire it, eliminating it by diversification would be hard to justify. When pooling several hedge funds in a portfolio, one should therefore be cautious not to diversify away the "biases" of the underlying hedge funds, as they correspond to the specific bets taken by their fund managers.

Note that this does not mean that diversification is useless. Just as choosing a bad manager may easily wipe out all the benefits of a hedge fund allocation, so too investing in only one hedge fund is likely to be sub-optimal. Diversification in hedge funds should therefore consist of finding *other* talented managers taking *other* specific and non-overlapping/non-compensating bets. In this context, the number of optimal hedge funds in a diversified portfolio becomes very much related to the *dimensionality* of the hedge fund universe, which is defined by (i) the time correlations for series of hedge funds considered as units of analysis, (ii) the space correlations among hedge funds, and (iii) the dynamics of these time and space correlations, which is modified by shocks and crises – see Lhabitant (2006). Not surprisingly, this dimensionality is much lower than for traditional equities, which suggest that a portfolio with a few well-selected hedge funds should be able to capture all the desired dimensions.

The second point to remember when building a portfolio of hedge funds is that their portfolios are not static, but dynamically managed and continuously rebalanced based on market conditions. As a result, the future behaviour of a hedge fund – including its correlation with other hedge funds or other asset classes – is extremely difficult to assess in absolute terms, but may be much easier to model using a relative perspective and this may facilitate the construction of effectively diversified well portfolios. As an illustration, several researchers have put forward the non-linear structure and option-like features of returns associated with hedge fund strategies. Fung and Hsieh (2001) suggested using lookback straddles to analyse commodity trading advisors, Mitchell and Pulvino (2001) evidenced the short put nature of merger arbitrageurs, and Agarwal and Naik (2003) generalised the option-based approach to other strategies. More recently, Kat and Palaro (2005) suggested a general procedure to design simple trading strategies in stock index, bond, currency and interest rate futures that generate returns with statistical properties very similar to those of hedge funds.

Clearly, this option-based approach seems extremely promising, especially for investors willing to build truly diversified portfolios. Indeed, if they can map hedge funds into portfolios of options or dynamic trading rules, they have a wonderful method of understanding their performance and the non-linear risks that can create and destroy their value. They can also see which kind of dynamic pay-off will be obtained at the end and can avoid cancelling trades. Say a hedge fund behaves like selling a put option on the market, while another hedge fund behaves like buying a put option on the same market. Their strategies may be fundamentally different – the first one could be a merger arbitrageur and the second a dedicated short manager that wants to limit its downside. But at the end of the day, they will produce opposite pay-offs. Should we combine them in a portfolio? Not really. Simultaneously buying and selling a put is neutral in the Black and Scholes world, but it is highly costly in the hedge fund world, as both managers will charge hefty management fees and one of them will get in addition at least 20% of the performance. Taking into account the dynamic and asymmetric nature of hedge funds, is therefore essential for successful diversification. And here again, one could say that there are not that many fundamentally different option strategies that hedge funds can be compared to, so that a small number of managers should be sufficient to represent them adequately.

As a summary, our opinion is clearly that (i) diversifying a portfolio of hedge funds is fundamentally different from diversifying a portfolio of stocks or bonds and (ii) only a small number of *carefully selected hedge funds* should do the work. Let us now see if this is confirmed by empirical data.

DIVERSIFICATION IN PRACTICE: OUR ANALYSIS

To provide a comprehensive representation of the hedge fund universe, we used the Altvest database and extracted the monthly returns for all hedge funds in activity during the 36 months of the May 2003–April 2006 period. In total, this gives a sample of 2,234 hedge funds. With this data, we created a series of equally weighted portfolios of increasing size ($N = 1, 2, \ldots, 50$ funds) of underlying hedge funds randomly selected. We calculated the time series of returns for each portfolio and used it to generate various statistics (average return, volatility, etc.). For each portfolio size, this process is repeated 5,000 times to obtain 5,000 observations of each statistic. This is necessary to estimate the "typical" behaviour of a portfolio of size N.

Due to the nature of our experiment, the return on the portfolio is not affected by the number of funds. This result is due to the linearity of the average operator. In a sense, the figure we obtain for a one-fund portfolio is the average of 5,000 hedge funds returns, while the figure for a two-fund portfolio will simply be the average of 10,000 hedge funds. We will therefore not analyse the evolution of the return here.

Figure 1 shows the effect of the number of funds on the volatility of the portfolio. The thick line represents the average of our sample, the two thin lines the 32% and 68% quantiles, and the two dotted lines the 5% and 95% quantiles. It is clear that the number of funds required to reduce the volatility is quite small. We find that approximately 10 to 15 hedge funds are enough to reduce most of the volatility. Adding more funds thereafter produces only marginal gains, particularly when one considers the cost of a real due diligence process. The variability of the results is considerable for single-fund portfolios, but decreases very quickly as the number of funds increases.

Figure 1 Impact of diversification on the volatility of a fund of funds portfolio

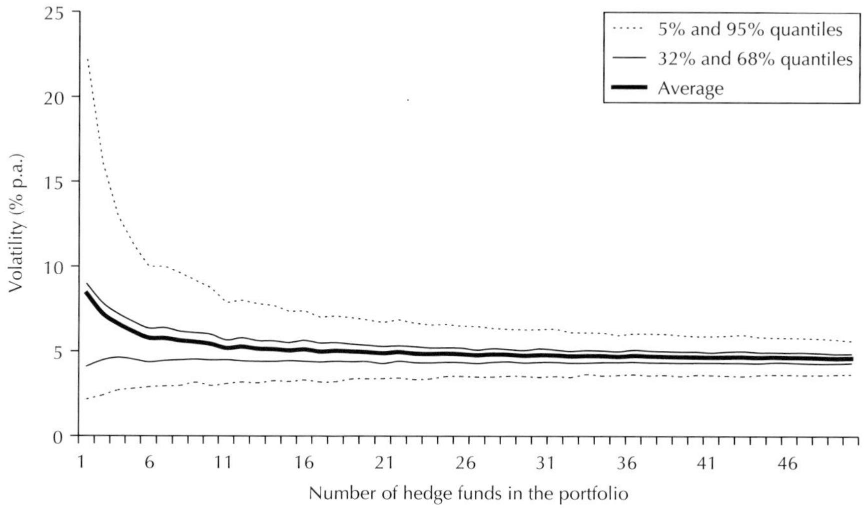

As mentioned above, hedge fund returns are generally not normally distributed. Asymmetry and fat tails in the return distribution are a result of the complexity of their trading styles. As illustrated by Scott and Horvath (1980), investors should prefer positive skewness and negative kurtosis. Of course, the characteristics of a hedge fund's past performance do not determine its future performance, as all disclosure statements continuously remind us. However, a hedge fund that is highly, positively skewed most certainly gives the investor a different gut feeling from one that is negatively skewed. For this reason, we have included the effect of the number of hedge funds in a portfolio on skewness and excess kurtosis in this study – see Figures 2 and 3. Our results tend to evidence that both skewness and excess kurtosis tend to decrease smoothly as the number of hedge funds increase, but this decrease is relatively slow.

We also analysed the behaviour of three generally accepted downside-risk statistics, the worst monthly return, the value at risk and the maximum drawdown. The worst monthly return is the greatest decline in net asset value for the portfolio for any one-month period during the time span considered. The maximum drawdown is the biggest percentage-losing period ("peak to valley") experienced by a particular portfolio, regardless of whether or not the

Figure 6 Impact of diversification on the maximum drawdown of a fund of funds portfolio

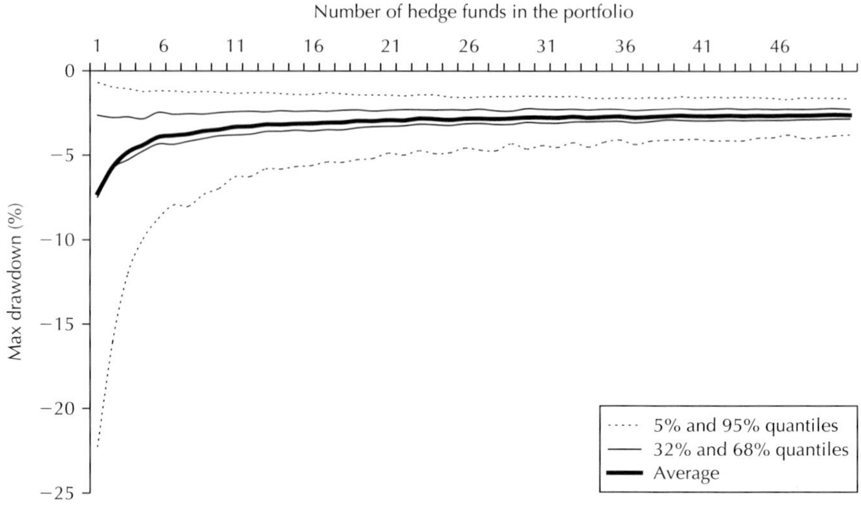

Figure 7 Impact of diversification on the correlation with the S&P 500 of a fund of funds portfolio

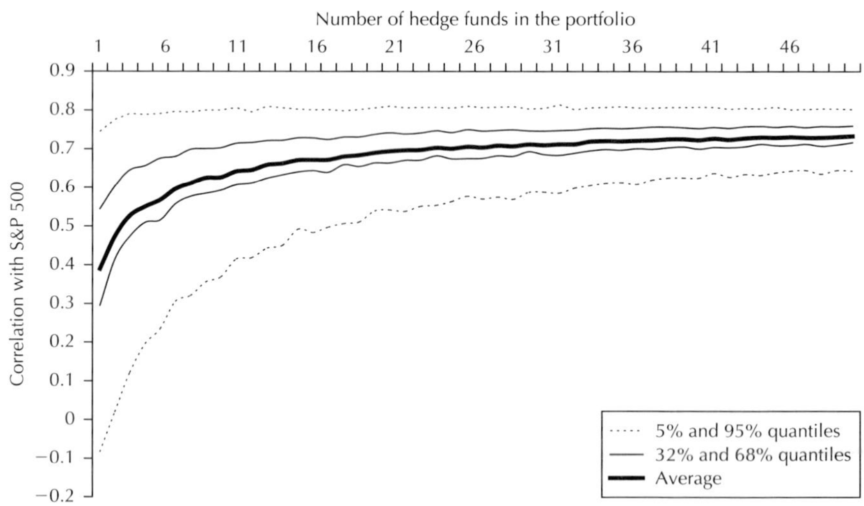

the maximum a particular portfolio could lose over a one-month period in normal market conditions. In our analysis, we defined "normal market conditions" as being 95% of the time and we calculated VAR by simply taking the 5% percentile of the empirical return distribution over the considered period (36 months).

All these risk measures gave the same answer: diversification seems to work well in terms of downside-risk reduction, and most of the diversification benefits are obtained with about 10 to 15 funds. Adding more funds still provides benefits, but the gains seem marginal compared to the drawbacks of managing the enlarged portfolio.

Finally, the last statistic we examined was the correlation with the S&P 500. Since investors generally still maintain an equity portfolio alongside their hedge fund allocation, it is essential to examine the impact of the number of funds in a portfolio on the correlation of its attributes with equity markets. As illustrated in Figure 8, it appears that diversification leads to a rapid increase in the correlation with the S&P 500 as the number of funds increases.

Although our analysis only focused on a unique database (Altvest) and on a specific period (May 2003–April 2006), its results are consistent with the findings of Henker (1998), Henker and Martin (1998), Schneeweis, Kazemi and Karavas (2003), Schneeweis, Karavas and Dubose (2005) and Lhabitant (2002, 2005) and Lhabitant and Learned (2003, 2004).

CONCLUSIONS

The proliferation of hedge funds, the increasing participation of investors in alternative investments, the growing collection of articles analysing hedge funds, and the ever-present uncertainty of future market conditions all give rise to a greater need to choose the right hedge funds when allocating to alternative assets. Although some level of diversification proves better than no diversification at all, investors should be cautious and limit the number of hedge funds in their portfolios to 10 to 15 if they want to truly benefit from diversification while maintaining the de-correlation properties of their hedge fund portfolios. Diversification looks like the only free lunch in Wall Street, but one should not eat too much to enjoy it. Particularly when sitting at the table has a hidden charge of two and twenty.

1 Note that if the average correlation between assets is equal to 1, there is no reduction in portfolio risk. If the average correlation is equal to zero, then the reduction in risk tends toward 100%, ie, a portfolio of zero risk. The closer the average correlation between assets is to zero, the greater is the reduction in risk.

REFERENCES

Agarwal, V. and N. Naik, 2003, "Risk and Portfolio Decisions Involving Hedge Funds", *Review of Financial Studies*, **17**, pp 63–98.

Artzner, Ph., F. Delbaen, J. M. Eber, and D. Heath, 1999, "Coherent Measures of Risk", *Mathematical Finance*, **9(3)**, pp 203–28.

Campbell, J. Y., M. Lettau, B. G. Malkiel, and Y. Zu, 2001, "Have Individual Stocks Become More Volatile? An Empirical Exploration of Idiosyncratic Risk", *The Journal of Finance*, **56**, pp 1–46.

Evans, J. L. and S. H. Archer, 1968, "Diversification and the Reduction of Dispersion: An Empirical Analysis", *The Journal of Finance*, **23**, pp 761–67.

Fama, E. F., 1965 "Portfolio analysis in a stable Paretian market", *Management Science A*, January, **11(3)**, pp 404–19.

Fung, W. and D. Hsieh, 2001, "Empirical Characteristics of Dynamic Trading Strategies: The Case of Hedge Funds", *Review of Financial Studies*, **10**, pp 275–302.

Henker, T., 1998, "Naive Diversification for Hedge Funds", *The Journal of Alternative Investments*, Winter, pp 33–38.

Henker, T. and G. Martin, 1998, "Naïve and Optimal Diversification for Managed Futures", *The Journal of Alternative Investments*, Fall, pp 25–39.

Kat, H. M. and H. P. Palaro, 2005, "Hedge Fund Returns: You can Make Them Yourself", Working paper, Cass Business School.

Levy, P., 1925, "Calcul des Probabilites", Gauthier-Villars, Paris.

Lhabitant, F. S., 2002, "Hedge funds: myths and limits", John Wiley & Sons, London.

Lhabitant, F. S., 2005, "Hedge Funds Diversification, in Handbuch Hedge Funds", in H. Dichtl, J. M. Kleeberg, Ch. Schlenger (eds), Uhlenbruch Verlag, Bad Soden, pp 197–211.

Lhabitant, F. S., 2006, "What is the Dimensionality of the Hedge Fund Universe?", Working Paper, Kedge Capital.

Lhabitant, F. S. and M. Learned, 2003, "Hedge Fund Diversification: How Much is Enough?", *The Journal of Alternative Investments*, Winter, **5(3)**, pp 23–49.

Lhabitant, F. S. and M. Learned, 2004, "Finding the Sweet Spot of Hedge Fund Diversification", *The Journal of Financial Transformation*, **10**, pp 31–9.

Malkiel, B. G., 2002, "How much Diversification is Enough?" AIMR Conference Proceedings on Equity Portfolio Construction, **5**, pp 18–28.

Markowitz, H. M., 1952, "Portfolio Selection", *The Journal of Finance*, **7**, pp 77–91.

Markowitz, H. M., 1959, "Portfolio Selection: Efficient Diversification of Investment", John Wiley & Sons, New York.

Mitchell, M. and T. Pulvino, 2001, "Characteristics of Risk and Return in Risk Arbitrage", *Journal of Finance,* **56(6)**, pp 2135–75.

Samuelson, P. A., 1967, "Efficient portfolio selection for pareto-lévy investments", *Journal of Financial and Quantitative Analysis,* June, **2(2)**, pp 107–22.

Scott, R. C. and P. A. Horvath, 1980, "On the Direction of Preference for Moments of Higher Order than the Variance", *The Journal of Finance,* **35**, pp 915–9.

Schneeweis, T., H. Kazemi, and V. Karavas, 2003, "Fund diversification in fund of funds investment: how many hedge funds are enough?" CISDM Working Paper, University of Massachusetts.

Schneeweis, T., V. Karavas, and R. DuBose, 2005, "Diversification in Fund of Funds Investment: How many Hedge Fund Managers are Enough to Represent a Strategy?", CISDM Working Paper, University of Massachusetts.

Statman, M., 1987, "How many Stocks Make a Diversified Portfolio?", *Journal of Financial and Quantitative Analysis,* **22**, pp 353–63.

Tole, T., 1982, "You can't Diversify Without Diversifying", *Journal of Portfolio Management,* **8**, pp 5–11.

17

The Risks of Systematic Trend Followers: When Markets Stop Trending!

Understanding High Intraday Volatility and its Impact on CTA Returns

John E. Dunn III

Thunderbird, The Garvin School of International Management

INTRODUCTION

Compared with some of the other hedge fund strategies, systematic trend following strategies, hereafter simply referred to as trend followers, have some very significant benefits both in terms of liquidity and lockups, potential significant returns in both up-trending as well as down-trending markets, as well as significant correlations benefits when combined with other hedge funds as well as traditional stock and bond portfolios. Yet during certain market scenarios, there can be significant drawdowns for trend followers, causing havoc to investors' portfolios, and keeping the uninitiated firmly on the investment sidelines. Although drawdowns in these trading strategies come with the turf, an understanding of the particular market conditions in which trend followers do very poorly can shed some light as to their risk profile. This short chapter presents some of the unique characteristics of systematic trend followers from the investment perspective, and explores how their return patterns can be negatively impacted during certain trading patterns in the financial markets.

TREND FOLLOW INVESTMENT PARADIGM

In addition to fairly high risk adjusted return streams in trending markets, trend followers offer significant benefits to both diversified hedge fund portfolios as well as to traditional portfolios. Over longer periods of time systematic trend followers tend to exhibit strong diversification utility to investors: for the period 1990 to 2001 the Center for International Securities and Derivatives Markets (CISDM) CTA index was negatively correlated −0.33 with S&P 500 during 48 worst months, and positive correlated 0.08 during the best 48 months. Additionally, trend followers have had better risk adjusted performance, with a Sharpe ratio of 0.85 for the CISDM CTA index during the latter half of the 1990s as compared with a 0.6 Sharpe ratio of the S&P 500. In most cases, trend followers also have a positive skew. Of note, while the majority of fund strategies are very highly correlated with each other when equity markets are falling and are not well hedged in down markets when liquidity dries up, the pattern of trend followers exhibit large and positive returns during worst performing months of the world equity markets, as illustrated by Table 1.

Moreover, because these strategies capture market trends, both on the upside as well as the downside, they can significantly improve portfolio diversification by providing returns when traditional markets decline sharply. Note however, that trend followers also show strong returns when traditional financial markets are also advancing, but have periods of losses whenever market direction changes significantly, and when there is little directionality in the market.

DISSECTING THE TREND FOLLOWING MODEL: SOURCE OF RETURNS

Trend followers are (systematic) mathematical models of market behaviour which put on market exposure when a market breakout or "trend" appears. Based on quantitative analysis of technical indicators, momentum, breakout indicators, pattern indicators and so forth, the existence and use of such models have been around for long periods of time and recent advances in computer firepower have meant that there have been a large number of new entrants into the field over the last decade. Yet all such trend models are based on variations of known and tested methodologies well documented in the financial and academic literature. Despite the claimed "proprietary" nature of

Table 1 CTA returns during worst months of global markets: December 1992–March 2006
CISDM asset weighted CTA Systematic Index against traditional financial market indexes

MSCI world (%)	0 year treasuries (%)	S&P 500 (%)	Russell 2000 (%)	HFRI composite (%)	CTA (%)	Date (%)
−14.01	−2.20	−14.46	−19.51	−8.70	6.33	Aug. 98
−10.97	−9.15	−10.87	−7.34	−1.54	1.10	Sep. 02
−9.13	−4.83	−8.08	−13.59	−2.83	0.19	Sep. 01
−8.41	−1.16	−9.12	−6.69	−2.21	−0.13	Feb. 01
−8.39	−5.68	−7.80	−15.18	−2.86	1.69	Jul. 02
−7.02	1.29	−5.60	2.19	0.34	−4.81	Aug. 97
−6.73	−4.12	−6.34	−5.03	−1.59	2.92	Mar. 01
−6.20	−0.35	−7.88	−10.39	−3.49	4.59	Nov. 00
−6.10	−4.46	−7.12	−5.08	−1.94	5.11	Jun. 02
−5.95	−2.90	−3.34	−4.48	−1.53	−1.25	Oct. 97
−5.49	−0.51	−5.28	−3.05	−1.24	−2.19	Sep. 00
−5.39	6.05	−5.02	−1.67	0.64	1.27	Jan. 00
−5.20	7.32	−0.95	−3.41	0.15	−0.21	Nov. 93
−4.77	−0.49	−5.87	−5.74	−0.21	3.07	Dec. 02
−4.60	−5.15	−6.26	−3.35	−0.41	1.13	Aug. 01
−4.49	8.54	−4.36	−5.40	−1.51	2.00	Mar. 94
−4.49	−4.31	−3.01	−6.08	−2.85	−1.22	Apr. 00
−4.45	2.72	−1.94	−3.53	0.59	−1.19	Mar. 92
−4.34	2.84	−3.64	−4.18	−1.27	3.42	Nov. 94
−3.74	−0.58	−4.42	−8.83	−2.08	−3.06	Jul. 96
−3.57	−1.76	−1.49	−4.88	−0.41	9.85	Jun. 92

Source: Pertrac and Altvest data

the individual trading models, the majority of trend following managers offer a fairly high level of transparency as to signalling methodology and trend recognition period, and with some simple intuitive reasoning, (as well as some careful due diligence) it can be (easily) inferred as to what a trend following manager is doing.

In simplistic terms, trend followers buy volatility, and thrive with market trends. Their return patterns exhibit long optionality and can best be compared to a lookback straddle, a common options trading methodology. To follow the similarity to long options trading and trend followers, in the latter a stop loss limits downside losses as one might lose an option premium if the option expires worthless, and as long as the trend runs it creates large profit opportunities. Even if a majority of trades the programme enters into are non-profitable and are stopped out, the strategy as a whole is profitable as long as the market trends that are captured outweigh the losses on any trades that are stopped out. Correspondingly in general, such programmes are extremely well diversified: to ensure the greatest chance to invest in trending markets, most systematic trend followers invest in all the world's large liquid markets, including global currency, interest rates, commodities, equity and bond markets, with the hope of finding at least one trend in a particular market at any one time. Stop loss positioning allows the profits to keep running until a trend reverses, at which time a position is stopped out. As such, most diversified globally invested trend following programmes will tend to all converge on the same financial market trends, and differences in returns from the different funds are mainly explained by the different position entry and exit signalling methodology, and certainly with different stop loss limits and trend exposure periods.

As such, success for a trend follower is dependent on several points. First, the natural risk premia from taking on hedging risk from hedgers, the amount of margin a manager decides to put to work and lastly, the manager's skill in developing models which can adequately predict market price patterns. Let's look at these three points in some detail.

INSURANCE SELLERS: TREND FOLLOWING IS NOT A ZERO SUM GAME!

Unlike the stock and bond markets, the majority of futures and options markets that a globally diversified trend follower will trade in are not zero sum games. Futures and options markets are composed of both speculators and hedgers, with the role of speculators being that of selling insurance to cover the business risks of hedgers, and taking risk premium out of the pocket of hedgers. Although hedging is generally thought of as encompassing operating businesses and multinationals hedging off their interest rate risk, currency risk or commodity risk, it also encompasses the hedging volumes of proprietary trading desks, market makers, investment banks and institutional investors. The volume of financial market hedging globally is enormous, and accompanies all sorts of transactions, and includes things such as convertible arbitrage traders hedging away equity risk by shorting the stock in a rising market and buying the stock in a falling market, option market makers delta hedging in the futures market and index arbitrage traders continuously trading the difference between the cash and the futures market. In sum, the existence of this large body of hedgers means that there are ample opportunities to earn a return greater than zero by trading in these markets, which is exactly what trend followers do.

THE IMPERATIVE OF TRADE SIZING

Returns to trend followers vary significantly from manager to manager, and to a large degree are designed into the system depending upon the amount of margin the manager wishes to put in play out of the total fund's equity, as with any futures or derivatives based trading programme. Typically, this would vary between 5% and 25% investable margin, and the rest would be kept as cash investments for eventual margin calls. This effect of leverage is important to us when considering comparing results of systematic trend followers to other investment management strategies; in short, one cannot compare apples and oranges without adjusting for how much juice is contained in each. Returns of any futures portfolio is very much a function of how much margin is put to work or how leveraged the model is, rather than the inherent success of a given investment model. As such, risk and return are designed into the system by the amount of margin with which a manager chooses to work, and this choice is to a large degree as much a marketing decision as it is an investment management decision. Those managers who put too much of their cash into play risk losing the whole amount if markets turn too sharply too quickly against them, so trade sizing is of paramount importance in assessing trend following managers.

TREND FOLLOWERS ARE BEHAVIOURALLY DESIGNED MARKET MODELS

Trend following models are created to profit from the observed patterns of market trends. Such models are nothing more than approximations of reality on behalf of their creators on how participants in the markets over time have driven prices up as well as down by their market transactions. Returns to a trend follower depend mainly upon the manager's skill in developing models that can detect sometimes complex but predictable market price patterns. There is as such, a high degree of skill in good trend following managers, as modelling is a skill which some managers do better than others. As such, such programmes are open to model risk, that is the risk that the model may not adequately portray investors' behaviour during certain market conditions, or may lose its effectiveness because the behaviour of market participants has fundamentally changed. Model risk, the risk that the model does not portray investor's current behaviour satisfactorily, is probably one of the most difficult aspects of considering a trend follower, and one of the biggest risks to the investment performance of trend followers.

DRAWDOWNS: THE ACHILLES HEEL – WHEN MARKETS STOP TRENDING

Unsettled financial markets and sharp market reversals in the financial markets are generally performance killers for the majority of systematic trend followers. In particular, when financial markets are sideways, and there is still a certain higher level of intraday or intraweek volatility in the markets, this more often than not, results in major drawdown periods for systematic trend followers.

Trend followers lose money when the model puts on a trade and a loss is realised when the trade is stop-lossed out. Sideways markets or in traders' lingo, "whipsaw" markets, accompanied by a significant amount of daily volatility are the worst market conditions for trend followers. Most trend following models take a certain amount of directional emphasis to put on a position. If the market does not know where it is going…and the trend breakout is delayed another day or another week because there is not enough steam (read market conviction) to push the position into breakout, such that at the end of the day the instrument returns to its original price and the trend follower's stop-loss is executed, the program will show a pattern of losses. Take a hypothetical stop loss limit of 3% stop-loss, leverage three times, apply to 100 different markets concurrently, and then the magnitudes of drawdowns which trend followers sometimes realise in sideways markets with a high intra-period volatility can readily be understood.

THE MIND OF THE FLOOR TRADER

Common sense and market savvy (or call it behavioural finance if you like) can give us some insight as to why this might happen. Consider a floor trader trading equity index positions today. His intuition might tells him to not be too long, to not step out too far from the rest of the crowd, but there is some enthusiasm in the market in the early hours, but as the day goes by market participants are not sufficiently enthusiastic to propel the market one way or the other. In the vernacular trader's lingo, when bulls come in the bears cream them, and when bears start selling, they find ready buyers. Intraday volatility or even intraweek volatility may be high, so there are no sustained breakouts developing into longer dated trends, hence systematic trend following models may put on positions, and later in the day or period, they may be stopped out because the market just does not have the enthusiasm to propel the trend forward. The pattern is quite simple: when intra-period, intraday or intraweek volatility is strong enough for models to put on positions but these trends do not continue for lack of market enthusiasm, systematic trend followers have drawdowns. When this pattern is repeated in all the major markets for a long period of time, systematic trend followers will have major drawdowns. The good news is that sideways markets do not last forever, but for only as long as markets participants to not have enough enthusiasm for trends to continue their breakouts. Quite frankly, it is not easy predicting how long such patterns might continue to last, and some may say, quite impossible.

MARKET PARTICIPANT'S BEHAVIOUR DURING SHARP REVERSALS

In addition to sideways markets, sharp reversals in market directions cause drawdowns, sometimes important ones, for trend followers. This is essentially caused during periods in which the markets have moved quite sharply to a new peak or new bottom, and reverse themselves sharply; a trading pattern characteristic of a market top or market bottom. Markets always react on the upside as well as the downside and in such cases are generally in far from equilibrium conditions for brief periods of times when the market is peaking or bottoming, such reversals generally happen quite quickly with strong volatility. Because volatility had been building up on the upside of the trend, this may have caused the model to recognise a sharper trend, and put on even more trades, such that when the trend reverses itself sharply, these trades are stopped out thus creating large losses.

CONCLUSION

Model tweaking and research continues at the majority of trend following managers. The manager who is able to create the model that can recognise and stay un-invested during periods of high intra-period market volatility and sharp reversals in the markets will create a veritable money machine which profits in each and every market scenario, in much the same way as an alchemist might make gold out of lead. Until now, however, current world class trend followers are the closest we have to this money machine! They deserve a role in every portfolio.

REFERENCES

Fung, W. and M. Hsieh, 2001, "The Risk in Hedge Fund Strategies: Theory and Evidence from Trend Followers", *The Review of Financial Studies,* **14(2)**, pp 313–41.

Gregoriou, G. N. and J. Zhu, 2005, *Data Envelopment Analysis: Evaluating Hedge Funds and CTAs* (Hoboken, NJ: John Wiley and Sons).

Harding, D. and G. Nakou, 2004, "Understanding the Relationship between Risk, Reward, and Margin/Equity Ratio in Managed Futures, and the Implications for Assessing their Attractiveness as an Asset Class", unpublished working paper (London: Winton Capital Management).

Jaeger, L., 2002, *Managing Risk in Alternative Investment Strategies* (London: Prentice Hall).

Rulle, M. S., 2003, "Trend Following: Performance, Risk, and Correlation Characteristics", in *Evaluating and Implementing Hedge Fund Strategies,* R. Lake, (ed.) (London: Euromoney Publications).

Weismann, A. and J. Abernathy, 1999, "The Danger of Historical Hedge Fund Data", Working Paper.

18

Selecting Last Year's Top Performing CTA as this Year's Choice: A Simple Trading Strategy

Greg N. Gregoriou

State University of New York (Plattsburgh)

INTRODUCTION

An important theme that has been the focus of immense discussion in recent years is the question of whether CTAs that have historically performed well are able to continue to do so in the future. Random walk theory suggests that having an in-depth knowledge of technical analysis such as, trying to predict peaks and bottoms, using past trends and market-timing are not feasible because stock markets adjust to information as it becomes instantly disseminated.

If investors are not able to predict future performance by using historical performance or selecting past winners then this proposed trading strategy may not provide any help for selecting top performing CTAs. Although there have been numerous studies demonstrating that CTAs exhibit little evidence of performance persistence over certain periods; a large number of studies are done pre-1999 during the US bull market (Schneeweis *et al*, 1996; Edwards and Ma, 1988; Elton *et al*, 1989; Irwin *et al*, 1992a; Irwin *et al*, 1992b). One of the more recent studies by Brorsen and Townsend (2002) confirm and also find a small amount of performance persistence using regression analysis during the 1990–1999 period. To ratify this the 1992–2004 period is used in this study, encompassing both bull and bear markets. Capocci (2004) adopts Carhart's (1997) decile classification and shows that most deciles do not outperform the CTA Global Index using a large database of 542 live and 1,350 defunct CTAs.

If investors can select a winning CTA, then over the long haul what will the investor's returns look like when compared with the Barclay BTOP 50 Index, Goldman Sachs Commodity Index (GSCI) and the S&P 500? Database vendors such as the Barclay Trading Group Ltd. publishes returns and other statistics of the top performing CTAs in a quarterly newsletter.

CTA returns have been the centre of attention since the collapse of the Russian ruble and the ensuing burst of the tech bubble in the spring of 2000 because of their positive returns during these negative market events. Managed futures have come back into fashion to cushion traditional stock and bond investment portfolios in bear markets for downside protection. As a result of their negative correlation to traditional stock and bond markets, CTAs can offer superior returns to hedge funds in bear markets, but will tend to underperform major market indices such as the S&P 500 in bull markets.

Do investors often get disappointed by selecting last year's top performing CTA as this year's choice? Although the above CTA studies have limited capabilities of predicting a top performing CTA in consecutive years, this chapter investigates returns of this strategy over a long-time frame using an initial hypothetical investment.

Despite the problems with performance measurement, CTAs are known for their bets on the managerial skill talent in their firm. A recent study, that examined the efficiency of CTAs using the number of trades per year per million, found that they possess a great deal of turnover regularly in terms of futures contracts (Gregoriou 2006). Behavioural finance literature has also makes a strong case that investors prefer to be associated with winning funds (Barber, Odean and Zheng 2000).

DATA AND METHODOLOGY

The data set consists of 534 live CTAs that reported monthly performance figures net of all fees to the Barclay Group database during the January 1992 to December 2004 period, a total of 156 months. It is also recognised that the data contain survivorship bias since dead funds are not examined, but Hallahan and Taff (2001) observe that even examining only live CTAs would have no bias effect on performance persistence.

Although the examination period is from 1992–2004, many CTAs have underperformed and outperformed the BTOP 50 Index, GSCI and the S&P 500 Index. How do these winning CTAs perform years later? Is a simple trading strategy able to provide superior returns than the S&P 500 and two investable commodity indices?

To prove whether winning CTAs have a tendency to repeat their performance, the annual returns are examined (net of all fees) of the CTA for the year after the CTA was the top performing fund. The average annualised arithmetic and geometric returns as well as the average annualised arithmetic standard deviation are then compared against the returns of the BTOP 50, the GSCI and the S&P 500. Therefore, if the return of the winning CTA for the following year turns out to be higher than the return of the stock market or the investable indices, then adhering to a simple trading strategy can be followed to provide superior returns for investors.

FINDINGS

The rate of return or ROR_t is the return the year the CTA was the best performer. The return of the CTA the following year is designated by ROR_{t+1}. The BTOP 50 Index, the GSCI and the S&P 500 ROR are the returns of the BTOP, GSCI and the S&P 500 for that particular year. The results are exhibited in Table 1 and indicate that the average annual arithmetic and geometric rates of return during the 1992–2004 period for CTAs the year after they were the top performing fund is 14.7400% and 8.9456% respectively with an annual arithmetic standard deviation of 37.0635%. The average annual arithmetic and geometric returns of the Barclay BTOP 50 Index and the GSCI were 8.3969%, 8.3953% and 6.6700%, 6.3426% respectively. The S&P 500 on the other hand produced a geometric and annual arithmetic average return of 12.2155% and 12.2315% respectively with annual arithmetic standard deviation of 14.2500%.

For the investigation period, the return of last year's winning CTA the following year surpasses both the return of the Barclay BTOP 50 Index and the GSCI the following year in seven out of 13 years, whereas for the S&P 500 index it is six out of 13 years. This implies that last year's top performing CTAs continue to be winners more than 50 per cent of the time versus the Barclay BTOP 50 Index and the GSCI and 46% of the time versus the S&P 500 Index. There were no CTAs that were top performers for two consecutive years.

Table 1 Rates of return of the top performing CTAs and various indices 1992–2004

Year	Top performing CTA	Rate of return ROR(*t*) (%)	Rate of return ROR(*t*+1) (%)	Value of US$1,000 invested in last year's winner (US$)	Barclay BTOP 50 CTA index rate of return (%)	Value of US$1,000 invested in Barclay BTOP 50 CTA index (US$)	Goldman Sachs Commodity index rate of return (%)	Value of US$1,000 invested in Goldman Sachs Commodity index (US$)	S&P 500 index rate of return (%)	Value of US$1,000 invested in S&P 500 index rate of return (US$)
1992	Ashley Capital Management (Financials)	201.38	20.31	**1,203.10**	2.55	**1,025.55**	−2.89	**971.10**	7.62	**1,076.20**
1993	Lawless Commodities (Diversified)	117.68	−10.10	**1,081.59**	13.42	**1,163.12**	−9.65	**877.39**	10.08	**1,184.68**
1994	Saxon Investment Corporation (Aggressive Diversified)	142.60	−50.13	**539.39**	−0.20	**1,160.79**	10.52	**969.69**	1.32	**1,200.32**
1995	Hirst Investment Management (Currency)	150.75	0.67	**543.00**	14.02	**1,323.54**	12.58	**1,091.68**	37.58	**1,651.40**
1996	Mangin Capital Management (Unassigned)	432.17	56.00	**847.08**	12.86	**1,493.75**	5.78	**1,154.78**	22.96	**2,030.56**
1997	Trading Solutions (Program #1)	189.23	0.54	**851.65**	11.97	**1,672.55**	−18.65	**939.41**	33.36	**2,707.95**

1998	Oxeye Capital Management FTSE 100 Futures/Options (Unassigned)	237.97	90.32	**1,620.86**	12.38	**1,879.61**	−25.55	**699.39**	28.58	**3,481.89**
1999	Mangin Capital Management (Unassigned)	121.89	6.43	**1,725.08**	1.64	**1,910.44**	46.25	**1,022.86**	21.04	**4,214.47**
2000	Forecast Trading Group (Discretionary)	253.18	44.14	**2,486.53**	6.60	**2,036.62**	26.92	**1,298.21**	−9.10	**3,830.96**
2001	Kinkopf Capital Management (Stocks)	66.83	−19.65	**1,997.92**	3.83	**2,114.62**	−31.50	**889.27**	−11.89	**3,375.46**
2002	Haar Capital Management (Discrestionary)	375.46	27.89	**2,555.14**	13.68	**2,403.990**	39.02	**1,236.26**	−22.10	**2,629.48**
2003	Monarch Capital Management (FX-Multi-Strategy)	164.15	−14.93	**2,173.66**	15.55	**2,777.71**	10.80	**1,369.78**	28.68	**3,383.62**
2004	Haar Capital Management (Discretionary)	105.20	40.13	**3,045.95**	0.86	**2,801.60**	19.16	**1,632.23**	10.88	**3,751.76**
	Geometric average return (%)		8.9456		8.3953		6.3426		12.2155	
	Arithmetic average return (%)		14.7400		8.3969		6.6700		12.2315	
	Arithmetic standard deviation		37.0635		10.2800		18.4900		14.2500	

By investing US$1,000 in 1993 in the top performing CTA of 1992, Ashley Capital Management at the end of 1992 the hypothetical investment of US$1,000 would have appreciated to US$1,203.10 by the end of 1993. By simultaneously investing the same amount in the Barclay BTOP 50 Index, the GSCI and S&P 500 Index would have returned US$1,025.55, US$971.10 and US$1,076.20 respectively. If this simple trading strategy of selecting last year's winning CTA as this year's choice is adhered to for 13 years, the initial investment of US$1,000 would have appreciated to US$3,045.95. This compares with a geometric average annual rate of return of 8.9456%. If the US$1,000 was invested in the BTOP 50 Index, the GSCI and S&P 500 Index, it would have appreciated to US$2,801.60, US$1,632.23 and US$3,751.76 respectively. It appears that the largest five (out of six) and efficient CTAs may not be taking on more risk because of the ample management and performance fees they receive.

CONCLUSION

The results demonstrate that simply purchasing last year's winning CTA could be considered as a trading strategy that will outperform the investable CTA indices but not the S&P 500 Index. The standard deviation of the returns of the top performing CTAs demonstrates that they are more volatile than both commodity indices and the S&P 500. This stands to reason, since top performing CTAs assume more risk. However, in general it is well documented that certain CTA classifications on average are generally less volatile than both CTA indices. Therefore, the main purpose of this simple trading strategy is to suggest to investors that investing in CTAs should be for the long and not the short-term.

ACKNOWLEDGEMENTS

The author would like to thank Rick Oberuc Sr. of Laporte Asset Allocation (www.laportesoft.com) for the use of his software and Sol Waksman of the Barclay Trading Group (www.barclaygrp.com).

The author would further like to thank www.pertrac.com for providing the BTOP 50 and the GSCI data.

Parts of this chapter have been reproduced from 'Last year's winning hedge fund as this year's selection: A simple trading strategy' by G. N. Gregoriou and F. Rouah in *Derivatives Use, Trading and Regulation*, Vol. 7, No. 3, 2001, pp 269–74.

REFERENCES

Barber, B. M., T. Odean, and L. Zheng, 2000, The Behavior of Mutual Fund Investors, Working Paper, University of California at Davis, Davis, CA.

Brorsen, B. W. and J. Townsend, 2002, "Performance Persistence for Managed Futures", *Journal of Alternative Investments*, **4(4),** pp 57–61.

Capocci, D., 2005, "CTA Performance, Survivorship Bias, and Dissolution Frequencies", in G. N. Gregoriou, V. N. Karavas, F-S. Lhabitant, and F. Rouah (eds) *Commodity Trading Advisors: Risk Performance Analysis and Selection* (Hoboken, NJ, John Wiley and Sons Inc).

Carhart, M., 1997, "On Persistence in Mutual Fund Performance", *Journal of Finance*, **52(1),** pp 57–82.

Edwards, F. R. and C. Ma, 1998, "Commodity Pool Performance: Is the Information Contained in Pool Prospectuses Useful?", *Journal of Futures Markets*, **8(5),** pp 589–616.

Elton, E. J., M. J. Gruber, and J. C. Rentzler, 1989, "New Public Offerings, Information, and Investor Rationality: The Case of Publicly Offered Commodity Funds," *Journal of Business*, **62(1),** pp 1–15.

Gregoriou, G.N., 2006, "Efficiency of Trading of CTAs Using Data Envelopment Analysis", *Derivatives Use, Trading and Regulation*, forthcoming.

Hallahan, T. A. and R. W. Taff, 2001, "Induced Persistence or Reversals in Fund Performance? The Effect of Survivorship Bias", *Applied Financial Economics*, **11(2),** pp 119–26.

Irwin, S., C. R. Zulauf, and B. Ward, 1992a, "The Predictability of Managed Futures Returns", *Journal of Derivatives*, **2(2),** pp 20–7.

Irwin, S., T. Krukemeyer, and C. R. Zulauf, 1992b, "Are Publicly Commodity Pools a Good Investment?", in C. C. Peter, (ed.) *Managed Futures: Performance evaluation and Analysis of Commodity Funds, Pools, and Accounts*, Chicago, IL: Probus Publishing.

Schneeweis, T., R. Spurgin, and D. McCarthy, 1996, "Survivor Bias in Commodity Trading Advisors' Performance", *Journal of Futures Markets*, **16(7),** pp 757–72.

19

Guaranteed Funds, Guaranteed Hedge Funds – How to Put Investment Efficiency to the Test?

Zsolt Berényi

R.I.S.C. Consulting

INTRODUCTION

During recent decades, alternative investment forms have literally been mushrooming and investors still put money in them with growing alacrity. Within the universe of alternative investments, assets with capital protection enjoy an increasing popularity as well. Guaranteed funds – essentially closed-end investment funds with some form of capital protection – are a relatively new phenomenon of growing interest, not just on matured but, in particular, on developing markets, like Asia or Central Eastern Europe.

The explanation for this lies at hand. On the one hand, investors are "hunting for yields" with a (seemingly) decreasing risk awareness. On the other hand, the subjective risk of a market "meltdown" perceived by the investors has been amplified by a number of events. This, in turn, has motivated the design of investment products with some form of capital protection. Funds with capital protection are designed for rather conservative investors not wanting to risk an overall market meltdown but willing to participate in upward market movements.

Guaranteed funds may follow different investment strategies. In some cases, guaranteed funds invest a considerable part of their investments in risk free assets (ie, the investment strategy secures the capital protection), and for the rest they take risky positions, eg in derivatives or hedge funds (which provides the chance for upside return). In other cases, principal guarantee is purchased from an external provider.

Because of the capital protection, which reduces downside risk, such assets compete rather with deposit products and conservative mutual funds. Thus, a direct comparison with hedge funds with conventional performance measures may produce at best controversial results. Exactly from this background, measuring the overall performance of such funds is a difficult task but is, in essence, comparable to measuring the performance of a pure derivatives fund.

Are guaranteed funds worth the money one puts in? The aim of the present chapter is to have a closer look at guaranteed investments: design, benchmark construction and evaluation of efficiency. I would like to show that using the moment-based replication approach, performance of guaranteed funds could be meaningfully assessed. Following this methodology, for each asset, a synthetic – optioned – benchmark portfolio is created.

For the analysis, a higher moment based replication methodology is used, in which statistical higher moments of the original return distribution are matched with that of the replicating portfolio. Certainly, as it will be pointed out later, the characteristics of guaranteed funds require certain modifications of the "classical" replication-based performance assessment.

REPLICATION-BASED PERFORMANCE EVALUATION

Fundamentals of performance assessment

What is the general idea of replication-based performance assessment? To answer this question, let us take a step back first to what performance evaluation really means. Measuring performance always implies a comparison: some (desirable or undesirable) characteristics of the (past or expected) return distribution have to be compared with other investments, in order to gain information on attractiveness of the original asset as investments.

If the relevant risk-return characteristics, while others are similar, differ in one dimension only, assets can easily be compared with each other directly. However, since this is seldom the case, a more sophisticated way is to build homogeneous asset groups in order to compare assets with each other within this group through benchmarks for each group.

An even more advanced approach for performance evaluation purposes is the idea of distributional performance assessment. In this concept, it is only the return distribution of the assets that counts, and, consequently, similar return distributions denote similar risk, for which an equal expected return should be offered.

Distributional performance evaluation

This latter concept has gained popularity only recently although it has its roots in the Payoff Distribution Pricing Model (Dybvig, 1988a, b). Dybvig proposed a pricing framework for assets with arbitrary return distributions, in which agents minimise the cost of any one-period return distribution, regardless of the factors that drive state probabilities. He labelled the price of the most efficient, ie, the minimum cost portfolio for any return distribution as "distributional price", to distinguish it from the normal asset price.

Within this framework, a wide spectrum of investments like equity, bond, real estate, money market investments, hedge funds and guaranteed funds, could, theoretically, be analysed. This methodology provides a common language in evaluating diverse assets and ensures a compatibility of different performance views.

What denotes this methodology today, what is the practical value of it? It can be reduced to the following: Having an efficient market with traded options, it is possible to re-create practically any risk-return shape, for literally any form of investment, provided the underlying return distribution for a particular holding period can be estimated with sufficient accuracy. The same is true for dynamic strategies as well (eg Amin and Kat, 2003), ie, dynamic strategies can similarly be used for replication purposes.

Re-creating an asset's risk shape with options naturally delivers a set of investments: a number of replicating portfolios as available, and competing, substitutes for the original asset. The most efficient optioned portfolio will be treated as the replicating benchmark asset for the particular fund. Thus, the expected return on this benchmark makes a good starting point for any efficiency analysis.

It is important to note that during this kind of analysis, we build on the implicit assumption of investors holding assets for the same period (eg one year). That is, for the evaluation the same holding period is used, and thus, performance of every asset can be compared with each other readily.

The Efficiency Gain/Loss Measure

Throughout, this chapter uses the concept of the so-called Efficiency Gain/Loss. The Efficiency Gain/Loss is a measure of value added created by a fund manager, and is defined as the differential between the expected return of the particular fund and that of its individually constructed, replicating benchmark.

The interpretation of the Efficiency Gain/Loss measure is a straightforward one. The expected return on the benchmark asset is the best alternative return one may achieve when holding the risk exposure constant. Since the optioned return may be realised without restrictions, it embodies the minimum acceptable return for a given risk profile. In other words, if using options, a fund's risk profile can be replicated with higher expected return, then it cannot be efficient, and vice versa, if it is efficient, then it cannot be replicated.

For mimicking any return distribution, a few statistical higher moments – eg up to the kurtosis – are often treated as sufficient. Certainly, it is also possible to include a greater number of moments or other characteristics (like eg, individual pins of the return distribution), but here the analysis is restricted to the variance, skewness and kurtosis. In addition, considering lower partial moments may also turn out to be necessary.

THE SPECIFIC FEATURES OF GUARANTEED FUNDS

Definition of guaranteed funds

Guaranteed funds and guaranteed hedge funds are part of the alternative investments universe. Besides, these terms are used interchangeably, ie, they cover similar investments. This is so even though most guaranteed funds do not necessarily invest *per se* in hedge funds. Rather, this term is justified by the investment structure of such assets in which alternative investors are able to invest, which is comparable with hedge funds, as one can see from the description of strategies.

For that reason, in the present framework there will be no difference in the performance evaluation of such assets even if one fund invests in hedge funds, funds of funds, pure options, or builds on a guarantee acquired from an external provider. It is only the resulting return distribution that counts. This is why both terms will be used simply in the sense of guaranteed funds.

Guaranteed funds serve basically two purposes: they both provide a chance for high absolute returns without having the overall risk of a market meltdown, and at the same time a good (ie not too risky) opportunity for investors previously not invested in alternative assets.

Now, what are the basic characteristics of guaranteed funds? These assets are, by definition, investment funds with a certain capital guarantee, where a significant portion of the capital invested (and in some cases, also a part of the return) is protected. However, it is important to know that capital protection refers to the invested capital at maturity. In case of an early withdrawal, investors receive the net asset value only.

Capital protection of such assets may cover a predetermined amount (eg 90% or 100%) of the capital invested, or it can denote a so-called "stepped", or variably adjusted, downside protection in which the downside is limited to a certain percentage (eg 10% or 15%) of the current asset price level. The vast majority of guaranteed funds are closed-end funds, although some providers also offer open-end guaranteed funds where the guaranteed threshold is adjusted dynamically (variably).

The first guaranteed products were designed as traditional mutual fund investment vehicles with the addition of a guarantee. That is, there is an external source of capital protection – and thus the investor runs, in this case, the risk of the guarantee provider.

Another possible form for guaranteed funds are funds with an intrinsic source of risk reduction, ie, where investment strategies secure a capital protection with a potential up-side return, which is linked to the performance of some underlying assets. That is, the risk of the fund value falling below the threshold amount at maturity is mitigated using a specific investment strategy like investing a significant portion of the fund in debt instruments, combined with some alternative investments, option positions, hedge funds, or other dynamic strategies.

Certainly, there are many forms of guaranteed funds, some even with innovative features like guaranteed coupon payments, investments in hedge funds, fund of funds, or compound options, funds with target redemption, funds with early capital repayment, or open-end continuous guaranteed funds. However, the basic formula remains the same.

(1) Do guaranteed funds offer superior performance when compared to optioned portfolios?
(2) In which case, if any, is positive performance achievable?
(3) Do the results in the first case (ie holding assets to maturity) differ from those in the second case significantly (ie holding assets for three months)? Or, put differently, does guarantee matter?

Performance of guaranteed funds

In order to assess the value created by the fund manager, as discussed above, the Efficiency Gain/Loss methodology is used with the higher moment-*LPM* (1) optimisation. That is, to every fund, a replicating portfolio was constructed, comprising an underlying index, options, and risk free asset.

Figure 1 contains the results of the first calculation for the Central European sample, while Figure 2 contains the same data for the Asian sample. Note that all the figures contain annualized data, sorted by their magnitude, for an easier understanding and interpretation.

In both cases, as the outline shows, as expected, the majority of the funds show considerable negative efficiency, but it is also possible to find investments with reasonably good (if not superior) performance. That is, there are some funds whose performance cannot be simply replicated within the current setting.

On the other hand, the efficiency lost can be in some cases substantial (even as high 50% per annum, which is an immense value). The majority of the funds under investigation produce negative performance of between −10% and −20% in magnitude per annum. However, a considerable part of this efficiency lost – about 8% to 10% per annum – is attributable to management and other fees, and the rest is simply bad luck. In fact, when looking at the universe of guaranteed funds, they all seem to have similar fee structures.

Therefore, for institutional investors, it is clearly not advisable to invest in the set of guaranteed funds investigated here. This is partly so because of the substantial costs and fees associated with guaranteed funds, which are not really depending on the actual investment strategy but on the fact that individual investors would rather swallow these costs.

Figure 1 Efficiency Gain/Loss calculation for the Central European sample

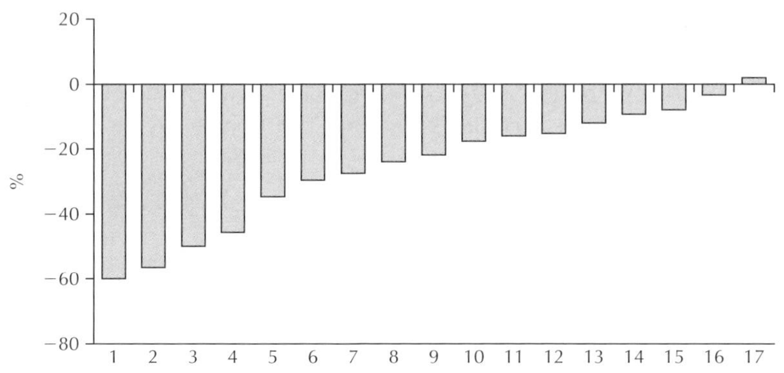

Figure 2 Efficiency Gain/Loss calculation for the HSBC Asian sample

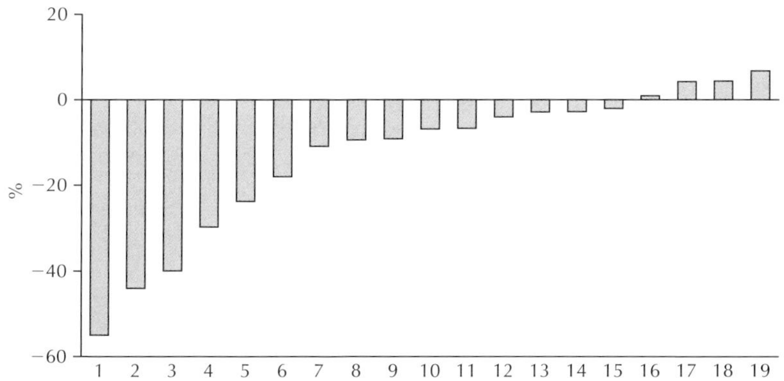

Certainly, we do not account for direct or indirect costs of building such optioned portfolios. As these costs and limitations can be substantial for private investors, they should carefully analyse these investment opportunities, because guaranteed funds might offer in some cases a good investment opportunity not accessible elsewhere.

The winning strategy

What would be the best advice where to put one's money? First of all, in the present framework (no serious investment constraints, lending and borrowing at risk-free rate, option prices calculated with

Black and Scholes, etc), guaranteed funds do not seem to show superior performance. However, based on the detailed results, it can be asserted that funds, whose net asset value is significantly below the guaranteed principal amount, still seem to offer a higher value added in terms of portfolio efficiency (Efficiency Gain/Loss measure) than the others.

This can intuitively be explained by the following. In such cases, capital protection grants a significant positive drift in return generating process for the holding period while retaining an overall return volatility (therefore the chance for higher returns) not very different from other "normal" investment funds. The capital protection is in essence a deep-in-the money option, which, oddly, seems to be cheaper than in the in-the-money or out-of-the money cases. That is, these are the circumstances where capital protection counts most.

On the other hand, for assets with relatively high actual net asset values compared to the guarantee threshold, the return distribution will be much alike a normal hedge fund. Here, the capital protection will play a lesser role at the calculated end-of-holding-period return distribution – however, the costs characteristic to a guaranteed fund will nevertheless be charged on it.

Does capital protection matter?

One last question is whether capital protection does indeed play a significant role in performance evaluation. That is, does accounting for the end-of-period capital protection deliver results significantly different from those obtained by assuming a uniform (three-month) holding period?

The chapter asserted earlier that guaranteed funds would probably not create much value in terms of investment efficiency. This is true even if considering the capital protection the funds are offering. Then, one should expect that neglecting the capital protection would definitely not enhance the Efficiency Gain/Loss measure.

The answer to this question can be seen in Figure 3. That is, in case of the Central European sample, the value added by guaranteed funds is in almost all cases negative (black bars) – as it should be. Furthermore, it also can be seen that the efficiency lost has a much lower variation, and that the rankings on both cases do not have a strong correlation. This is probably due to the fundamental

Figure 3 Efficiency Gain/Loss comparison for the Central European sample

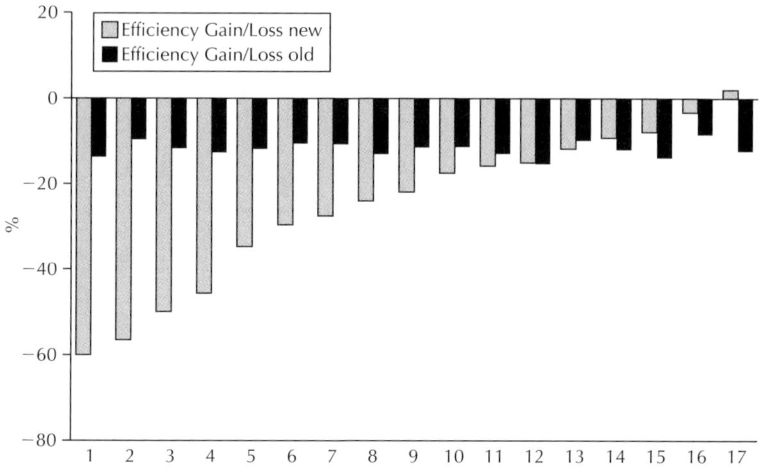

differences in both models (regarding the underlying distribution, the option prices, and the different holding period views).

Thus, one can assert that the answer is affirmative; capital protection does matter – in calculating the ranking of different guaranteed funds. The simpler methodology will only deliver a rudimentary approximation for the efficiency of funds with capital protection.

CONCLUSIONS

This chapter has investigated the performance of guaranteed funds with the Efficiency Gain/Loss methodology. What are the conclusions? The findings can be summarised as follows.

First, the methodology presented here seems to offer a useful tool when evaluating guaranteed funds. In addition, it has been made clear that investors should assess such assets assuming a hold-to-maturity view, and then normalise (annualise) the obtained results.

Second, for institutional investors, it is clearly not advisable to invest in the set of guaranteed funds investigated here. Institutional, high net-wealth investors would do better building up their own optional, "guaranteed-like" portfolios. This is because of the substantial costs and fees associated with (and charged for) guaranteed funds.

Third, for private individuals, these investments might be interesting but not without caution. That is, for private investors with limited market access, guaranteed funds may offer an attractive investment opportunity in quite a few cases. In this case, we would advise buying guaranteed funds whose current asset price is substantially below the guaranteed payment at the end of the holding period, and then buying them to maturity.

REFERENCES

Amin, G. and H. Kat, 2003, "Hedge Fund Performance 1990–2000: Do the Money Machines Really Add Value?", *Journal of Financial and Quantitative Analysis*, **38(22)**, pp 251–74.

Dybvig, P. H., 1988a, "Inefficient Dynamic Portfolio Strategies or How to Throw Away a Million Dollars in the Stock Market", *Review of Financial Studies*, **1(1)**, pp 67–88.

Dybvig, P. H., 1988b, "Distributional Analysis of Portfolio Choice", *Journal of Business*, **61(3)**, pp 369–93.

Part Four

Asset Allocation

20

Blending Hedge Funds with Traditional Stock and Bond Portfolios: Investment Management in a New World

R. McFall Lamm Jr

Global Investment Management, Deutsche Bank

INTRODUCTION

The strong increase in hedge fund investing over the past decade has accelerated the demise of mainstream portfolio management techniques as epitomised by modern portfolio theory (MPT). The reason is that the traditional MPT approach to asset allocation, which relies on mean variance (MV) analysis or its derivatives, breaks down when allocations to hedge funds are included. The major problem is that MV presumes that return distributions are normal, whereas hedge fund returns and investor preferences are asymmetrical.

This is clear from recent research. For example, Brooks and Kat (2002) have demonstrated that the returns for some hedge fund strategies – such as fixed income arbitrage, convertible arbitrage, and distressed debt – exhibit negative skew, while others – equity long/short and CTAs/managed futures, for instance – are positively skewed. Negative skew is a particularly troubling problem in that its presence indicates that downside risk is greater than upside potential. Therefore, if one relies on MPT to construct portfolios that combine hedge funds with traditional assets, investor risk may be greater than perceived.

At the same time, behavioural finance champions contend that investors experience greater distress from losses than satisfaction from wins of the same magnitude (Kahneman and Tversky 1974, 1979). In other words, investors prefer positive asymmetry in portfolio return payoffs. This is reflected by their willingness to buy call options and principal-protected securities. Clearly, this behavioural predilection needs to be taken into account if portfolio design is to be robust.

The failure of MPT to incorporate non-normal market returns and asymmetric investor preferences has stimulated the rise of post-modern portfolio theory (PMPT), which explicitly takes into account these factors in building portfolios. In this regard, researchers have suggested using modified value-at-risk approaches for incorporating asymmetry in hedge fund allocations (Favre and Galeano 2002; Signer and Favre 2002; Lamm 2003). Others propose optimising higher-order power and exponential utility functions to derive efficient portfolios (Jondeau and Rockinger 2002; 2005). Numerous alternative PMPT techniques have also been suggested.

This chapter addresses these issues by presenting a generalised PMPT approach to the portfolio design problem in which hedge funds are blended with conventional assets such as stocks and bonds. The method described – polynomial utility optimisation – takes into account the return asymmetry exhibited by hedge fund strategies, as well as asymmetries in investor preferences. The technique is applied both retrospectively and prospectively to identify how allocations differ when hedge fund strategies are added to the portfolio mix. In addition, the effect of translating hedge fund allocations into aggregate primary asset exposure is reported. The key conclusion is that the approach offers a novel tool for portfolio management but that the critical decision remains simply including hedge funds in one's portfolio.

POST MODERN PORTFOLIO THEORY

It is now widely acknowledged that the addition of hedge funds to portfolios needs to address two issues. First, hedge funds exhibit asymmetrical returns with some strategies showing negative skew. This implies that downside risk is greater than it appears if one only considers mean and variance. Second, investors prefer positive asymmetry and eschew large negative tail events. This trade-off between investor preferences and market reality is illustrated in Figure 1.

Fortunately, much effort in the past few years has focused on addressing these concerns. The various proposals for dealing with asymmetry can be grouped essentially into two categories. First, are

Figure 1 Asymmetries in return vs. preferences

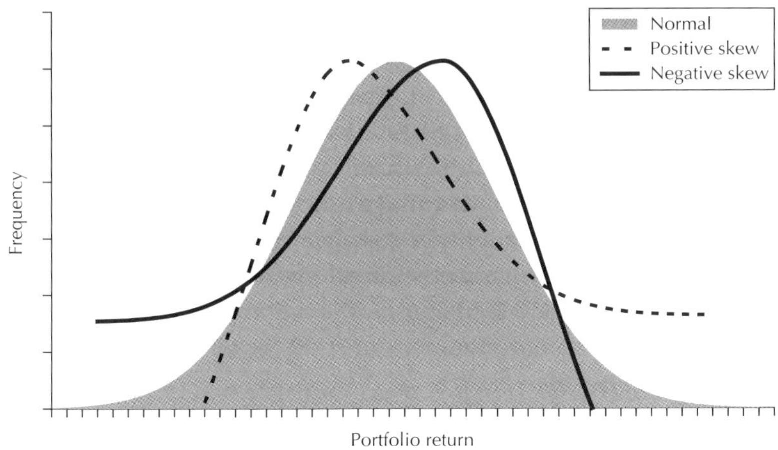

the more rigorous approaches based on the maximisation of wealth given specific utility functions. The basic ideas were developed some time ago (Jean 1971, 1973) but were recently extended to include a specific analytic solution to the three-moment asset allocation problem, attained by elegantly stacking the return co-skew cube into a sideways matrix (Athayde and Flores 2004). Jondeau and Rockinger go further, describing a specific solution to the four-moment allocation problem in the specific case where the utility of wealth is represented by either a power or exponential function.

In the second type of approach, no explicit utility function is specified and optimal portfolios are generated by varying target risk over a selected spectrum. For example, Favre and Galeano (2002), Signer and Favre (2002) and Lamm suggest using modified value-at-risk methodologies for incorporating asymmetry in hedge fund allocations. Another option is polynomial goal programming (Davies *et al* 2005), which focuses only on the asymmetric behaviour of constituent assets in constructing optimal portfolios. The issue with all these techniques is that, by neglecting the form of the utility function, they are atheoretical. As a consequence, one cannot assess whether the underlying investor possesses sensible behavioural characteristics. Furthermore, these approaches are largely numerical and therefore have a black box nature that limits interpretation. Explicit utility optimisation is more transparent and intuitive.[1]

measured by the Merrill high yield master index, commodities as measured by the CRB index, and real estate as proxied by the NAREIT index. Cash yield is the return on the Merrill 3-month Treasury index.

The plain-vanilla hedge fund strategies include equity market neutral, fixed income arbitrage, convertible arbitrage, merger arbitrage, distressed debt, equity long/short, global macro, and CTAs/managed futures. The hedge fund data are from Hedge Fund Research (HFR) with the exception of CTA returns, which come from Barclays. I employ monthly data covering the period from January 1990 to December 2005. While this is not an extremely lengthy period, it none the less represents the interval over which reasonably reliable hedge fund data are available.

To avoid the common complaint that hedge fund data overstate actual returns due to survivor bias, corrections are made based on prior studies that have attempted to quantify the extent of bias. I rely primarily on Amin and Kat (2003) who find overall survivor bias for the major hedge fund strategies of approximately 2% per annum. For individual strategies, the Amin and Kat estimates of survivor bias are roughly proportionate to the volatility of the underlying strategy. I therefore take their estimate of overall survivor bias and apply proportionate scaling to arrive at the adjustments indicated in Table 1, which also presents the distribution statistics for the raw data used for the optimization.

To simplify the presentation of the results, optimal look-back portfolios are produced for a limited number of cases. These include: (a) a MV optimisation applied only to traditional assets (with θ, γ, and all hedge fund strategy weights set to zero); (b) a MV optimisation applied to the universe of all assets including plain vanilla hedge fund strategies (with $\theta, \gamma = 0$); (c) a series of optimisations using polynomial utility where the value of the skew preference parameter θ is gradually increased holding volatility preference constant (with $\gamma = 0$); and (d) an optimisation in which, for given volatility and skew preferences, a kurtosis preference is introduced. In addition, the maximum skew ($\lambda, \gamma = 0$) and minimum kurtosis portfolios ($\lambda, \theta = 0$) are produced as points of reference. The initial starting value for λ is set to produce an optimal portfolio with 8% volatility with θ derived via a grid search to assure declining ARA, RRA and marginal utility.[5]

Table 1 Strategy distribution statistics, 1990–2005

Strategy	Return (%)	Survivor bias (%)	Volatility (%)	Skew	Kurtosis	JB test	Asymmetry
Long large caps	11.1	–	14.5	−0.42*	0.69	9.4*	Weakly negative
Long small caps	10.7	–	18.6	−0.49*	0.85*	13.7*	Weakly negative
Long bonds	7.1	–	4.5	−0.46*	0.65	10.1*	Weakly negative
Long high yield	9.2	–	7.0	−0.54*	3.68*	117.7*	Strongly negative
Convertible arb	10.0	0.3	3.6	−1.11*	1.92*	68.9*	Strongly negative
Fixed income arb	10.5	0.4	3.4	−0.31	5.18*	217.7*	Strongly negative
Equity mrkt. neutral	9.2	0.3	3.1	0.16	0.43	2.3	None
Merger arb	10.1	0.5	4.3	−2.60*	11.37*	1249.9*	Strongly negative
Distressed debt	15.1	1.1	6.0	−0.64*	5.72*	274.9*	Strongly negative
Long/short equity	17.2	2.3	8.8	0.18	1.43*	17.3*	Weakly positive
Global macro	16.2	2.1	8.2	0.37*	0.63	7.7*	Weakly positive
CTAs/mngd. futures	8.1	4.1	11.6	0.63*	1.25*	25.4*	Positive
Commodities	2.3	–	8.7	0.23	−0.09	1.7	None
Long REITs	13.2	–	13.2	−0.29	1.16*	13.4*	Weakly negative
Cash	4.4	–	0.6	−0.01	−0.60	2.9	None

*significance with 95% confidence.

Table 2 Optimal retrospective portfolios for various investor preferences

Measure	MV (xHFs)	MV	Polynomial				Max skew	Min kurt
			I	II	III	IV		
Strategy:				*Weight*				
Long large caps	42.6%	–	–	–	–	–	13.0%	–
Long small caps	10.4%	–	–	–	–	–	–	–
Long bonds	47.0%	–	–	–	–	–	–	–
Convertible arb	–	–	–	–	–	–	–	3.4%
Fixed income arb	–	–	–	–	–	–	9.0%	–
Equity mrkt. neutral	–	–	–	–	–	–	25.2%	7.3%
Merger arb	–	–	–	–	–	–	–	0.4%
Distressed debt	–	42.1%	21.6%	16.3%	9.8%	26.2%	1.6%	–
Long/short equity	–	40.2%	64.9%	71.2%	79.0%	59.3%	–	–
Global macro	–	17.7%	13.6%	12.5%	11.2%	14.5%	–	–
CTAs/mngd. futures	–	–	–	–	–	–	33.4%	–
Long real estate	–	–	–	–	–	–	1.2%	–
Cash	–	–	–	–	–	–	16.6%	89.0%
Portfolio:								
Return	9.5%	13.8%	14.0%	14.0%	14.1%	13.9%	7.4%	4.8%
Volatility	8.0%	6.4%	7.2%	7.5%	7.9%	7.1%	4.4%	0.7%
Skew	−0.37*	−0.25	−0.01	0.04	0.11	−0.07	1.04*	−0.14
Kurtosis	0.30	2.24*	1.63*	1.53*	1.44*	1.74*	3.14*	−0.93*
Utility	0.886	0.897	0.910	0.912	0.914	0.909	0.905	0.904
λ	−0.112	−0.112	−0.112	−0.112	−0.112	−0.112		
θ			0.013	0.015	0.017	0.015	1	
γ						−0.001		−1

The results are presented in Table 2 and are essentially what one would expect – the optimal traditional asset portfolio is split nearly equally between stocks and bonds. The portfolio produces an average return of 9.8% annually over the period with statistically significant negative skew. In addition, the portfolio's return stream shows the pattern experienced by most investors over the 1990 to 2005 period with robust performance in the 1990s and substantial negative returns during the bubble sell-off from 2000 to early 2002.

In the second optimisation, the MV analysis is repeated with hedge funds admitted to the candidate universe. The results are dramatically different – no traditional assets enter the optimum portfolio and holdings are concentrated in three hedge fund strategies. These include distressed debt, long/short equity and global macro. Compared with the traditional asset portfolio, average returns rise to 14.0%, volatility falls to 6.2%, and portfolio skew is not statistically significant. This is an extraordinary degree of improvement and is produced using the same volatility preference parameter as in the initial MV case.

While a traditionalist might cringe at a portfolio consisting of 100% hedge funds, many investors in alternative assets would not find this so extreme. Indeed, Edwards and Liew (1999) made a very strong case for large allocations to hedge funds. Furthermore, Lamm (1999) even suggested a 100% hedge fund allocation that proved prescient during the 2000 to 2002 bear market when hedge funds dramatically outperformed conventional portfolios.

Moreover, it is important to realise that while the optimal allocations are 100% to hedge funds, there is an uncanny subterfuge of traditionalism – in reality the portfolio is still split primarily among fixed income and equities. It is just that the fixed income allocation is in distressed debt and the equity allocation is relinquished to equity long/short managers, who are well-known to carry a significant long bias to stocks. The added smaller allocation to global macro provides broad exposure to currencies and a variety of other assets. As a result, presuming the 100% hedge fund allocation is well-dispersed among a sufficient number of managers whose composite behavioural characteristics are similar to the industry, the outcome is more diversification than a standard long-only stock and bond portfolio.

The next optimisation focuses on identifying portfolios which exhibit positive asymmetry. This is done by using the same value for the investor's volatility preference but adding a weight on skew preference and raising it incrementally. Three optimal portfolios are presented – labelled as polynomial I, II and III with the latter representing the strongest preference for positive skew. The results indicate that the same hedge fund strategies enter the optimum mix as in the case of unconstrained MV optimisation but the portfolio weights shift away from distressed debt, which is negatively skewed. This is exactly as it should be. However, volatility rises with greater skew preference illustrating that there is a cost associated with achieving positive asymmetry.[6]

The last polynomial optimisation allows for kurtosis aversion by including a non-zero value for γ and allows it to rise incrementally. This generally has only a limited impact on allocations due to the interaction of the parameters in Equation 4, so just one result (IV) is shown. Lastly, the maximum skew and minimum kurtosis portfolios – the extrema – are found to further illustrate the trade-offs implicit in the multi-moment problem.

The short conclusion is that – with the benefit of hindsight – the key portfolio management decision over the last decade and a half was simply to include hedge funds in one's portfolio. This would likely have improved performance by any measure provided allocations were not hugely off the efficient frontier. Stock and bond investors who avoided hedge funds suffered significant lost returns, higher portfolio volatility and larger downside risk than was necessary.

Importantly, postmodern portfolio theory is not required to produce this revelation. MV analysis alone – with hedge funds admitted – would have generated superior portfolios and better results for investors (Figures 3 and 4). Using polynomial utility does incrementally improve the results by yielding slightly higher returns and positive asymmetry but this comes at the cost of greater portfolio volatility. That said, polynomial utility forces a conscious choice between conflicting portfolio characteristics and illustrates clearly what costs must be incurred in the pursuit of asymmetry.

FORWARD-LOOKING OPTIMISATION

Identifying the best portfolio to have held in the past, while interesting, is to some extent a futile exercise – the historical optimum is unlikely to outperform in the future. Indeed, it can be argued that

Figure 3 Optimum portfolio returns for various utility functions

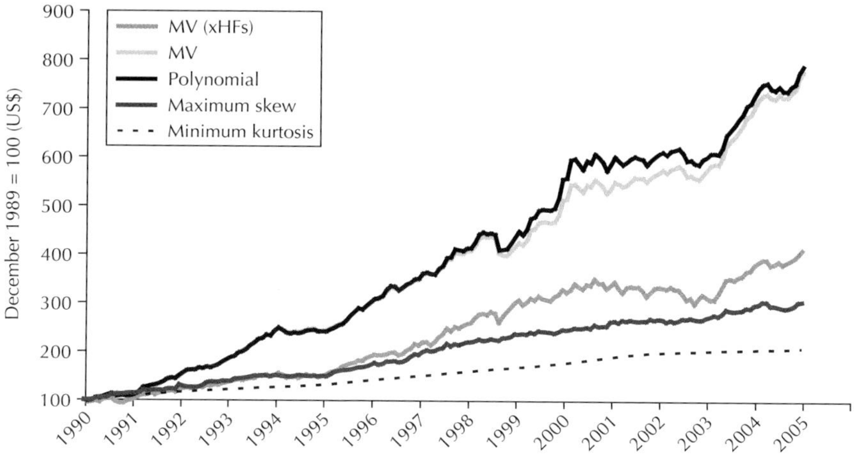

Figure 4 Histograms for various utility functions

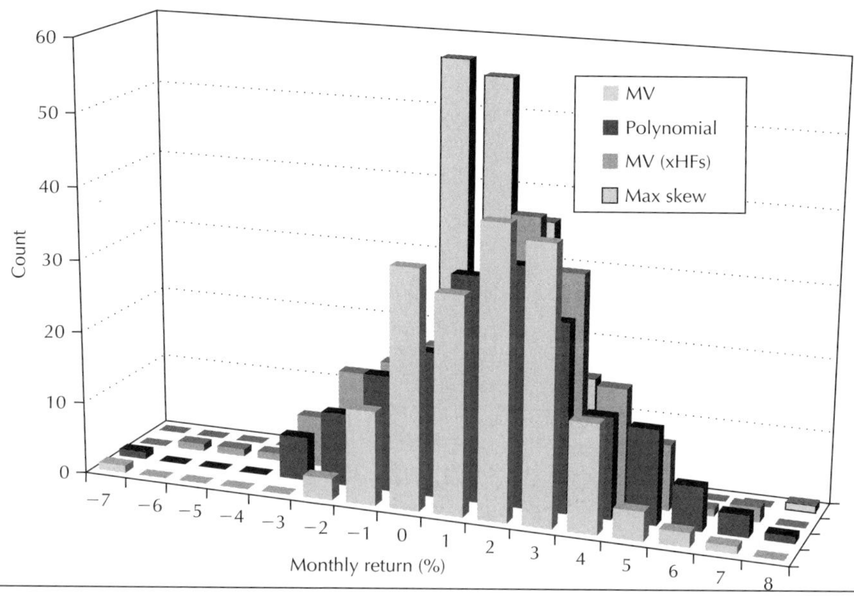

substantial investment flows into hedge funds have the potential to dilute future performance and one would expect that past superior risk-adjusted returns will eventually be arbitraged away via normal market adjustment dynamics. That said, the unique characteristics of different hedge fund strategies suggest that they will continue to be important portfolio constituents for some years to come.

Turning to the forward-looking portfolio construction problem, one needs an objective basis from which to begin. In this regard, the classic Black and Litterman (1990) approach of re-engineering implied asset returns from given portfolio weights is employed. Market capitalisation is usually employed in this exercise but because many investors are constrained from hedge fund investing – either directly via institutional restrictions or indirectly via small size – high net worth (HNW) investor allocations are taken as the starting point and implied returns derived.

High net worth investor allocations are a suitable reference since this group dominates hedge fund investing. Furthermore, HNW investors are not constrained by boards, which may be dominated by naïve or uninformed individuals, and are therefore free to seek out performance wherever it may be. Many HNW portfolios are also quite large and often quasi-institutional in operational structure.

The annual asset allocation survey conducted by the Institute of Private Investors (IPI) is one of the few sources available on HNW investor holdings. It shows for 2005 an average allocation of 23% to hedge funds, with the remainder invested in stocks, bonds, private equity and real estate. Because reported IPI asset classifications do not correspond exactly with the categories considered here, a few liberties are taken in producing a base allocation. These include: (a) presuming the 23% hedge allocation is allocated proportionate to strategy market capitalisation as reported by HFR; (b) adding the private equity allocation to long-only small cap exposure; (c) assuming the fixed income allocation is proxied by Treasury debt; (d) using REITs as a surrogate for real estate exposure; and (e) adding the small "other" allocation to reported cash exposure.[7] Furthermore, a cash yield of 5% is used to produce nominal rather than excess expected returns.

Table 3 presents the outcome of this exercise. The first column of weights is the base strategy allocation derived from the IPI data. The distribution statistics for this portfolio – return, volatility, skew, and kurtosis – are generated from the re-engineered expected returns and the sample covariance, coskew, and cokurtosis matrices employed in the retrospective analysis. The key presumption here is that coskew and cokurtosis are similar to covariance in that they are fairly stable over time. While this might not necessarily be

Table 3 Prospective optimal portfolios: adding incremental positive asymmetry

Measure	**Percentage of maximum attainable skew from base**						**Expected returns (%)**
	0% (base)	**10%**	**20%**	**30%**	**50%**	**100%**	
Strategy		*Weight*					
Long large caps	32.8	32.2	31.6	31.1	30.0	27.2	8.1
Long small caps	14.1	12.7	11.3	9.9	7.1	–	8.9
Long bonds	13.5	12.1	10.8	9.4	6.7	–	5.1
Long high yield	1.1	1.0	0.9	0.8	0.6	–	6.0
Convertible arb	1.6	1.5	1.3	1.1	0.8	–	5.3
Fixed income arb	1.5	1.3	1.2	1.0	0.7	–	5.5
Equity mrkt. neutral	1.4	2.2	3.0	3.9	5.5	9.7	5.2
Merger arb	1.3	1.2	1.1	0.9	0.7	–	5.6
Distressed debt	2.1	1.9	1.7	1.5	1.0	–	5.9
Long/short	9.9	9.0	8.0	7.0	5.0	–	6.9
Global macro	2.4	2.2	1.9	1.7	1.2	–	6.1
CTAs/futures	2.7	8.7	14.8	20.8	32.9	63.1	4.8
Long real estate	9.4	8.4	7.5	6.6	4.7	–	8.9
Long cash	6.3	5.6	5.0	4.4	3.1	–	5.0
	100	100	100	100	100	100	
Hedge fund weight	23.0	28.0	33.0	37.9	47.8	72.8	
Portfolio							
Return	7.0	6.9	6.7	6.6	6.4	5.7	
Volatility	8.6	8.1	7.7	7.4	7.2	8.8	
Skew	−0.54	−0.49	−0.41	−0.27	0.13	0.94	
Kurtosis	1.12	1.11	1.10	1.09	1.07	1.02	

the case in the future, it avoids the complex problem of forecasting neutral higher-moment expectations.

The subsequent columns of the table show portfolio weights obtained by progressively increasing the skew preference parameter θ until the maximum skew portfolio is reached. The rationale is that since positive asymmetry is the focus – and the critical step in attaining this is producing a positively skewed portfolio – one wants to see the cost as simply as possible in terms of sacrificed return and volatility. Off the prospective optimisation, this is achieved by increasing the weights on positive asymmetry hedge fund strategies – most obviously CTAs/managed futures.

The evidence suggests that the cost of attaining modestly greater positive asymmetry is not very high. For example, moving from the base IPI allocation to a portfolio with 50% of attainable skew produces allocations to all traditional and hedge fund strategies, but with a strong tilt to CTAs/managed futures. The expected portfolio return declines from 7.0% to 6.4%, expected volatility falls from 8.6% to 6.4%, and expected portfolio skew rises from negative 0.54 to a positive 0.13. A more risk averse investor might prefer such a portfolio to the base in order to avoid tail risk and to obtain a higher return than could be obtained by adding cash. Notice importantly that, unlike in MV analysis, risk reduction is accomplished not by adding cash and reducing allocations to riskier assets but by rotating to positive asymmetry strategies.

Of course, in actuality one would likely end up with portfolios fundamentally different from the base IPI portfolio since one would want to scrutinise implied returns and interpose their own expectations. None the less, this example illustrates the process and the possible extent of changes necessary to transform the portfolio into one that possesses more favourable characteristics.

CRUDE BETA EXPOSURE

To this point the discussion has ignored the fact that hedge fund strategies contain beta exposure to primary asset markets. That this is important has been discussed by Schneeweis and Spurgin (1998), Fung and Hseih (2002, 2004), Lamm (2002), Schneeweis *et al* (2002), Agarwal and Naik (2004), Jaegar and Muller (2004) and others. For example, equity long/short hedge fund managers on average carry derivative net long stock exposure. This consists of a long small cap portfolio offset in part by short positions in large cap stocks. While individual managers may add alpha on top of this position and their beta exposure may vary, this does not change the fact that for the average portfolio an allocation to long/short equity subtracts from large caps and adds to the small cap net allocation.

The way to account for beta exposure is to treat hedge fund positions as derivative on primary markets and extract the common asset exposures. This is often referred to as "alpha/beta separation" and is well-documented by Dopfel (2005) and Liew and French (2005). In its simplest form, the linkage between hedge fund strategies and primary markets is represented by the relationship $\mathbf{r}_h = \boldsymbol{\alpha} + \boldsymbol{\beta}\mathbf{r}_p + \boldsymbol{\varepsilon}_h$ where the components of $\boldsymbol{\beta}$ represent strategy exposures to traditional assets, $\mathbf{r}_h$ is hedge fund strategy returns, and $\mathbf{r}_p$ is traditional asset returns. This is classic asset-based factor analysis and allows one to explicitly estimate alpha contribution.

Ignoring asymmetry, the overall portfolio allocation can be split into two components $\mathbf{w}^T = [\mathbf{w}_p{}^T \mid \mathbf{w}_h{}^T]$ with the optimum $\mathbf{w}^* = \lambda^{-1}\mathbf{V}^{-1}\mathbf{r}$. With $\mathbf{r}^T = [\mathbf{r}_p{}^T \mid \mathbf{r}_h{}^T] = [\mathbf{r}_p{}^T \mid (\boldsymbol{\alpha} + \boldsymbol{\beta}\mathbf{r}_p + \boldsymbol{\varepsilon}_h)^T]$ and $\boldsymbol{\Omega}$ the covariance of $\mathbf{r}_p$, then as long as $\boldsymbol{\varepsilon}_h \neq \mathbf{0}$ the covariance of $\mathbf{r}_h$ is $\boldsymbol{\beta\Omega\beta}^T + \boldsymbol{\varepsilon}_h\boldsymbol{\varepsilon}_h{}^T$ and $\mathbf{V}$ can be inverted for a solution. One can then derive the primary asset exposure using $\hat{\mathbf{w}}^* = \boldsymbol{\beta}^T\mathbf{w}_h^* + \mathbf{w}_p^*$. Note that it is not necessary – and unlikely – that the asset exposures in $\hat{\mathbf{w}}^*$ sum to unity since various hedge fund strategies employ leverage and may be long or short.

Unfortunately, one cannot reverse the process and engineer an optimal portfolio consisting of long positions in primary assets and hedge funds. The reason is that the number of strategies will almost always exceed the number of primary assets. That said, one can examine the implied primary asset exposure given any strategy allocation as a reality check on the true dimensions of portfolio exposure.

Table 4 presents estimates of the primary market exposure for the prospective allocations already presented. Estimates of $\boldsymbol{\beta}$ are made on the basis of simple regressions of hedge fund strategy returns on primary market returns covering the sample. The fit for each strategy varies significantly with the highest R^2 found for long/short equity at 83.4% and the lowest value of 11.1% for equity market neutral. Using smaller samples covering more recent data significantly improves the fit – hedge fund exposures evolve

Table 4 Implied beta exposure to primary market assets

Primary asset market	Percentage of maximum attainable skew from base					
	0%	10%	20%	30%	50%	100%
Large caps	32.1	32.0	32.0	32.1	32.2	32.3
Small caps	16.5	14.4	12.2	10.0	5.6	−5.5
Bonds	18.1	20.9	23.8	26.6	32.3	46.6
High yield	−0.2	−1.1	−2.0	−2.9	−4.8	−9.4
Commodities	2.7	3.4	4.1	4.7	6.1	9.6
Dollar	2.9	0.9	−1.1	−3.1	−7.1	−17.0
Real estate	9.4	8.4	7.5	6.6	4.7	0.0
Cash	−1.9	−4.5	−7.1	−9.6	−14.7	−27.5

through time as market conditions and opportunities change. While one might prefer to forecast beta exposure from recent data rather than the entire sample, the latter approach is followed here in an effort to simply extract long-term averages. The effort is therefore a necessarily crude approximation.[8]

The results indicate that if one examines the base IPI strategy allocation, the investor might be surprised to discover there is more small cap exposure than believed. This comes primarily from the long/short equity hedge funds bias to small caps. In addition, indications are that investors will have long commodity and short dollar exposure. Somewhat surprisingly, the results show that cash exposure is negative. However, this is attributable to the well known fact that many hedge fund strategies – especially CTAs/managed futures – employ leverage.

As one increases skew preference to the maximum, the analysis reveals a substantial hidden exposure to bonds, as well as nontrivial long commodity and short dollar exposure. This is largely attributable to the progressively larger allocation to CTAs which profited from such exposures in the past. The short exposures in small caps and high yield arise from the lack of extensive CTA trading of these assets.

CONCLUSION

The principal conclusion from this analysis is that properly defining the admissible strategy domain for portfolio construction is of critical importance for successful investment management. Certainly this is the case over the 1990 to 2005 period during which the inclusion of hedge fund strategies would have dramatically improved portfolio performance. Indeed, holding the optimal traditional asset portfolio would have produced a quadrupling of initial wealth with compounding. However, allocating to the optimal hedge fund strategy mix would have multiplied wealth by seven times for a similar amount of volatility risk.

Using more advanced postmodern portfolio techniques is not critical to achieve these results – mean variance analysis alone would have done nearly as well, presuming of course, that one had perfect foresight and considered hedge funds as part of the admissible universe. That said, postmodern portfolio management techniques would have added substantial value by allowing one to further reduce downside risk.

A major benefit of postmodern portfolio theory is to make explicit the trade-off between returns, variance and asymmetry. In this regard, it appears that downside risk can be reduced for more conservative investors by the judicious use of hedge fund strategies to transform portfolios into higher-returning positive asymmetry forms in ways that avoid carrying large amounts of risk-free cash holdings.

Lastly, the analysis also suggests that it is important to examine the full information contained in hedge fund beta exposure to primary asset markets to fully comprehend how returns and positive asymmetry are generated. In specific circumstances, investors may want to re-examine their portfolio allocations in light of their hedge funds implicit beta exposure to primary markets.

1 There are other eclectic approaches where nonstandard utility functions and various constraints are employed in the optimisation process. The best example is Cremers *et al* (2005) where downside and upside utility are characterised by different functions around a loss limit, producing an asymmetrical kink in utility. Other more exotic utility function specifications such as the power expo (Saha,1993) have not been widely applied empirically, however, due to intractability in the case of higher-order moments.

2 Quadratic is a special case of polynomial utility. This can be seen by substituting $\delta_3 = \delta_4 = 0$ in Equation 4 and noting that $E(r)$ in the resulting expression will generally be small.

3 Note that if an investor irrationally does not care about asymmetry, then $\theta = \gamma = 0$ and $E[U(W)]$ reduces to the standard quadratic utility form. In addition, one can generate the efficient frontier by varying λ, θ, and γ in the usual way. Also, note that variance, skew and kurtosis as used here are central moments. The results presented in the tables which appear later use more convention definitions with variance $= \sigma^2/n - 1$, skew $= [n/[(n-1)$

$(n-2)]\Sigma[r - E(r)]/\sigma']^3$ and kurtosis $= [n(n+1)]/[(n-1)(n-2)\,(n-3)]\Sigma[r - E(r)]/\sigma']^3 - 3(n-1)^2/\,[(n-1)(n-2)]$ where σ' is conventional standard deviation.

4 One solution is to exploit the fact that **S** and **K** are likely to be sparse and include only statistically significant entries with others zeroed out. That is, $s^3 = \Sigma\Sigma\Sigma w_i w_j w_k s_{ijk}$ and $k^4 = \Sigma\Sigma\Sigma\Sigma\, w_i w_j w_k w_l k_{ijkl}$ need be summed only for the small subset of all possibilities where $s_{ijk} \neq 0$ and $k_{ijkl} \neq 0$. However, even this approach is computationally intensive.

5 The initial MV target volatility of 8% is similar to what many traditional investors actually experienced over the 1990 to 2005 period.

6 Normally one would also expect that higher skew would also come at a cost of lower returns. This occurs when one progressively increases skew preference beyond that shown here.

7 Note that small cap returns are normally used as a benchmark for private equity buy-out fund performance.

8 The approach used here also ignores the fact that hedge fund betas are nonlinear – being generally lower in up markets and higher in down markets. In addition, serial correlation may affect the quality of the estimates (Getmansky *et al*, 2004).

REFERENCES

Agarwal, V. and N. Naik, 2004, "Risks and Portfolio Decisions Involving Hedge Funds," *The Review of Financial Studies*, **17(1)**, pp 63–98.

Amin, G. S. and Harry M. Kat, 2003, "Welcome to the Dark Side: Hedge Fund Attrition and Survivorship Bias Over the Period 1994–2001," *The Journal of Alternative Investments*, **6(1)**, pp 57–73.

Athayde, G. M. and R. G. Flores Jr., 2004, "Finding a Maximum Skewness Portfolio – A General Solution to Three-Moments Portfolio Choice," *Journal of Economic Dynamics and Control*, **28(6)**, pp 1335–52.

Black, F. and R. Litterman, 1990, "Asset Allocation: Combining Investor Views with Market Equilibrium," Goldman Sachs Fixed Income Research, September.

Brooks, C. and H. M. Kat, 2002, "The Statistical Properties of Hedge Fund Return Index Returns and Their Implications for Investors," *The Journal of Alternative Investments*, **5(3)**, pp 26–44.

Cremers, J.-H., M. Kritzman, and S. Page, 2005, "Optimal Hedge Fund Allocations: Do Higher Moments Matter?" *Journal of Portfolio Management*, **32(1)**, pp 70–81.

Davies, R., H. M. Kat, and S. Lu, 2005, "Fund of Hedge Funds Portfolio Selection: A Multiple-Objective Approach," unpublished paper, September.

Dopfel, F. E., 2005, "How Hedge Funds Fit," *Journal of Portfolio Management*, **32(2)**, pp 9–20.

Edwards, F. R. and J. Liew, 1999, "Hedge Funds Versus Managed Futures as Asset Classes," *Journal of Derivatives*, **6(1)**, pp 45–64.

Favre, L. and J.-A. Galeano, 2002, "Mean-Modified Value at Risk Optimization with Hedge Funds," *The Journal of Alternative Investments*, **5(2)**, pp 21–5.

Fung, W. and D. Hsieh, 2002, "Asset-Based Style Factors for Hedge Funds," *Financial Analysts Journal*, **58(5)**, pp 16–27.

Fung, W. and D. Hsieh, 2004, "Hedge Fund Benchmarks: A Risk Based Approach," *Financial Analysts Journal*, **60(5)**, pp 65–80.

Getmansky, M., A. W. Lo, and I. Makarov, 2004, "An Econometric Model of Serial Correlation in Hedge Fund Returns," *Journal of Financial Econometrics*, **74(4)**, pp 529–609.

Jaegar, L. and S. Muller, 2004, "Sources of Systematic Return in Hedge Funds," *Altternative Investment Quarterly*, **4(1)**, pp 43–54.

Jean, W. H., 1971, "The Extension of Portfolio Analysis to Three or More Parameters," *Journal of Financial and Quantitative Analysis*, **6(5)**, pp 505–15.

Jean, W. H., 1973, "More on Multidimensional Portfolio Analysis," *Journal of Financial and Quantitative Analysis*, **8(5)**, pp. 475-490.

Jondeau, E. and M. Rockinger, 2002, "The Allocation of Assets Under Higher Moments," research paper, International Center for Financial Asset Management and Engineering, Geneva, December.

Jondeau, E. and M. Rockinger, 2005, "Conditional Asset Allocation under Nonnormality: How Costly is the Mean-Variance Criterion?" research paper, International Center for Financial Asset Management and Engineering, Geneva, December.

Kahneman, D. and A. Tversky, 1974, "Judgment under Uncertainty: Heuristics and Biases," *Science*, **185**, pp 1124–31.

Kahneman, D. and A. Tversky, 1979, "Prospect Theory: An Analysis of Decisions under Risk," *Econometrica*, **47(2)**, pp 263–91.

Lamm, R. M., 1999, "Why Not 100% Hedge Funds?" *The Journal of Investing*, **8**(4), pp 87–97.

Lamm, R. M., 2002, "How Good Are Equity Hedge Managers," *Alternative Investments Quarterly*, **2(1)**, pp 17–25.

Lamm, R. M., 2003, "Asymmetric Returns and Optimal Hedge Fund Portfolios," *The Journal of Alternative Investments*, **6(4)**, pp 9–21.

Liew, J. and C. French, 2005, "Quantitative Topics in Hedge Fund Investing," *Journal of Portfolio Management*, **32(2)**, pp 21–32.

Saha, A., 1993, "Expo-Power Utility: A Flexible Form for Absolute and Relative Risk Aversion," *American Journal of Agricultural Economics*, **75(4)**, pp 905–13.

Schneeweis, T. and R. Spurgin, 1998, "Multi-Factor Analysis of Hedge Funds, Managed Futures, and Mutual Fund Return Characteristics," *The Journal of Alternative Investments*, **1(3)**, pp 1–24.

Schneeweis, T., H. Kazemi, and G. Martin, 2002, "Understanding Hedge Fund Performance: Research Issues Revisited – Part 1," *The Journal of Alternative Investments*, **5(4)**, pp 6–22.

Signer, A. and L. Favre, 2002, "The Difficulties of Measuring the Benefits of Hedge Funds, *The Journal of Alternative Investments*, **5(2)**, pp 31–42.

21

Long-Term Co-Movements Between Hedge Funds and Financial Asset Markets

Roland Füss; Dieter G. Kaiser; Heinz Rehkugler; Irina Butina

University of Freiburg; Benchmark Alternative Strategies GmbH; University of Freiburg; University of Freiburg

INTRODUCTION

Hedge funds are under the constant scrutiny of investors and researchers. In the past decade they have already grown from a small number of firms managing several hundred million dollars to more than 8,000 hedge funds totalling more than US$1 trillion in assets under management (HFR 2006). It is often argued that one of the key drivers behind this substantial growth are the diversification benefits to a traditional portfolio that hedge funds contribute to due to their low correlation structure (Zask 2000; Morley 2001; Brooks and Kat 2002). However, applying correlation analysis to hedge funds deserves a second look. Kat (2002) argues that correlation coefficients are reliable only if the variables have a normal distribution. In general, hedge fund indices are far from being elliptically distributed. As Kat and Lu (2002) show, they exhibit non-zero skewness and/or excess kurtosis. Therefore, the lower and upper bounds of a correlation coefficient may be narrower than ±1 (Kat 2002). This makes the often-quoted advantage that hedge funds have low correlation with stock market indices simply unreliable. When using mean-variance methods as pioneered by Markowitz (1959), return series are also analysed assuming the property of stationarity. In addition, returns must be normally

results of cointegration relationships between hedge funds and portfolios of conventional and alternative financial assets are presented. In this context, we also point out the incorrect inferences taken from correlation results and its subsequent implications for a portfolio optimisation approach, respectively. The final section concludes.

TACTICAL VERSUS STRATEGIC ASSET ALLOCATION

Normally, in the finance literature we distinguish between three levels of asset allocation – the benchmark, the strategic, and the tactical asset allocation. As a result of financial decision-making, asset allocation strives to realise the best possible risk/return profile of a portfolio consisting of financial assets. In the case of benchmark asset allocation or so-called indexing, the portfolio manager invests exactly according to the assets weights of the benchmark index. On the other hand, strategic asset allocation is based on long-term opinions of asset class performance, usually with a five-year horizon. Since the weights are determined by long-term forecasts, there is no annual update of the forecast and hence no rebalancing of the portfolio. Tactical asset allocation refers to short-term deviations from the strategic weights, usually one month to one quarter. Since indexing is always value-weighted, thus altering portfolio weights only slightly, the variation in investment weights increases with the strategic program. In regard to the strategic asset allocation, there are slow evolving weights in order to maintain the strategic objective by rebalancing the portfolio within a year. In contrast, weight changes for tactical asset allocation are highly dynamic.

Whereas, no conditioning information is used to determine the weights in benchmark allocation, it is generally employed in strategic and tactical asset allocation. In addition, strategic allocation decisions are sometimes based on unconditional information by simply assuming that historical returns will reflect the next five years of returns, which could be dangerous since it is assumed that no other information is relevant. In the context of portfolio optimisation, the use of ex-post data leads to a fixed weight portfolio. The opposite is true for both strategic and tactical asset allocation where short- and long-term expected returns induce weight changes unless the conditioning information has no predictive ability (Dahlquist and Harvey 2001).

In order to establish a solid investment policy, investors have to assess the future uncertainty in their financial decision-making process by using quantitative models. In doing so, time series models possess the attractive feature that their future behaviour is explained by its own past and by the past of related time series. Consequently, no or only some prior knowledge about related (exogenous) economic variables is needed. More precisely, this chapter focuses on long-term co-movements between hedge funds and financial asset markets, and the effects of long-term and short-term planning horizons. In doing so, cointegration reveals the existence of long-run equilibrium relations between hedge funds and other financial series. On the other hand, the error correction mechanism describes how series react to temporary deviations from the long-term equilibrium relations. Assuming risk-averse investors, it follows that for strategic asset allocation, they can benefit from the knowledge of cointegrating relationships, ie, that asset prices will stay together on a long-run basis. Cointegrating relations of financial time series show less long-term variability, and therefore, less long-term risk (Lucas 1997). By contrast, for tactical asset allocation the reaction to a temporary state of disequilibrium can be incorporated into the calculus. If time series are cointegrated then an error correction mechanism exists, which allows the portfolio manager to predict and to anticipate some of the near future developments. This means that the conditioning information is given by the adjustment coefficient of the temporary deviations from the equilibrium. However, if the process that adjusts hedge funds and financial asset markets takes decades, passive long-term investors could be better off focusing on error correction instead of cointegrating vectors, and active investors could probably ignore the presence of cointegration.

ECONOMETRIC METHODOLOGY

Augmented Dickey–Fuller tests

In the context of the long-run properties of financial time-series, researchers are particularly focused on the characteristics of asset prices, ie, whether they can be characterised as random walk (unit root) or mean reversion (trend stationary) processes. If asset prices follow a mean-reverting process there must be a tendency for the price level, after a transitory deviation, to reverse to its trend path (or mean return) over time. This suggests that future returns can be predicted using information on past returns. In contrast, a random walk process presupposes that any shock to an asset price is permanent and there is no tendency for the price level to return to a trend path over time. Thus, in a random walk framework, future returns based on historical observations are unpredictable, meaning that the most recently observed return is the best indicator of future returns. A further characteristic of random walks is that the longer the time horizon, the more likely it is that prices will wander far from their trend path. In the long run, this inestimable growth in the volatility of asset prices characterises the non-stationarity of random walks, which in turn has important implications for the pricing of assets and the portfolio allocation decision.

In general, to test whether asset prices follow a random walk or mean-reverting processes, the augmented Dickey–Fuller (ADF) (1979, 1981) test is applied. To obtain this statistic, let us consider the following process:

$$X_t = \mu + \gamma X_{t-1} + \beta t + \varepsilon_t \qquad \text{with } \varepsilon_t \sim \text{iid}(0, \sigma^2) \tag{1}$$

where X_t is the asset price, μ is a constant parameter and β is a trend parameter. If $\gamma = 1$ and $\mu = \beta = 0$ asset prices follows a pure random walk without any deterministic component. Alternatively, they can be described as random walks with a drift ($\gamma = 1$, $\mu \neq 0$, $\beta = 0$) when the prices fluctuate around a constant mean. If the prices fluctuate around a linear deterministic trend, they follow a random walk with drift and trend ($\gamma = 1$, $\mu \neq 0$, $\beta \neq 0$). By contrast, if $\gamma < 1$ the time series is stationary and mean-reverting, respectively. Tests of stationarity are often characterised as unit roots, where Equation (1) is manipulated in differences and the following regressions are estimated (Dickey and Fuller 1981; Dickey and Pantula 1987):

$$\Delta X_t = \mu + \beta t + \gamma^* X_{t-1} + \varepsilon_t \tag{2}$$

where $\gamma^* = (\gamma - 1)$ and $\varepsilon_t \sim \text{iid}(0, \sigma^2)$.

If $\gamma^* = 0$, ie, γ is equal to one, then the X series is said to have a unit root and be non-stationary, and the ΔX_t series will be stationary, $I(1)$. Hence, if the hypothesis $\gamma^* = 0$ is rejected, γ is less than one, and the time series does not have a unit root and is integrated of order 0 (stationary), $I(0)$. The parameters μ and β test for the presence of drift and trend components. Although unit root tests are robust against moderate degrees of heteroscedasticity, they do not account for autocorrelation. The problem of autocorrelation in the residuals is corrected by using the augmented Dickey–Fuller test. This approach incorporates lagged changes in the values of the dependent variable X_t in the regression equation, with a sufficient number of lags $(p - 1)$ being included to remove the autocorrelation in the residuals and to ensure random residuals.

$$\Delta X_t = \mu + \beta t + \gamma^* X_{t-1} + \sum_{i=1}^{p-1} \delta_i \Delta X_{t-i} + \varepsilon_t \tag{3}$$

μ and β are coefficients of the constant, and the time trend respectively, δ_i are coefficients of the $p - 1$ order lagged differenced X_t series and the error term is $\varepsilon_t \sim \text{iid}(0, \sigma^2)$.

For financial decisions on optimal asset allocation, the property of a time series is of major relevance, and the results above naturally involve the correct choice concerning the (non-)stationarity.

The Johansen test

In order to evaluate whether hedge funds exhibit potential benefits of diversification in traditional portfolios over the long-term, we need to investigate whether common stochastic trends are present. The concept of cointegration was introduced by Granger (1981) and Engle and Granger (1987). Cointegration is a property possessed by some non-stationary time series. If two non-stationary time series are cointegrated, then a linear combination relationship exists which is stationary. In the context of portfolio theory this implies that if the value series of a fixed weight portfolio of assets with non-stationary prices is stationary, then the assets will form a cointegrated set. The set of asset weights within such a portfolio is called the cointegrating vector.

Cointegration implies that despite permanent departures from the equilibrium in the short-run, there is some long-run equilibrium relation tying time series together. According to the ADF test of stationarity for a single time series, cointegration exists when there is mean reversion in the price spread(s) of two (or more) assets. Johansen (1988, 1991) and Johansen and Juselius (1990, 1991) developed the multivariate test for cointegration and the error correction model. The Johansen test is a maximum likelihood estimation of a fully specified error correction model. Hence, this methodology is based on a vector autoregressive specification, VAR(k) for the $n \times 1$ vector of $I(1)$ stochastic variables, X_t, with $n \times 1$ iid Gaussian error vector (Maddala and Kim 1998):

$$X_t = \mu + A_1 X_{t-1} + \cdots + A_k X_{t-k} + \varepsilon_t \tag{4}$$

where X_{t-k} are assumed to be predetermined, A_i are $n \times n$ matrices of parameters, μ is a $n \times 1$ vector of constant, ε_t is a vector of normal distributed error terms with a mean of zero and constant variance Ω, and k is the maximum number of lag length processing the white noise.

In order to receive the vector error correction model in transitory form, the system in Equation (4) is rewritten in differences by defining $\Delta \equiv 1 - L$ where L is the lag operator (see Johansen and Juselius 1990):

$$\Delta X_t = \mu + \Gamma_1 \Delta X_{t-1} + \cdots + \Gamma_{k-1} \Delta X_{t-k+1} + \Pi X_{t-1} + \varepsilon_t \tag{5}$$

where

$$\Gamma_i = -(\mathrm{I} - \mathrm{A}_1 - \cdots - A_i), \quad i = 1, \ldots, (k-1)$$
$$\Pi = -(\mathrm{I} - \mathrm{A}_1 - \cdots - A_k)$$

ΔX_t exhibits the vector of price changes in period t, Γ represents the short-run dynamics, I is an identity matrix, and Π is the long-run impact matrix, which summarises the long-run information in the X_t process by relating the change, ΔX_t, to the levels X_{t-k}, of k periods earlier. The number of stationary linear combinations of X_t, ie, the cointegrating vectors is determined by the rank of this matrix. If Π is of full rank, $r(\Pi) = n$, the assumed stationarity of the error term in Equation (5) requires that all n linearly independent stationary combinations must be stationary. This can only happen if the deviations of X_t around the deterministic components are stationary. If the rank of Π is zero, no linear combination exists to make ΠX_t stationary, except for the trivial solution. Hence, Equation (5) is reduced to a standard vector autoregressive model in first differences. An applicable case occurs when Π is of intermediate rank, $0 < r(\Pi) = r < n$, so that r linear combinations of non-stationary variables are stationary, ie, there are r cointegrating vectors, or equivalently, $n - r$ stochastic trends. Because the matrix does not have full rank, two $n \times r$ matrices α and β can be factored such that $\Pi = \alpha\beta'$, where $'$ denotes transposition. Consequently, Equation (5) can be rewritten as

$$\Delta X_t = \mu + \sum_{i=1}^{k-1} \Gamma_1 \Delta X_{t-1} + \alpha\beta' X_{t-1} + \varepsilon_t \qquad \textbf{(6)}$$

In this factorisation, the r columns of β can be defined as cointegrating vectors, ie, the linearly independent combinations of X_t that are stationary. This factorisation results from Equation (6), where $\beta' X_{t-1}$ must be stationary as ΔX_t and ε_t are stationary processes (Johansen 1991). Moreover, the r linear combinations $\beta' X_t$ of the n possibly non-stationary time series X_t, so-called equilibrium relations, are stationary (Lucas 1997). α is the matrix of the error correction terms that shows the impact of r cointegrated vectors on ΔX_t. In other words, the elements of $\beta' X_t$ yield the deviations of the long-term equilibrium, which represents the equilibrium error. Using parameterisation of the error correction model in Equation (6), the equilibrium error is defined as $\beta' X_{t-1}$. Hence, if $\beta' X_{t-1} \neq 0$, then X_t will adjust towards the equilibrium, and the ith row of α shows the direction and strength of the adjustment process. From this the evidence of the error correction mechanism for tactical asset allocation decisions is quite obvious. If X_t is in a transitory state of disequilibrium, ie, $\beta' X_t \neq 0$, then a part of the future developments of X_t can be predicted due to the functioning of the error correction mechanism (Lucas 1997).

To determine the rank r of estimated matrix $\hat{\Pi}$, the eigenvalues $\tilde{\lambda}_i$ have to be calculated at first. The number of significant non-zero eigenvalues shows the rank of the matrix $\hat{\Pi}$ and can be evaluated by the trace and the maximal eigenvalue test. As Kasa (1992) explains, the two tests differ in what they assume about the alternative hypothesis. The *trace statistic* is the result of testing the restriction $r \leq q$ ($q < n$) against the completely unrestricted model $r \leq n$.

$$\lambda_{\text{trace}} = -T \sum_{i=q+1}^{n} \ln(1-\tilde{\lambda}_i) \qquad \textbf{(7)}$$

where T is the sample size and $\tilde{\lambda}_{r+1}, \ldots, \tilde{\lambda}_n$ are the $n - r$ smallest squared canonical correlations. The second restricted maximum likelihood ratio test is referred to as the maximal eigenvalue test statistic. The $\lambda_{\max}$ is found by again testing the null hypothesis of at most q cointegrating vectors against the alternative of one additional cointegrating vector (ie, $r \leq q + 1$):

$$\lambda_{\max} = -T \ln(1-\tilde{\lambda}_{q+1}) \qquad \textbf{(8)}$$

where $\tilde{\lambda}_1^*, \ldots, \tilde{\lambda}_q^*$ are the largest squared canonical correlations. In comparison to the trace test, the maximal eigenvalue test produces more clear-cut results, since the former does not utilise the information detected in the eigenvalues, which have been found, do not differ significantly from zero (Johansen and Juselius 1990).

In conclusion, these technical derivations allow us to now set up a relationship to the framework of optimal asset allocation. For illustrative purposes, let us consider an investor with a quadratic risk aversion utility function, where conditional mean and variance of portfolio returns over the investment horizon matters. Further, it is assumed that the vector of log asset prices X_t follows a VAR process of order one:

$$\Delta X_t = \mu + \Pi X_{t-1} + \varepsilon_t \qquad \text{with } \varepsilon_t \sim \text{iid}(0, \Omega) \qquad \textbf{(9)}$$

For $\Pi = 0$ we receive the standard model with iid returns, whereas $\Pi = \alpha\beta'$ in Equation (9) represents a cointegrated system of asset prices. Given a constant holding vector x in the assets over an investment horizon H, the conditional mean and the conditional variance are defined as:

$$x'E_0(X_H - X_0) = \sum_{t=0}^{H-1} x'(I+\Pi)^t \mu \qquad \textbf{(10)}$$

$$x'V_0(X_H - X_0)x = \sum_{t=0}^{H-1} x'(I+\Pi)^t \Omega (I+\Pi')^t x \qquad \textbf{(11)}$$

respectively. When $\Pi = 0$ (no cointegration), we get the standard formulation $Hx'\mu$ and $Hx'\Omega x$ for the mean and variance respectively, from which the usual mean-variance analysis pioneered by Markowitz (1959) follows. When the asset prices are cointegrated ($\Pi = \alpha\beta'$), mean-variance analysis still applies, but with different formulas and values for conditional moments that generate a shift in the mean-variance frontier. Thus, the relevance of cointegration for asset allocation will depend on the holding period of the investment, rebalancing frequency of the portfolio, and the risk attitude of investor. In the case of strategic asset allocation with a static (no-rebalancing) long-term investment decision, as shown in the example above, the portfolio can be constructed with weights corresponding to cointegrating vectors in $\beta' X_{t-1}$. Thereby, the uncertainty is lower compared with no cointegration due to the lower long-term variability. These portfolios are particularly interesting for long-term investors with a highly risk-averse attitude. By contrast, from the perspective of tactical asset allocation, portfolio managers can anticipate the temporary deviations of asset prices from long-run equilibrium and can effectively rebalance the portfolio using the matrix α.

DATA AND EMPIRICAL RESULTS

The data used in this study are monthly total return indexes denominated in US$, covering the period from December 1993 to December 2005, with each series containing 145 end of the month observations. The hedge fund composite index is taken from CS/Tremont, while the other financial asset-class indices are represented by *S&P 500* Composite Index, *NASDAQ* Composite (DS calculated), Wilshire All *Growth*, Wilshire All *Value*, Wilshire *Large* Cap 750, Wilshire *Small* Cap 1750, J.P. Morgan Government *Bond* Index, Goldman Sachs *Commodity* Index, FTSE/EPRA NAREIT All *REITS*, and S&P/IFCG *Emerging Markets* Composite Index. The traditional as well as the alternative asset classes have been chosen to create different types of portfolios depending on the risk attitude of the investors.

Since we use a hedge fund index as a proxy for hedge fund performance, the time series is subject to different biases. These biases derive from the fact that hedge funds are not legally required to make information about returns and strategies public (self-selection bias), and because hedge funds that stop reporting to the data vendors are excluded from the data bases (survivorship bias). Further discussion on the biases in existing hedge fund indices can be found in the contribution of Heidorn *et al* (Chapter 1 of this volume). These biases result in an overestimation of expected returns and lead to underestimated expected variance. Since hedge fund managers also invest in illiquid instruments, they often choose to report the last price for these positions, which might not correspond to the real value. This approach creates a smoothing effect, which is called the autocorrelation bias. As a result of this marking-to-market problem (positive autocorrelation), the volatility of hedge funds is underestimated.

In terms of the cointegration analysis, these biases affect the values of the cointegrating vectors and error-correction model coefficients. However, the general result of cointegration or the absence of cointegrated relationships still holds. Moreover, in this study the CS/Tremont Hedge Fund Composite Index is used, where the autocorrelation effects can be neglected since the autocorrelation coefficients of first order (0.121) up to order 30 (0.014) are not significant. Nevertheless, the CS/Tremont indices are affected in particular by the survivorship and self-selection bias (Lhabitant 2004). In addition to the presence of several biases, it should also be mentioned that broad-based hedge fund style indexes generally understate the diversity of trading styles and overstate the risk of style convergence which is outweighed by using a fund of hedge funds index.

Descriptive statistics

The logarithms of the indices levels are depicted in Figure 1. As can be seen from the first graph, the stock markets series exhibit overall similar increasing trend behaviour, whereas the US bond market, the commodity futures market and the emerging stock market follow a clearly different trend. In comparison to the US stock markets, the alternative assets in the second graph exhibit a steady linear trend. In addition, the indices and in particular the emerging markets index show sharp declines at the time of the Asian financial crisis in 1997/1998, and a recovery in the aftermath. Even at this preliminary stage of the analysis, it would appear that not all assets follow a common trend, suggesting that, certainly amongst these

Figure 1 Evolution of financial market indices

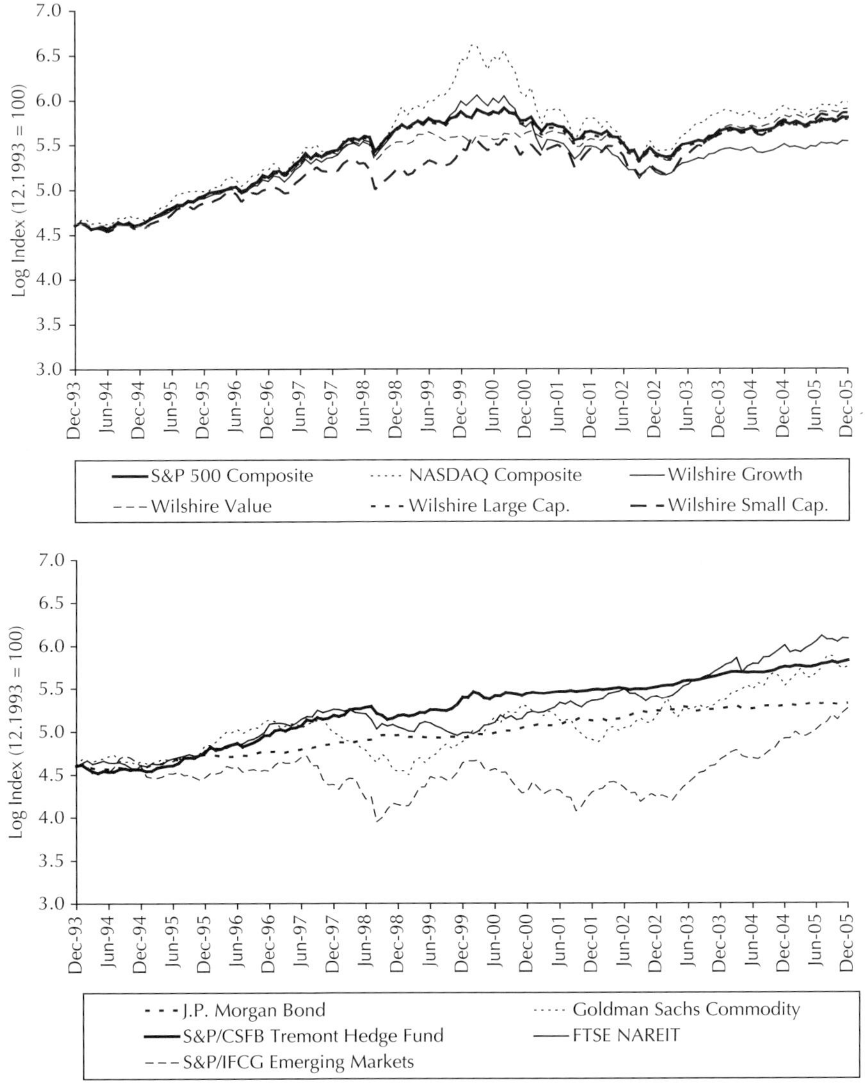

Source: Thomson Financial Datastream

financial assets, benefits to diversification may be present not only in the short-term but may also persist in the long-run.

However, most of the indices increase continuously over the given period, implying a high rate of return. The summary

Table 1 Statistical properties of the time series, 01/1994–12/2005

	Mean (in% p.a.)	Std. dev. (in % p.a.)	Skewness	Excess kurtosis	Sharpe ratio	J.–B. test
Δln(Hedge fund comp.)	10.160	7.810	−0.026	2.247	1.301	30.32***
Δln(S&P 500 comp.)	10.007	14.853	−0.730	0.919	0.674	17.85***
Δln(NASDAQ comp.)	11.412	26.868	−0.628	1.181	0.425	17.83***
Δln(Wilshire growth)	7.800	18.218	−0.885	1.470	0.428	31.78***
Δln(Wilshire value)	10.826	14.582	−0.892	2.423	0.742	54.31***
Δln(Wilshire large cap.)	9.834	15.089	−0.769	1.022	0.652	20.44***
Δln(Wilshire small cap.)	10.452	18.930	−0.770	1.743	0.552	32.47***
Δln(J.P. Morgan bond)	6.018	4.755	−0.588	1.081	1.266	15.32***
Δln(GS commodities)	9.586	19.930	−0.066	0.043	0.481	0.12
Δln(FTSE NAREIT)	12.290	13.128	−0.844	2.652	0.936	59.31***
Δln(S&P/IFCG emerg. M.)	5.500	21.403	−1.076	3.053	0.257	83.72***

Based on monthly continuously compounded total returns for 144 observations. ***, **, * denote significance at 1%, 5%, and 10% levels, respectively (rejection of the normal distribution); the Sharpe ratio is defined as coefficient of mean and standard deviation without adjustment of risk-free rate.

statistics for hedge fund, stock, bond, commodity and real estate index returns are reported in Table 1. First, the FTSE NAREIT real estate index displays the highest continuously compounded average return; whereas in terms of risk-adjusted return, ie, the simple Sharpe ratio defined as coefficient of mean and standard deviation, the CS/Tremont Hedge Fund Composite and the JP Morgan Bond index highly outperform the other financial assets. In comparison to the low annualised mean of 5.5% for the S&P/IFCG Emerging Equity Market index, the US stock market indices range between 10.83% for value and 7.80% for growth stocks. At the same time, the NASDAQ composite is the most volatile asset, with annualised standard deviation of 26.87%, which is nearly four times higher than for the hedge fund index.

In addition note that the emerging stock markets possess extremely high volatility compared with their low mean return. However, almost all asset classes exhibit asymmetric return patterns with negative skewness and positive excess kurtosis, with the exception of the Goldman Sachs Commodity index. The Jarque–Bera test shows the degree to which returns deviate from the normal distribution. A high value for the test statistics suggests that the returns do not follow a normal distribution at 1% significance levels. The results show again that there is a substantial variation between the different asset classes. For this reason, the use of standard deviation as single measure of risk may result in a distortion of the true performance. Moreover, in the context of portfolio optimisation this makes standard deviation an incomplete measure of risk and may lead to inferior asset allocation decisions.

Finding the optimal portfolio weights in mean-variance analysis also requires that the return correlations between assets are stable. However, correlation analysis is only valid for stationary variables. Most of the financial data are stationary by taking the first differences of the prices or by de-trending the variables; thus, asset prices are integrated order one. This in turn has the disadvantage that valuable information is lost, because de-trending eliminates any possibilities of detecting common trends in prices. In addition, due to their trading strategies, hedge funds typically are non-linear functions of traditional markets, so that the use of linear correlation coefficients as a measure of dependence seems unreliable (Lhabitant 2004). However, the use of the correlation coefficient as an indicator for the dependence among random variables is problematic due to the fact that only linear dependence is measured. Moreover, the result is only meaningful if the multivariate distribution is elliptic as noted by Embrechts *et al* (1999, 2002) and Kat (2002). Since most of the hedge fund strategies, as is apparent in Table 1, have a positive or negative skewness and/or an excess kurtosis, the joint distribution is far from being elliptic, and thus the correlation coefficient is not an adequate measure for the structure of dependence between two assets. Furthermore, if the distribution is not elliptic, the correlation coefficient does not exhaust the full interval $[-1,+1]$, eg, the interval is much smaller for certain distributions. This in turn means that the correlation coefficients are underestimated and a very low dependence will be falsely concluded, even though the variables are perfectly correlated. In contrast, the cointegration approach works directly on asset prices compared to returns and makes no assumption about the distributional properties or stationarity of the asset value series.

Table 2 provides the correlation matrix between the various financial assets under consideration, regardless of its disadvantages mentioned above. First, it can be observed that only the monthly bond returns are negatively correlated with the other

Table 2 Contemporaneous correlations between monthly returns, 01/1994–12/2005

	Hedge fund comp.	S&P 500 comp.	NASDAQ comp.	Wilshire growth	Wilshire value	WS large cap.	WS small cap.	J.P. Morgan bond	GS commodity	FTSE/ NAREIT	S&P/IFCG EMMA
Hedge fund comp.	1										
S&P 500 comp.	0.489	1									
NASDAQ comp.	0.514	0.810	1								
Wilshire growth	0.512	0.926	0.935	1							
Wilshire value	0.440	0.923	0.622	0.744	1						
WS large cap.	0.509	0.996	0.836	0.944	0.916	1					
WS small cap.	0.583	0.773	0.839	0.802	0.759	0.802	1				
J.P. Morgan bond	0.112	−0.108	−0.180	−0.131	−0.121	−0.114	−0.182	1			
GS commodity	0.162	0.009	0.103	0.033	0.031	0.017	0.141	0.091	1		
FTSE/NAREIT	0.241	0.318	0.185	0.208	0.454	0.312	0.449	0.056	0.006	1	
S&P/IFCG EMMA	0.503	0.652	0.632	0.614	0.657	0.659	0.697	−0.220	0.147	0.367	1

WS = Wiltshire; GS = Goldman Sachs.

assets – with the exception of commodities. It is also expected that the stock indices would be highly correlated, in particular with the S&P 500 index. The hedge fund index has high positive correlation with the NASDAQ index, growth and small companies as well as the equity markets of developing countries, whereas low correlations accompany the bond, commodity and real estate markets. Overall, the alternative investment classes exhibit very low correlation amongst themselves. Finally, it also well documented that due to the nature of real estate equities, they are increasingly correlated with small and value companies.

Irrespective of the problems associated with correlations, it is essential to recognise that cointegration and correlation are related, yet individual concepts. Accordingly, high correlation does not imply high cointegration, and vice versa. Thus, higher correlation is neither a necessary nor a sufficient condition for higher cointegration between the assets. In fact, cointegrated series can have correlations that are sometimes quite low (Füss and Herrmann 2005).

Testing for unit roots

Before applying the Johansen cointegration methodology, it is necessary to test whether the time series is integrated of the same order, or rather, if each series requires the same degree of differencing to achieve stationarity. As discussed by Engle and Granger (1987), a series is said to be integrated of order d, $I(d)$, if the d times differenced series has a stationary invertible ARMA representation. Tests of stationarity are often characterised as unit roots. If the hedge fund index and the financial market indices data exhibit a unit root they will be integrated, ie, $I(1)$. In determining the order of integration of a time series, the Dickey–Fuller-test (Dickey and Fuller 1979) and the Augmented Dickey–Fuller t-tests (ADF) (Dickey and Fuller 1981, Said and Dickey 1984) are applied. The ADF values for each time series are calculated by estimating regression equations for a random walk, a random walk with drift, and a model with drift and trend, respectively (Dickey and Pantula 1987). Thus, according to Equation (3), we test the null hypothesis of difference-stationary AR($p - 1$) process against the alternative trend-stationary AR(p) process. If asset returns exhibit the property of random walk, temporary shocks in the returns persist over time and do not dissipate when asset returns revert to mean levels.

Table 4 VAR lag order selection – *portfolio I* (1993/12–2005/12)

Lag	0	1	2	3	4	5	6	7	8
FPE	1.63E−12	5.11E–19[a]	5.28E–19	5.19E–19	5.97E–19	7.18E–19	7.71E–19	7.53E–19	8.94E–19
AIC	−12.96	−27.93[a]	−27.73	−27.92	−27.78	−27.61	−27.56	−27.60	−27.46
SIC	−12.85	−27.29[a]	−26.73	−26.21	−25.55	−24.84	−24.25	−23.77	−23.10
HQ	−12.91	−27.67[a]	−27.42	−27.23	−26.88	−26.49	−26.21	−26.05	−25.69

[a] indicates lag order selected by the criterion Akaike information criterion (AIC), Schwarz information criterion (SIC), Hannan-Quinn information criterion (HQ), and final prediction error (FPE).

whereas the Chow breakpoint test indicates significant structural breaks for S&P 500, NASDAQ, growth and large stocks during the time period 1998/11 to 2001/02, and for emerging stock markets in the period 1998/07 to 2001/04. Thus, the tests were carried out for the entire period as well as for the two sub-samples 1993/12 to 1997/12 (before the Asian and Russian crises), and 2001/12 to 2005/12 (after new economy bubble) to avoid spurious results from parameter instability.

The specification of the unrestricted VAR model's order is based on the Akaike information and the final prediction error criterion (see Lütkepohl 1991). As can be seen from Table 4 (representative for the whole sample), all information criteria refer to a VAR model of order one. Hence, the vector error correction model (VECM) involves $k - 1 = 0$ terms in differences. The result of $k - 1 = 0$ also holds for the sub-samples and in the case of portfolio II.

According to the ADF test, the distribution of the test statistics from trace and maximal eigenvalue tests depend on the existence of the deterministic components drift and trend in the system. Given the weak trend behaviour in Figure 1, a model was chosen without deterministic components, ie, also without a constant. From an economic point of view, this seems to be reasonable since a constant in the return relationship would imply increasing returns over time.

The cointegration results for the conventional portfolio (*portfolio I*) are reported in Table 5. For the whole sample, the maximal eigenvalue test does not reject the hypothesis of the presence of a single cointegration vector at the 1% level, while for the trace test a significant cointegrating relationship is detected at the 5% level only. The same result holds for the first sub-sample, indicating that there is one common stochastic trend driving the financial assets for which the variance is bounded. However, the test statistics are significantly higher in the second sub-period, where λ_{trace} suggests no more than three cointegrating vectors since we fail to reject $r \leq 3$. In contrast, the λ_{max} indicates four long-term equilibriums at the 5% significance level, with the exception of a single cointegrating vector at the 1% level. When considering the cointegrating vector normalised on the first component hedge fund index for the current period (in Table 5), the coefficient of the value stock index is very close to zero. Thus, it may be the case that this asset class does

Table 5 Johansen's maximum likelihood test – *portfolio I*

H_0	Eigenvalues	Trace Test – λ_{trace}			Maximal Eigenvalue Test – λ_{max}		
		Estimated statistics	5% critical value	1% critical value	Estimated statistics	5% critical value	1% critical value
Panel A: The whole sample from 1993/12 to 2005/12							
$r = 0$	0.2258	65.20*	59.46	66.52	36.86**	30.04	35.17
$r \leq 1$	0.1032	28.34	39.89	45.58	15.69	23.80	28.82
$r \leq 2$	0.0507	12.65	24.31	29.75	7.50	17.89	22.99
$r \leq 3$	0.0298	5.16	12.53	16.31	4.36	11.44	15.69
$r \leq 4$	0.0056	0.80	3.84	6.51	0.80	3.84	6.51
Cointegrating vector (normalised on Hedge Fund Composite in parentheses)							
Hedge F.	S&P 500	Value	Large Cap.	Bond			
−0.4278	−4.6387	−0.9609	5.0483	2.2255			
(1.0000)	(10.842)	(2.2459)	(−11.800)	(−5.2019)			
Normalised α coefficients representing speed of adjustment to equilibrium							
Hedge F.	S&P 500	Value	Large Cap.	Bond			
0.0037	0.0035	0.0035	0.0034	0.0022			
Panel B: The sub-sample from 1993/12 to 1997/12							
$r = 0$	0.5424	65.82*	59.46	66.52	37.53**	30.04	35.17
$r \leq 1$	0.2856	28.30	39.89	45.58	16.14	23.80	28.82
$r \leq 2$	0.1755	12.16	24.31	29.75	9.26	17.89	22.99
$r \leq 3$	0.0583	2.90	12.53	16.31	2.89	11.44	15.69
$r \leq 4$	0.0002	0.01	3.84	6.51	0.01	3.84	6.51

Table 5 (continued)

Cointegrating vector (normalised on Hedge Fund Composite in parentheses)							
Hedge F.	S&P 500	Value	Large Cap.	Bond			
27.820	−45.734	−26.663	44.912	15.477			
(1.0000)	(−1.644)	(−0.958)	(1.614)	(0.556)			
Normalised α coefficients representing speed of adjustment to equilibrium							
Hedge F.	S&P 500	Value	Large Cap.	Bond			
−0.4752	−0.3122	−0.3383	−0.3275	−0.1609			
Panel C: The sub-sample from 2001/12 to 2005/12							
$r = 0$	0.6464	109.4**	59.46	66.52	50.93**	30.04	35.17
$r \leq 1$	0.4302	58.46**	39.89	45.58	27.56*	23.80	28.82
$r \leq 2$	0.3167	30.90**	24.31	29.75	18.66*	17.89	22.99
$r \leq 3$	0.2206	12.24	12.53	16.31	12.21*	11.44	15.69
$r \leq 4$	0.0010	0.03	3.84	6.51	0.03	3.84	6.51
Cointegrating vector (normalised on Hedge Fund Composite in parentheses)							
Hedge F.	S&P 500	Value	Large Cap.	Bond			
−46.966	−99.629	−14.375	137.91	52.853			
(1.0000)	(2.121)	(0.306)	(−2.937)	(−1.125)			
Normalised α coefficients representing speed of adjustment to equilibrium							
Hedge F.	S&P 500	Value	Large Cap.	Bond			
−0.3300	−0.2858	−0.5944	−0.3136	0.1480			

** and * indicate that the null hypothesis of no cointegration can be rejected at the 1% and 5% significance levels, respectively. λ_{trace} and λ_{max} statistics are performed under the assumption of no deterministic trend (ie, without a constant in the cointegrating vector). Critical values for the Johansen test are from Osterwald-Lenum (1992); r refers to the number of cointegrated vectors in the model; $k = 1$, k refers to number of lags in the unrestricted VAR.

Table 6 Testing the entering in and the adjustment to the relevant cointegrating vector – *portfolio I*

Panel A: The whole sample from 1993/12 to 2005/12			
$\beta_{\text{Hedge Fund}} = 0$	$\chi^2(1) = 0.0090$	$\alpha_{\text{Hedge Fund}} = 0$	$\chi^2(1) = 12.0736^{**}$
$\beta_{\text{S\&P 500}} = 0$	$\chi^2(1) = 0.3550$	$\alpha_{\text{S\&P 500}} = 0$	$\chi^2(1) = 4.0986^{*}$
$\beta_{\text{Value}} = 0$	$\chi^2(1) = 0.0785$	$\alpha_{\text{Value}} = 0$	$\chi^2(1) = 4.3631^{*}$
$\beta_{\text{Large Cap.}} = 0$	$\chi^2(1) = 0.3423$	$\alpha_{\text{Large Cap.}} = 0$	$\chi^2(1) = 3.8066$
$\beta_{\text{Bonds}} = 0$	$\chi^2(1) = 0.2026$	$\alpha_{\text{Bonds}} = 0$	$\chi^2(1) = 12.1614^{**}$
Panel B: The sub-sample from 1993/12 to 1997/12			
$\beta_{\text{Hedge Fund}} = 0$	$\chi^2(1) = 18.2399^{**}$	$\alpha_{\text{Hedge Fund}} = 0$	$\chi^2(1) = 16.5925^{**}$
$\beta_{\text{S\&P 500}} = 0$	$\chi^2(1) = 7.0080^{**}$	$\alpha_{\text{S\&P 500}} = 0$	$\chi^2(1) = 3.7414^{*}$
$\beta_{\text{Value}} = 0$	$\chi^2(1) = 1.1358$	$\alpha_{\text{Value}} = 0$	$\chi^2(1) = 4.8080^{*}$
$\beta_{\text{Large Cap.}} = 0$	$\chi^2(1) = 2.3837$	$\alpha_{\text{Large Cap.}} = 0$	$\chi^2(1) = 4.3086^{*}$
$\beta_{\text{Bonds}} = 0$	$\chi^2(1) = 4.9787^{*}$	$\alpha_{\text{Bonds}} = 0$	$\chi^2(1) = 8.0626^{**}$
Panel C: The sub-sample from 2001/12 to 2005/12			
$\beta_{\text{Hedge Fund}} = 0$	$\chi^2(1) = 16.1994^{**}$	$\alpha_{\text{Hedge Fund}} = 0$	$\chi^2(1) = 12.6073^{**}$
$\beta_{\text{S\&P 500}} = 0$	$\chi^2(1) = 18.1612^{**}$	$\alpha_{\text{S\&P 500}} = 0$	$\chi^2(1) = 0.8008$
$\beta_{\text{Value}} = 0$	$\chi^2(1) = 2.2496$	$\alpha_{\text{Value}} = 0$	$\chi^2(1) = 3.0981$
$\beta_{\text{Large Cap.}} = 0$	$\chi^2(1) = 17.4346^{**}$	$\alpha_{\text{Large Cap.}} = 0$	$\chi^2(1) = 1.0000$
$\beta_{\text{Bonds}} = 0$	$\chi^2(1) = 21.0173^{**}$	$\alpha_{\text{Bonds}} = 0$	$\chi^2(1) = 1.3743$

not enter the common stochastic trend. A formal likelihood ratio (LR) test enables one to analyse the nature of the cointegrating vectors and the adjustment coefficients. To this end, Table 6 shows results from tests of restrictions on the composition of the cointegrating vector present in each sample, and tests of restrictions on the reaction of an asset's returns to the common trend.

The results from Panel C reveal that value stock prices do not share common trends with the remaining stock prices. By imposing this restriction, one obtains the normalised cointegrating vector {1; 1.563; 0; −2.021; −1.002}. It can also be noted that the coefficient for bonds is close to −1, so that the restricted cointegrating vector finally reads as {1; 1.558; 0; −2.017; −1}. The formal test of the joint imposition of the restrictions yield a test statistic of 2.251, which is $\chi^2(2)$ distributed, ie, the restrictions cannot be rejected at the 5% level. This in turn implies that there is a proportional relationship between hedge funds and bonds. In contrast, only the returns of the hedge funds react significantly to the common trend as supposed by the α coefficient. To sum up, this information is useful in developing forecasts on hedge fund prices.

Table 7 Johansen's maximum likelihood test – *portfolio II*

H_0	Eigenvalues	Trace Test – λ_{trace}			Maximal Eigenvalue Test – λ_{max}		
		Estimated statistics	5% critical value	1% critical value	Estimated statistics	5% critical value	1% critical value
Panel A: The whole sample from 1993/12 to 2005/12							
$r = 0$	0.3098	149.0**	109.99	119.80	53.39**	41.51	47.15
$r \leq 1$	0.2269	95.61**	82.49	90.45	37.06*	36.36	41.00
$r \leq 2$	0.1412	58.55	59.46	66.52	21.92	30.04	35.17
$r \leq 3$	0.1291	36.62	39.89	45.58	19.90	23.80	28.82
$r \leq 4$	0.0643	16.72	24.31	29.75	9.57	17.89	22.99
$r \leq 5$	0.0334	7.15	12.53	16.31	4.88	11.44	15.69
$r \leq 6$	0.0126	2.27	3.84	6.51	2.27	3.84	6.51
Cointegrating vector (normalised on Hedge Fund Composite in parentheses)							
Hedge F.	NASDAQ	Growth	Small Cap.	Emerg. M.	Commod.	Real Estate	
7.3481	−2.0637	3.4888	−8.1944	3.7243	−4.6562	2.2319	
(1.0000)	(−0.2809)	(0.4748)	(−1.1152)	(0.5068)	(−0.6337)	(0.3037)	
Normalised α coefficients representing speed of adjustment to equilibrium							
Hedge F.	NASDAQ	Growth	Small Cap.	Emerg. M.	Commod.	Real Estate	
−0.0516	0.0833	0.0337	−0.0057	0.0174	0.0150	−0.0969	
Panel B: The sub-sample from 1993/12 to 1997/12							
$r = 0$	0.6062	131.0**	109.99	119.80	44.73*	41.51	47.15
$r \leq 1$	0.5404	86.22*	82.49	90.45	37.32*	36.36	41.00
$r \leq 2$	0.2823	48.90	59.46	66.52	15.92	30.04	35.17
$r \leq 3$	0.2662	32.98	39.89	45.58	14.86	23.80	28.82
$r \leq 4$	0.2076	18.12	24.31	29.75	11.17	17.89	22.99
$r \leq 5$	0.0972	6.96	12.53	16.31	4.91	11.44	15.69
$r \leq 6$	0.0418	2.05	3.84	6.51	2.05	3.84	6.51

Table 7 (continued)

H_0	Eigen values	Trace Test – λ_{trace}			Maximal Eigenvalue Test – λ_{max}		
		Estimated statistics	**5% critical value**	**1% critical value**	**Estimated statistics**	**5% critical value**	**1% critical value**
Cointegrating vector (normalised on Hedge Fund Composite in parentheses)							
Hedge F.	NASDAQ	Growth	Small Cap.	Emerg. M.	Commod.	Real Estate	
−5.1329	−15.6482	12.2291	3.6766	3.8802	1.6116	3.4605	
(1.0000)	(3.0486)	(−2.3825)	(−0.7163)	(−0.7559)	(−0.3140)	(−0.6742)	
Normalised α coefficients representing speed of adjustment to equilibrium							
Hedge F.	NASDAQ	Growth	Small Cap.	Emerg. M.	Commod.	Real Estate	
0.0757	0.0504	0.0804	0.0696	−0.0385	0.0268	0.0850	
Panel C: The sub-sample from 2001/12 to 2005/12							
$r = 0$	0.5940	124.8**	109.99	119.80	44.17*	41.51	47.15
$r \leq 1$	0.4350	80.66	82.49	90.45	27.98	36.36	41.00
$r \leq 2$	0.3536	52.68	59.46	66.52	21.38	30.04	35.17
$r \leq 3$	0.3162	31.30	39.89	45.58	18.62	23.80	28.82
$r \leq 4$	0.1425	12.68	24.31	29.75	7.53	17.89	22.99
$r \leq 5$	0.0986	5.15	12.53	16.31	5.08	11.44	15.69
$r \leq 6$	0.0013	0.06	3.84	6.51	0.06	3.84	6.51

Table 7 (continued)

Cointegrating vector (normalised on Hedge Fund Composite in parentheses)						
Hedge F.	NASDAQ	Growth	Small Cap.	Emerg. M.	Commod.	Real Estate
−35.6446	22.2427	−1.5600	−24.7274	3.4937	2.5109	16.2454
(1.0000)	(−0.6240)	(0.0438)	(0.6937)	(−0.0980)	(−0.0704)	(−0.4557)
Normalised α coefficients representing speed of adjustment to equilibrium						
Hedge F.	NASDAQ	Growth	Small Cap.	Emerg. M.	Commod.	Real Estate
−0.2575	−0.0028	−0.0166	−0.5179	−0.8241	−0.4360	−0.2877

** and * indicate that the null hypothesis of no cointegration can be rejected at the 1% and 5% significance levels, respectively. λ_{trace} and λ_{max} statistics are performed under the assumption of no deterministic trend (ie, without a constant in the cointegrating vector). Critical values for the Johansen test are from Osterwald-Lenum (1992); r refers to the number of cointegrated vectors in the model; $k = 1$, k refers to number of lags in the unrestricted VAR.

Table 8 Testing the entering in and the adjustment to the relevant cointegrating vector – *portfolio II*

Panel A: The whole sample from 1993/12 to 2005/12			
$\beta_{\text{Hedge Fund}} = 0$	$\chi^2(1) = 2.3752$	$\alpha_{\text{Hedge Fund}} = 0$	$\chi^2(1) = 8.6130^{**}$
$\beta_{\text{NASDAQ}} = 0$	$\chi^2(1) = 0.2832$	$\alpha_{\text{NASDAQ}} = 0$	$\chi^2(1) = 1.8770$
$\beta_{\text{Growth}} = 0$	$\chi^2(1) = 0.8866$	$\alpha_{\text{Growth}} = 0$	$\chi^2(1) = 0.7399$
$\beta_{\text{Small Cap.}} = 0$	$\chi^2(1) = 11.8326^{**}$	$\alpha_{\text{Small Cap.}} = 0$	$\chi^2(1) = 0.0220$
$\beta_{\text{Emerg. M.}} = 0$	$\chi^2(1) = 3.2098$	$\alpha_{\text{Emerg. M.}} = 0$	$\chi^2(1) = 0.1553$
$\beta_{\text{Commod.}} = 0$	$\chi^2(1) = 12.5930^{**}$	$\alpha_{\text{Commod.}} = 0$	$\chi^2(1) = 0.1200$
$\beta_{\text{Real Estate}} = 0$	$\chi^2(1) = 0.4335$	$\alpha_{\text{Real Estate}} = 0$	$\chi^2(1) = 11.5715^{**}$
Panel B: The sub-sample from 1993/12 to 1997/12			
$\beta_{\text{Hedge Fund}} = 0$	$\chi^2(1) = 0.0880$	$\alpha_{\text{Hedge Fund}} = 0$	$\chi^2(1) = 4.8296^{*}$
$\beta_{\text{NASDAQ}} = 0$	$\chi^2(1) = 1.6571$	$\alpha_{\text{NASDAQ}} = 0$	$\chi^2(1) = 1.7632$
$\beta_{\text{Growth}} = 0$	$\chi^2(1) = 0.3301$	$\alpha_{\text{Growth}} = 0$	$\chi^2(1) = 6.5440^{*}$
$\beta_{\text{Small Cap.}} = 0$	$\chi^2(1) = 0.3558$	$\alpha_{\text{Small Cap.}} = 0$	$\chi^2(1) = 5.1132^{*}$
$\beta_{\text{Emerg. M.}} = 0$	$\chi^2(1) = 1.1790$	$\alpha_{\text{Emerg. M.}} = 0$	$\chi^2(1) = 0.8445$
$\beta_{\text{Commod.}} = 0$	$\chi^2(1) = 0.4049$	$\alpha_{\text{Commod.}} = 0$	$\chi^2(1) = 0.7180$
$\beta_{\text{Real Estate}} = 0$	$\chi^2(1) = 0.2374$	$\alpha_{\text{Real Estate}} = 0$	$\chi^2(1) = 6.0525^{*}$
Panel C: The sub-sample from 2001/12 to 2005/12			
$\beta_{\text{Hedge Fund}} = 0$	$\chi^2(1) = 11.1868^{**}$	$\alpha_{\text{Hedge Fund}} = 0$	$\chi^2(1) = 10.1464^{**}$
$\beta_{\text{NASDAQ}} = 0$	$\chi^2(1) = 8.4406^{**}$	$\alpha_{\text{NASDAQ}} = 0$	$\chi^2(1) = 0.0001$
$\beta_{\text{Growth}} = 0$	$\chi^2(1) = 0.0592$	$\alpha_{\text{Growth}} = 0$	$\chi^2(1) = 0.0050$
$\beta_{\text{Smal Cap.}} = 0$	$\chi^2(1) = 8.4835^{**}$	$\alpha_{\text{Small Cap.}} = 0$	$\chi^2(1) = 3.1847$
$\beta_{\text{Emerg. M.}} = 0$	$\chi^2(1) = 1.1736$	$\alpha_{\text{Emerg. M.}} = 0$	$\chi^2(1) = 9.2334^{**}$
$\beta_{\text{Commod.}} = 0$	$\chi^2(1) = 0.7815$	$\alpha_{\text{Commod.}} = 0$	$\chi^2(1) = 1.1711$
$\beta_{\text{Real Estate}} = 0$	$\chi^2(1) = 9.4481^{**}$	$\alpha_{\text{Real Estate}} = 0$	$\chi^2(1) = 1.1624$

The results for the trace and the maximal eigenvalue tests for the alternative *portfolio II* are summarised in Table 7. Two highly significant cointegrating vectors are detected by the trace test for the first sample period, whereas the maximal eigenvalue statistic rejects the null hypothesis of $r = 0$, but fails to reject the next higher order null hypothesis of $r \leq 1$ at the 1% level. It is obvious that the values of the estimated statistics are decreasing over time. This may be explained by the fact that high tech, real estate, and growth companies for instance are no longer comprised of small irrelevant stocks, but rather more or less stand-alone asset classes.

The normalised cointegrating vectors from Panel C of Table 7 shows that there are very small values for growth stocks, the emerging equity and commodity market. The results are confirmed in Table 8 by imposing restrictions on these assets which implies that the hedge fund composite and NASDAQ index as well as small and real estate stocks share a common stochastic trend in the alternative investment portfolio. Indeed, imposing these restrictions jointly, $\beta_{Growth} = \beta_{Emerg.\,M.} = \beta_{Commod.} = 0$, yields the following cointegratig vector {1; −0.536; 0; 0.595; 0; 0; −0.606} suggesting that there is no proportional relationship between hedge funds and NASDAQ, small-capitalised and real estate stocks. Furthermore, NASDAQ and real estate stocks tend to have an inverse (or negative) long-run relationship with hedge funds, whereas small-capitalised stocks are positively related to hedge funds. Furthermore, only hedge funds and stocks of emerging markets are influenced significantly by the common trend.

In comparison to the conventional portfolio, a smaller number of assets entering the cointegrating vector particularly in the actual period. Thus, the traditional portfolio has lower long-run variability, and as a result of lower uncertainty risk-averse investors should prefer such a strategic asset allocation when considering hedge funds. In contrast, while the adjustment coefficients in the portfolio of progressive assets (portfolio II) are much lower, active investors can anticipate the information on the short-term movements of asset prices.

CONCLUSIONS

Investors and researchers often consider hedge funds as a way to diversify portfolios otherwise consisting of bonds and stocks, because hedge fund indices show low correlation with these markets. While alternative investments might well entail diversification benefits, low correlation will hardly be a verifiable reason. Hedge fund returns are often significantly non-normally distributed; therefore, correlation analysis is inappropriate. In this context, standard deviation does not fully reveal the risk structure and correlation coefficients might have different bounds.

This study confirms the existence of cointegration between hedge funds and traditional as well as alternative financial assets. In other words, it examines common stochastic trends that move hedge funds and US stock and bond market indices as well as alternative assets to common equilibrium after each terminal shock. To do so, the Johansen cointegration test is employed and the error-correction mechanism is analysed. Active investors can use the former in the framework of tactical decision making and the latter in strategic asset allocation planning. The existence of cointegration lowers uncertainty; therefore, risk-averse investors should prefer cointegrated assets as opposed to non-cointegrated assets. The empirical results suggest that, in the case of the traditional portfolio, the hedge fund index not only enters the cointegrating vector but also its returns react to the common trend. Thus, risk-averse investors with a long-term investment horizon do not increase their risk position by including hedge funds.

In contrast, in the portfolio consisting of alternative assets, hedge funds share a common trend with NASDAQ listed companies, small-capitalised stocks and real estate equities. However, only the returns of hedge funds and emerging equity markets react significantly to the common trend, therefore the impact that any common trend has on these assets is not highly substantial. Overall, one can conclude that in both traditional and alternative portfolios, the investor can benefit from risk diversification.

REFERENCES

Alexander, C. O., 2001, *Market Models: A Guide to Financial Data Analysis* (New York: John Wiley & Sons).

Arshanapalli, B. and J. Doukas, 1993, "International Stock Market Linkage: Evidence from Pre- and Post-October 1987 Period", *Journal of Banking and Finance*, **17(1)**, pp 193–208.

Campbell, J. Y., Y. L. Chan, and L. M. Viceira, 2003, "A Multivariate Model of Strategic Asset Allocation", *Journal of Financial Economics*, **67**, pp 41–80.

Bossaerts, P., 1988, "Common Nonstationary Components of Asset Prices", *Journal of Economic Dynamics and Control*, **12(2–3)**, pp 347–64.

Brooks, C. and H. Kat, 2002, "The Statistical Properties of Hedge Fund Index Returns and Their Implications for Investors", *Journal of Alternative Investments*, **5(2)**, pp 26–44.

Corhay, A., A. T. Rad, and J.-P. Urbain, 1993, "Common Stochastic Trends in European Stock Markets", *Economics Letters*, **42(4)**, pp 385–90.

Dahlquist, M. and C. R. Harvey, 2001, "Global Tactical Asset Allocation", *Emerging Markets Quarterly*, **5(1)**, pp 1–16.

Dickey, D. A. and W. A. Fuller, 1979, "Distribution of the Estimators for Autoregressive Time Series with a Unit Root", *Journal of American Statistical Association*, **74(366)**, pp 427–31.

Dickey, D. A. and W. A. Fuller, 1981, "Likelihood Ratio Tests for Autoregressive Time Series with a Unit Root", *Econometrica*, **49(4)**, pp 1057–72.

Dickey, D. A. and S. G. Pantula, 1987, "Determining the Order of Differencing in Autoregressive Processes", *Journal of Business and Economic Statistics*, **5(4)**, pp 455–61.

Embrechts, P., A. McNeil, and D. Strautmann, 1999, "Correlation: Pitfalls and Alternatives", *RISK Magazine*, **12(5)**, pp 69–71.

Embrechts, P., A. McNeil and D. Strautmann, 2002, "Correlation and Dependence in Risk Management: Properties and Pitfalls", in: M. Dempster (ed.), *Risk Management: Value at Risk and Beyond* (Cambridge: Cambridge University Press), pp 176–223.

Engle, R. F., and C. W. J. Granger, 1987, "Co-integration and Error Correction: Representation, Estimation and Testing", *Econometrica*, **55(2)**, pp 251–76.

Füss R. and F. Herrmann, 2005, "Long-Term Interdependence between Hedge Fund Strategy and Stock Market Indices", *Managerial Finance*, **31(12)**, pp 29–45.

Garret, I. and Spyrou, S. 1999, "Common Stochastic Trends in Emerging Equity Markets", *The Manchester School*, **67(6)**, pp 649–60.

Granger, C. W. J. 1981, "Some Properties of Time Series Data and Their Use in Econometric Model Specification", *Journal of Econometrics*, **16(1)**, pp 121–30.

Gregoriou, G., F. Rouah, and K. Sedzro, 2001, "Do Hedge Fund Returns Follow Random Walks?" *Derivative Use, Trading & Regulation*, **7(3)**, pp 241–50.

Gregoriou, G. and F. Rouah, 2001, "Do Stock Market Indices Move the Ten Largest Hedge Funds? A Cointegration Approach", *The Journal of Alternative Investments*, **3(3)**, pp 61–6.

HFR, 2006, HFR Industry Report Q4 2005, Chicago.

Johansen, S. 1988, "Statistical Analysis of Cointegration Vectors", *Journal of Economic Dynamics and Control*, **12(2–3)**, pp 231–54.

Johansen, S. 1991, "Estimation and Hypothesis Testing of Cointegration Vectors in Gaussian Vector Autoregression Residuals", *Econometrica*, **59(6)**, pp 1551–81.

Johansen, S. and K. Juselius, 1990, "Maximum Likelihood Estimation and Inference on Cointegration: with Applications to the Demand for Money", *Oxford Bulletin of Economics and Statistics*, **52(2)**, pp 169–210.

Johansen, S. and K. Juselius, 1991, "Estimation and Hypothesis Testing of Cointegration Vectors in Gaussian Vector Autoregressive Models", *Econometrica*, **59(6)**, pp 1551–80.

Kanas, A., 1998, "Linkages between the US and European Equity Markets: Further Evidence from Cointegration Tests", *Applied Financial Economice*, **8(6)**, pp 607–14.

Kasa, K., 1992, "Common Stochastic Trends in International Stock Markets", *Journal of Monetary Economics*, **29(1)**, pp 95–124.

Kat, H. M., 2002, "The Dangers of Using Correlation to Measure Dependence", Working Paper No 0010, Alternative Investment Research Centre, Cass Business School, City University, October 9.

Kat, H. M. and S. Lu, 2002, "An Excursion into the Statistical Properties of Hedge Fund Returns", Working Paper, University of Reading, 19 July.

Lhabitant, F. -S., 2004, *Hedge Funds: Quantitative Insights* (New Jersey: John Wiley & Sons).

Lucas, A., 1997, "Strategic and Tactical Asset Allocation and the Effect of Long-run Equilibrium Relations", Research Memorandum, Vrije University, August.

Lütkepohl, H., 1991, *Introduction to Multiple Time Series Analysis* (Berlin: Springer Publishing).

distribution of hedge fund returns. Different parametric and non-parametric models (eg, NIG or Johnson distributions) are used to fit the empirical distribution of hedge fund returns.[3] Although these models are able to closely resemble the *static* behavior of hedge fund returns, they are not designed to capture their dynamic behavior. *Dynamic models*, on the other hand, try to capture the evolution of hedge fund returns over time, ie, the dynamics of the *conditional* distribution. Cvitanic *et al* (2003), eg, use a geometric Brownian motion to describe hedge fund dynamics. Though appealing from an analytical perspective, lognormal processes are clearly not appropriate to describe hedge fund returns. As a general conclusion, none of the above models can capture all the empirically observable features of hedge fund returns. As such, the existing models are only of limited use to hedge fund investors.

The model presented here uses a *Markov-switching autoregressive process* to describe the dynamic evolution of hedge fund returns. Stock and bond returns are modeled by a lognormal random walk. We show that this model can reproduce most of the observable features of hedge fund time series. In particular, it produces serially correlated returns with non-normal (unconditional) distributions. The model can easily be fitted to historical data using moment-matching techniques.

To measure the risk/reward tradeoff associated with a portfolio consisting of hedge funds and traditional assets, we employ several *performance metrics*, including the Omega measure suggested by Keating/Shadwick (2002), and expected utility. These measures reflect the whole portfolio return distribution and not only the first two moments as it is the case in the mean-variance setup. Monte-Carlo simulation is used to compute these measures.

The paper is organised as follows: In the second section, we examine the historical return time series of various hedge fund indices and determine their main (statistical) properties. The third section describes the model, shows how to estimate the model parameters, and compares the model properties with the empirically observable properties of hedge funds. In the fourth section, we apply the model to derive the optimal allocation of bonds, stocks, and hedge funds in a portfolio. A summary and concluding remarks are found in the fifth section.

Table 1 Descriptive statistics of monthly log returns of HFRI indices over the period January 1990 to April 2006

	Mean (%)	Volatility (%)	Skewness	Excess Kurtosis	Min (%)	Max (%)
Convertible Arbitrage	0.80	1.02	−1.13	2.00	−3.24	3.28
Fixed Income Arbitrage	0.66	1.21	−1.89	11.62	−6.67	4.59
Equity Market Neutral	0.73	0.89	0.15	0.36	−1.68	3.53
Event Driven	1.15	1.88	−1.44	5.35	−9.32	5.00
Merger Arbitrage	0.83	1.24	−2.62	11.55	−6.68	3.07
Distressed Securities	1.19	1.71	−0.84	6.34	−8.88	6.82
Global Macro	1.22	2.33	0.26	0.59	−6.61	7.58
Short Selling	0.12	5.98	−0.17	1.72	−23.84	20.57
Emerging Markets	1.26	4.23	−1.22	5.77	−23.60	13.80
Equity Hedge	1.34	2.49	0.04	1.26	−7.96	10.33
FoF Composite	0.80	1.59	−0.42	4.50	−7.76	6.63
MSCI World	0.58	4.12	−0.61	0.70	−14.33	9.98
S&P 500	0.85	4.10	−0.62	1.05	−15.62	10.83
LB Global Aggregate	0.58	0.91	−0.31	0.29	−2.08	3.43

PROPERTIES OF HEDGE FUND RETURNS

The aim of this section is to characterise the hedge fund asset class. We use publicly available index data from Hedge Fund Research (HFR) to identify the main statistical properties of hedge fund (index) returns so that we can afterwards propose a model that is suitable to capture these features.[4]

Hedge fund data

Data description

HFR is a hedge fund research and consulting firm that has collected data on more than 5,500 different hedge funds. It calculates 37 equally weighted performance indices (HFRI indices). These indices reflect the monthly net of fee returns of a basket of hedge funds in USD.[5] Our sample comprises monthly index data of 11 HFRI sub-indices representing the most important hedge fund strategies over the period January 1990 to April 2006. To study the relationship of hedge funds with traditional asset classes, our sample also includes monthly time series of the MSCI World index, the S&P 500 index, and the Lehman Brothers Global Aggregate Bond index (LB Global Aggregate).[6] In total, our sample consists of $N = 196$ monthly returns.

Table 1 shows the mean, volatility or standard deviation, skewness, excess kurtosis, minimum, and maximum of the monthly log returns $r_t = \ln(X_t) - \ln(X_{t-1})$, where X_t denotes the asset price at time t, for each of the 11 HFRI hedge fund indices, and the three traditional asset class indices within the sample period.[7]

Obviously, different hedge fund styles show distinctly different risk/return characteristics. It is also evident from Table 1 that the risk profile of hedge funds cannot be sufficiently described by volatility alone. Higher moments of the return distribution have to be considered as well. It can further be observed, that there is a tendency for a low volatility to go together with relatively low skewness and high (excess) kurtosis.

Data biases

It is well known that hedge fund data is subject to a number of severe biases.[8] The three main biases that arise in analysing hedge fund data are survivorship bias, selection bias, and backfill bias. *Survivorship bias* arises when a sample of hedge funds, eg, a hedge fund index, includes only funds that are operating at the end of the period and excludes funds that have ceased operations during that period. Hence, the poorer performing hedge funds tend to disappear and thus historical returns are likely to be biased upward. Liang (2000), using hedge fund data bases of HFR and TASS, estimated the survivorship bias to exceed two percentage points a year in returns. This is consistent with the studies of Brown *et al* (1999) and Fung/Hsieh (2002) for other databases.

A *selection bias* may occur because the funds can decide on their own if they want to be included/excluded in a database and hence the selection of funds may not be representative of the whole population of hedge funds. Presumably, only those funds that have good track records and still want to grow may opt to be included in a database to attract more investors. Therefore, hedge funds in a database tend to have better performance than those that were excluded. On the other hand, very good hedge funds may not be participating in a database because they are not looking to attract new investors. These hedge funds are probably better performing than the average hedge fund. The net effect of selection bias on hedge fund returns is somewhat ambiguous.

When a new hedge fund is added to a database or index, historical returns are often back filled. As the fund can choose the entry date into the database, it may cause an upward bias – ie, *backfill*

Figure 1 Histogram of monthly log returns of the HFRI Convertible Arbitrage index. Sample period: January 1990–December 2005. Superimposed is a normal curve having the same mean and the same variance as that estimated from the sample

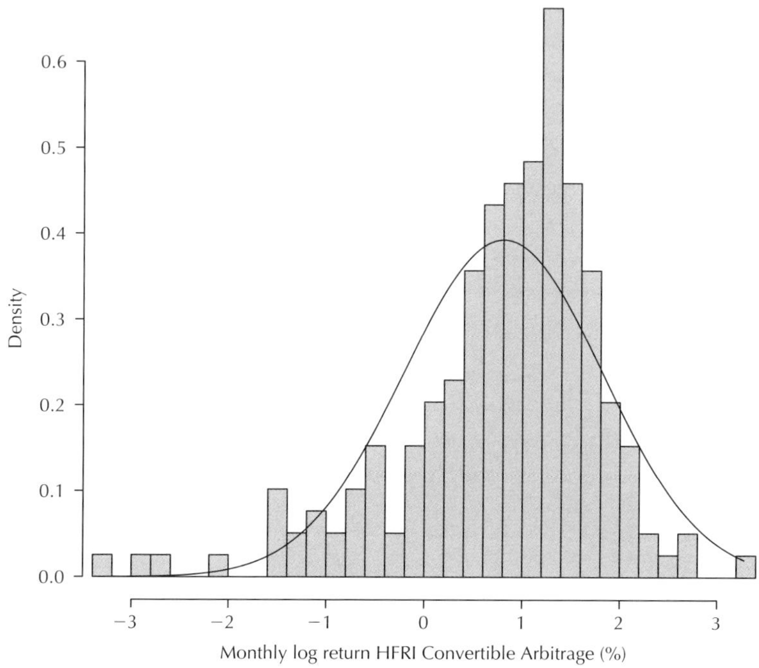

bias, also called instant-history bias. Using data from the TASS database, Fung/Hsieh (2000) estimated the backfill bias to be 1.4 percentage points a year in returns.

Statistical Properties

Non-normality

The skewness and kurtosis values in Table 1 indicate a non-normal distribution for hedge fund (index) returns – nearly all hedge fund strategies show *negatively skewed* return distributions with *positive excess kurtosis*. Figure 1 illustrates these findings graphically for the HFRI Convertible Arbitrage index. Clearly, the empirical density function deviates from a normal curve (solid line) with the same mean and the same variance as that estimated from the sample.

Negative tail events seem underestimated by the normal distribution. This is particulary true for arbitrage strategies as well as for the event-driven and Distressed Securities styles. Although graphical inspection of the empirical density function is a useful tool for detecting deviations from normality, the method is necessarily imprecise. To check more rigourously, we perform Jarque–Bera and Shapiro–Wilk tests. The null hypothesis of a normal distribution is rejected at the 1% level (5% level for the Equity Hedge style using a Jarque–Bera test) for all hedge fund strategies, except of the Equity Market Neutral style. This formally proves that, in general, hedge fund returns follow a non-normal distribution. Note that the Gaussian assumption is also rejected for the two stock indices MSCI World and S&P 500 but not for the bond index LB Global Aggregate.

Non-normality in the context of hedge funds can be explained by the use of leverage, Short Selling, dynamic trading strategies, and derivatives by hedge fund managers. For example, when a put option is added to a long-only equity portfolio, this creates asymmetry in the return distribution and hence leads to a non-normal distribution.

Serial correlation

Table 1 shows the sample autocorrelation function $\hat{\rho}(h)$ of monthly log returns r_t up to lag $h = 3$, and the Ljung–Box statistics $Q(n)$ of the joint null hypothesis that all of the first $n = 5$ and $n = 10$ autocorrelations are zero. Under the assumption that returns are independent and identically distributed, an autocorrelation coefficient is statistically significant different from zero for a sample size of $N = 196$ at the 5% level, if it lies outside the interval $[-0.14; 0.14]$.

Similar to the results of other studies in the field, eg, Brooks/Kat (2002), we find monthly log returns of many hedge fund indices to be highly serially correlated. First-order autocorrelation coefficients range from 0.08 for Short Selling to 0.56 for Convertible Arbitrage. Except of the Short Selling and Equity Hedge style, the Ljung–Box statistics $Q(5)$ and $Q(10)$ for all hedge fund indices indicate significant autocorrelation at the 5% level. For the stock market indices, we find very little evidence of statistically significant autocorrelation. This is consistent with informationally efficient markets, where price changes must be unpredictable if they are properly anticipated by market participants. The autocorrelation coefficient at lag 1 for the LB Global Aggregate bond index is significant at the 5% level, indicating positive first-order autocorrelation. However, the Ljung–Box statistics $Q(5)$ and $Q(10)$ are not significant at the 5% level.

The most likely explanation for the observed positive autocorrelation in hedge fund return series is *illiquidity exposure*, ie, investments in securities that are not actively traded and for which market prices are not readily available.[9] When hedge funds face this problem, they either use the last reported transaction price or an estimated price of the current market price (eg, a model price), which may easily create lags in the evolution of the net asset value and hence positive serial correlation. This would explain why the Convertible Arbitrage, Fixed Income Arbitrage, and Distressed Securities style indices exhibit the highest autocorrelation. Another explanation for the positive autocorrelation in hedge fund returns is that funds may intentionally report less volatile returns. This behavior is sometimes referred to as *performance smoothing*.

Time series of financial returns often exhibit the *volatility clustering* property: large changes in prices tend to follow large changes and small changes tend to follow small changes. To test on the existence of volatility clustering effects in hedge fund data, we compute the first-order autocorrelation $\hat{\rho}(1)$ and the Ljung–Box statistic $Q(5)$ of squared log returns r_t^2 for all hedge fund indices, and for comparison also for the traditional investments. The right part of Table 2 shows the results. For the majority of hedge fund indices the null hypothesis of no autocorrelation up to lag 5 is rejected at the 5% level. This may serve as an indicator for the existence of volatility clustering effects in hedge fund data. It should be noted that volatility clustering can also account for some but not all of the excess kurtosis observed.

Correlation with traditional asset classes

Table 3 shows the (linear) correlations between the HFRI hedge fund indices, bonds, and stocks. Apart from the relative value hedge fund styles Convertible Arbitrage, Fixed Income Arbitrage, and Equity Market Neutral, the indices show surprisingly high (absolute) correlations with equities over the sample period January 1990–April 2006.[10] For example, the correlation between the S&P 500 and the Equity Hedge index is 67%. This is

Table 2 Autocorrelations of monthly log returns r_t and squared log returns r_t^2 over the period January 1990 to April 2006; $\hat{\rho}(h)$ is the sample autocorrelation of lag h, $Q(n)$ is the Ljung–Box statistic for autocorrelation up to order n

	r_t					r_t^2	
	$\hat{\rho}(1)$	$\hat{\rho}(2)$	$\hat{\rho}(3)$	$Q(5)$	$Q(10)$	$\hat{\rho}(1)$	$Q(5)$
Convertible Arbitrage	0.56	0.26	0.06	76.18	85.54	0.15	10.41
Fixed Income Arbitrage	0.39	0.12	0.12	38.52	44.95	0.43	38.24
Equity Market Neutral	0.07	0.10	0.16	11.15	42.54	−0.03	34.55
Event Driven	0.28	0.05	0.01	16.79	17.96	−0.04	5.44
Merger Arbitrage	0.19	0.05	0.08	10.36	18.42	0.02	16.79
Distressed Securities	0.49	0.14	0.02	51.76	56.25	0.25	20.77
Global Macro	0.17	0.00	0.01	12.87	17.81	0.10	33.72
Short Selling	0.08	−0.05	−0.02	7.93	9.82	0.05	79.71
Emerging Markets	0.31	0.10	0.04	21.59	28.47	0.03	10.41
Equity Hedge	0.15	0.07	0.03	7.53	13.69	0.08	37.05
FoF Composite	0.31	0.11	0.00	23.17	26.48	0.10	13.36
MSCI World	0.00	−0.05	0.02	2.46	6.43	0.11	14.26
S&P 500	−0.04	0.01	0.02	3.11	7.86	0.08	18.85
LB Gobal Aggregate	0.21	0.05	0.06	10.26	12.91	0.05	2.90
5% critical value	±0.14	±0.14	±0.14	11.07	18.31	±0.14	11.07

Table 3 Correlations between HFRI hedge fund indices and traditional asset classes over the time period January 1990–April 2006

	MSCI World	**S&P 500**	**LB Global Aggregate**
Convertible Arbitrage	0.26	0.29	0.22
Fixed Income Arbitrage	0.00	−0.05	−0.14
Equity Market Neutral	0.10	0.13	0.19
Event Driven	0.61	0.65	0.10
Merger Arbitrage	0.43	0.48	0.13
Distressed Securities	0.40	0.41	0.04
Global Macro	0.41	0.39	0.41
Short Selling	−0.65	−0.69	−0.03
Emerging Markets	0.63	0.58	0.04
Equity Hedge	0.63	0.67	0.10
FoF Composite	0.45	0.45	0.10

not astonishing, as it is well-known that Equity Hedge type hedge funds often exhibit a significant long bias. Hedge funds often claim that their returns are market-neutral, ie, uncorrelated with equity and bond market risk. While this may be true for single hedge funds carrying high unsystematic risk, Table 3 shows that this is not so for the majority of hedge fund indices. For most hedge fund indices, a substantial part of their risk is equity market risk. This is an important point to investors, since nowadays most of them invest into fund of funds rather than single funds. In sum, it can be stated that the diversification benefits of hedge funds are generally overstated.

The quantification of the diversification level through linear correlations can be improved by looking more closely at the actual dependence structure. Statistical analyses reveal that the relationship between hedge fund returns and returns of traditional asset classes typically exhibits some *non-linearities*.[11]

Implications for modelling hedge fund returns

To sum up, hedge fund log return time series are characterised by the following distinct features:

(1) Data biases: Survivorship bias, selection bias, and backfill bias
(2) Non-Normality: Negative skewness and excess kurtosis
(3) Serial correlation: Mainly of lag 1 and to a minor extent of lag 2
(4) Volatility clustering: Significant autocorrelation of squared log returns.

Property 1 implies that return expectations derived from historical hedge fund return series are generally upward biased. Since hedge fund returns are non-normally distributed (*Property 2*), all tools based on the normality assumption are no longer appropriate. In particular, the mean-variance approach is no longer suitable to derive the optimal asset allocation. Assuming that investors dislike negative skewness and positive excess kurtosis, this means that hedge funds become less attractive than in the mean-variance framework when higher-order moments of the return distribution are considered.[12] *Property 3* implies that reported hedge fund returns will tend to be smoother than true economic returns, which will understate volatility and increase risk-adjusted performance. When modelling hedge fund returns, the volatility clustering effect (*Property 4*) has also to be considered. It basically implies time-varying conditional volatilities.

From the above discussion the need for an alternative asset allocation framework is obvious.

THE MODEL

Model description

Based on the empirical results of the previous section, we propose a stochastic model for the joint evolution of hedge fund, stock and bond returns. The main focus of the model is thereby on the realistic modelling of the hedge fund asset class.

Let us consider a financial market where investors are allowed to trade at discrete times $t = 0, 1, \ldots, T^*$. The uncertainty in the financial market is characterised by the complete probability space $(\Omega, \mathcal{F}, \mathbb{P})$, where Ω is the state space, $\mathcal{F}$ is the σ-algebra representing measurable events, and $\mathbb{P}$ is the (objective or real-world) probability measure. The traded assets in our model are a bond index B, a stock index S, and a hedge fund (index) H with time $t \in \{0, \ldots, T^*\}$ prices B_t, S_t, and H_t and time t log returns $r_{B,t} = \ln B_t - \ln B_{t-1}$, $r_{S,t} = \ln S_t - \ln S_{t-1}$, and $r_{H,t} = \ln H_t - \ln H_{t-1}$.[13]

Denoting by $\epsilon = \{\epsilon_t : t \in [0, T^*]\}$, $\epsilon_t = (\epsilon_{B,t}, \epsilon_{S,t}, \epsilon_{H,t})'$ a three-dimensional Gaussian zero-mean white noise process with unit variance and positive semi-definite correlation matrix[14]

$$\Xi = (\varrho_{i,j})_{i \in \{B,S,H\}, j \in \{B,S,H\}}$$

we make the following assumptions on the evolution of the bond and stock:

$$r_{B,t} = \mu_B + \sigma_B \epsilon_{B,t}, \quad t \in \{0, \ldots, T^*\} \tag{1}$$

$$r_{S,t} = \mu_S + \sigma_S \epsilon_{S,t}, \quad t \in \{0, \ldots, T^*\} \tag{2}$$

where $\mu_B, \mu_S \in \mathbb{R}$ and $\sigma_B, \sigma_S > 0$ are the means and standard deviations of the bond and stock log returns.

The hedge fund evolution is given by the first-order Markov-switching autoregression:[15]

$$r_{H,t} = \mu_{H,s_t} + \phi(r_{H,t-1} - \mu_{H,s_{t-1}}) + \sigma_{H,s_t} \epsilon_{H,t}, \quad t \in \{0, \ldots, T^*\} \tag{3}$$

where ϕ, $|\phi| < 1$, is the autocorrelation parameter, $\mu_{H,s_t} \in \mathbb{R}$ and $\sigma_{H,s_t} > 0$ are state- or regime dependent location and dispersion parameters. The state or regime s_t, $t \in \{0, \ldots, T^*\}$, is modeled as the outcome of an unobserved 2-state discrete Markov chain with s_t independent of ϵ_t.[16] If $s_t = 1$ then the process is in regime 1, while $s_t = 2$ means that the process is in regime 2. The transition probabilities between states 1 and 2 are defined by

$$\mathbb{P}(s_{t+1} = j | s_t = i, s_{t-1} = k, \ldots) = \mathbb{P}(s_{t+1} = j | s_t = i) = p_{i,j}$$

$$0 \leq p_{i,j} \leq 1, \quad \sum_{j=1}^{2} p_{i,j} = 1, \quad i = 1, 2$$

This implies that the Markov chain is homogenous. For convenience, we collect the transition probabilities in the transition matrix $P = (p_{i,j})_{i,j=1,2}$. If we assume that the Markov chain is ergodic, ie, if $p_{1,1} < 1$, $p_{2,2} < 1$, and $p_{1,1} + p_{2,2} > 0$, then there exists a unique stationary distribution and the unconditional probabilities that the process will be in state 1 or 2 at any given time is given by:

$$p_1 = \frac{p_{2,1}}{1 - p_{1,1} + p_{2,1}} \text{ and } p_2 = 1 - p_1 \tag{4}$$

The model defined by Equations (1), (2), (3) and by the parameter vector

$$\theta = (\mu_B, \sigma_B, \mu_S, \sigma_S, \mu_{H,1}, \mu_{H,2}, \sigma_{H,1}, \sigma_{H,2}, p_{1,1}, p_{2,2}, \phi, \varrho_{B,S}, \varrho_{S,H}, \varrho_{B,H})$$

can be simulated with standard Monte Carlo methods.

Estimation method

Given T observations of the return vector $r_t = (r_{B,t}, r_{S,t}, r_{H,t})$, we employ the Method of Moments (MoM) to estimate the parameter vector θ. The MoM estimate of θ is the value $\hat{\theta}_T$ for which the unobservable population moments of r_t are equated to the sample moments of r_t. Because the number of unknown parameters is 14, the number of moment conditions is also required to be 14.[17]

The population mean and the variance of the bond and stock return are given by

$$E[r_{i,t}] = \mu_i, \quad i \in \{B, S\} \tag{5}$$

$$Var[r_{i,t}] = \sigma_i^2, \quad i \in \{B, S\} \tag{6}$$

and the correlation between bond and stock returns is

$$Cor[r_{B,t}, r_{S,t}] = E[\epsilon_{B,t} \times \epsilon_{S,t}] = \varrho_{B,S} \tag{7}$$

Equating the population moments $E[r_{i,t}]$, $Var[r_{i,t}]$, $i \in \{B, S\}$, and $Cor[r_{B,t}, r_{S,t}]$ with the sample moments $\hat{\mu}_i, \hat{\sigma}_i^2, i \in \{B, S\}$, and $\hat{\varrho}_{B,S}$ we obtain the first five moments conditions. The computation of the parameter estimates is straightforward. In practice, it is often more appropriate simply to impose a value for the mean return of bonds and stocks rather than using the sample estimate. For example, we do not expect bonds or stocks to have an ex-ante equilibrium return that is negative, regardless of the sample mean in a given set of data.

Next, we derive the moment conditions for hedge fund returns. If we assume that the hedge fund process (3) is in steady state, we obtain the following expressions for the population mean, the population variance and the centered moments of order 3 and 4:

$$E[r_{H,t}] = p'\mu \tag{8}$$

$$Var[r_{H,t}] = p'\left((\mu - E[r_{H,t}]\mathbf{1}) \odot (\mu - E[r_{H,t}]\mathbf{1}) + \frac{\sigma^2}{1-\phi^2}\right) \tag{9}$$

$$\begin{aligned} E[(r_{H,t} - E[r_{H,t}])^3] = {} & p'((\mu - E[r_{H,t}]\mathbf{1}) \odot (\mu - E[r_{H,t}]\mathbf{1}) \odot (\mu - E[r_{H,t}]\mathbf{1})) \\ & + 3\phi^2 p'((P(I_2 - \phi^2 P)^{-1}\sigma^2) \odot (\mu - E[r_{H,t}]\mathbf{1})) \\ & + 3p'((\mu - E[r_{H,t}]\mathbf{1}) \odot \sigma^2) \end{aligned} \tag{10}$$

$$\begin{aligned} E[(r_{H,t} - E[r_{H,t}])^4] = {} & 6p'((\mu - E[r_{H,t}]\mathbf{1}) \odot (\mu - E[r_{H,t}]\mathbf{1}) \odot \sigma^2) \\ & + p'((\mu - E[r_{H,t}]\mathbf{1}) \odot (\mu - E[r_{H,t}]\mathbf{1}) \odot (\mu - E[r_{H,t}]\mathbf{1}) \odot (\mu - E[r_{H,t}]\mathbf{1})) \\ & + \phi^4 p'(I_2 - \phi^4 P)^{-1}(3\sigma^4 + 6\phi^2 (P(I_2 - \phi^2 P)^{-1}\sigma^2) \odot \sigma^2) \\ & + 6\phi^2 p'((P(I_2 - \phi^2 P)^{-1}\sigma^2) \odot (\mu - E[r_{H,t}]\mathbf{1}) \odot (\mu - E[r_{H,t}]\mathbf{1})) \end{aligned} \tag{11}$$

where $p = (p_1, p_2)'$, $\mu = (\mu_{H,1}, \mu_{H,2})'$, $\sigma = (\sigma_{H,1}, \sigma_{H,2})'$, $P = (p_{i,j})_{i,j=1,2}$, $\mathbf{1} = (1, 1)'$, I_2 is the 2×2 identity matrix, and $\odot$ is the element-by-element multiplication operator.

Normalizing expressions (10) and (11) yields the population skewness and excess kurtosis of hedge fund returns:

$$Sk(r_{H,t}) = \frac{E[(r_{H,t} - E[r_{H,t}])^3]}{E[(r_{H,t} - E[r_{H,t}])^2]^{\frac{3}{2}}} \tag{12}$$

$$K(r_{H,t}) = \frac{E[(r_{H,t} - E[r_{H,t}])^4]}{E[(r_{H,t} - E[r_{H,t}])^2]^2} - 3 \tag{13}$$

To capture the serial correlation that is observed in empirical hedge fund data, we match the first- and second-order model autocorrelations to the empirical autocorrelations. The model autocorrelation $\rho_{r_{H,t}}(n)$ of order n is defined by:

$$\rho_{r_{H,t}}(n) = \frac{E[(r_{H,t} - E[r_{H,t}])(r_{H,t-n} - E[r_{H,t-n}])]}{Var[r_{H,t}]}, \qquad n \in \{1, 2\} \tag{14}$$

with:

$$E[(r_{H,t} - E[r_{H,t}])(r_{H,t-n} - E[r_{H,t-n}])] = p'((P^n(\mu - E[r_{H,t}]\mathbf{1})) \odot (\mu - E[r_{H,t}]\mathbf{1})) + \phi^n p'(I_2 - \phi^2 P)^{-1}\sigma^2 \tag{15}$$

Since hedge fund returns show volatility clustering features, we also include the first-order serial correlation of squared returns in our set of moment conditions. It is given by:

$$\rho_{r^2_{H,t}}(1) = \frac{E[(r^2_{H,t} - E[r^2_{H,t}])(r^2_{H,t-1} - E[r^2_{H,t-1}])]}{E[(r^2_{H,t} - E[r^2_{H,t}])^2]} \tag{16}$$

with:

$$\begin{aligned} E[(r^2_{H,t} - E[r^2_{H,t}])\,(r^2_{H,t-1} - E[r^2_{H,t-1}])] &= \phi^2 p'(((I_2 - \phi^2 P)^{-1}\sigma^2) \odot \mu^2) \\ &+ \phi^2 p'(I_2 - \phi^4 P)^{-1}(3\sigma^4 + 6\phi^2((P(I_2 - \phi^2 P)^{-1}\sigma^2) \odot \sigma^2)) \\ &+ p'((P(I_2 - \phi^2 P)^{-1}\sigma^2) \odot \mu^2) + p'((P\mu^2) \odot \mu^2) \\ &+ p'((P(I_2 - \phi^2 P)^{-1}\sigma^2 + P\mu^2) \odot \sigma^2) \\ &+ 4\phi p'(((P(I_2 - \phi^2 P)^{-1}\sigma^2) \odot \mu) \odot \mu) \\ &- (Var[r_{H,t}] + E[r_{H,t}]^2)^2 \end{aligned} \tag{17}$$

and:

$$\begin{aligned} E[(r^2_{H,t} - E[r^2_{H,t}])^2] &= p'\mu^4 + 6\phi^2 p'(((P(I_2 - \phi^2 P)^{-1}\sigma^2) \odot \mu) \odot \mu) \\ &+ 6p'(\mu^2 \odot \sigma^2) + p'(I_2 - \phi^4 P)^{-1}(3\sigma^4 + 6\phi^2((P(I_2 - \phi^2)^{-1}\sigma^2) \odot \sigma^2)) \\ &- (Var[r_{H,t}] + E[r_{H,t}]^2)^2 \end{aligned} \tag{18}$$

The dependence structure of hedge fund returns and the returns of the traditional asset classes is fully specified by the correlations $\varrho_{B,H}$ and $\varrho_{S,H}$ In our model they are given by

$$Cor[r_{i,t}, r_{H,t}] = \frac{p'\sigma}{\sqrt{Var[r_{H,t}]}} \varrho_{i,H}, \quad i \in \{B, S\} \tag{19}$$

Equating the population moments of hedge fund returns given by Equations (8), (9), (12), (13), (14), (16), and (19) to their sample moments yields the following system of equations:

$$\begin{aligned}
&E[r_{H,t}] = \hat{E}[r_{H,t}] \\
&Var[r_{H,t}] = \hat{V}ar[r_{H,t}] \\
&Sk(r_{H,t}) = \hat{S}k(r_{H,t}) \\
&K(r_{H,t}) = \hat{K}(r_{H,t}) \\
&\rho_{r_{H,t}}(1) = \hat{\rho}_{r_{H,t}}(1) \\
&\rho_{r_{H,t}}(2) = \hat{\rho}_{r_{H,t}}(2) \\
&\rho_{r^2_{H,t}}(1) = \hat{\rho}_{r^2_{H,t}}(1) \\
&Cor[r_{B,t}, r_{H,t}] = \hat{C}or[r_{B,t}, r_{H,t}] \\
&Cor[r_{S,t}, r_{H,t}] = \hat{C}or[r_{S,t}, r_{H,t}]
\end{aligned} \tag{20}$$

where the sample moments are marked by a "^". The system (20) can be solved to obtain the hedge fund related parameter estimates, eg, by applying numerical root finding techniques.

Model properties

When comparing the model properties with the empirical properties of hedge fund returns as summarised in previously, we find:

- To account for data biases in hedge fund data, we adjust downwards the historically observable returns and set the model parameters $\mu_{H,1}$, $\mu_{H,2}$ accordingly (*Property 1*).
- The Markov-switching component of the model accounts for non-normality in hedge fund returns. To see this, suppose that $\phi = 0$. In that case Equation (3) reduces to:

$$r_{H,t} = \mu_{H,s_t} + \sigma_{H,s_t} \epsilon_{H,t} \tag{21}$$

When the process is in regime i, $i = 1, 2$, the observed return r_t is presumed to have been drawn from a $N(\mu_{H,i}, \sigma_{H,i})$ distribution. Since the unconditional probability to be in state i is p_i, the unconditional distribution of $r_{H,t}$ is a mixture of two normal distributions. Gaussian mixtures can produce distributions with non-zero skewness and excess kurtosis (*Property* 2).

- The autoregressive structure of the model captures the main part of the (first-order) serial correlation detected in empirical hedge fund data. The remaining part is captured by the Markov-switching component (*Property* 3).
- The volatility clustering effect is modeled by fitting the model to the serial correlation of squared hedge fund returns (*Property* 4).

To sum up, the model is able to capture most of the empirically observable characteristics of hedge fund returns.

OPTIMAL ALLOCATION TO HEDGE FUNDS: A CASE STUDY

The investment problem

In this section, we consider the optimal allocation to hedge funds to a traditional portfolio of bonds and stocks. We use our Markov-Switching Autoregressive model (MSAR) to capture the specific characteristics of hedge fund returns. For comparison, we consider the classic mean-variance model (MV).

The reference portfolio of traditional assets consists of 70% bonds and 30% stocks, represented by the Lehman Brothers Global Aggregate Bond index and the MSCI World index, respectively. For bonds, we assume a mean return of $\hat{\mu}_B = 0.33\%$ per month or 4% per year and for stocks $\hat{\mu}_S = 0.63\%$ per month or 7.5% per year.[18] The volatility and correlation parameters are estimated from historical data (see Section 2, Table 1). They are $\hat{\sigma}_B = 0.91\%$ per month or 3.15% per year, $\hat{\sigma}_S = 4.12\%$ per month or 14.27% per year, and $\hat{\varrho}_{B,S} = 0.13\%$.

We consider three different hedge fund investments: a Convertible Arbitrage fund (CA), an Equity Hedge/long short equity fund (EH), and a multi-strategy fund of fund (FoF). They are represented by the HFRI Convertible Arbitrage index, the HFRI Equity Hedge index and the HFRI Fund of Fund index, respectively. These hedge fund styles are chosen to cover a broad spectrum of different hedge fund characteristics. Fund of funds

Table 4 Estimated model parameters for three different hedge fund styles

	$\hat{\mu}_{H,1}$	$\hat{\mu}_{H,2}$	$\hat{\sigma}_{H,1}$	$\hat{\sigma}_{H,2}$	$\hat{p}_{1,1}$	$\hat{p}_{2,2}$	$\hat{\phi}$	$\hat{\varrho}_{B,H}$	$\hat{\varrho}_{S,H}$
CA	0.009	−0.008	0.005	0.010	0.917	0.621	0.538	0.217	0.258
EH	0.011	0.013	0.023	0.050	0.972	0.374	0.170	0.096	0.634
FoF	0.003	0.007	0.025	0.003	0.608	0.797	0.319	0.450	0.105

are included, because of its popularity among hedge fund investors. Based on monthly data of HFR as described earlier, we calibrate three different models – one for each hedge fund style. Since hedge fund index data carries survivorship, selection, and backfill biases, average returns estimated from historical data overestimate "true" returns. To account for these biases, we reduce the historical mean for each index by 4% per year.[19] This yields return expectations of 5.6% for the Convertible Arbitrage fund and for the multi-strategy Fund of Fund, and 12.08% for the Equity Hedge fund. The other moments that are needed to solve the system of Equations (20) equal their sample moments. Table 4 summarises the parameter estimates.

To ensure the comparability of results, we set the expected return in the mean-variance model MV equal to the expected return in the MSAR model, ie, the MV model also accounts for data biases in historical hedge fund data. The same is true for the covariance structure, ie, the estimates for the volatility and correlation parameters are the same than those used in calibrating the MSAR model.[20]

To measure the risk/reward tradeoff associated with a portfolio of hedge funds and traditional assets, we employ four different criteria:

- *Sharpe ratio*: Excess return per unit of volatility risk, ie,

$$\text{Sharpe ratio} = \frac{E[r_{PF}] - r_f}{\sqrt{Var[r_{PF}]}} \tag{22}$$

where r_{PF} denotes the (log) portfolio return and r_f is the continuously compounded risk-free rate.[21]

- *Omega measure*: Expected upside per unit of expected downside, ie,

$$\text{Omega} = \frac{\int_L^{\infty} (1 - \mathbb{P}(r_{PF} \le x))\mathrm{d}x}{\int_{-\infty}^{L} \mathbb{P}(r_{PF} \le x)\mathrm{d}x} \tag{23}$$

  where L is the threshold return that separates "positive" and "negative" returns. We set L equal to 3% p.a.[22]
- *Conditional Value at Risk* (CVaR): Maximum return for a fixed level of risk, defined by the 99% CVaR of the traditional portfolio consisting of 70% bonds and 30% stocks. The CVaR at a confidence level of 99% is defined by

$$CVaR(99\%) = E[r_{PF} \mid r_{PF} \le \sup\{z \mid \mathbb{P}(r_{PF} \le z) \le 0.01\}] \tag{24}$$

- *Power Utility*: The power utility function is defined by

$$U(r_{PF}) = \frac{1}{1-\lambda}(\exp(r_{PF}))^{(1-\lambda)} \tag{25}$$

where the risk aversion parameter λ was chosen such that the traditional 70% bonds/30% stocks portfolio is optimal.

The Sharpe ratio considers only the first two moments of the return distribution, ie, mean and variance. As such, it is only of limited use in the context of hedge funds. In contrast, the Omega, CVaR and power utility criterion consider the entire return distribution and are thus more appropriate to assess the benefits of hedge funds.

In a final step, we simulate the joint evolution of bonds, stocks, and hedge funds in the MSAR model, using a Monte Carlo approach with 10,000 paths. Applying numerical optimisation techniques, we obtain the optimal asset allocation between the three asset classes.

Empirical results

The optimal asset allocation of bonds, stocks, and hedge funds is shown in Table 5 for three different time horizons – 1, 3, and 5 years.[23]

A further observation refers to the composition of the optimal portfolio. The Convertible Arbitrage style exhibits more bond-like characteristics and hence tends to substitute bonds. On the other hand, Equity Hedge has more stock-like features and thus tends to substitute stocks. When we look at the optimal allocation to hedge funds for different time horizons, we see that for the omega criterion the optimal hedge fund allocation tends to decrease when the time horizon increases. This is mainly due to the serial correlation in hedge fund returns, leading to a stronger increase in variance than in the i.i.d. case. This makes hedge funds relatively less attractive for longer time horizons. However, this effect is rather weak, as it is superimposed by other contrary effects.

SUMMARY AND CONCLUSION

Hedge fund investors are increasingly sophisticated and are requiring the same rigor in portfolio construction that is utilised in constructing portfolios of traditional assets. The problem is that hedge funds and their indices exhibit a number of distinctive features such as data biases, negative skewness, excess kurtosis, and serial correlation. This presents difficulties to traditional mean-variance asset allocation models. Such models tend to overallocate to hedge funds and overestimate the attainable benefits from incorporating hedge funds in a portfolio of traditional assets.

In this chapter, we introduce a more effective way of modelling hedge funds in an asset allocation context. Describing the evolution of hedge fund returns by a Markov-switching autoregression, the model is able to reproduce most of the salient features of hedge fund returns. The model is flexible enough to deal with different hedge fund styles and can be easily estimated using moment-matching techniques.

We applied the model to find the optimal asset allocation to bonds, stocks, and hedge funds of different styles. The results suggest a substantial allocation to hedge funds even with consideration for positive autocorrelation, negative skewness, and excess kurtosis. Compared to the results obtained from the mean-variance model, however, the optimal hedge fund allocations are significantly lower. This can be explained by the fact, that the hedge fund investor typically reduces risk as measured by dispersion around the mean (volatility), but increases risk as measured by the probability of large negative losses (negative skewness and high kurtosis). The different risk/return profiles of the various hedge funds styles translate in distinctly different allocations to hedge funds.

Realistic modelling of hedge fund characteristics becomes even more important when the construction of optimal hedge fund of fund portfolios is considered. Our model can be easily extended to deal with a number of correlated hedge funds of different styles. This proves to be an interesting area for future research.

1 See Amenc *et al* (2003).
2 See, eg, Fung/Hsieh (2000), Getmansky *et al* (2003), and Amo *et al* (2002).
3 See, eg, Beus *et al* (2003) and Perez (2005).
4 See Brooks/Kat (2002) for a detailed analysis of the statistical properties of hedge fund returns.
5 For more information on HFR and HFRI indices, see www.hedgefundresearch.com and Amenc/Martellini (2002).
6 To eliminate currency effects the LB Global Aggregate is hedged to US$. Because the equity volatility is significantly higher than the bond volatility, and thus currency effects play a minor role, the MSCI World is left unhedged.
7 Throughout the paper we measure asset returns as log (or continuously compounded) returns. For simplicity, we use the notions return and log return interchangeably.
8 See, eg, Fung/Hsieh (2000) and Fung/Hsieh (2002).
9 See Getmansky *et al* (2003).
10 See also Brooks/Kat (2002).
11 See Lo (2001).
12 See Scott/Horvath (1980).
13 The model can easily be extended to include other asset classes. For brevity, we henceforth speak of a bond, a stock, and a hedge fund.
14 x' denotes the transpose of the vector x.
15 The model was introduced by Lam (1990).
16 For a brief introduction to Markov chains in the context of regime-switching models, see Hamilton (1994), Chapter 22.
17 When the number of moment conditions is the same as the number of unknown parameters, the MoM estimator equals the Generalised Method of Moments (GMM) estimator, since the weighting matrix has no impact. See Hamilton (1994), Chapter 14. Alternative techniques to estimate the parameter vector θ are Maximum Likelihood Estimation or Markov Chain Monte Carlo (MCMC) methods.
18 In fact, we expect an inflation rate of 2% p.a., a real bond return of 2% p.a., and a risk premium of stocks over bonds of 3.5% p.a.
19 For a similar approach, see Amenc, Martellini (2003) and Popova *et al* (2006).
20 We assume that returns are normally distributed. Note that the mean variance model is also valid when the representative agents have a quadratic quadratic utility function.
21 We omitted time indices, for brevity.
22 For an in-depth derivation and discussion of the omega measure, see Keating/Shadwick (2002).
23 The risk aversion parameter λ in the power utility model is 6.7 for a 1 year time horizon, 7.2 for a three year horizon, and 7.5 for a five year horizon.
24 By convention, the CVaR is expressed as a positive number.

REFERENCES

Amenc, N., S. Curtis, and L. Martellini, 2003, "The Alpha and Omega of Hedge Fund Performance Measurement", *Working paper*, EDHEC.

Amenc, N. and L. Martellini, 2002, "The Brave New World of Hedge Fund Indexes", *Working paper*, EDHEC.

Amenc, N. and L. Martellini, 2003, "Optimal Mixing of Hedge Funds with Traditional Investment Vehicles", *Working paper*, EDHEC.

Amo, A.-V., H. Harasty, and P. Hillion, 2002, "Hedge Funds and Funds of Hedge Funds: Are they Worth the Risk?", *Working paper*, Lombard Odier & Cie.

Beus, P., M. Bressers, and T. Graaf, 2003, "Alternative Investments and Risk Measurement", *Working paper*, Ernst & Young Actuaries, Asset Risk Management.

Brooks, C. and K. M. Kat, 2002, The Statistical Properties of Hedge Fund Index Returns and Their Implications for Investors", *The Journal of Alternative Investments*, **5(3)**, pp 26–44.

Brown, S. J., W. N. Goetzman, and R. G. Ibbotson, 1999, "Offshore Hedge Funds: Survival and Performance 1989–95", *Journal of Business*, **72**, pp 91–117.

Cvitanic, J., A. Lazrak, L. Martellini, and F. Zapatero, 2003, "Optimal Allocation to Hedge Funds: An Empirical Analysis", *Quantitative Finance*, **3**, pp 1–12.

Fung, W. and D. A. Hsieh, 2000, "Performance Characteristics of Hedge Funds and Commodity Funds: Natural vs. Spurious Biases", *Journal of Financial and Quantitative Analysis*, **35(3)**, pp 291–307.

Fung, W. and D. A. Hsieh, 2002, "Hedge-Fund Benchmarks: Information Content and Biases", *Financial Analysts Journal*, **58(1)**, pp 22–34.

Getmansky, M., A. W. Lo, and I. Makarov, 2003, "An Econometric Model of Serial Correlation and Illiquidity in Hedge Fund Returns", *Working paper*, National Bureau of Economic Research.

Hamilton, J. D., 1994, *Time Series Analysis*, Princeton University Press, New Jersey.

Keating, C. and W. Shadwick, 2002, "A Universal Performance Measure", *Journal of Performance Measurement*, **6(3)**, pp 59–84.

Lam, P.-S., 1990, "The Hamilton Model with a General Autoregressive Component: Estimation and Comparison with Other Models of Economic Time Series", *Journal of Monetary Economics*, **26(3)**, pp 409–32.

Liang, B., 2000, "Hedge Funds: The Living and the Dead", *Journal of Financial and Quantitative Analysis*, **35(3)**, pp 309–26.

Lo, A. W., 2001, "Risk Management for Hedge Funds: Introduction and Overview", *Financial Analysts Journal*, pp 16–33.

Perez, P. G., 2005, "An Approach to the Non-normal Behavior of Hedge Fund Indices Using Johnson Distributions", *Working paper*, ITAM.

Popova, I., D. Morton, E. Popova, and J. Yau, 2006, Optimal hedge fund allocation with asymmetric preferences and distributions, *Working paper*, Albers School of Business and Economics Seattle.

Schneeweis, T. and R. Spurgin, 1998, Multi-factor models of hedge fund, managed futures and mutual fund return and risk characteristics, *Journal of Alternative Investments*, **1(1)**, pp 1–24.

Scott, R. and P. Horvath, 1980, On the direction of preference for moments of higher than variance, *The Journal of Finance*, **35(4)**, pp 915–19.

23

The Effect of Hedge Funds on the Risk Profile of Global Portfolios

Peter Oertmann

Vescore Solutions Inc, University of Basle

INTRODUCTION

We are concerned with the question of whether hedge funds affect the risk profile of a globally diversified portfolio and, if so, how. In theory, unrelated asset risks cancel each other out as their number in a portfolio increases indefinitely. Hence, a portfolio inherits from its assets only those risks that are related. In practice, one cannot increase the number of assets held indefinitely, of course, but the gist of the argument remains: the investor should concentrate on general risks. Given a sufficiently large and diversified portfolio, specific risks are less important. The risk profile of a portfolio therefore represents only risks that cannot be diversified even by pooling many assets. From this perspective, it is not immediately clear that hedge funds affect a portfolio's risk profile.

On the one hand, some argue that hedge fund returns are mostly made up of alpha, ie, driven by a manager's skill in exploiting market inefficiencies. Following this line of argument, even very volatile hedge funds would not increase a portfolio's risk: if the return is attributed to the manager, it cannot be related to the returns of other assets. Hedge funds could thus be added to a portfolio with impunity, ie, with no significant effect on its risk profile (provided the number of hedge funds in the portfolio is large). Among the more extreme views is a study by Morgan Stanley (Peskin *et al*, 2000) that explains up to 98% of observed hedge fund returns with the managers' "ability to exploit structural inefficiencies in the markets".

On the other hand, beginning with the pioneering paper of Fung and Hsieh (1998), academic research explains more and more of hedge fund returns with exposure to so-called alternative risks. According to this view, missing the risks captured by such factors may lead to a misperception of hedge fund returns as a sort of "free lunch". Notably, the alpha becomes smaller and smaller as researchers get a better grip on the risks of hedge funds. A case in point, in their latest paper on the subject Fung and Hsieh (2004), embed contingent risk factors defined over traditional assets in an Arbitrage Pricing Theory (APT) framework. This allows them to explain up to 90% of the monthly variation of diversified hedge fund portfolios.

If hedge funds are driven by systematic risk exposure, then this must have implications for their integration in portfolios. In particular, if it is true that hedge funds are exposed to alternative risk factors, then what is the relation of this alternative risk to its counterpart, "traditional" risk? It is not clear why or how alternative risk factors should differ from other asset risks.

In our view, hedge funds seem to carry a bundle of common as well as specific risks. Contrary to the view that hedge funds insulate themselves from general market movements, significant hedge fund exposure is found to traditional risk factors. In particular, it is found that they explain the co-movements between hedge funds and equity investments relatively well. In accordance with the current research literature, it is also found that the residual correlations of hedge funds indicate alternative, hedge fund-specific risk factors. Performing a principal component analysis on the residuals of hedge funds, it is found that the first two components look similar to long and short straddles on two traditional risk factors. If this observation is valid, the suspected risk factors could reflect the sensitivity of situations-based strategies to macroeconomic disturbances and the trend-following exposure of another set of traders respectively.

This fits in well with both the empirical properties of hedge fund returns and theoretical considerations as to their payoff structure. Theoretically, payoffs to dynamic trading strategies may differ from those of buy-and-hold investments. In particular, they can exhibit option-like, non-linear payoffs when expressed as functions of the appropriate risks or assets (Merton, 1981). Empirically, conditional correlations between hedge funds and stocks seem to differ from their unconditional counterparts (Kat, 2003). Simple graphical analysis also indicates non-linear relationships between some strategies and markets. In addition, hedge fund returns deviate significantly from the normal form. Exposure to non-linear risk factors, defined over traditional ones, could offer a plausible explanation for all of these empirical and theoretical observations.

The two suspected additional risk factors seem to reflect systematic and alternative macro-risks of certain hedge fund strategies. They are alternative in the sense that they seem to apply to trading strategies rather than original assets. They are macroeconomic in that they are defined over factors that affect and are affected by the economy as a whole. And they are systematic in that they cannot be diversified by simply adding more assets.

The last point in particular has implications for the integration of hedge funds into principal portfolios: If the two additional factors are valid, the multi-factor-efficient portfolio *with* hedge funds has to be defined over (at least) two more dimensions in the investor's risk-return space than the one *without* hedge funds. The effect of hedge funds on the risk profile of a global portfolio is thus to both enter and extend it.

ASSET CLASS UNIVERSE

We use a broad universe of traditional asset classes to illustrate our discussion consisting of international equity and bond market indexes. We use monthly returns during the April 1994–April 2004 period. To isolate the active risk contribution of hedge funds, the perspective of a US$ investor is adopted as hedge funds are still mostly American-dominated. Therefore the returns are all on a US$ basis and expressed as excess returns, where the 1 month Treasury-bill rate is used as the risk-free rate. The traditional equity and bond indexes are taken from Data-stream.

The bond universe consists only of government bonds, split into five regions and three maturity ranges (1–3 Y, 3–5 Y and 7–10 Y) respectively and is invested globally in Europe (EUR), Switzerland (CHF), Japan (JPY), Britain (GBP) and the United States (US$). However, the bond universe is not hedged against currency fluctuations. The resulting foreign exchange risk will be captured through an explicit currency risk factor. The equity universe is represented by 13 stock indexes from the most important markets in Europe,

America and Asia. The international equity returns are not hedged against foreign exchange fluctuations because the currency risk is to be captured explicitly in a later section. The hedge fund strategies are taken from CSFB/Tremont's index services. There exists a growing literature on the relative advantages and disadvantages of the various hedge fund indexes available today (Ross and Oberhofer, 2002; Kat and Brooks, 2002; Amenc and Martinelli, 2003).

Table 1 includes an overview of the asset classes used in the study. Figure 1 shows the relative performances of selected indexes between April 1994 and April 2004.

THE RISK OF GLOBAL PORTFOLIOS

Global risk factors

To measure the risk contribution of an asset to a portfolio, basic portfolio theory is followed and the variance of the joint distribution of assets used. In particular, the focus is on co-movements between assets. Given the relatively advanced state of financial market integration and international trade, one would expect significant correlations between the international assets under consideration here (Figure 2).

In order to summarise this risk in an economically meaningful way, we postulate a linear relationship between any asset's excess return and a set of common risk factors. This relationship is represented by a multi-factor model

$$r_{it} = a_i + \sum_j \beta_{ij} \cdot \delta_{jt} + \varepsilon_{it} \qquad \textbf{(1)}$$

with risk factors denoted by δ_{jt}, average specific influences a_i, noise terms ε_{it}, where $i = 1, \ldots, n$ and $j = 1, \ldots, k$. No matter how large the number n of assets, the dimension of the portfolio risk measure is now fixed at the number of common risk factors k.

Although it is clear that pooling many assets will reduce the number of risks, little is known about the remaining risk factors. The proposed specification includes four global risk factors which are meant to capture the macroeconomic risks reflected by four big asset markets:

- world equity market ($\delta_{1t} = \delta_{WM,t}$);
- interest rate ($\delta_{2t} = \delta_{IR,t}$);

Table 1 Asset classes used in the study. The traditional equity and bond indexes are taken from Datastream. The hedge fund strategies are taken from CSFB/Tremont's index services

Bonds	Stocks	Hedge funds
Bond EUR 1–3 Y	Stock CAC 40	Convertible arb.
Bond EUR 3–5 Y	Stock DAX	Dedicated short
Bond EUR 7–10 Y	Stock Eurostoxx	Distressed
Bond CHF 1–3 Y	Stock FTSE 100	Event driven multi
Bond CHF 3–5 Y	Stock Hang Seng	Emerging markets
Bond CHF 7–10 Y	Stock IBEX 35	Equity market neutral
Bond JPY 1–3 Y	Stock MSCI SG	Event driven
Bond JPY 3–5 Y	Stock Nasdaq	Fixed income arb.
Bond JPY 7–10 Y	Stock Nikkei 225	Global macro
Bond GBP 1–3 Y	Stock OMX	Long-short equity
Bond GBP 3–5 Y	Stock SMI	Managed futures
Bond GBP 7–10 Y	Stock S&P 500	Multi-strategy
Bond US$ 1–3 Y	Stock TSE 60	Risk arb.
Bond US$ 3–5 Y		
Bond US$ 7–10 Y		

Figure 1 Relative performance of selected indices (S&P 500, datastream bond US$ 7–10 Y, CSFB/Tremont hedge fund composite) between April 1994 and April 2004

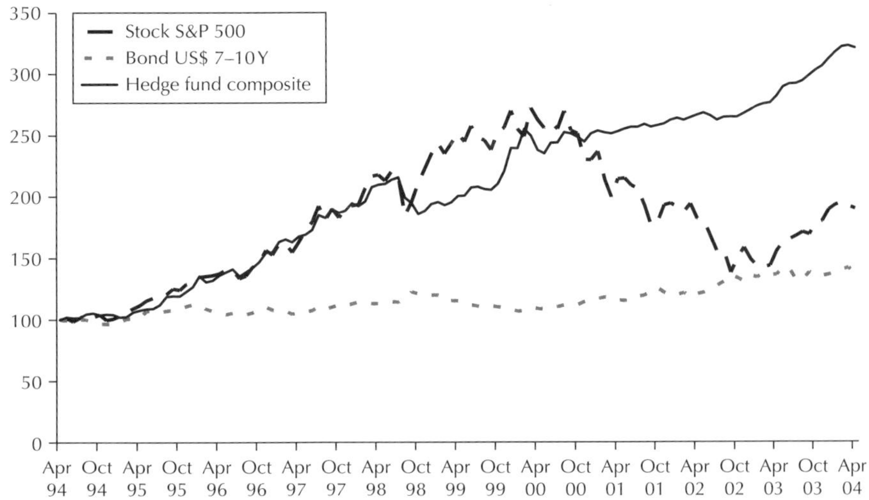

Figure 2 Frequency distribution of correlation estimates within the bond and equity universes – 105 bond, 78 equity coefficients in total

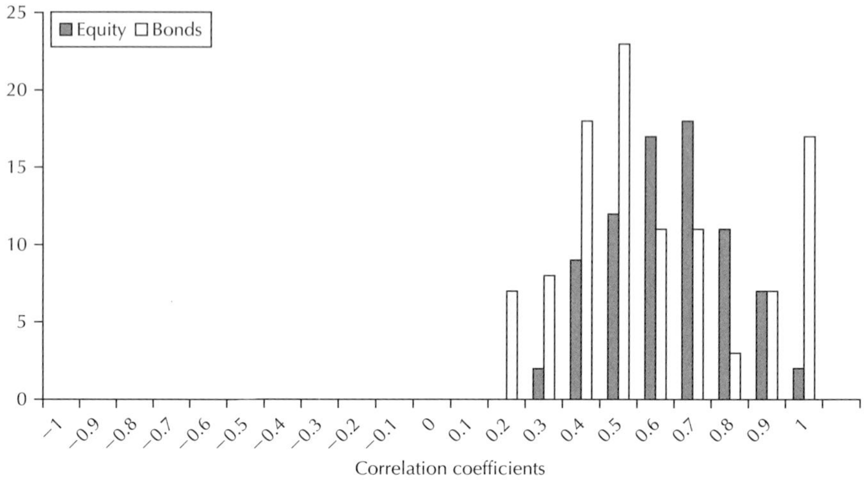

- ❑ commodity ($\delta_{3t} = \delta_{COM,t}$); and
- ❑ currency ($\delta_{4t} = \delta_{FX,t}$).

The specification is guided by the idea that movements in the largest international asset markets should be related to movements in national asset prices globally. In particular, it seems plausible that the dependencies between the latter will be explained well through a set of global risk factors. There is an extensive academic literature on the macroeconomic motivation of these factors (Oertmann, 1997).

The world market risk factor is represented by the relative change of the MSCI World index over one-month periods:

$$\delta_{WM,t} = \frac{Index_{MSCI,t} - Index_{MSCI,t-1}}{Index_{MSCI,t-1}} \tag{2}$$

The global interest rate factor is represented by weighted absolute interest rate changes in 10Y government bonds, measured over monthly periods:

$$\delta_{IR,t} = \sum_{k=1}^{5} w_k (y_{10Y,k,t} - y_{10Y,k,t-1}) \quad \text{with} \quad w_k = \frac{GDP_k}{\sum_k GDP_k} \tag{3}$$

The denominator of the weighting factors is the total GDP of the EUR-region and the four G7 countries outside of it. Note that this sum still represents over two-thirds of total world GDP. The numerators are given by each country's respective GDP. The weights are re-calculated each year with a lag of one period.

The global commodity factor is represented by relative changes of the Goldman Sachs index for industrial metals:

$$\delta_{COM,t} = \frac{Index_{Ind.Metals,t} - Index_{Ind.Metals,t-1}}{Index_{Ind.Metals,t-1}} \quad \textbf{(4)}$$

The global currency risk factor is represented by the weighted relative change of the most important exchange rates, measured against the US$:

$$\delta_{FX,t} = \sum_{k=1}^{4} w_k \frac{(FX_{k,t} - FX_{k,t-1})}{FX_{k,t-1}} \quad \text{with} \quad w_k = \frac{GDP_k}{\sum_k GDP_k} \quad \textbf{(5)}$$

The weighting scheme is equal to the scheme used for the interest rate factor. Exchange rates are expressed as the ratio between foreign currency units and US$. The currency basket consists of CAD, EUR, GBP and JPY.

The risk profile before introducing hedge funds

The regression results show that the four global risk factors have considerable explanatory power for the set of equity and bond investments. The residual sum of squares varies over the cross-section, being relatively low for the S&P 500 (which is not surprising given the construction of our equity factor) and relatively high for Asian equity markets, for example. Since we concentrate on co-movements, we consider the F-statistic more pertinent. As the F-statistic is rather high even for assets with low R-squared values, this is registered as a first piece of evidence for the hypothesis that the postulated risk factors capture common risks (see Table 2).

Because the equity and bond investments do not co-move significantly to begin with (a point that will be looked at in more detail later), the correlations within the equity and bond classes are presented for more direct evidence. As the frequency distributions of t-statistics for the correlation estimates in Figures 3 and 4 show,

Table 2 R-squared and F-statistics for bond and stock indexes, as calculated from OLS regressions based on Equation (1) with independent variables as in Equations (2)–(5)

	R^2(%)	F-stat		R^2(%)	F-stat
Bond EUR 1–3 Y	73.68	81.16	Stock CAC 40	67.65	60.65
Bond EUR 3–5 Y	74.79	86.02	Stock DAX	67.64	60.60
Bond EUR 7–10 Y	74.28	83.76	Stock Eurostoxx	75.40	88.87
Bond CHF 1–3 Y	73.17	79.09	Stock FTSE 100	72.56	76.68
Bond CHF 3–5 Y	72.34	75.86	Stock Hang Seng	44.62	23.36
Bond CHF 7–10 Y	68.52	63.11	Stock IBEX 35	54.63	34.91
Bond JPY1–3 Y	70.71	70.01	Stock MSCI SG	37.09	17.10
Bond JPY 3–5 Y	69.17	65.07	Stock Nasdaq	60.63	44.67
Bond JPY 7–10 Y	66.51	57.58	Stock Nikkei 225	43.26	22.11
Bond GBP 1–3 Y	43.02	21.89	Stock OMX	63.25	49.91
Bond GBP 3–5 Y	48.71	27.54	Stock SMI	47.88	26.64
Bond GBP 7–10 Y	51.99	31.41	Stock S&P 500	91.68	319.61
Bond US$ 1–3 Y	69.37	65.69	Stock TSE 60	67.31	59.72
Bond US$ 3–5 Y	82.52	136.88			
Bond US$ 7–10 Y	86.48	185.50			

Figure 3 Significance distribution of correlation estimates for equity universe – 78 estimates in total for each set

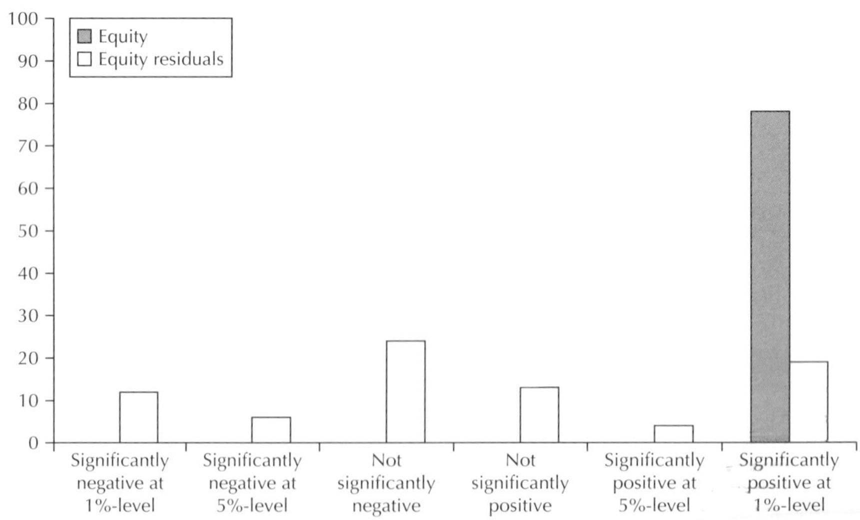

Figure 4 Significance distribution of correlation estimates for bond universe. 105 estimates in total for each set

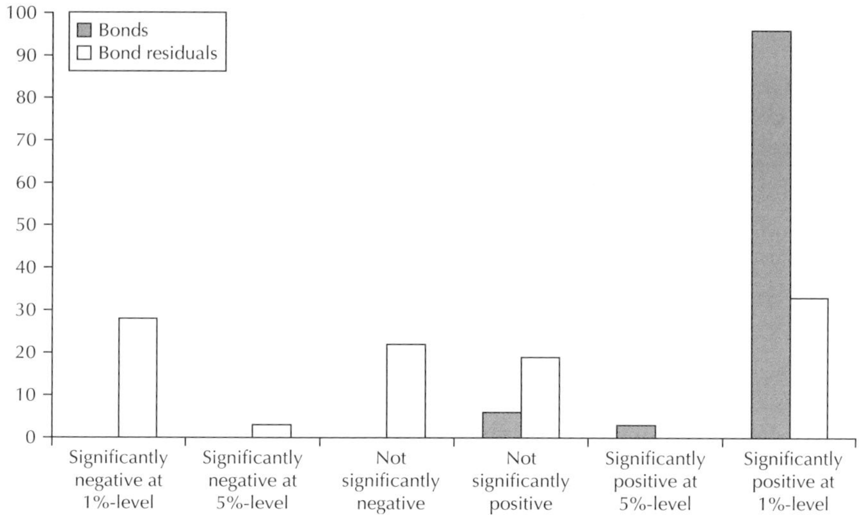

the number of significantly positive relationships between assets drops dramatically once one accounts for their exposure to the set of global risk factors.

The partition is at the 1% and 5% levels of significance respectively.[1] One can clearly see that the residuals of both equity and bond classes are less correlated with each other than the unadjusted returns. These frequency distributions are interpreted as confirmation that the co-movements of our set of traditional assets are well explained by the proposed set of global risk factors.

Noting that some of the risk factors are measured in relative terms while others are in absolute terms, the regression is repeated on standardised variables to make the interpretation of risk profiles more complete. All else being equal, a beta of 0.83 implies that the asset's return will move by 0.83 standard deviations if the corresponding factor moves by one standard deviation. It may also be noted that under the assumption of no collinearity, the regression coefficients now are simply the correlation coefficients between the assets and the risk factors. Since the risk factors are slightly correlated with each other, this relation holds only sporadically.

Recall that the primary motivation for the risk factors is to capture co-movements between assets. If the evidence is valid, then a large part of a global portfolio's variation stems from only a few systematic risk factors. One can note, however, that the number of remaining dependencies in both classes is high enough to suspect additional risk factors. A look at the residual correlations indicates that these could be regional in nature.

A portfolio's exposure to any factor is simply the weighted sum of constituent asset exposures. It follows that the risk contribution of any asset to a global portfolio can be read directly from its own risk profile. Within this framework, we will now analyse the effect of hedge funds on the risk of global portfolios.

The linear risk of hedge funds

According to a common perception, hedge funds are not risky because they are not correlated to traditional assets or benchmarks. Researchers have found lower correlations among hedge funds than mutual funds. On an absolute and a relative level more positive correlations are found within both equity and bond universes than among the different strategies followed by hedge funds. For example, the average coefficient estimate for the bond and equity universe is 0.54 and 0.59 respectively, but for hedge fund strategies it is only 0.21. Figures 5 and 6 also illustrate that effective diversification seems to be easier between hedge funds than between equities or bonds when taken by themselves.

In the context of a portfolio, however, we are interested in the co-movement between hedge fund strategies and the remaining traditional assets. Weighing the diversification benefits of the bond, equity and hedge fund universes relative to each other, a different picture emerges. Even unconditional correlations show significant co-movement between hedge funds and international equities. Conditioning correlations on the world equity market factor, as will be examined later, indicates that their co-movement properties could be inferior.

To illustrate, the correlations between equities and bonds are compared with those between equities and hedge funds. Figure 7 shows the respective frequency distributions, ordered by statistical significance. The critical values for the test statistic have been selected at the 5% and 1% levels respectively. While the relationship

Figure 5 Frequency distribution of correlation estimates within bond and hedge fund universes – 105 bond coefficients, 78 hedge fund coefficients in total

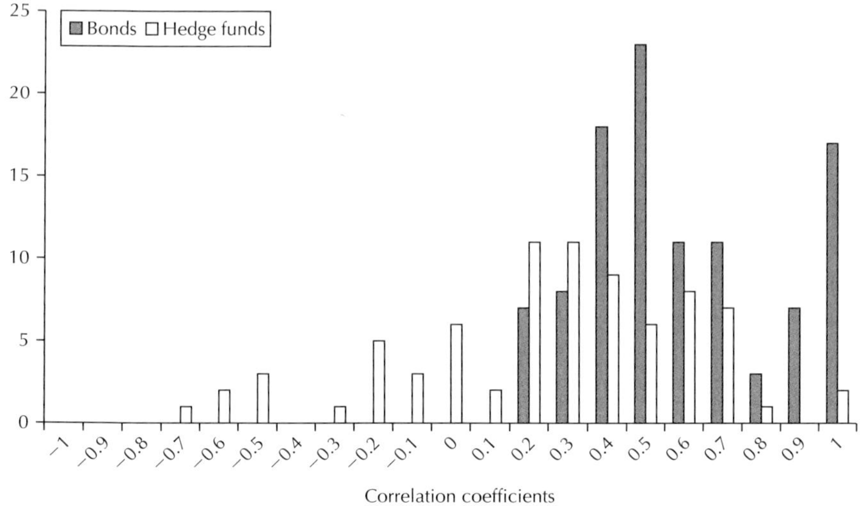

Figure 6 Frequency distributions of correlation estimates within equity and hedge fund universes – 78 equity coefficients, 78 hedge fund coefficients in total

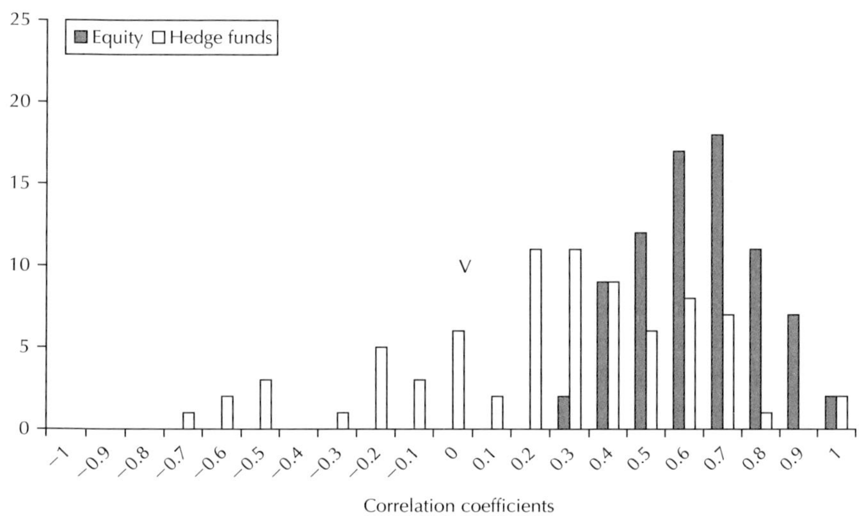

could be explained on purely technical rather than economic grounds.

Hedge fund deviations from normality

Hedge funds deviate much more from standard distributional assumptions than traditional investments. Samples generated from a normal population should have skewness close to zero and kurtosis close to three. None of the traditional investments are perfectly normally distributed, but when compared with hedge funds, it seems that the distributional deviations of hedge funds cannot be safely ignored.

In particular, higher moments of marginal hedge fund distributions could lead to joint distribution properties that make correlation only a partial measure of co-movement. Hence hedge fund skewness and leptokurtosis may lead investors to overestimate their diversification benefits.

Non-linear relationships between hedge funds and markets

Most traditional fund managers pursue long-only strategies in well-defined markets. As a result of this strategy, their performance can usually be expressed as a linear function of their respective benchmark.

In contrast, hedge funds pursue a variety of strategies with little outside limitations or interference as to their choice of markets. As a result, there is no pre-ordained relationship between their returns and the markets in which they trade. Merton (1981) has first shown that dynamic trading may result in non-linear payoff structures, ie, in non-linear relationships between the payoff to the strategy and the payoff to the assets traded. The intuition is that a trading strategy defined over a set of assets or their outcomes is similar to an option position in that both their payoffs are contingent on the underlying asset. Linearity, it turns out, is just a special case of the general dependence between strategy and assets.

Building on this insight, some researchers such as Mitchell and Pulvino (2001) have sought to model hedge fund returns in a contingent claims framework. To illustrate, there are second-order polynomials on the scattergram of merger arbitrage and world market returns. The graph in Figure 11 indicates that merger arbitrage returns seem contingent on equities in an (uncovered) short-put like fashion.

Figure 11 Scattergram and second-order polynomial line fitting of the merger arbitrage hedge fund strategy (y-axis) and the world market factor (x-axis)

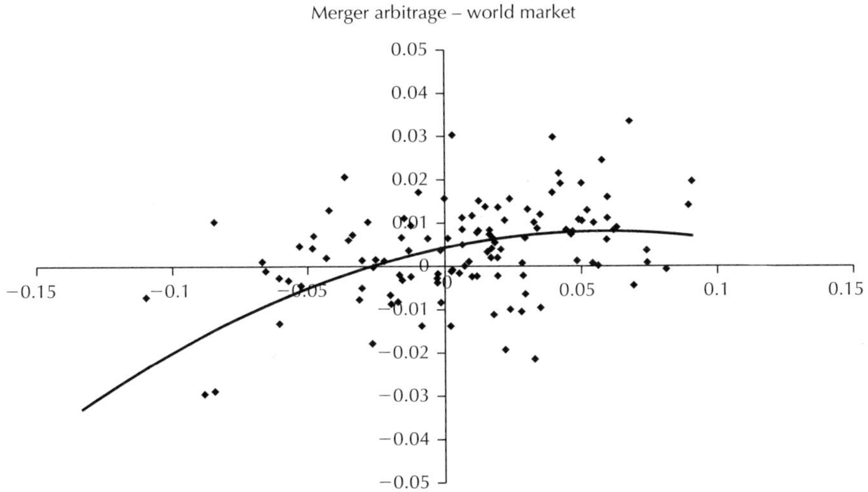

In principle, a variety of non-linear relationships can be defined over a variety of assets. For example, Figure 12 seems to indicate a short-straddle like dependence of the fixed income arbitrage strategy on the world market factor. To see the potential of a contingent claims approach to hedge funds, compare this with the linear fitting. While the former seems to reveal a significant relationship, the latter is flat and would lead to an inference of zero.

Can the three observations be related to each other?

Intuition tells us that the three highlighted phenomena could be related. In particular, it is suspected that hedge fund exposure to non-linear risk factors could offer a plausible explanation for all of them.

To motivate the idea, we propose a thought experiment: consider a normally distributed random variable to which both hedge funds and equity markets are related. While equity markets are linearly related to it, however, hedge funds have linear as well as non-linear exposure to it. Assume this non-linear exposure resembles a linear exposure to a short-straddle position defined

Figure 12 Scattergram, first- and second-order polynomial line fitting of the fixed income arbitrage hedge fund strategy (y-axis) and the world market factor (x-axis)

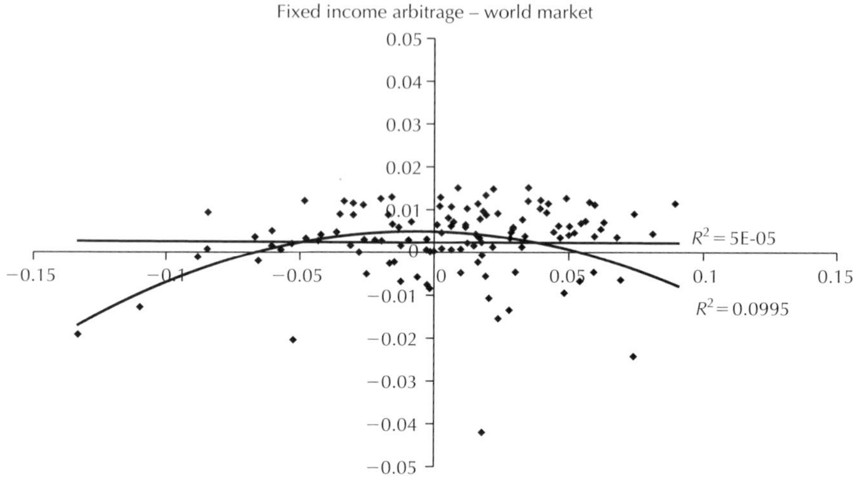

over the original variable and that it is symmetrical over the entire domain. Then we would find that:

- ❑ correlations between equity markets and hedge funds are higher when the variable moves down than when it moves up;
- ❑ hedge fund return distributions are negatively skewed and possibly leptokurtic; and
- ❑ hedge fund returns are related to equity market returns in a non-linear fashion.

First, if we divide the hypothetical sample into halves on the basis of movements of the variable, then it obviously follows that there are more negative equity market observations in the lower half than in the upper half, and vice versa. If hedge funds are related to a short-straddle position on the risk variable, however, there will be more negative observations in the lower half than positive ones in the upper half, both in absolute and in relative terms. As a result, conditional correlations between equity markets and hedge funds will be higher when equity markets move down and lower when they move up.

Second, if hedge funds were only linearly related to the risk variable, they would simply inherit its normal distribution. Because they also have non-linear exposure, however, their up-moves will be less positive than otherwise; correspondingly, their down-moves will be more frequent or more pronounced. As a result of this asymmetry, their distributions will be negatively skewed. In addition, one could expect a relatively high concentration of observations around the mean if the linear relationship dominates the non-linear one, thus the hypothetical hedge fund distributions could also contain fat tails.

As for the third point, hedge funds are related to equity markets in a non-linear fashion. This relationship is more obvious than the others. Note, however, that it is not primary but derived from the linear and non-linear exposures to the underlying risk variable. More to the point, if a strategy is found to exhibit some option-like payoff distribution defined over some market that does not necessarily mean the strategy is contingent on that market.

The crucial term in the equation is, so to speak, the risk variable. Can it be established that hedge funds are exposed to meaningful economic risk factors of the desired form?

THE NON-LINEAR RISK OF HEDGE FUNDS

Alternative risk factors of hedge funds

We have performed a principal component analysis on the correlations between the regression residuals of hedge funds. The first three principal components (PCs) together explain about 59% of the residual variation. In light of the tentative nature of this analysis, they are viewed as statistical proxies for hypothetical alternative risk factors. In other words, we temporarily disregard that PCs have no economic content whatsoever, and assume they can be related to alternative risk factors. With this in mind, it seems natural to extend the original regression models by the new artificial "risk factors".

Unsurprisingly, the *R*-squared values of the new, extended models rise significantly. This, however, is not meaningful in itself. Therefore, incremental contributions are assigned to the explained sum of squares to each new regressor. Note that the nature of the analysis allows this. First, the analysis was done on the residuals, which precludes correlations between the PCs and the original risk

Figure 13 Interest rate quantile averages and sub-sample averages (rescaled) for the first component

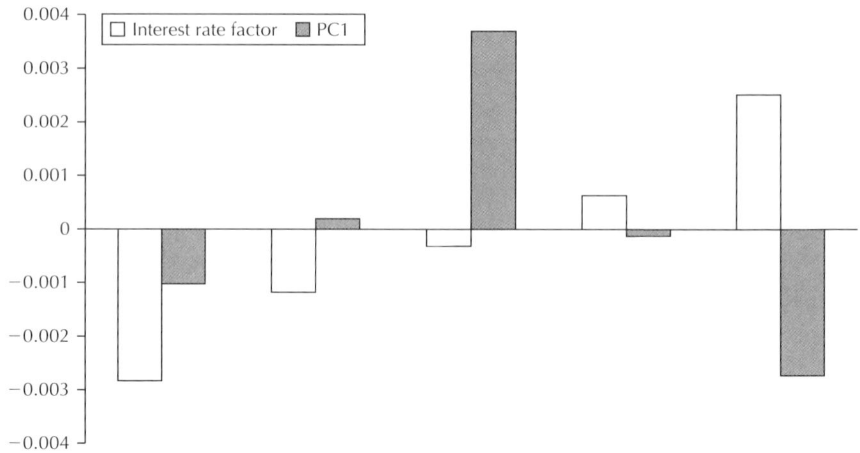

first two PCs. In particular, we would like to get a firmer grip on their economic content. That is, can we make the hypothesised risk factors to which we have intuitively related them more specific?

Interpretation of first component

We have tried to relate the first component to the original global risk factors, but it turns out that it seems related to the interest rate factor. Ordering the sample observations by this factor and averaging the quintile values of the first component results in Figure 13. Interestingly, it seems to resemble a short straddle position on the interest rate factor.

According to the pattern shown in Figure 13, the first group of strategies seems to be exposed to the risks captured by large movements of the interest rate factor. The strategies are apt to do badly in extreme interest rate environments. Alternatively, they seem to be short interest rate volatility. This pattern agrees with the previous suspicion, based on the groupings and qualitative strategy descriptions, that the first PC is related to an event-risk factor.

Why should this be so? Recall that the interest rate factor is defined as the weighted average of absolute changes on ten-year government bond yields in the five most important currencies.

Figure 14 History of global interest rate factor, as in Equation (3), between April 1994 and April 2004

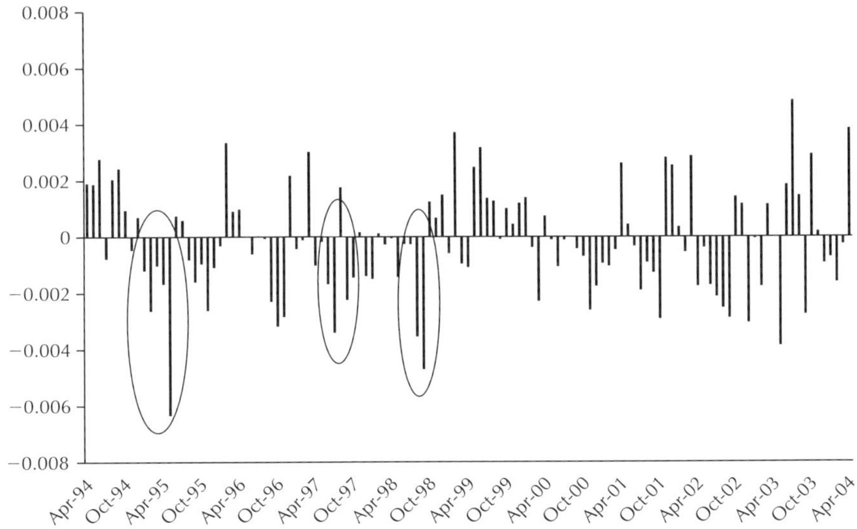

One would expect then that large positive moves are induced by financial crisis situations and corresponding "flights to quality". Alternatively, as the factor reflects macroeconomic developments in the most important economic regions of the world, higher volatility could also be induced by unexpected economic developments.

Figure 14 shows that at least some of the large downward moves are indeed connected to financial crises or high general uncertainty. For example, we have highlighted three periods marked by international financial crises: the peso crisis in 1995, the Asian crisis beginning in mid-1997, and the Russia/LTCM crisis in 1998.

The evidence points towards the presence of an alternative risk factor that is statistically related to the first PC and economically resembling a short straddle position on global interest rates, seems to reflect common hedge fund exposure to event-risk. Overall, this pattern makes sense. Corporate events tend to go in unlikely directions and spread distortions tend to persist or even exacerbate if significant risk events occur. Thus, managers betting on situations or spreads should be expected to do badly in such environments, all else being equal.

Figure 15 Commodities factor quintile averages and sub-sample averages (rescaled) for the second component

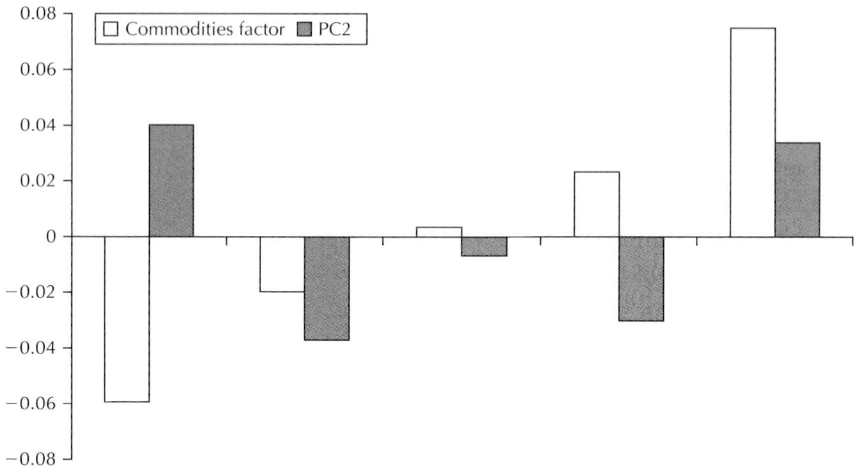

Figure 16 Significance distribution of the correlations within the hedge fund universe, unadjusted, adjusted for global risk exposure, and adjusted for both global and "local" risk factors. Seventy-eight estimates in total for each set

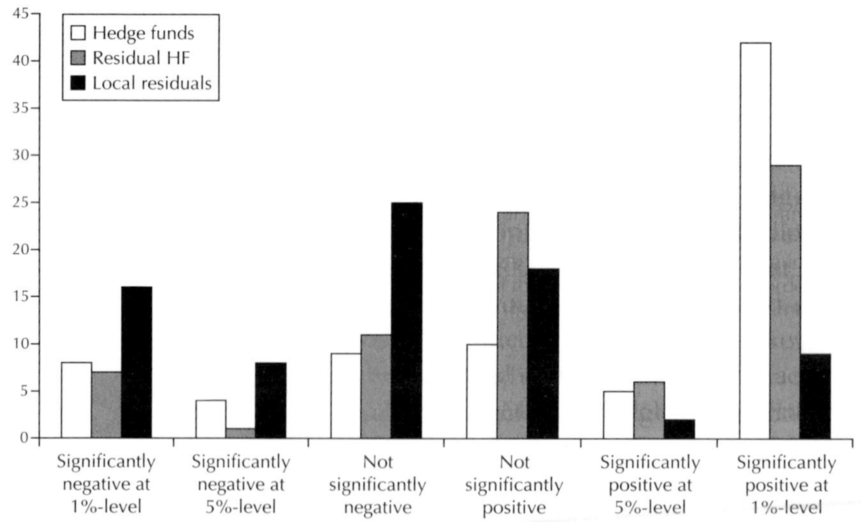

Interpretation of second component

We have also attempted to relate the second component to the original risk factors. However, it seems related to the commodities factor. Ordering the sample observations by this factor and averaging the quintile values of the second PC results in a pattern resembling a long straddle position on the commodities factor. For the moment ignoring the strange shape around the middle, could this make sense?

Consider that CTAs seem to be largely trend-followers (Fung and Hsieh, 1998; Fung and Hsieh, 2001; Darius *et al*, 2003) whereby they seek to detect and profit from sustained price moves in any direction. To do well they need large moves. Frequent small moves, randomly spread over positive and negative signs, are bad environments for trend-followers; "breakout" moves and non-random stretches of either positive or negative signs, by contrast, are good environments for trend-followers. The connection between global macro managers and the second PC could indicate that they are largely trend-followers as well. The membership of the EMN strategy in this group could be explained by the connection between commodities prices and the business cycle. If spreads between "good" and "bad" companies within an industry do indeed rise in pronounced phases of the business cycle, and if the commodities factor is partly explained by the stage of the business cycle, then a straddle-like exposure of EMN managers to the commodities factor could make sense.

Accounting for risk exposure and residual correlations

Once a parsimonious set of common risk factors have been identified, one can account for the systematic risk of a well-diversified portfolio. The remainder in terms of individual variation should be noise and hence unimportant in a portfolio context. This section concludes with an illustration of the frequency distributions of unadjusted and adjusted hedge fund correlations for global risk exposure, as well as adjusted for traditional and "quasi"-alternative risk factors. Obviously, this distribution should be taken with a pinch of salt, given the artificial nature of the analysis.

Hedge funds and the portfolio risk profile

To the extent that hedge funds bear standard asset risks, as represented through the set of four global risk factors, their fund-level risk

Longin, F. and B. Solnik, 2001, "Extreme Correlation of International Equity Markets", *Journal of Finance*, **56(2)**, pp 649–76.

Merton, R. C., 1981, "On Market Timing and Investment Performance. I. An Equilibrium Theory of Value for Market Forecasts", *Journal of Business*, **54(3)**, pp 363–406.

Mitchell, M. and T. Pulvino, 2001, "Characteristics of Risk and Return in Merger Arbitrage", *Journal of Finance*, **56(6)**, pp 2135–75.

Oertmann, P., 1997, *Global Risk Premia on International Stock and Bond Markets*, (Wiesbaden: Gabler Verlag).

Peskin, M. W., M. S. Urias, S. I. Anjilvel, and B. E. Boudreau, 2000, *Why Hedge Funds Make Sense*, (New York: Morgan Stanley Quantitative Strategies).

Ross, L. B. and G. Oberhofer, 2002, *What the Indexes Don't Tell You about Hedge Funds*, (Tacoma, WA: Russell Institutional Investors).

24

The Benefits of Hedge Funds in Asset-Liability Management

Lionel Martellini, Volker Ziemann

EDHEC Risk and Asset Management Research Center

INTRODUCTION

Recent difficulties have drawn attention to the risk management practices of institutional investors in general, and defined benefit pension plans in particular. A perfect storm of adverse market conditions over the past three years has devastated many corporate defined benefit pension plans. Negative equity market returns have eroded plan assets at the same time as declining interest rates have increased the market-to-market value of benefit obligations and contributions. In extreme cases, this has left corporate pension plans with funding gaps as large as, or larger than, the market capitalisation of the plan sponsor. For example, in 2003, the companies included in the S&P 500 and the FTSE 100 Index faced a cumulative deficit of US$225 billion and £55 billion, respectively (Credit Suisse First Boston, 2003; Standard Life Investments, 2003), while the worldwide deficit reached an estimated US$1,500 to US$2,000 billion (Watson Wyatt, 2003).

Because institutional investors have been so dramatically affected by market downturns, major changes have taken place in institutional money management including, notably, the need for an increased focus on asset-liability management (ALM). In this context, institutional investors in general, and under-funded pension funds in particular, are desperately seeking new asset classes or investment styles that could be cast in a surplus optimisation context and that would offer access to an equity-like premium without all the associated downside risks.

Because of their focus on absolute performance and risk control, hedge funds are typically suggested as a natural alternative to stocks and bonds. While long-only investment strategies can only generate a simple linear exposure to the return on underlying asset classes (go up and down with the indexes), the main benefits of hedge fund strategies is that they actually allow for a non-linear exposure with respect to stock and bond returns in such a way that the downside risk is typically limited.[1] This is because hedge fund managers, who operate in the absence of regulatory constraints, can incorporate a variety of dynamic investment strategies and/or investments in derivatives likely to generate non-linear payoffs (Fung and Hsieh, 1997).

While the assessment of the benefits hedge funds offered when included in an investor's portfolio has given rise to a burgeoning literature (eg, Agarwal and Naik, 2004), this question has not been examined in an ALM framework. This chapter attempts to fill this void.

Overall, the results in this chpater strongly suggest that when added to bonds and stocks, suitably designed portfolios of hedge funds can allow for significant benefits in an ALM context, as can be measured in terms of the reduction of the expected mismatch between assets and liabilities. This impact is more pronounced when the relevant objective turns to extreme risks. In fact, we show that the probability of extreme deficits (value of the assets falling below 75% of the value of liabilities) can be reduced by 50% by allocating 20% to hedge funds. These results should be taken into account by investors that are constrained to meeting liabilities.

The rest of this chapter is organised as follows. The next section presents an overview of ALM techniques as well as a presentation of the model used. We then present a formal surplus optimisation model followed by an introduction to hedge funds and test for their impact in terms of surplus optimisation benefits.

OVERVIEW OF ALM TECHNIQUES

ALM denotes the adaptation of the portfolio management process in order to handle the presence of various constraints relating to the commitments that figure in the liabilities of an institutional investor's balance sheet (ie, commitments to paying pensions, insurance premiums, etc). There are therefore as many types of liability constraints as there are types of institutional investors, and thus as many types of approaches to ALM.

ALM-type management techniques can be classified into several categories. A first approach called *cash-flow matching* involves ensuring a perfect match between the cash flows from the portfolio of assets and the liabilities commitments. Let's assume for example that a pension fund has a commitment to pay out a monthly pension to a retired person. Leaving aside the complexity relating to the uncertain life expectancy of the retiree, the structure of the liabilities is defined simply as a series of cash outflows to be paid, the real value of which is known today, but for which the nominal value is typically matched with an inflation index. It is possible in theory to construct a portfolio of assets whose future cash flows will be identical to this structure of commitments. To do so, assuming that securities of that kind exist on the market, would involve purchasing inflation-linked, zero-coupon bonds with a maturity corresponding to the dates on which the monthly pension instalments are paid out, with amounts that are proportional to the amount of real commitments.

This technique, which provides the advantage of simplicity and allows, in theory, for perfect risk management, nevertheless presents a number of limitations. First of all, it will generally be impossible to find inflation-linked securities whose maturity corresponds exactly to the liability commitments. Moreover, most of those securities pay out coupons, which leads to the problem of reinvesting the coupons. To the extent that perfect matching is not possible, there is a technique called *immunisation*, which allows the residual interest rate risk created by the imperfect match between the assets and liabilities to be managed in an optimal way. This interest rate risk management technique can be extended beyond a simple duration-based approach to fairly general contexts, including, eg, hedging non-parallel shifts in the yield curve (see Martellini *et al*, 2003), or to simultaneous management of interest rate risk and inflation risk (Siegel and Waring, 2004). It should be noted, however, that this technique is difficult to adapt to hedging non-linear risks related to the presence of options hidden in the liability structures, and/or to hedging non-interest rate related risks in liability structures.

Another, probably more important disadvantage of the cash-flow matching technique (or of the approximate matching version represented by the immunisation approach) is that it represents a positioning that is extreme and not necessarily optimal for the investor in the risk/return space. In fact, we can say that the cash-flow matching approach in asset-liability management is the equivalent of investing in the risk-free asset in an asset management context. It allows for perfect management of the risks, namely, a capital guarantee in the passive management framework, and a guarantee that the liability constraints are respected in the ALM framework. However, the lack of return, related to the absence of risk premia, makes this approach very costly, which leads to an unattractive level of contribution to the assets.

In an effort to improve the profitability of the assets, and therefore to reduce the level of contributions, it is necessary to introduce into the strategic allocation asset classes (stocks, government bonds and corporate bonds) that are not perfectly correlated with the liabilities. It will then involve finding the best possible compromise between the risk (relative to the liability constraints) thereby assumed, and the excess return that the investor can hope to obtain through the exposure to rewarded risk factors. Different techniques are then used to optimise the surplus, ie, the excess value of the assets compared with the liabilities, in a risk/return space. In particular, it is useful to turn to stochastic models that allow for a representation of the uncertainty relating to a set of risk factors that impact the liabilities. These can be financial risks (eg, inflation, interest rate, stocks) or non-financial risks (demographic ones in particular). When necessary, agent behaviour models are then developed, which allows the impact of decisions linked to exercising certain implicit options to be represented. For example, an insured person can (typically in exchange for penalties) cancel his/her life assurance contract if the guaranteed contractual rate drops significantly below the interest rate level prevailing at a date following the signature of the contract, which makes the amount of liability cash flows, and not just their current value, dependent on interest rate risk.

Different optimisation models are used by institutional investors within the framework of ALM (eg, see Mulvey *et al* (2005)), and it is impossible to provide an exhaustive list here.[2]

FORMAL SURPLUS OPTIMISATION MODEL

A surplus optimisation model is basically founded on optimising the match between the asset and liabilities sides of financial structures in companies.

Instead of making assumptions on the detailed allocation to single assets or funds in investors' portfolios, proxies are used for the different asset classes. In this exercise, three asset classes are considered (in addition to hedge funds): stocks, nominal bonds and inflation-indexed bonds (TIPS). The portfolio return R_{PF} is then given as:

$$R_{PF,t} = \sum_{i=1}^{n} \omega_i R_{i,t} \qquad t = 1, \ldots, T$$

where i represents the proxy for the asset class i and ω_i its weight in the portfolio.

The purpose of surplus optimisation is to find the allocation that minimises at the horizon T (here taken to be equal to 10 years) the relative expected shortfall SF beyond a certain target α, which is defined as follows:

$$SF(\alpha) = -E\left(\frac{R_{PF,T} - L_T}{L_T} \middle| \frac{R_{PF,T} - L_T}{L_T} < \alpha \right)$$

where L denotes the company's liabilities.

In the remaining sections, the optimal allocation will be obtained by resolving the following objective function:

$$\omega^* = \arg\min_{\omega} SF(0)$$

In order to optimise expected values of the portfolio distribution, we need to generate from an ex-ante basis, stochastic scenarios both for the asset and the liability side. On the asset side, Monte Carlo analysis is used to generate 10,000 random paths for each asset class using geometric Brownian motions and we generate scenarios:

$$S(t) = S(0)\exp\left(\left(\mu - \frac{1}{2}\sigma^2\right)t + \sigma B(t)\right)$$

where $B(t)$ is a Brownian motion with $\Delta B(t) \sim N(0, \Delta t)$ so that:

$$S(t+s) = S(t)\exp\left(\left(\mu - \frac{1}{2}\sigma^2\right)t + \sqrt{s}N\right)$$

with $N \sim N(0, \sigma^2)$.

In order to take the correlation of the underlying asset classes into account, we introduce the 3-dimensional geometric Brownian motion:

$$S_a(t+s) = S_a(t)\exp\left(\left(\mu_a - \frac{1}{2}\sigma_a^2\right)t + \sqrt{s}N_a\right)$$
$$S_b(t+s) = S_b(t)\exp\left(\left(\mu_b - \frac{1}{2}\sigma_b^2\right)t + \sqrt{s}N_b\right)$$
$$S_c(t+s) = S_c(t)\exp\left(\left(\mu_c - \frac{1}{2}\sigma_c^2\right)t + \sqrt{s}N_c\right)$$

with the three-dimensional Gaussian:

$$\begin{pmatrix} N_a \\ N_b \\ N_c \end{pmatrix} \sim N\left(\begin{pmatrix} 0 \\ 0 \\ 0 \end{pmatrix}, \begin{pmatrix} \sigma_a^2 & \sigma_a\sigma_b\rho_{ab} & \sigma_a\sigma_c\rho_{ac} \\ \sigma_a\sigma_b\rho_{ab} & \sigma_b^2 & \sigma_b\sigma_c\rho_{bc} \\ \sigma_a\sigma_c\rho_{ac} & \sigma_b\sigma_c\rho_{bc} & \sigma_c^2 \end{pmatrix}\right)$$

The calibration of the model is performed using long-term estimates (see Table 1). For mean return and volatility on stocks, bonds and TIPS, we have used Dimson *et al* (2002) 1900–2000 estimates; for volatility on TIPS, and for the correlation matrix, we have used Kothari and Shanken (2004) 1953–2000 estimates.[3]

Table 1 Long-term parameter estimates

Correlation	Stocks	Bonds	TIPS
Stocks	1		
Bonds	0.24		
TIPS	−0.05	0.52	1
Mean	10.4%	5.8%	4.3%
Volatility	16.5%	8.5%	6.58%

On the liability side, in an attempt to focus on a stylised institutional investor, we take the return on liabilities to be equal to the return on inflation-indexed bonds to which we add 300 basis points. This is because most institutional investors' liabilities are impacted by two main risk factors, inflation and interest rates. As a result, in our model, liabilities are perfectly correlated with return on TIPS. In practice, TIPS are certainly the asset class that exhibits the highest correlation with liabilities, even though the correlation is not perfect due to the presence of a number of extraneous sources of risk beyond inflation and interest rates.

The relative expected shortfall is then given as:

$$SF(0) = -\frac{1}{n}\sum_{s=1}^{10,000}\left(\frac{R_{PF,t}^{s} - L_{T}^{s}}{L_{T}^{s}} \cdot 1_{\{R_{PF,T}^{s} - L_{T}^{s} < 0\}}\right)$$

where the exponent s denotes the scenario and n is the number of scenarios yielding deficits after 10 years:

$$n = \sum_{s=1}^{10,000}\left(1_{\{R_{PF,T}^{s} - L_{T}^{s} < 0\}}\right)$$

ALLOCATION TO HEDGE FUNDS IN THE CONTEXT OF SURPLUS OPTIMISATION

There are two possible approaches that lead to the inclusion of hedge funds in an ALM context.

A first approach consists of considering hedge funds as an *additional* asset class that can be added to stocks and bonds in a surplus optimisation ALM exercise. This approach, however, faces a number of conceptual and technical difficulties. First, from a technical standpoint, it must be recognised that, in spite of the recent progress of academic literature (eg, Fung and Hsieh, 2002 or Agarwal and Naik, 2004), there are not yet any truly satisfying models for representing the dynamics of hedge fund returns that can be used in an ex-ante Monte Carlo simulation approach. This technical difficulty can be somewhat mitigated by the introduction of non-parametric bootstrapping techniques that allow one to generate a multitude of scenarios based on the random sampling of some history of hedge fund returns. This latter solution is not fully satisfactory, however, as it remains strongly sample-dependent. Moreover, and perhaps more importantly, the afore-mentioned approach to hedge fund investing in an ALM context is implicitly based upon the assumption that hedge funds can be treated as a coherent asset class in an ALM stochastic simulation exercise. This is certainly not satisfying from a conceptual standpoint, and a strong case can be made that hedge funds do not constitute a homogeneous new asset class, but rather a set of very diverse investment strategies.

Because of all these reasons, we advocate a competing approach that does not treat hedge funds as an *addition*, but rather as a *complement* to traditional asset classes (stocks and bonds). This alleviates the concern over ex-ante modelling of hedge fund returns: hedge funds only enter the surplus optimisation exercise through the impact they have on risk parameter estimates for stocks and bonds.[4]

Previous research (eg, Amenc *et al*, 2005) has actually shown that some hedge fund strategies mix well with either stocks or bonds in terms of risk reduction benefits, where risk is measured not only in terms of portfolio volatility, but also in terms of impact on higher moments of portfolio distribution. In order to take this diversification into account, we follow the suggestion in Amenc *et al* (2005) to first select the strategies that allow for the optimal risk reduction benefits and then optimise the allocation so as to generate the highest possible reduction in risk. They show that adding 5% to 35% of a suitably designed portfolio of hedge funds (labelled *equity diversifier*) to stocks reduces the volatility of that asset class by 5% to 37%. The respective risk reduction for bonds

Table 2 Evolution of volatility of stocks and bonds as a function of the proportion allocated to hedge funds in the stock and bond portfolios

	0% HF (%)	5% HF (%)	15% HF (%)	25% HF (%)	35% HF (%)
Stocks	16.50	15.62	13.75	11.99	10.34
Bonds	8.50	7.98	7.21	6.70	6.18
TIPS	6.58	6.58	6.58	6.58	6.58

yielded 6% to 27% when a suitably designed portfolio (labelled bond diversifier) is used.

Below, we model the introduction of hedge funds in a surplus optimisation context through the impact in terms of reduction of the volatility parameter for stocks and bonds. Based on estimates from Amenc *et al* (2005), we obtain the corresponding parameter (σ) estimate (see Table 2) as a function of the portion of hedge funds added to the traditional asset classes, which we use in the surplus optimisation exercise.

It should be noted that we have chosen not to consider the impact in terms of expected returns in the context of this surplus optimisation exercise. While the addition of hedge funds to a stock or to a bond portfolio is likely to have an impact on performance, the alpha benefits of hedge funds are not robust enough to be incorporated in a long-term allocation exercise.

For each of these parameter values, we created 10,000 scenarios and ran the same optimisation problem as in the previous section. For the optimal portfolio allocation as well as the benefits in terms of relative expected shortfall and probability of extreme losses we obtained the results in Table 3.

From these numbers, we learn that the introduction of hedge funds allows for a significant improvement of the risk management process in an ALM context. For example, introducing 25% of hedge funds in the stock and bond allocation portions of the investor's portfolio allows for a decrease of 7.82% of the expected shortfall. The impact is even more spectacular with a focus on extreme risks, as the introduction of 25% of hedge funds in the stock/bond allocation allows for a 27.02% decrease in the probability of a shortfall greater than 25% (ie, a deficit worse than 75%).

Table 3 Evolution of optimal asset allocation, expected relative shortfall and probability of a shortfall greater than 25% as a function of the proportion allocated to hedge funds in the stock and bond portfolios

	Stocks (%)	Bonds (%)	TIPS (%)	Exp. relat. shortfall (%)	Benefit of HFs (%)	Prob (SF > 25%) (%)	Benefit of HFs (%)
0% HF	15.71	29.11	55.19	17.81	0	19.58	0
5% HF	16.93	24.90	58.17	17.57	1.36	18.66	4.70
15% HF	18.24	29.20	52.55	17.04	4.36	17.09	12.72
25% HF	27.83	18.39	53.78	16.42	7.82	14.29	27.02
35% HF	32.89	14.49	52.62	15.66	12.09	11.89	39.27

Table 4 Evolution of effective allocation to hedge funds in the global portfolio as a function of the proportion allocated to hedge funds in the stock and bond segments

	Stocks (%)	Bonds (%)	TIPS (%)	Hedge funds (%)
0% HF	15.71	29.11	55.19	0.00
5% HF	16.09	23.66	58.17	2.09
15% HF	15.51	24.82	52.55	7.12
25% HF	20.88	13.79	53.78	11.56
35% HF	21.38	9.42	52.62	16.58

A 25% allocation to hedge funds might be perceived as unusually high. It should be noted, however, that the implicit introduction of hedge funds has been carried out only for bonds and stocks, and not for TIPS. Consequently, the effective amount invested to hedge funds is lower than mentioned in the upper tables (5–35%). According to the obtained portfolios, the effective allocation to hedge funds is described in Table 4. For example, introducing 25% hedge funds in the stock and bond portions of the portfolios, only leads to a very reasonable 11.56% of the total funds allocated to hedge funds.

Summarises the relative benefits in terms of the expected relative shortfall and the probability of extreme losses.

Overall, these results strongly suggest that, when added to bonds and stocks, suitably designed portfolios of hedge funds can allow for significant benefits in an ALM context, that can be

Figure 1 Improvement of expected relative shortfall and probability of a shortfall greater than 25% as a function of the effective proportion allocated to hedge funds

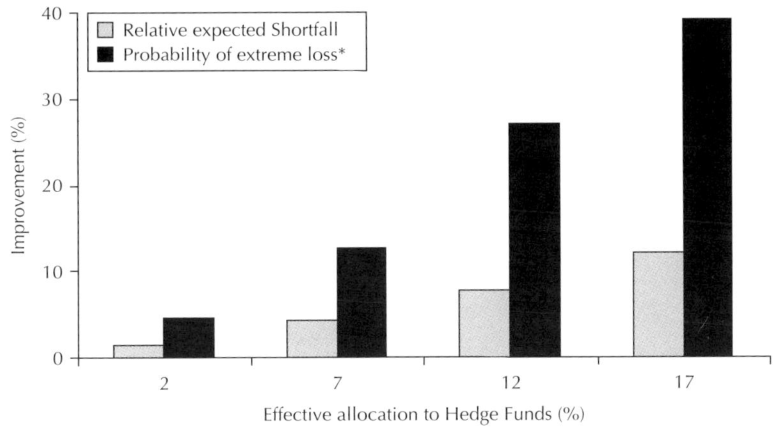

measured in terms of the reduction of the expected mismatch between assets and liabilities. This impact is more spectacular when the relevant objective turns to extreme risks. Perhaps our most important finding is that even limited levels of investment in hedge funds allow for a significant decrease in extreme risks. In fact, we show that the probability of extreme deficits (value of the assets falling below 75% of the value of liabilities) can be reduced by as much as 50% by allocating not more than 20% to hedge funds.

CONCLUSION

While most institutional investors are looking into hedge funds as a possible solution to the challenges posed by asset liability management in the presence of serious concerns over the size of the equity and bond premium and the associated risks, very little is known on how to include these alternative investment styles in an ALM context. This study provides evidence for the contribution of hedge funds in a surplus optimisation context. To this end, what we have proposed is a pragmatic approach that does not treat hedge funds as an *addition*, but rather as a *complement* to traditional asset classes (stocks and bonds) that alleviates the concern over modelling of hedge fund return distribution and parameter estimation. Our conclusion is that suitably designed hedge fund portfolios can be particularly attractive when the objective of optimising expected returns is constrained to meeting liabilities. This is due to hedge funds' benefits in terms of diversification properties, related to their appealing behaviours in terms of impact on tail-distribution and the extreme risks of stock and bond portfolios.

1 It has recently been shown that financial products that offer non-linear return profiles are particularly useful in an ALM context (see eg Draper and Shimko, 1993).
2 Finally, and for the sake of completeness, it is appropriate to mention non-linear risk-profiling management techniques, the goal of which is to provide a compromise between a risk-free and return-free approach on the one hand, and a risky approach that does not allow the liability constraints to be guaranteed on the other (see, in particular, Leibowitz and Weinberger (1982a,b) for the contingent optimisation technique or Amenc *et al* (2004) for a generalisation in terms of a dynamic core-satellite approach).
3 For stocks, we have used data on world markets. For bonds, because of the impact of high inflation period in some European countries in the vicinity of the Second World War, we have focused on the US estimate, and have added a 0.4% credit spread to the 2.1% real rate plus 3.3% inflation estimate. For the return on TIPS, we used the US inflation rate (3.3%) plus the real short-term rate (1%), in the absence of a reliable estimate of long-term risk premium for that asset class.
4 Because the *raison d'être* of TIPS is to be as correlated as possible with liabilities, we do not see it as desirable to include hedge funds within the TIPS allocation. In other words, the introduction of hedge funds is motivated by the reduction of risk related to investment in the risky – in an ALM sense, that is with respect to liabilities-asset classes (ie, stocks and bonds).

REFERENCES

Amenc, N., F. Goltz, and L. Martellini, 2005, "Hedge Funds from the Institutional Investor's Perspective", in G. Gregoriou, N. Papageorgiou, G. Hübner, and F. Rouah, *Hedge Funds: Insights in Performance Measurement, Risk Analysis, and Portfolio Allocation* (Chichester, UK: John Wiley).

Amenc, N., L. Martellini, and P. Malaise, 2004, "Revisiting Core-Satellite Investing – A Dynamic Model of Relative Risk Management", *Journal of Portfolio Management*, **31(1),** pp 64–75.

Agarwal, V. and N. Naik, 2004, "Risk and Portfolio Decisions involving Hedge Fund", *Review of Financial Studies*, **17(1)**, 63–98.

Credit Suisse First Boston, 2003, "The Magic of Pension Accounting, Part II", *Equity Research Report*, 15 October.

Dimson, E., P. Marsh, and M. Staunton, 2002, *Triumph of the Optimists* (Princeton, NJ: Princeton University Press).

Draper, D. and D. Shimko, 1993, "On the Existence of Redundant Securities", *University of Southern California Working Paper.*

Fung, B. and D. Hsieh, 1997, "Empirical Characteristics of Dynamic Trading Strategies: The Case of Hedge Funds", *Review of Financial Studies*, **10**, 275–302.

Kothari, S. P. and J. Shanken, 2004, "Asset Allocation with Inflation-Protected Bonds", *Financial Analyst Journal*, **60(1)**, pp 54–70.

Leibowitz, M. and A. Weinberger, 1982a, "Contingent Immunization – Part I: Risk Control Procedures", *Financial Analysts Journal*, pp 17–31, November–December.

Leibowitz, M. and A. Weinberger, 1982b, "Contingent Immunization – Part II: Problem Areas", *Financial Analysts Journal*, pp 35–50, January–Februar.

Martellini, L., P. Priaulet, and S. Priaulet, 2003, *Fixed-Income Securities – Valuation, Risk Management and Portfolio Strategies* (Chichester: John Wiley & Sons).

Mulvey, J., F. Fabozzi, W. Pauling, K. Simsek, and Z. Zhang, 2005, "Modernizing the Defined-Benefit Pension System", *Journal of Portfolio Management*, **31(2)**, pp 73–82.

Siegel, L. and B. Waring, 2004, "TIPS, 'The Dual Duration and the Pension Plan' ", *Financial Analysts Journal*, **60(5)**, pp 52–64.

Standard Life Investments, 2003, "Bridging the Pensions Gap", *Global Bytes*, can be downloaded at http://uk.standardlifeinvestments.com/content/strategy/strategy_index.html

Watson Wyatt, 2003, Global Asset Study (ongoing); as cited by "Finanz und Wirtschaft" (28/01/2004), can be downloaded at http://www.finanzinfo.ch

25

Portable Alpha – Separation and Recombination of Alpha and Beta

Georg Wessling

Harcourt Investment Consulting AG

INTRODUCTION

The so-called portable alpha concept has received a lot of attention recently. Initially developed by traditional long-only asset managers, the concept is now increasingly applied by hedge funds and funds of hedge funds. This chapter will first describe the theoretical foundations of the concept. Second, it will discuss the alpha potential in traditional long-only asset management and in hedge fund management. Finally, it will point out how the portable alpha concept could be utilised.

THEORETICAL FOUNDATION

The differentiation between alpha and beta has its foundation in the Capital Asset Pricing Model (CAPM) which was developed by William Sharpe in the early 1960s.[1] This section will recapitulate the findings of the CAPM along with its extensions. Based on this academic work it will explain how – from a theoretical standpoint – alpha and beta can be separated and recombined.

SHARPE'S CAPM

CAPM explains the relationship between the price of an asset and its sensitivity to an asset class. The basic idea behind the CAPM is that in a market equilibrium investors are only compensated for systematic risk. On the other hand unsystematic or idiosyncratic risk earns no return because it can be eliminated by investing in a larger number of securities. In Sharpe's CAPM beta is the measure for the systematic risk and is defined as follows:

$$\beta_i = \frac{Cov(r_i, r_M)}{\sigma_M^2}$$

with

β_i	beta of security i;
$Cov(r_i,r_M)$	covariance between the returns of security i and the returns of the market portfolio M;
σ_M^2	variance of the returns of the market portfolio M.

The expected (excess) return of a security i is then defined by the following formula:

$$E(r_i) - r_f = \beta_i (E(r_M) - r_f)$$

with

r_f	return of a risk free asset
$E(r_i)$	expected return of security i
$E(r_M)$	expected return of the market portfolio M

The CAPM is based on some strong assumptions (asset markets are in equilibrium; investors have homogeneous beliefs about means and variances and select mean-variance efficient portfolios). If these assumptions hold the market portfolio is the optimal portfolio to invest in. But if the assumptions do not hold securities returns can deviate from the expected returns and investors can generate an extra return by deviating from the market portfolio.

In an extension to Sharpe's CAPM, Jensen (1968) has defined alpha as a measure for the risk-adjusted return of a portfolio which deviates from the market portfolio. The alpha can be identified with the following regression equation:

$$r_{P,t} - r_{f,t} = \alpha_P + \beta_P (r_{M,t} - r_{f,t}) + \varepsilon_P$$

with

α_P	alpha of portfolio P
ε_P	noise term with a mean of zero

Alpha measures the excess return of a portfolio which cannot be explained by its sensitivity to the market (β). The noise term represents any unsystematic or idiosyncratic risk which does not add an additional return.

Many portfolios are exposed to more than one market or more than one risk factor. Therefore the regression equation has to be extended to a multi-market/multi-factor model:

$$r_{P,t} - r_{f,t} = \alpha_{P,t} + \sum_{m,n} \beta_P^{m,n} (r_{m,t} - r_{n,t}) + \varepsilon_P$$

where $(r_m - r_n)$ can represent any systematic risk premium.

The models discussed so far all imply a constant market or risk factor exposure. But asset managers try to add value through market timing as well. Treynor and Mazuy (1966) were the first to propose the following regression equation to analyse the timing effect:

$$r_{P,t} = \alpha_P + \beta_P r_{M,t} + \gamma_P r_{M,t}^2 + \varepsilon_P$$

with

γ_P market timing ability of portfolio P

The square of the third term turns negative values to positive ones. Therefore, a positive gamma implies that the manager of the portfolio can generate a positive return also in negative market environments. Combining Treynor and Mazuy's (1966) approach with the multi-factor regression equation one obtains:

$$r_{P,t} - r_{f,t} = \alpha_P + \sum_{m,n} \beta_P^{m,n} (r_{m,t} - r_{n,t}) + \sum_{m,n} \gamma_P^{m,n} (r_{m,t} - r_{n,t})^2 + \varepsilon_P$$

Following the CAPM and its enhancements the return of a portfolio has three main sources:

- the alpha, ie, the added value due to stock picking;
- the beta, ie, the return due to systematic exposure to any risk factor; and
- the gamma, ie, the added value due to market timing.[2]

In practice it is not always easy to differentiate between returns generated from alpha, beta and gamma. This is especially true for hedge funds which have exposures not only to traditional risk factors like stocks, bonds and currencies but also to various non-traditional risk factors like commodities, (il)liquidity, volatility, event and insurance risks and so on.

Separation of alpha and beta

For a traditional, single asset class mutual fund the separation of alpha and beta is straightforward. If we take as an example an actively managed equity portfolio the equity market beta may be hedged out of the portfolio by going short the equity index. A common way to do this is through a total return swap which exchanges the total return of the equity index against the risk-free rate (Libor). If the beta of the equity portfolio is equal to one the long-only portfolio has the following return:

$$\begin{aligned} r_{equity\ long\text{-}only} &= \alpha_{equity\ long\text{-}only} + r_f + \beta_{equity\ long\text{-}only}(r_{equity\ index} - r_f) \\ &= \alpha_{equity\ long\text{-}only} + r_{equity\ index} \end{aligned}$$

By combining the long-only portfolio with a total return swap we get:

$$\begin{aligned} r_{separated\ alpha} &= \alpha_{equity\ long\text{-}only} + r_{equity\ index} \underbrace{-r_{equity\ index} + r_f}_{total\ return\ swap} \\ &= \alpha_{equity\ long\text{-}only} + r_f \end{aligned}$$

This alpha-only return can also be considered to be the return of a market neutral hedge fund.

$$r_{hedge\ fund} = \alpha_{hedge\ fund} + r_f$$

A main difference between the long-only fund and the hedge fund is that the volatility of the hedge fund's alpha is usually much higher than the volatility of the alpha of a long-only fund.[3] While both the long-only manager as well as the hedge fund manager can amplify the volatility of their alpha by increasing the size of certain positions and by running a more concentrated portfolio only the hedge fund manager can utilise leverage to multiply his alpha.[4]

The fact that both mutual funds as well as hedge funds usually don't maintain a constant beta to any market is a first challenge in separating alpha and beta. Rather the funds try to add value through market timing. If the respective manager has timing skills we argue that this timing alpha should not be hedged out. Instead the swap should only eliminate the (expected) average beta exposure, denoted by $\hat{\beta}_{fund}$:

$$\begin{aligned} r_{separated\ alpha} &= \alpha_{fund} + \beta_{fund}(r_M - r_f) + r_f \underbrace{- \hat{\beta}_{fund}(r_M - r_f)}_{total\ return\ swap} \\ &= \alpha_{fund} + \underbrace{(\beta_{fund} - \hat{\beta}_{fund})(r_M - r_f)}_{market\ timing\ alpha} + r_f \end{aligned}$$

Even more challenging are multi-asset class portfolios with changing asset class allocations. As already mentioned, hedge funds exhibit different traditional and non-traditional beta exposures which vary over time. In theory all undesirable risk can be hedged out, but the more exotic the risks, the more expensive the hedge may be. Therefore it may not be worthwhile hedging out all beta risk. The individual investor therefore has to exactly define which beta, $\hat{\beta}^{m,n}_{fund}$, should be hedged with a swap.

$$\begin{aligned} r_{separated\ alpha} &= \alpha_{fund} + \sum_{m,n} \beta^{m,n}_{fund}(r_m - r_n) + r_f \underbrace{- \sum_{m,n} \hat{\beta}^{m,n}_{fund}(r_m - r_n)}_{total\ return\ swap} \\ &= \alpha_{fund} + \sum_{m,n} (\beta^{m,n}_{fund} - \hat{\beta}^{m,n}_{fund})(r_m - r_n) + r_f \end{aligned}$$

Recombination of alpha and beta

In the same way as alpha and beta can be separated they can also be (re)combined. As a first example we take the alpha from the long-only equity fund and combine it with a bond index:[5]

$$\begin{aligned} r_{bond\ plus} &= \alpha_{equity\ long\text{-}only\ fund} + r_{equity\ index} \underbrace{- r_{equity\ index} + r_{bond\ index}}_{total\ return\ swap} \\ &= \alpha_{equity\ long\text{-}only\ fund} + r_{bond\ index} \end{aligned}$$

This simple two asset class portable alpha concept can be extended to any multi-asset class portable alpha concept:

$$\begin{aligned} r_{portable\ alpha} &= \alpha_{fund} + \sum_{m,n} \beta_{fund}^{m,n}(r_m - r_n) \\ &\quad + \underbrace{r_f - \sum_{m,n} \hat{\beta}_{fund}^{m,n}(r_m - r_n) + \sum_{o,p} \hat{\beta}_{fund}^{o,p}(r_o - r_p)}_{total\ return\ swap(s)} \\ &= \alpha_{fund} + \sum_{m,n} (\beta_{fund}^{m,n} - \hat{\beta}_{fund}^{m,n})(r_m - r_n) + \sum_{o,p} \hat{\beta}_{fund}^{o,p}(r_o - r_p) + r_f \end{aligned}$$

with

$\hat{\beta}_{fund}^{m,n}$ beta exposure hedged out of the portfolio
$\hat{\beta}_{fund}^{o,p}$ beta exposure transferred into the portfolio

The first return component of the portable alpha portfolio is the stock picking alpha generated by the alpha generating portfolio. The second return component is the value added by the alpha generating portfolio through market timing. Given the beta exposures maintained by the alpha generating portfolio and the beta exposure hedged out through the total return swap, the portable alpha portfolio may have a positive or negative net exposure to the different risk factors. A positive market timing return is generated if an overweighed (underweighted) risk factor is generating a positive (negative) return and vice versa. The final return component is the long beta exposure which is transferred into the portable alpha portfolio through the total return swap.

OPTIMAL ALPHA GENERATION

As has been shown alpha can be generated both in traditional mutual funds as well as in hedge funds. For an investor considering a portable alpha solution the question is which of these two fund types has the best foundations for optimal alpha generation. This section will elaborate how the different opportunity sets of hedge funds and mutual funds influence their alpha potential. In a second step the merits of multi-manager approaches are explained.

Different opportunity sets

If we compare mutual funds and hedge funds we find three important restrictions for mutual funds, where hedge funds are not restricted at all: mutual funds typically have to consider a limited investment universe, are not allowed to sell securities short or to use leverage.

To assess the consequences of these restrictions three funds are considered: one market neutral equity hedge fund and two equity mutual funds. One equity mutual fund has a low tracking error (enhanced index fund) whereas the other equity mutual fund has a high tracking error limit (aggressive equity fund). We assume that the three funds are managed by the same manager with the same skills (Information Ratio of 1.0)[6] and that the investment universe for all three funds is the S&P 500.[7]

For the hedge fund portfolio the manager will build long and short positions for a large number of S&P 500 stocks. It is assumed that the hedge fund portfolio holds in total 150% (as a percentage of the money invested in the hedge fund) of short positions and 150% of long positions. In aggregate the portfolio will be beta neutral to the S&P 500 and will have no sector and style exposure. The 150% long and short positions add up to a 300% gross exposure or a 3:1 leverage. As the short selling requires some borrowing costs we assume an adjusted information ratio of 0.9.

For the enhanced indexing portfolio the manager will build overweight and underweight positions for the same stocks as he built long and short positions in the hedge fund portfolio. But because of the short selling and leverage constraints the relative overweight and underweight to the S&P 500 will be small. The maximum underweight for each single stock is limited by the respective index weight.[8] It is assumed that the manager will limit the aggregate underweight positions to 10% also to control risk. As long as the portfolio is fully invested in stocks the aggregated overweight positions will also have to be 10%. Therefore the sum of the overweight and underweight positions relative to the S&P 500 is only 20%.

To increase the tracking error for the aggressive equity portfolio the manager has to increase the position size of some stocks and to reduce the overall number of positions in the portfolio. Let's assume he is investing only in his 50 favourite stocks. As the manager is not investing in 450 stocks of his investment universe the aggregated underweight positions relative to the S&P 500 can be quite significant.[9] The sum of the underweight (and overweight) positions is assumed to be 75%. The manager has to underweight stocks which

Table 1 Alpha potential of a market neutral hedge fund compared with two mutual funds

Fund	Sum of under- (short) and overweight (long) positions (%)	Tracking error (%)	Information ratio	Excess return (%)
Market Neutral Hedge Fund	300	15.0	0.9	13.5
Enhanced Indexing Mutual Fund	20	1.0	1.0	1.0
Aggressive Equity Mutual Fund	150	7.5	0.8	6.0

he overweighs in the enhanced indexing portfolio. It is therefore assumed that his information ratio is decreasing to 0.8.

Table 1 shows how the different investment approaches translate into different information ratios and into different excess returns. The tracking error for the hedge fund portfolio is equal to its volatility as the benchmark is the risk free return. It is assumed that the tracking error is 5% if the sum of under- (short) and overweight (long) positions is 100%.

The difference between the hedge fund performance and the mutual fund performance lies in the fact that the information ratio of the mutual fund decreases with increasing tracking error while the information ratio of the hedge funds keeps pretty stable. The reason behind this are the restrictions the mutual funds have to observe. Figure 1 generalises this finding: Whereas the risk-adjusted return of a hedge fund portfolio is scalable the risk-adjusted return of mutual funds is not.

The fundamental law of active management[10]

For an investor who is looking for added value with limited active risk the scalability of hedge fund returns seems to be negligible. In fact, it is not! If it is possible to find a number of hedge funds with the same investment talent but with uncorrelated excess returns we can build a portfolio of hedge funds (a fund of funds) with reduced risk and increased information ratio. The excess return of the fund of funds is defined as followed:

$$r_{fund\ of\ funds} - r_f = \sum_{i=1}^{N} w_i * (r_{hedge\ fund\ i} - r_f) = \sum_{i=1}^{N} w_i * \alpha_{hedge\ fund\ i}$$

Figure 1 Relationship between excess return and tracking error for hedge funds and mutual funds

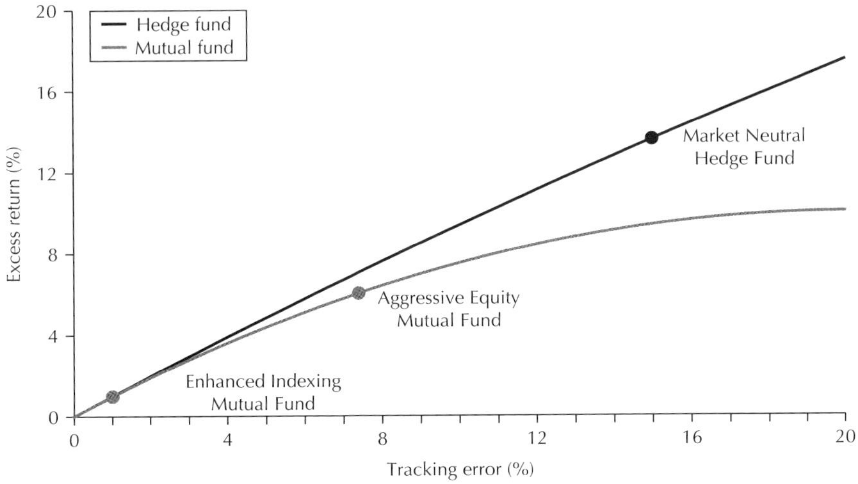

with

N number of underlying hedge funds

If we assume that all hedge funds, i, have the same alphas and are equally weighted this formula becomes:

$$r_{fund\ of\ funds} - r_f = \sum_{i=1}^{N} (1/N) * \alpha_{hedge\ fund\ i} = \alpha_{hedge\ fund\ i}$$

For the tracking error of the fund of funds we get:

$$\sigma(r_{fund\ of\ funds} - r_f) = \sigma\left[\sum_{i=1}^{N} w_i * (r_{hedge\ fund\ i} - r_f)\right]$$

$$= \sqrt{\sum_{i=1}^{N}\sum_{j=1}^{N} w_i * w_j * \sigma(r_{hedge\ fund\ i} - r_f) * \sigma(r_{hedge\ fund\ j} - r_f)\,\rho(r_{hedge\ fund\ i} - r_f;\ r_{hedge\ fund\ j} - r_f)}$$

If we assume that the returns of all hedge funds have the same volatility and are uncorrelated this formula becomes:

$$\sigma(r_{fund\ of\ funds} - r_f) = \sqrt{\sum_{i=1}^{N} (1/N)^2 * \sigma(r_{hedge\ fund\ i} - r_f)^2}$$

$$= \sqrt{(1/N)} * \sigma(\alpha_{hedge\ fund\ i} + \varepsilon_{hedge\ fund\ i})$$

Figure 2 Tracking error and information ratio subject to the number of managers

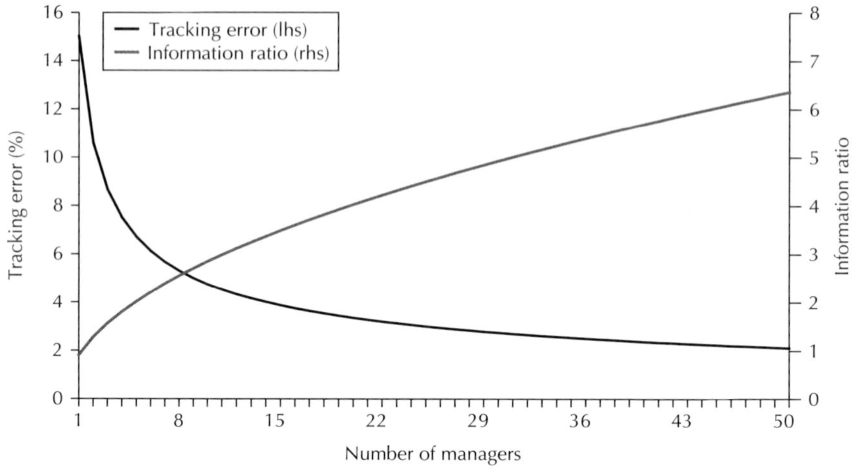

Now we can calculate the information ratio of the fund of funds:

$$IR_p = \frac{r_{fund\ of\ funds} - r_f}{\sigma(r_{fund\ of\ funds} - r_f)} = \sqrt{N} * \frac{\alpha_{hedge\ fund\ i}}{\sigma(\alpha_{hedge\ fund\ i} + \varepsilon_{hedge\ fund\ i})}$$
$$= \sqrt{N} * IR_{hedge\ fund\ i}$$

This means that the information ratio can be doubled with four uncorrelated hedge funds and the information ratio can be tripled with nine uncorrelated hedge funds and so forth. Figure 2 shows the effect graphically.

Given that the selected hedge funds are following a similar risk return profile as the one shown before (ie, expected excess return of 13.5% and volatility of 15%) the tracking error respective the volatility will be reduced from 15% to 5% with only nine funds. With excess return unchanged we reach an information ratio of 2.7. Even if we detract typical fund of funds fees of 1.0% (management fee) and 10.0% (performance fee) we keep an excess return of 11.25% with an information ratio of 2.25. Actually, the number of uncorrelated hedge funds which can be found is limited. Therefore the information ratio cannot be increased infinitely.

Of course the tracking error could also be reduced for a portfolio of enhanced indexing funds. But because the tracking error for a single enhanced indexing fund is already quite small the effect is less useful than in the case of the hedge funds. Furthermore, the costs of selecting and monitoring the enhanced indexing funds will have a higher impact on the excess return.

PRACTICAL IMPLEMENTATION

After the theoretical foundation and some thoughts on optimal alpha generation this section describes instruments that are used in practice to transfer alpha or beta and which types of portable alpha solutions are provided by financial intermediaries.

Instruments for alpha and beta transfer

In practice there are several instruments which could be used to separate and recombine alpha and beta. The most common instruments used are futures and swaps. Futures are standardised contracts traded on public exchanges. In the context of the portable alpha concept the most interesting ones are futures on bond and equity indices. These contracts are settled by cash delivery and the trader has to maintain a margin account with the clearing house. For a portable alpha portfolio which targets a 100% exposure to an equity index and which invests the money in a hedge fund portfolio this means that less than 100% of the nominal can be invested in the underlying (ie, 100% minus the required margin).[11] If losses occur on the futures position additional cash might be needed to maintain the margin. Additionally, futures allow only exposure to a limited number of markets. On the contrary futures usually comprise low costs and high liquidity.

A swap arrangement obligates two counterparties to exchange cash flows at one or more future dates. As swaps are not standardised the counterparties can agree to exchange each cash flow which can be well defined. Examples are:

- ❑ Libor;
- ❑ return of an equity index;
- ❑ return of a bond index;
- ❑ return of a hedge fund portfolio; and
- ❑ return of a liability portfolio.

The cash flows take place on a predefined frequency (monthly, quarterly, annually). Depending on the volatility of the respective index this can lead to more or less substantial cash flows. If the underlying portfolio is invested in liquid securities it might be easy to sell securities to the extent that cash is needed. But if the underlying is less liquid, as is usually the case for a hedge fund portfolio, some cash has to be held in reserve to serve cash settlement.[12] It has also to be taken into account that the counterparty for the swap might require collateral. The costs of swaps can differ substantially. They depend on the rating of the counterparty, on the replicability of the return the counterparty has to pay and on the quality of the collateral.

The use of a swap which exchanges a beta return for Libor is equivalent to the use of leverage. Therefore some portable alpha solutions might not be permitted for certain investors.

Classification of Portable Alpha solutions

As has been shown on pp 000–0 and 000–0 alpha and beta can be separated and recombined in many different ways. This section will explain four types of portable alpha solutions which are often found in practice.[13]

Alpha separation

In this solution the money is invested in one or several actively managed mutual funds. The beta coming along with the funds will be hedged out of the portfolio by using either futures or swaps. The investor receives as return the alpha plus the risk free return. This solution might be compared with a market neutral hedge fund.

Alpha transfer

In this solution money is invested in a portfolio which contains the desired beta exposures. The alpha is transferred to the portfolio from an alpha generating portfolio through a swap. The swap counterparty holds or replicates the alpha generating portfolio which for this solution is most likely a hedge fund or a fund of hedge funds. The investor receives from the swap counterparty the performance of the alpha generating portfolio in return for the

Libor. The advantage for the investor is that the existing beta portfolio can be kept and therefore transaction costs can be minimized. The disadvantage is that the swap might be quite expensive as the (fund of) hedge fund(s) might not be easy to replicate for the swap counterparty.

Standard beta transfer

The money is invested in an alpha generating portfolio which can be either an actively managed mutual fund or a (fund of) hedge fund(s). In the case of a mutual fund the return of the undesired beta is exchanged for the return of desired beta by either using futures or swaps. In the case of a hedge fund investment only the desired beta is transferred into the portfolio. The investors receive as return the alpha plus the desired beta. A product like this is an alternative to a traditional actively managed mutual fund. The alpha is typically transferred to an asset class where the generation of alpha is more difficult than in the asset class where the alpha is transferred from.

Customised beta transfer

Institutional investors who like pension funds which have to finance certain liabilities might be interested in more complex beta transfer. Let's first assume a pension fund which has defined a strategic asset allocation which allows it to match the liabilities with a high probability. Instead of investing the accumulated contributions and earnings along the strategic asset allocation the pension fund might invest the money in an alpha generating portfolio. This physical investment might be combined with a synthetic investment in the strategic asset allocation through a customised swap with an investment bank.

Alternatively we assume that a pension fund can match its liabilities through a total return swap with an investment bank. Instead of investing the accumulated contributions and earnings just in cash it could invest this money in an alpha generating portfolio. It pays the investment bank Libor and receives the liability cash flows.

To the extent the alpha generating portfolio generates alpha the pension fund might either increase the benefits or decrease the contributions.

CONCLUSION

Based on the CAPM and its extensions the basic idea behind the portable alpha concept is that the return of an actively managed portfolio can be dismantled into a return which is based on manager skills and a return which is based on systematic market exposure. These returns can be recombined in a way that each investor ends up with an allocation of alpha and beta which is optimal for his targets. Obviously, such optimal solutions are only feasible for large investors like pension funds. But also retail investors can invest in standard beta transfer products which potentially deliver better returns than standard mutual funds.

We also showed that hedge funds are better suited to generate alpha as they are not limited by certain regulations. Although the portable alpha concept was developed by traditional asset management it is believed that it unfolds its full potential only in the combination with hedge fund investments. Key for a success of a portable alpha product is always to find managers who are able to generate sustainable alpha.

1 Sharpe (1964).

2 Going forward we will denote all skill based returns (ie, stock picking and market timing) as alpha.

3 The same is true for the funds' beta. Whereas the beta of a long-only fund is typically close to one, the beta of a hedge fund can be both negative and significantly higher than one.

4 On pp 000–0 this aspect will be analysed in more detail.

5 This concept is usually called portable alpha. Literally speaking it is a portable beta concept because the beta is ported to the alpha generating portfolio and not the alpha to the beta portfolio. But you can also find solutions where the swap is exchanging the total return of a alpha generating portfolio against Libor and therefore porting alpha to a beta portfolio. See also pp 000–0.

6 The information ratio is usually defined as $IR_P = \frac{r_P - r_B}{\sigma(r_P - r_B)}$ with:

$r_P - r_B$ excess return, ie, difference between the return of a portfolio, P, and the return of a benchmark, B;

$\sigma(r_P - r_B)$ tracking error, ie, standard deviation of the excess return.

The information ratio sets the excess return of a portfolio over a benchmark return in relation to the tracking error. If one assumes that the beta of a long-only fund to the benchmark portfolio is 1 and that the benchmark for a market neutral hedge fund is the risk free rate we can convert the formula in the following way:

$$IR_P = \frac{r_P - r_B}{\sigma(r_P - r_B)} = \frac{\alpha_P}{\sigma(\alpha_P + \varepsilon_P)}$$

7 In this case the hedge fund manager does not use the advantage of an unlimited investment universe.

8 As of 29th June, 2006, only 15 stocks had an index weight of more than 1% which together amounted for 25.1% of the portfolio. On the other hand, almost 250 stocks had an index weight of less than 0.1% and the smallest 250 components of the index had an aggregate weight of only 13.4%. Source: www.indexarb.com, 1st July, 2006.

9 The largest 450 components of the index have an aggregated weight of almost 99%.

10 This title refers to Grinold (1989) who analysed the relationship between investment skill and number of independent investment decisions.

11 Alternatively the margin could be financed with a credit line.

12 If a cash line is available it could be used to bridge finance the cash settlement until the underlying investments can be liquidated.

13 For a similar classification see Goricki *et al* (2006).

REFERENCES

Amenc, N., P. Malaise, and L. Martellini, 2005, "From Delivering to the Packaging of Alpha", EDHEC Working Paper.

Arnott, R. D., 2002, "Risk Budgeting and Portable Alpha", *The Journal of Investing*, **11**, pp 15–22.

Fung, W. and D. A. Hsieh, 2004, "Extracting Portable Alpha from Equity Long/Short Hedge Funds", *Journal of Investment Management*, **2**, pp 1–19.

Goricki, W., D. Soehnholz, M. Storr, and V. Weber, 2006, "Portable Alpha: Hedge Fund Index Based Alpha Overlay as the most Appropriate Solution?" Working paper Feri Institutional Advisors, Bad Homburg/Germany, February 24.

Grinold, R., 1989, "The Fundamental Law of Active Management", *Journal of Portfolio Management*, **15**, pp 30–7.

InvestHedge, 2005, "Mosers Opts for Diversified Separation of Alpha & Beta", *InvestHedge*, November, pp 14–15.

InvestHedge Roundtable Discussion, 2005, "Portable Alpha: The Answer to Institutional Investors' Needs?", June.

Jensen, M. C., 1968, "The Performance of Mutual Funds in the Period 1945–1964", *Journal of Finance*, **23**, pp 389–416.

O'Hara, N., 2005, "Portable Alpha and Hedge Funds – A Case Study", *Futures Industry*, Sep/Oct, pp 24–7.

Sharpe, W., 1964, "Capital Asset Prices: A Theory of Market Equilibrium", *Journal of Finance*, **19**, pp 425–42.

Treynor, J. L. and K. Mazuy, 1966, "Can Mutual Funds Outguess the Market", *Harvard Business Review*, **44**, pp 131–6.

value of an investment based on conclusions drawn from a fundamental analysis of a company's assets and business model. While the means of applying an activist investment programme remain beyond the financial wherewithal of the average investor, the basic concept is one that should ring clearly with all shareholders. The second section is a discussion of the basic philosophy that drives an active investment strategy and a consideration of the dynamics involved in the engagement of an underperforming management by a well-prepared active investor. The third section is an operational journal of three of the author's investment projects.

THE PHILOSOPHY OF ACTIVE VALUE INVESTING

An understanding of the philosophical underpinnings of an investment strategy is critical in assessing its methodology and the ultimate success or failure of the strategy as an investment discipline. In order to properly consider the active investment approach, the reader must first do away with any preconceived notions, whether fueled by the financial press or even the apparent behaviour of activists themselves, that the strategy is defined by confrontation for the sake of short term gain, and understand that activism is indeed a long term discipline. This common misconception is fueled in part by confusion over the function of the engagement process. The activist engages management not to disrupt a long term business plan, but to create one that will ultimately deliver a greater value to shareholders by more fully utilising the assets and businesses under management's control. A call for the disposal of assets for example, is not predicated on the desire for a short-term payout, but rather on the need to redirect a floundering management to a path that will allow shareholders to benefit from the profit stream of a more cohesive blend of assets.

A good portion of the image that comes to mind at the mention of the words "activist investor" is a consequence of their characterisation by managements who view themselves as under siege by "insurgent shareholders", "rabble rousers", "raiders" or whatever needlessly shrill image they choose to anchor their initial resistance to a vocal shareholder. The reflex reaction by managements to recoil at the sound of a shareholder's voice is the immediate hurdle that an active investor faces. Too often, managements and shareholders who are in discussions over the future course of a company's direction, are portrayed as rival factions, simply competing for dominance over a company's board or seeking to unilaterally control the future of a business plan. This is precisely the type of overly dramatic description, usually concocted by someone outside of the discussions, that actually serves to poison the well of relations between shareholders and management. The activist should not seek to initially antagonise management any more than a management should initially seek to silence a shareholder, and any communication with management must be based on a comprehensive and expertly researched understanding of the business at hand. Equally thorough must be the presentation provided by the activist, as it will serve as the foundation for all future discussions with management. Ideally, after an initial meeting, the ensuing weeks and months will produce a useful exchange of ideas and an honest consideration by management of the activist's proposal. This is activism in its purest and unfortunately, least common form, for the state of relations between shareholders and management, while improving, has not reached the level of cooperation that would make such a sequence of events the norm.

Often, shareholders who seek to realign a management's focus are required to present their proposals in a more forceful manner than they had initially hoped, and the activist has no shortage of tools at his disposal to, if necessary, present his ideas directly to the shareholders. This is the point at which the discussion may slip into public view. No activist should ever seek out a public conflict with management as it creates a costly distraction for both the active investor and the target company, but by no means should an activist ever abandon an investment simply because there appears to be a need for this type of approach. The guiding principle must be a determination to table a proposal based not on animosity or a childish war of wills with a management, but on the validity of the idea and the right of the shareholders to participate, to the extent that they are permitted under the law, in the corporation's future direction.

An activist who seeks to challenge management in an open forum needs expert legal counsel, especially in jurisdictions outside of the US, where the regulatory environment, if not fully understood, can result in embarrassing and possibly fatal missteps. Conducting an engagement in a manner that is in keeping with the regulatory requirements of the relevant jurisdiction is part of the professionalism that is required of an activist. An activist needs to do more than simply catch the attention of management, he needs to hold it, and the surest way to do that is to establish, through the quality of his presentation, a posture that demands attention. Surely the corporate world would not benefit from, nor listen to a parade of amateurish portfolio managers seeking to inundate managements with their latest "off the cuff" ideas to boost a stock price. Such managers are simply a distraction and muddy the waters for the serious activist; frankly the investment community would be better off without them.

The essential validity of an idea works to focus not only management, but also the shareholder community. This common focus can produce the single most useful element in persuading a management to act: alliances. The formation of alliances among like-minded investors presents a recalcitrant management with a more powerful block of investors who can use their considerable voting power to great effect. In forming alliances both in the US and abroad, an activist must, again, take great care to heed the advice of counsel to ensure that no communication or action results in the allegations of concert-action violations that are frequently leveled at allied activists, particularly in European jurisdictions. Again, a properly researched proposal and course of action will prevent such missteps.

Activists who are challenging management often resort to a board nominee who, if accepted by the shareholders, will provide a voice for an alternative approach in any boardroom discussion. Multiple nominees can serve the function, if necessary, of actually forcing a management into action by effectively blocking the continuation of an undesirable business plan. The unfortunate necessity of, at times, resorting to hostile action toward a board of directors, is one that merits further examination. Why does an activist face such hurdles when presenting, as a shareholder, a proposal that simply provides an alternative voice to a company's management? Why do so many managements refuse to accept the voice of their shareholder base? The answer lies in the irrational perception of an active shareholder base as a threat to a company and its management.

Managements who resist the involvement of an activist shareholder are in fact, unwittingly, turning their backs on a valuable asset that is at the disposal of any management. This asset is the collective sensibility and expertise of a group of professional money managers who, having thoroughly studied a company's balance sheet, have become believers in its potential profitability. The adversarial tone of many encounters is quite simply, misplaced. The remedy will most likely not be found in one or two instances of successful active engagements, but in a prolonged period during which newly empowered and more vocal hedge funds and other significant stakeholders, spurred on by a ravenous private equity community, succeed in improving the fortunes of the companies in which they invest and in enriching the long term shareholders who have entrusted their capital to management.

The concept of effective management must be expanded to include a willingness to hear the alternative views of those shareholders who wish to present them. It is the success of the activist that will alter the perceptions of management, eventually dispel any sense of vocal shareholders as adversaries of the corporation, and prove that a vocal shareholder base can be an asset in improving the efficiency of management. As the most effectively managed companies are logically the repositories for great sums of investor capital, one can easily envision the knock-on effect of improved management across the corporate landscape of any geographic locale, necessarily increasing competition, and drawing capital to that region. Activism is, at its core, a demand for efficiency; capital will inevitably find the efficient management.

Of course, not all countries receive the active investor in the same manner, nor do all require their presence with the same urgency. The US and the UK for example, while possessing no shortage of companies requiring improved management, are policed by fairly robust regulatory bodies that prevent some of the more glaring governance malfunctions commonly found in European markets. While in the US there has been a relaxation of regulations that now allows large shareholders to more easily work together in approaching management, and while there is certainly no shortage of activist investors, the European markets, in particular Germany and France, greet the activist manager with a landscape that resembles, in terms of shareholder rights, the US in the 1950s. With the additional challenges that these countries present, comes a greater profit margin to the activist manager with a keen sense of value and a willingness to pursue it in even the least hospitable environments.

As capital markets around the world improve their infrastructures, laws, regulations, and governance structures, more investment managers are beginning to take stakes in under-performing companies and are pushing for reform. Continental Europe is becoming an increasingly interesting forum for active initiatives and as successes increase in this realm, the pressure will only become more intense at under-performing companies.

There are a number of structural reasons why Europe is becoming increasingly attractive for active investors. It is widely acknowledged in financial circles that an effective guarantor of good corporate governance and effective management oversight is an unfettered market for corporate control. Corporate executives who consistently destroy value in a free market are replaced by good managers, often through takeovers. Potential bids are a 'Sword of Damocles' dangling over incompetent managers. And further on, a unified takeover code covering all members of the EU was meant to ease cross-border acquisitions and help the rationalisation of many of Europe's fragmented industries. Frits Bolkestein fought valiantly during his tenure as the EU's Internal Market Commissioner to pass legislation that would enshrine such a code and prevent managements from entrenching themselves with measures to deter takeover. But this effort was undermined by German members of the European Parliament eager to sustain Lower Saxony's obtuse law protecting Volkswagen from a takeover. The scheme eventually adopted by the EU in 2005, is a toothless hodgepodge that allows countries to determine individually if anti-takeover measures can be applied locally.

Internal Market Commissioner McCreevey says, "The European Union is threatening the French government, which is planning to block foreign takeovers in specified industries, indicating that the proposal would crimp competition and economic growth."[1] What this type of action creates is a parochial market for corporate control that is preventing cross-border rationalisation of various sectors across Continental Europe. While this is unfortunate for strategic buyers, it is providing a windfall for financial buyers – private equity, which has invested pools of approximately €250 billion in equity seeking acquisitions across the Continent. These are the natural allies of active investors, who, when they act as lightning rods or catalysts surrounding a particular listed company, will often play into the hands of a private equity or LBO group. The absence of strategic buyers because of the aforementioned impediments to cross-border activity thus lays the groundwork for active investing in Continental Europe.

Secondly, there is a serious question of relative value between Continental Europe and the US. In the latter, we have a situation where premiums over book value predominate. In Europe, there are substantial discounts to book or net asset values. Companies in Germany and Switzerland have been over-reserving and hiding assets for over 200 years. Also, in the US, there are more lawyers than citizens. The US is therefore a very litigious environment and poses a threat to any activist intervention. This is not the case in Europe, where lawsuits are not yet part of the culture, and can involve serious penalties unless the charges have merit. Also, on the legal front, resolutions proposed at annual meetings in Europe are binding resolutions. In the US they are strictly voluntary, in most instances. Therefore, it is much more serious and much more dangerous for management to face shareholders at annual or special meetings in Europe.

Thirdly, a number of European countries do not have adequate pension schemes. One hears that in most countries 40–50% of the total equity within a country is owned by Anglo-Saxon portfolio managers. Why not? Who else would buy the shares, in the absence of local pension funds? America's ERISA system and the British pension funds are replacing the non-existent local funds. What this means is that there is a captive audience when an activist appears on the scene to create value for a particular company. This captive audience will naturally vote and may even increase its stake as it follows the machinations of the active investor.

Fourth, because of Europe's archaic voting system, which requires shares to be blocked (immobilised) in order to be able to vote at a shareholder's meeting, the man on the street simply will not vote. Only the professionals and the aforementioned Anglo-Saxon portfolio managers will vote. The resulting quorum at most annual meetings is therefore in the range of 40–45% of the shares. An active investor who has done his homework should not have too much trouble in forming a coalition with 25% of the shares,

Figure 1 An operational journal

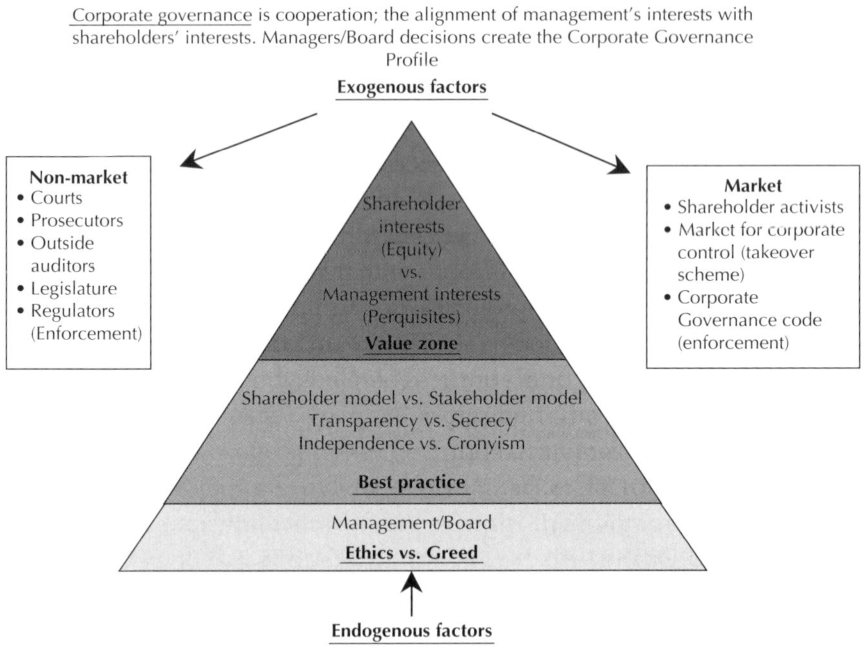

which assures him a fairly easy victory in almost every circumstance. The local institutions simply do not have the firepower to overcome the foreign, non-local interests.

In Figure 1 the reader will note three areas that define the corporate governance structure of the modern corporation. At the base is "Ethics." This is not an area where we concentrate because we assume that if the managers of a corporation have not been raised properly, there is nothing we can do about it. You cannot teach people ethics. The next area above "Ethics" is called "Best Practice." This is also not an area for active investing. We leave it to the CalPERS of this world with their Focus Lists to identify companies that have some issues with transparency, inappropriate corporate committee structure, director salaries, corporate jets, etc. The real issue for the active investor is what I call the "Value Zone," this is the area in which the rubber hits the road; i.e. where the value is truly created by aligning the incentives of management with the anticipation of shareholders. This is the real struggle that is occurring in Europe today between the owners of the business and its managers. This is defined as the principal-agent problem, which exists due to the separation of ownership and control of the private corporation. The agency problem exists in economics when "principals" who own an asset must delegate responsibility for it to "agents," whose stake, interests and understanding are different. Active investing then attempts to adequately harmonise the interests of both groups.

Identifying the "Value Gap"

Given the aforementioned background factors relevant to Europe, the critical element for the active investor in any given situation is to identify the "Value Gap." This gap or "spread" is the difference between the current market price and the unencumbered potential or expected restructured value of a particular company's shares. Four different types of analysis are used to arrive at an assessment of the value gap. First is obviously a fundamental analysis to determine what a more traditional value investor would call the "margin-of-safety." Also, it is this analysis that determines the strategic shortcomings or failures of a particular enterprise, which may be one of the reasons for the under-valuation. Second is a corporate governance analysis that attempts to determine the corporate governance breakdown that may have occurred. The third is a merger-arbitrage analysis, which seeks to establish the parameter of the value gap and the time element involved in yielding the return on investment and risk-reward calculations. Finally is a technical analysis that aids in determining the entry points, the potential accumulation strategy, and the formulation of an exit strategy. All of these factors point to the reasons for the under-valuation. It is then the job of the active investor to determine whether he can have an impact in closing that value gap or "spread" and over what period of time. If there is potential appreciation of 50% envisaged and the initiator believes he can capture that differential in a two-year period, then he is obviously looking at a 25% return on investment.

Friendly vs. Not

Once the active investor has determined that a potential target is an attractive one, he discretely accumulates his position and then, once he has crossed a reporting threshold, makes the appropriate filings with local government authorities and attempts to make contact with the management of the target company. The purpose of this contact is to explain what the active investor sees as strategies for enhancing shareholder value and to attempt, in a cooperative manner, to convince management to pursue and apply these strategic changes. When managers resist to such an extent that polemics lead to a more aggressive approach on the part of the active investor, a heated media campaign or, in a bitter turn, a proxy battle will ensue. This is of course what has recently happened in the IWKA situation in Karlsruhe, Germany.

IWKA case study

We began building a stake in IWKA on 1st September, 2003. Recognising the inefficiencies in the complicated conglomerate structure of IWKA AG and the potential to significantly maximise shareholder value, we acquired a 5% position in the company and began exerting pressure on management to initiate changes in the company's structure.

IWKA was run as a portfolio holding company with an inefficient and antiquated reporting structure. There were limited, if any, synergies across the divisions. Through the course of our diligence process, we recognised that there were a number of catalysts for creating value within the company, including operational restructuring and spin-offs of both specific assets and, potentially, entire divisions.

KUKA Robotics was the company's marquis asset. KUKA possesses a widely admired proprietary Windows-based operating system for its robots. The company also had years of valuable intellectual capital generated from strong relationships with automobile manufacturers. The quality and reputation of its robots was high and the company had strong market positions, particularly in Europe. KUKA Robots were number three worldwide in 2003 and number one in Europe. Despite its strong position, we believed the unique position of KUKA Robotics could be better exploited. Massive competition from Fanuc, Yaskawa and ABB necessitated a bigger focus on KUKA. We wanted to see the robotics broken out from the other production technology assets and reported as its own division. We also emphasised the need to expand KUKA

Robotics into a greater number of industries, diversifying away from its heavy reliance on the automotive sector. Additionally, we felt that KUKA needed to expand geographically into the US and Asian markets.

There were a number of underperforming assets within the remainder of the Production Technology Division. The division was highly dependent on the automotive industry and had several companies that had not been profitable for several years. We pushed for a comprehensive review of the portfolio and for a sale of activities that, at a minimum, were not earning at least their cost of capital.

We believed that the Packaging Technology Division faced a number of issues as well. The division had been built by a series of acquisitions and consisted of almost 20 different companies, each with their own management, procurement and sales forces, and manufacturing facilities. There was a clear need to eliminate redundancies, share capacity, streamline operations and integrate procurement activities. We pushed the company to either restructure or sell the division.

The Process Technology Division, in our view, sold largely commodity products and had become largely ineffective in its markets due to larger international competitors. We pushed to have the assets in this division sold off.

Finally, in our talk with IWKA management, we were unconvinced that the current management was even realising basic cross-divisional synergies and had little desire or focus on improving the structure of the company. Talks with management in late 2003 and early 2004 produced few results. We turned to a campaign of public pressure, using the press to draw attention to the situation at IWKA.

At the 2004 Annual General Meeting, we used the opportunity to speak to the shareholders to press forward our ideas on the need for change at IWKA. We stated that we intended to vote against management and encouraged other shareholders to do so as well. At the end of the voting, 37% had voted against management and over 22% had voted against the supervisory board, among the highest levels ever registered at a German annual meeting.

IWKA took the vote as a strong signal and subsequently addressed a number of our concerns during the weeks following the annual meeting and during the third quarter conference call on 9th November, 2004. The robotics were broken out into their own division (Robot Technology), and the company announced a plan to restructure the Packaging Division. The 18 companies in the Packaging Division were to be divided into three "market oriented business units" (Food, Dairy, and Pharmaceuticals & Cosmetics) and the company promised to eliminate redundant sales personnel, integrate their engineering teams, optimise their manufacturing capabilities and bundle their procurement activities. Finally, the Process Technology Division was transferred into a "Non-core Assets" Division and labeled for sale.

We remained unimpressed with IWKA management's performance at the end of 2004 and early 2005. The company appeared to be dragging its feet on asset sales and had not put enough emphasis on realising synergies within any of the three divisions. Talks with mid-level management, engineers and sales representatives confirmed our suspicion. Determined to push forward the restructuring process at IWKA, we decided to put forward a vote of no confidence in management at the 2005 Annual General Meeting as well as put forward two "dissident directors" – with the objective of replacing two of the existing Supervisory Board members, including the Chairman of the Supervisory Board, Reinhard Engel.

Faced with the increased pressure, CEO Hans Fahr resigned the morning of the annual meeting. As a gesture of good faith, we withdrew the measure to replace the Board members as long as the board reconstituted itself within 90 days.

For several months following the annual general meeting, the leadership of IWKA underwent a significant transition. With CEO Hans Fahr resigning, CFO Hans Lampert assumed the role of temporary CEO. Further developments to the makeup of the Management Board occurred, including: (1) on 15th July when the Supervisory Board announced that all six members would step down following the election of a new Supervisory Board at a November extraordinary general meeting; (2) on 29th July, when Wolfgang Dietrich Hein was appointed as Chairman of the Executive Board; and (3) on 28th October when CFO Hans Lampert resigned.

While there was a significant degree of uncertainty encompassing these changes, we viewed them as significant positive developments

Figure 2 Case study – KUKA

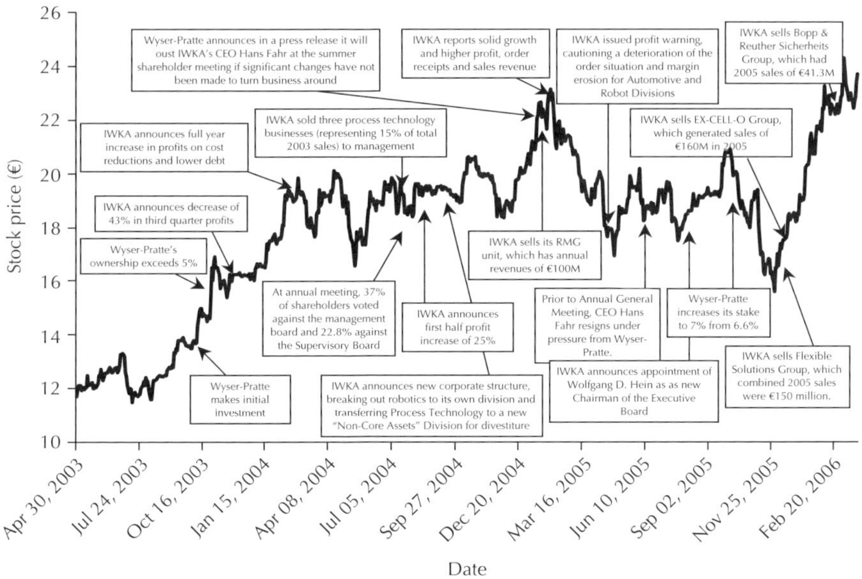

in terms of being able to move forward with making long awaited and much needed changes in IWKA's strategy. On 9th September, Hein assumed his role as CEO and then on 9th November, six shareholder representatives were elected to replace the six that were resigning.

In late October, management finally approved the sale of EX-CELL-O, one of IWKA's underperforming businesses that we had for months pressured the previous management to do. Given the short period of time elapsed since the new management members assumed their roles and the fact that they approved the sale of EX-CELL-O with a very clear purpose, it was a good indication to us that IWKA's management was finally taking a comprehensive look at the entire company and eliminating wasteful assets.

Our engagement of IWKA's management provides perhaps the best example of combining all of the tools at the activist's disposal to improve the fortunes of a company and its shareholder base. In this example it became necessary to combine a structural analysis of the company with not only a coalition of like minded investors which incidentally, was vetted by counsel, but also with use of a proxy contest to force sweeping management changes. All of the components of an activist programme were at work and the net effect on the stock is evident. The activist in this case proved himself to be an asset to the company.

Case study: Vendex

Figure 3 depicts our participation in the Vendex situation, which began when we determined the extreme under-valuation of Vendex relative to its peer-group, and more interestingly an under-valuation due to what is known as the "Dutch discount" for shares incorporated under the "Structured Regime." Every company so situated trades at a discount to its peer-group. We purchased 2% of the shares and went to the first annual meeting in June 2002. In a friendly but very firm manner told the entire Dutch community and Vendex management that there was something wrong with the Dutch being out voting in a general election on the very day that we were sitting as shareholders unable to vote, since shares incorporated under this regime are not shares but only certificates requiring the approval of the trust's administrator to allow shares to vote. Thus the discount: no accountability. We created such a furor that within three months the company changed its bylaws and allowed us to vote. Interestingly a number of Dutch companies followed suit. There was, however, still work to be done. For the next annual meeting, we decided that the company was still trading at depressed levels and decided to attack the company's strategy, which involved spending €350 million for Capex on a market cap of €1 billion. Totally inappropriate. This time, however, we had the proxy of K Capital of Boston, representing now a total of 14%. We made a thorough slide presentation at the annual meeting and undoubtedly, the management decided that at the next annual meeting they would see me with a 50% coalition and decided enough was enough. They shortly thereafter agreed to sell the company to KKR, the LBO firm.

Our successful engagement of Vendex illustrates several critical points. An activist does not require a controlling stake in a company in order to present a compelling proposal to management. Success is determined by the validity of the idea, not the size of the stake held. As was mentioned earlier, alliance or coalition building can be an integral component of an activist's engagement of management. K Capital's additional voice presented management with

Figure 3 Case study – Vendex

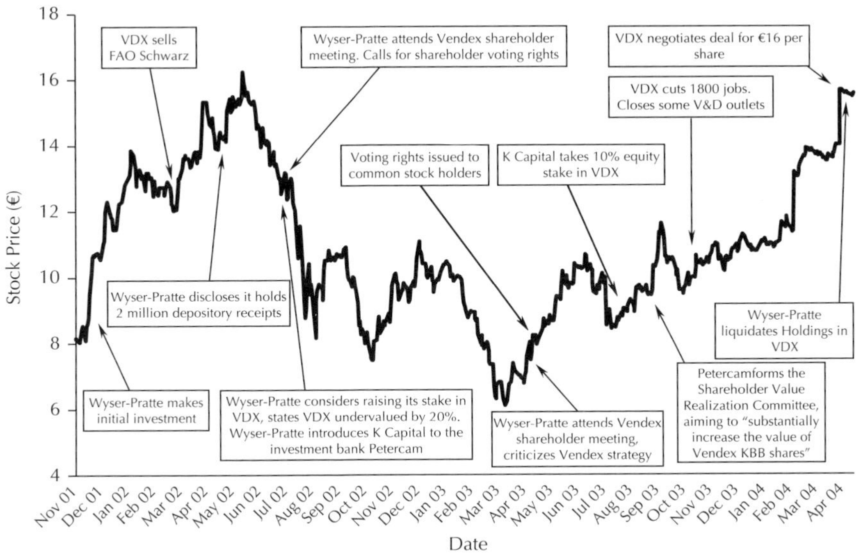

a block of activists rather than a lone manager and increased the volume of the shareholder dissension confronting the board. Additionally, when we first engaged management, we requested a change that would lay the groundwork for a future voice in the company's dealings. We did not arrive seeking outwardly to challenge the company's capex. First we needed to tend to the issue of voting structure in order to eventually proceed with a more specific programme. An activist investor requires a strategic composure throughout the process of engaging an unwilling management.

Case study: Taittinger, S.A.

Taittinger was the most celebrated of the French patrimonial companies controlled through interlocking holdings between subsidiaries. This company was tremendously undervalued at the outset of our interest. Net Asset Values ranged anywhere between €1,500–2,000 per share versus the then-current market price of €320. The company suffered from the dual discounts associated with the typical holding company structure and familial control. We sought to draw attention to the values inherent in the various luxury brands and luxury hotels (Le Crillon) as well as its valuable champagne empire. We sought to ultimately convince the majority owners to create value, or for potential bidders such as LVMH Moet Hennessy, Luis Vuitton, Pinot Printemps and the European and US hotel companies to make offers for various assets in order to increase shareholder value. We began accumulating shares at €320 in May of 1997 and eventually wound up acquiring a 5% interest, which we declared publicly. The stock would eventually double in the following year. In February of 2000, we changed tactics and joined forces with a well-known raider, Asher Adelman, who owned 15% of the 67% Taittinger-held subsidiary, Société du Louvre, and with Hoche Participation announcing a concert-party action to maintain pressure on Taittinger's majority shareholder. This began to have an effect as I was subsequently invited to meet Claude Taittinger in Rheims. Finally we changed tactics in November of 2000 in order to increase the public pressure on the company and to execute our exit strategy. We launched a private road show with some of the leading hotel and real estate operators in Europe, exhibiting newly calculated asset values between €2,500 and €3,000 per share. Our aim was to have someone join us in order to acquire a 30% total interest and have me placed on the Taittinger board. The strategy was eventually effective as Anne-Claire Taittinger, Claude's niece, convinced Albert Frère, the famous Belgian industrialist, to buy our shares at €800 (€160 post a five-per-one split) per share, which we sold to him on 29th December, 2000. In 2006, Frère forced the Taittinger family to sell the entire company at €336.24 per share. He had in fact doubled the price over a five-year period after our having tripled the shares in a four-year period.

Our involvement with the management of Taittinger was based on the type of thoroughly researched proposal that the activist investor, as was discussed earlier, is advised to present. Our conviction that the Net Asset Value of the company exceeded the stock price by an inexcusable margin, provided us with the confidence to prepare and present a road show to the relevant industry players. Again, the importance of alliances was never more apparent than in this case, and as hoped, provided the necessary leverage to cause the company to react. Patience, a long-term focus, and the determination to see this investment produce the value that we expected sustained this engagement.

Figure 4 Case study – Taittinger

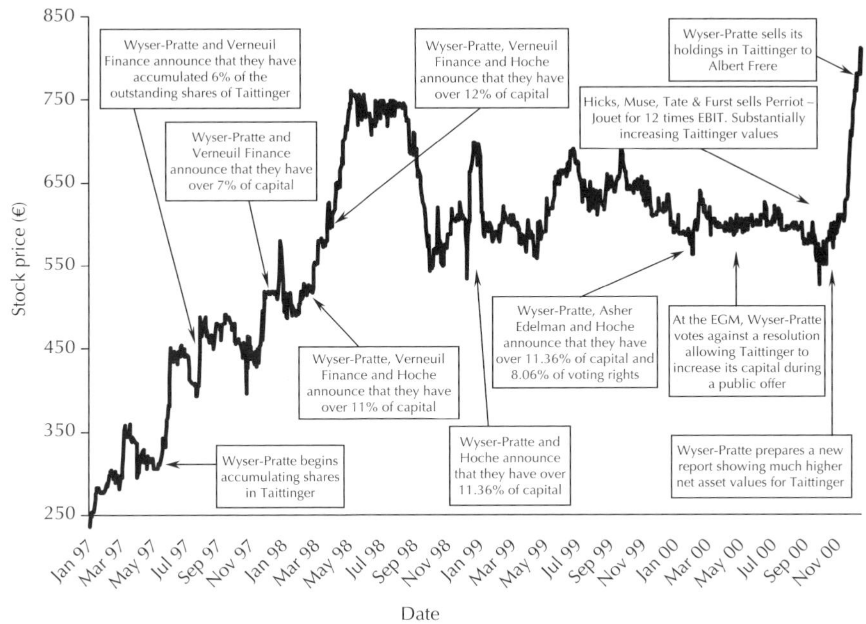

CONCLUSION

The cases presented in the preceding pages share a common thread. That is, a management that initially resisted the proposals of an activist investor, relented either by way of good sense, or as is sometimes required, by force, and accepted an alternative view of the proper management of the company. The net effect in each case was to increase the value of the corporation and enrich the shareholders who had entrusted their capital to these managements. It is time for the discussion of the economic benefits that a fully engaged shareholder community provides, to move beyond the circles of academic debate and editorial pages, to become a central principle of asset management. The solution to preventing potentially catastrophic lapses on the part of management will be found in all managers' actions rather than in the press reports of a handful of successful activists. We must have the objective of establishing a culture in which the terms "shareholder community" and "activist community" become synonymous.

The frequency of successful engagements of underperforming managements must increase beyond the occasional high profile contest, to a level that ingrains such events in the normal course of business. The change that is necessary is one that will render obsolete the public relations approach to assuaging the concerns of an activist, and along with it, any perception that underperforming or unresponsive management can survive by simply appeasing the occasional vocal shareholder. A true and lasting change in the dynamic between managers and owners, one that will extinguish the impulse to recoil at the sound of a shareholder's voice, will only be established by a steadily rising tide of managers who demand without exception, a proper place in the affairs of their investments.

1 15th September, 2005 Bloomberg article entitled, "EU May Sue France Over Merger Defenses".

Index